G0-EXB-193

Abstraction and the Classical Ideal, 1760–1920

The University of Delaware Press
Studies in Seventeenth- and Eighteenth-Century
Art and Culture

Advisory Board to the University of Delaware Press
Board of Editors
Elise Goodman, General Editor

Joseph Baillio
Sarah R. Cohen
Anthony Colantuono
Philip Conisbee
Wayne Franits
Alden R. Gordon
Walter Liedtke
Steven F. Ostrow
William L. Pressly
Anne L. Schroder

Books in This Series

Art and Culture in the Eighteenth Century
edited by Elise Goodman

Dugdale and Hollar: History Illustrated
by Marion Roberts

Piety and Politics: Imaging Divine Kingship in Louis XIV's Chapel at Versailles
by Martha Mel Stumberg Edmunds

Changing Minds: The Shifting Perception of Culture in Eighteenth-Century France
by John C. O'Neal

Utility and Beauty: Robert Wellford and Composition Ornament in America
by Mark Reinberger

From Savage to Citizen: The Invention of the Peasant in the French Enlightenment
by Amy S. Wyngaard

Abstraction and the Classical Ideal, 1760–1920
by Charles A. Cramer

Jacques-Louis David: New Perspectives
edited by Dorothy Johnson

Antoine Watteau: Perspectives on the Artist and the Culture of His Time
edited by Mary Sheriff

Caravaggio: Realism, Rebellion, Reception
edited by Genevieve Warwick

Abstraction and the Classical Ideal, 1760–1920

Charles A. Cramer

DELAWARE

Newark: University of Delaware Press

WITHDRAWN
OHIO UNIVERSITY LIBRARY ATHENS OHIO

© 2006 by Rosemont Publishing & Printing Corp.

All rights reserved. Authorization to photocopy items for internal or personal use, or the internal or personal use of specific clients, is granted by the copyright owner, provided that a base fee of $10.00, plus eight cents per page, per copy is paid directly to the Copyright Clearance Center, 222 Rosewood Drive, Danvers, Massachusetts 01923. [0-87413-935-X/06 $10.00 + 8¢ pp, pc.]

Other than as indicated in the foregoing, this book may not be reproduced, in whole or in part, in any form (except as permitted by Sections 107 and 108 of the U.S. Copyright Law, and except for brief quotes appearing in reviews in the public press).

Associated University Presses
2010 Eastpark Boulevard
Cranbury, NJ 08512

The paper used in this publication meets the requirements of the American National Standard for Permanence of Paper for Printed Library Materials Z39.48-1984.

Library of Congress Cataloging-in-Publication Data

Cramer, Charles A., 1968–
Abstraction and the classical ideal, 1760–1920 / Charles A. Cramer.
p. cm. — (University of Delaware Press studies in 17th- and 18th-century art and culture)
Includes bibliographical references and index.
ISBN-10: 0-87413-935-X (alk. paper)
ISBN-13: 978-0-87413-935-8 (alk. paper)
1. Art, Abstract. 2. Classicism. I. Title. II. Series.
N6465.A25C73 2006
709.04'052–dc22 2005028719

PRINTED IN THE UNITED STATES OF AMERICA

Contents

Illustrations

Acknowledgments

This book began as a dissertation at the University of Texas at Austin, and I would like to thank the professors there for their considerable support: Jeffrey Barnouw, Michael Charlesworth, John R. Clarke, Linda D. Henderson, Susan Rather, and especially Richard Shiff. The research for and writing of this book were also supported by a Travel Award from the Department of Art and Art History at the University of Texas at Austin, a Samuel H. Kress Foundation Travel Fellowship in the History of Art, a University Continuing Graduate Fellowship from the University of Texas at Austin, a Sherry and Tommy Jacks Graduate Art History Scholarship, and a course release provided by the College of Arts and Sciences at Suffolk University, Boston. Financial assistance with the cost of acquiring reproductions of the images was provided in part by the Department of Humanities and Modern Languages at Suffolk University. I would also like to thank some individuals who were particularly generous with their time and assistance: Nick Savage, Helen Valentine, and Laura Valentine at the British Royal Academy Library; the anonymous lenders of Emile Bernard's *Buckwheat Harvest* and of Reynolds's *Justice* and *Fortitude*; and the readers, editors, and staff at the University of Delaware Press and Associated University Presses. Most of all I thank my parents, Barton E. and Elizabeth LaVarge Cramer, and Kim T. Grant, to whom this book is dedicated.

Abstraction and the Classical Ideal, 1760–1920

Introduction

The title of this book, *Abstraction and the Classical Ideal*, appears to be an oxymoron. In art-historical terms, abstraction is an achievement of the aggressively radical and forward-looking modernists, while the classical ideal connotes a fundamentally conservative aesthetic program based in threadbare academic dogma and a reverence for the past. It is the intent of this study to demonstrate that these two concepts were in fact closely linked in the period between around 1760 and 1920, and indeed to demonstrate that abstraction was a route to the classical ideal, and that idealization was a route to abstract art.

The first hints of this link can be found in the art theory of Joshua Reynolds, who argued in 1770 that the artist must purify natural objects of their "accidental deficiencies, excrescences, and deformities" in order to render what he called an "abstract idea of their forms more perfect than any one original."[1] As David Morgan has noted, few scholars have remarked the use of the terms "abstract" and "abstraction" in the late eighteenth-century discourse on art.[2] Morgan has traced a history of this usage to the empirical philosophy of John Locke, has examined the widespread and very diverse application of the term in eighteenth- and nineteenth-century German, French, and British art theory, and has suggested some continuities with better-known theories of abstraction in the late-nineteenth and early-twentieth centuries.[3] However, the connections that Morgan suggests remain purely theoretical and very diffuse, encompassing many very different meanings and uses of the term abstraction.[4] This study concentrates on one specific use of the term and concept of abstraction within an aesthetic discourse composed of the following linked ideas: (1) the goal of discovering and depicting a visual model or archetype of essential and universally-valid truth and beauty: that which is often called the "ideal" in art theory; (2) the notion that all knowledge originates with sensory or "empirical" observation of a highly varied and imperfect nature; and (3) the articulation of a certain process, frequently called "abstraction" or "generalization," for achieving that goal by means of eliminating or attenuating those imperfections.[5] I argue that this process of abstracting toward the ideal forms a coherent aesthetic discourse between around 1760 and 1920, appearing within the larger body of thought of a number of committed proponents, including the British Academic artists Joshua Reynolds, John Opie and James Barry, the French art theorists Denis Diderot and Quatremère de Quincy, the natural scientists Geoffroy Saint-Hilaire and Richard Owen, the French Symbolists Maurice Denis and Emile Bernard, and the Dutch modernist Piet Mondrian—and within the body of thought of a number of equally-committed opponents, such as William Blake, William Hazlitt, and John Ruskin. This is a singularly heterogeneous personnel, but it is frequently valuable to cut across established periods, doctrines, and disciplines in order to examine ideas and practices in a new light. I hope especially to shed new light on two of the most important concepts of art-historical inquiry: idealization and abstraction. As we shall see, the discourse of abstracting toward the ideal had a wide range of theoretical and practical effects, significantly modulating and in some cases utterly transforming almost every aspect of the longstanding classical tradition of idealization, and serving as the nucleus of fundamental and highly acrimonious debates about the philosophy of mind, the relationship between the Ancients and the Moderns, the nature of human racial and functional variety, the nature of God's creative ideas, the use of brushwork in painting, the validity of abstraction in art, and the visual appearance of ideal truth and beauty.

* * *

The notion that the artist should depict the ideal rather than the real, the enduring essence of things rather than their ever-changing appearances, can be traced to Ancient Greek art theory. For Plato, underlying the diversity and deformity of natural objects is a set of Ideas or Forms that are somewhat like universal templates from which all individual objects are derived. The Idea-form of a given object instances that object in its essential truth and perfect beauty, such as it never appears on earth. In his dialog *Timaeus* (27d–29d), Plato correspondingly distinguishes between two sorts of knowledge: a low-order knowledge that is "conceived by opinion with the help of sensation," and a higher order of knowledge, based on the Ideas, that is "apprehended by intelligence and reason." The former cannot constitute either truth or reality, for opinions and appearances are always "becoming and perishing," always changing. By contrast, the Ideas are "always in the same state," offering a secure grounding for an eternal, universal truth. Plato thus asserts that those who conceive their works from the unchanging pattern of the Ideas will produce works that are "fair and perfect," while those who merely copy the appearances of things will founder in the shadow-world of deformity.[6] Although his overall philosophical system was very different, Aristotle makes much the same point in distinguishing between history and poetry in his *Poetics* (1451a1–b1). The historian records the way things happened in fact, while the poet has the liberty to alter the facts. Such poetic license could result in works of mere fantasy, but for Aristotle the implication is that poetry can be "more philosophic" than history, for "its statements are of the nature rather of universals, whereas those of history are singulars."[7] For both Plato and Aristotle, then, the artist should represent the ideal rather than the real, the universal truth rather than the singular occurrence, the eternal essence rather than the transitory appearance of nature.

In keeping with long historical usage, I call this aesthetic goal the "classical ideal," but contrary to most previous scholarship I mean no automatic reference to the *locus classicus* of idealizing art and art theory in Classical Greece and Rome. A terminological distinction will help to clarify one of my aims here: I will use the term "classical" to refer to the art and art theory that has as its primary concern the representation of ideal nature, and "neo-classical" to refer to the art and art theory that advocates a close conformity to the works and doctrines of Ancient Greece and Rome. The conflation of these two concepts has been a major cause of confusion in the scholarship, or more precisely has induced easy answers to what was in fact a complex problem. The history of idealization in the visual arts has almost exclusively been traced as a matter of imitating certain canonical works such as the *Doryphoros* and the *Apollo Belvedere*, or of closely emulating the formal qualities they embodied, such as precisely-defined and invariable proportions in the human figure, especially when combined with Ancient drapery and iconographic attributes; a rigidly controlled and composed style most famously defined by Heinrich Wölfflin as "linear, planar, closed, multiplicitous and clear;" and a restrained but momentous emotional tone most famously described by Johann Winckelmann as "noble simplicity and quiet grandeur."[8] Works such as the Parthenon frieze (c. 447–438 B.C.E.), the *Ara Pacis Augustae* (c. 13–9 B.C.E.), Raphael's *School of Athens* (1509–11, figure 1), Poussin's *Et in Arcadia Ego* (c. 1655), and Ingres's *Apotheosis of Homer* (1827, figure 2) clearly exemplify these qualities, and seem to offer a fixed countenance for ideal beauty across more than two millennia of Western history. It would appear that the difficult project of discovering and depicting universal truth and beauty was permanently solved by the Greeks, and that the practice of idealization in art can safely be conflated with neoclassicism, a constant, deferential recycling of Ancient achievement.

This formulaic understanding of the tradition of idealization has served not only historians of latter-day classical art, but also historians of modernist art. Because the characteristics of idealizing art are apparently so stable, and because their Greco-Roman genealogy is so easily traced as mere "borrowing," it is not surprising that the classical tradition has been seen as a primary antagonist to the revolutionary originality and rapid changes of style that characterized the modernist tradition. The Romantics, we are told, rebelled against the fixed contours and shallow reason of classicism with their painterly brushwork and intense expression; the Realists rebelled against its retrogressive orthodoxy with their contemporaneity and subversive politics, and so forth. Social historians of the tradition of idealization have also been complicit in this project, often reducing the theory and practice of idealization to unreflective dogma, the intellectual poverty of which

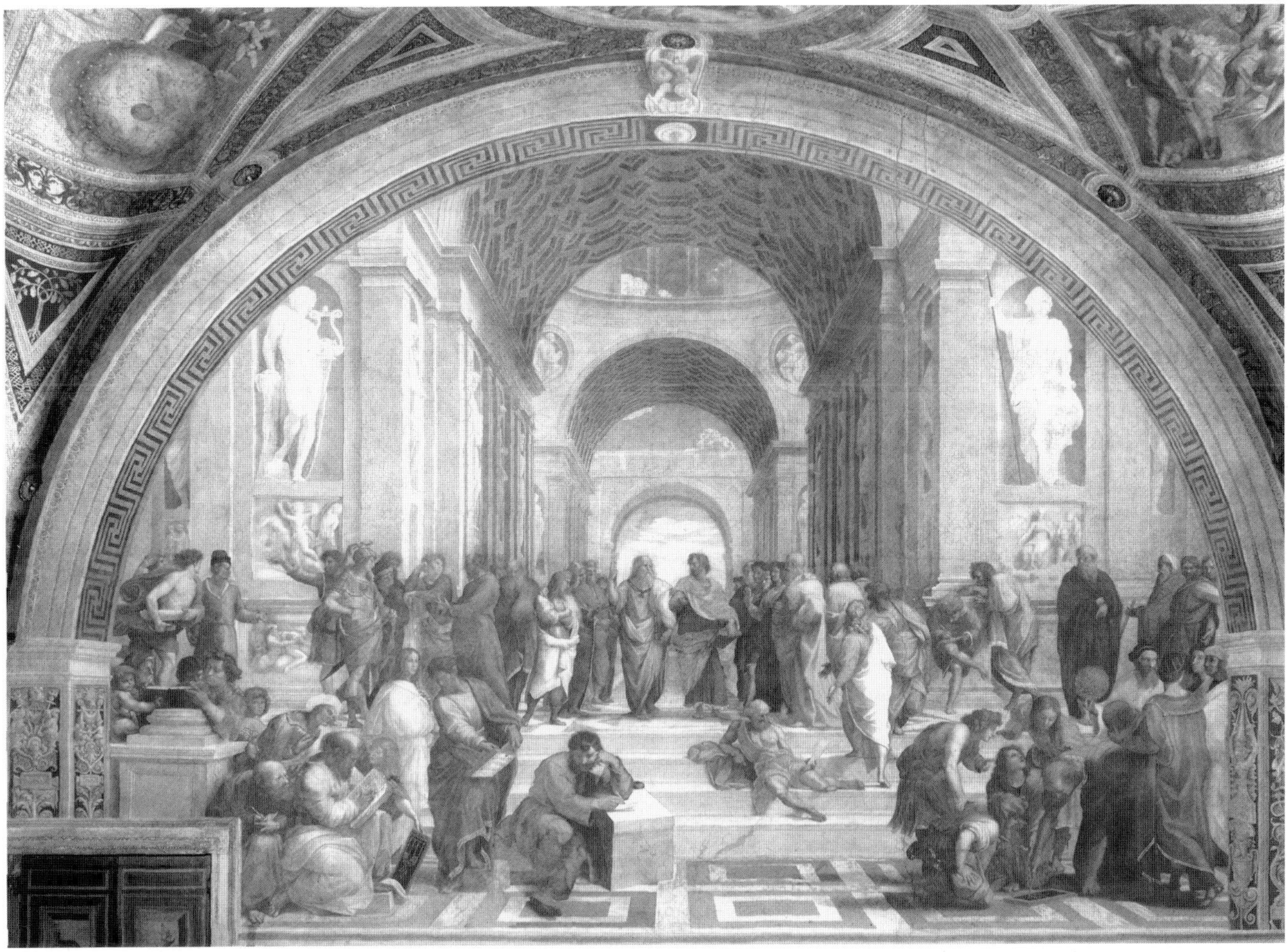

1. Raphael, *The School of Athens*, 1509–11. Stanza della Segnatura, Vatican Palace. Photo Credit: Scala/Art Resource, NY.

matches its pernicious social effects. In other words, the tradition of idealization in Western art has been demoted from the philosophical mission imagined by Plato and Aristotle to a mere rhetorical commonplace, a straw man against which all originality, all intellectual, social, and aesthetic engagement can be measured in high and sympathetic relief.

This study approaches the idealizing tradition from a different direction, a direction that will question the apparent philosophical poverty and monolithic stability of the theory and practice of idealization, especially during the modern period, when its stultification in dogma is usually taken for granted. Rather than tracing the history of idealizing art as a recycling of certain invariable formal, iconographic or expressive qualities, this study begins by investigating the *process of idealization*. While the appearance of the ideal seems to have remained fixed for millennia in Western art and imagination, this ostensive fixity has obscured radical changes in theories of idealization. The primary question asked and taken seriously by this study is this: how did artists visualize ideal form? Artists who depicted the ideal produced value for their audience on three simultaneous fronts: their works were not only aesthetically beautiful, but also philosophically true and morally exemplary. However, to produce such value is extraordinarily difficult. Instances of real objects abound on all sides and are immediately available to the artist through the simple act of perception, but nowhere in this world are Plato's Ideas or Aristotle's universals similarly available.[9] How, then, can the artist rise above the constant change, variety, and deformity of natural appearances and render universal truth and beauty?[10]

There have been three fundamentally differ-

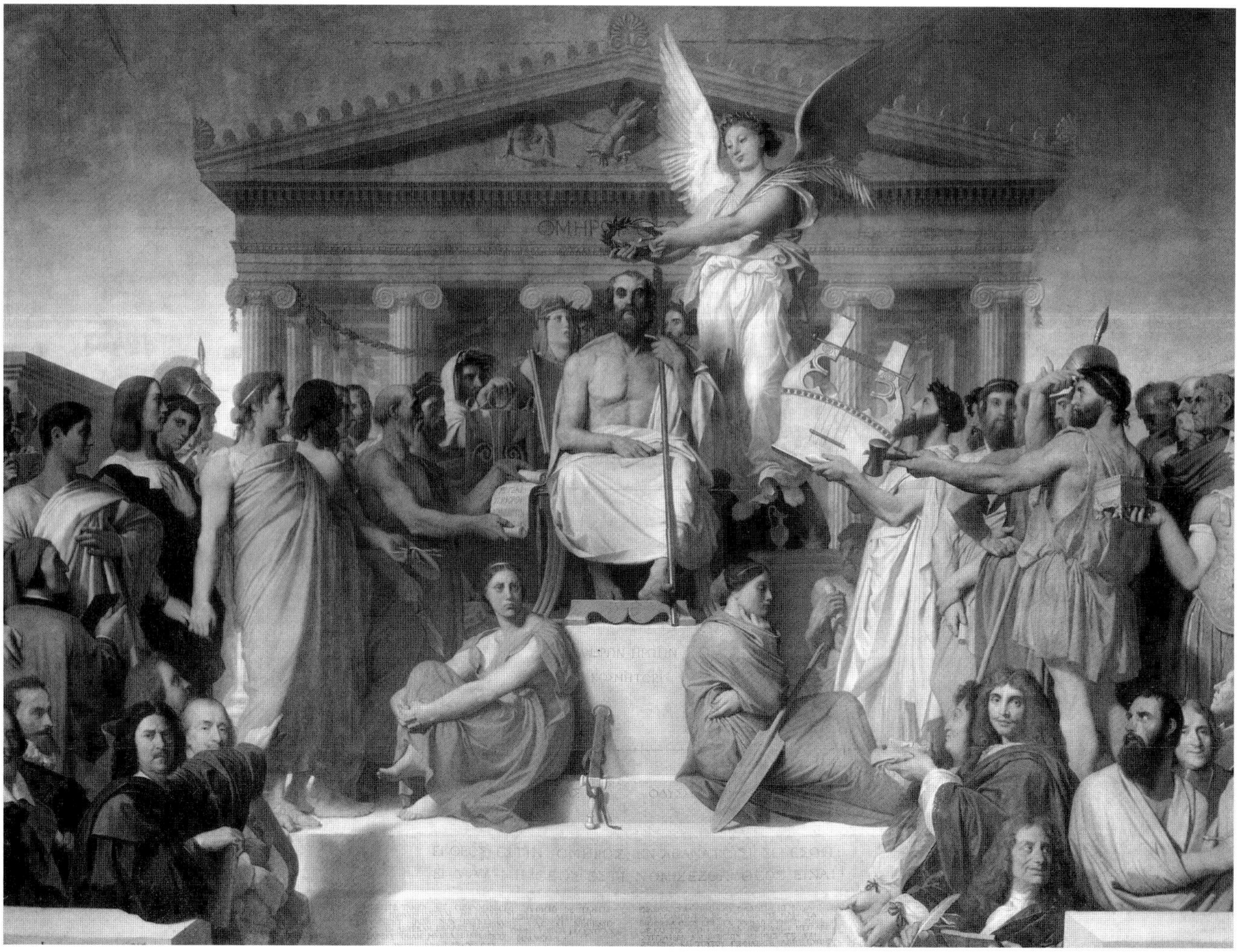

2. Jean Auguste Dominique Ingres, *The Apotheosis of Homer*, 1827. Louvre, Paris. Photo Credit: Erich Lessing/Art Resource, NY.

ent answers to this question in art theory since Ancient times, which I will call "imitation" (or neoclassicism), "transcendent classicism," and "empirical classicism." Explicitly recognizing the differences between these approaches will begin to indicate the heterogeneity and complexity of the Western practice of idealization.

A cursory review of the primary and secondary literature on classical art quickly reveals the process of imitation as one route to ideal form. The artist who wishes to render ideal beauty should simply copy the works of those who have done so already: Phidias, Raphael, Poussin, and their like. Classical art theory is replete with such advice, as in Bellori's admonition that "a study of the most perfect antique Sculptures is . . . necessary to guide us to the emended beauties of nature,"[11] Roger de Piles's counsel that "the painter cannot do better than to attempt to plumb the excellence of [ancient] Works, in order to know the purity of Nature,"[12] and Winckelmann's bald assertion that "The only way for us to become great or, if this be possible, inimitable, is to imitate the ancients."[13] The constant recourse in classical art theory to the authority of past masters has bolstered the scholarly assumption that the ideal was conclusively embodied by the Ancients and could admit no new form or idea into its predetermined contours. We shall return to the process of imitation as a route to the ideal, for its continuing presence in late eighteenth- and early nineteenth-century classical art theory cannot be denied. However, for the moment it is sufficient to remark that imitation was not the only answer to the question of how the artist can render ideal form. Indeed, as many theorists in this study will note, that answer begs the question of how Ancient artists, who had no prior models, *discovered* the ideal. The retrogressive appeal to prior authority can only recede so far. At some point in history at least—and thus potentially in the present as well—there must have been what seems to be almost a contradiction in terms: an *original* classicism, a process that has the potential to discover the ideal rather than merely reiterate a standard type.

Theories of original classical process divide roughly into two major types, corresponding to a longstanding philosophical debate about the origin and nature of human knowledge. In the set of processes that I will collectively call *transcendent classicism*, which is most closely associated with Plato and with Neoplatonists such as Plotinus, Marsilio Ficino, and Giovanni Paolo Lomazzo, humankind cannot directly access the Ideas through their senses, but must instead rely on communication from some otherworldly or "transcendent" source.[14] Although Plato largely denied artists the ability to know the Ideas, subsequent Neoplatonic art theorists derived from his writings concrete processes for achieving ideal knowledge. One is the process of "inspiration," in which a vision of ideal beauty is transferred to the artist's mind directly from some otherworldly source such as a muse or god, much as medieval manuscript illustrations would depict Saint Matthew as guided by an angel in writing his Gospel.[15] A second is the process generally called "unforgetting," which is derived from Plato's notion that before birth the human soul swam in a supercelestial place in direct contact the Ideas.[16] When the soul is born into the corrupt world of the senses, ideal knowledge is displaced by mere worldly knowledge, but traces of the Ideas linger and an internal, ratiocinative process can help to recollect or "unforget" them. Although in this version there is no direct, present-tense contact with an otherworldly source, unforgetting is still a fundamentally transcendent process, for knowledge of the ideal still relies on prior contact with such a source.

In sharp contrast to these transcendent processes is what I will call *empirical classicism*. The basic principle of empirical philosophy is that all knowledge must be derived from sensory experience of this world. The infant's mind is a clean slate at birth, having no innate ideas whatsoever and only a limited set of mental tools that are, barring abnormality, precisely the same as those of every other child. If there is such a thing as the ideal, and if it is knowable, then it must be discovered a posteriori, that is, directly or indirectly derived from worldly experience. While the artistic process of the transcendent classicist relies on otherworldly powers, that of the empirical classicist must be focused on this world and based on normative mental activity.

Both transcendent and empirical theories of idealization are relatively common already in Ancient art theory. In his *Orator ad Brutum* (2.7ff.), the Roman rhetorician Cicero asserted that in rendering the perfect beauty of his *Zeus* and his *Athena*, Phidias "did not look at a [real] human being whom he could imitate, but in his own mind there lived a sublime notion of beauty; this he beheld, on this he fixed his attention, and according to its likeness he directed his art and hand." Citing Plato, Cicero insists that perfect ideas such as these do not "come into being," are not acquired from experience, but rather "exist eternally, being contained in our intellect," suggesting that Phidias's process was one of unforgetting.[17] Notions of a transcendent route to the ideal are also evident in sixteenth-century Neoplatonist circles, most famously in the art theory of Michelangelo, who wrote in one of his later poems:

> As a trustworthy model for my vocation,
> At birth I was given the ideal of beauty,
> which is the lamp and mirror of both my arts.
> If you think otherwise, that opinion's wrong:
> for this alone can raise the eye to that height
> which I am preparing here to paint and sculpt.
> Even though rash and foolish minds derive
> beauty (which moves every sound mind
> and carries it to heaven) from the senses,
> unsound eyes can't move from the mortal to the divine,
> and in fact are fixed forever in that place
> from which to rise without grace is a vain thought.[18]

This passage contains many of the commonplaces of transcendent classical art theory: the ideal of beauty is the proper model of artistic production and (fortunately) was given to Michelangelo at birth. No quantity or quality of empirical observation can account for it or replace it, and indeed worldly vision distracts from the contemplation of the ideal. The only way to achieve ideal beauty in art is through divine intervention, through "grace."

Although current Western thought largely

denies the postulate of divine inspiration, and although few today would hold, with Plato, that there are ideal forms of objects floating somewhere in our heads or in a supercelestial place, the transcendent formulation of classical process has had many adherents throughout history, and understandably so. A superlative idea may occasionally occur suddenly, without any apparent linear reasoning or previous trial-and-error experience. Such an idea gives every appearance of having been received from a source outside the artist's own mind. The notion of artistic genius as a matter of inspiration, in other words, is a responsible explanation of a certain phenomenon that many people may have experienced in some degree, and as such is credible. Furthermore, the postulate that certain individuals have innate ideas or transcendent abilities was very convenient to the social tactics of postmedieval artists. Such individuals are by birthright above or beyond the norms of society, and should be granted status accordingly. For these reasons at least, it is not particularly fantastic that artists would have formulated or been responsive to transcendent explanations of their craft. The empiricist, however, will re-explain such "inspired" moments, and reground the status of the artist in other criteria. The sudden, perfect idea, although this may not be immediately evident, is always the result of past experience; "inspiration" can be explained as the sudden coalescence of multiple prior experiences forgotten by the conscious memory, and of multiple prior experiments indirectly related to the current situation. The status of artists is to be predicated on the breadth or depth of their worldly experience, and grounded in their acquired (not given) ability to mold that experience into artistic form.

An empirical explanation of artistic process is obviously relevant to modes of art that focus on the actual world or on subjective human experience. But when the goal of the artist is to present a metaphysical or transcendent quality such as the ideal, a transcendent process is perhaps more immediately cogent. Empiricism, in other words, appears to be a fundamentally secular doctrine, suitable only to worldly and human truths, and not to ideal truths. While the transcendent artist receives knowledge of the ideal from a source outside of the subjectivity of the human mind and beyond the contingencies of worldly objects, empirical experience is fundamentally subjective, and attains knowledge only of the imperfect objects of the real world. How, then, can the empirical classicist, in consultation only with a subjective experience of an imperfect nature, nonetheless transcend subjectivity and surpass nature?

The most often cited fully empirical solution to this problem is that suggested by the ancient story of Zeuxis and the maidens of Croton. Charged with the task of representing Helen of Troy, Zeuxis could find no single woman who embodied such exceptional beauty, so he formed his idea of beauty by selecting the most perfect parts of the five most beautiful women of Croton.[19] Similarly, in Zenophon's *Memorabilia* (3.10.1–5), Socrates suggests that in order to render perfect beauty, the artist must "take the most beautiful features from each of many models and thus make the whole body appear beautiful."[20] In *selection-theory*, then, the artist's idea of perfect beauty is fully empirical: it is derived from sensory experience and the ordinary mental function of selection. The artist refers only to nature and uses no special mental gifts, but nonetheless produces a work more perfect than the source material. Selection-theory has a subsequent history at least as long as that of imitation and inspiration. It was reiterated by theorists such as the sixteenth-century humanist and art critic Ludovico Dolce, by Giovanni Pietro Bellori in his treatise "The Idea of the Painter, Sculptor and Architect, Superior to Nature by Selection from Natural Beauties" (1672), and continued to be cited well into the eighteenth and nineteenth centuries, as we shall see.

These three processes—imitation, inspiration, and selection—are the mainstays of classical art theory and are widely recognized in the scholarship. There was, however, a fourth method, rarely recognized in the scholarship and rarely expounded in the source literature before the late-eighteenth century: the empirical process of *abstraction* or *generalization*. Aristotle had proposed this process in his theory of mental concepts,[21] and glancing references to such a process are discernable in the writings of the Greek physician Galen in the second century C.E. and in the art theory of the architect and humanist Alberti in the fifteenth century, but the notion of abstraction as a route to the ideal is thoroughly explored in art theory only starting in the later decades of the eighteenth century. After that time, however, its spread was rapid, especially in England and France, and its effect on the theory and practice of classicism was revolutionary, as we shall see.

The process of abstraction or generalization essentially defined the ideal as the average or minimum common denominator of all objects of a given type. This is already somewhat surprising: in what sense can the superlative beauty and truth of the ideal be associated with an average or minimum common denominator?[22] In *De temperamentis* (1.9), Galen explicitly makes this equation, asserting that "modellers and sculptors and painters, and in fact image-makers in general, paint or model beautiful figures by observing an ideal form in each case, that is, whatever form is most beautiful in man or in the horse or in the cow or in the lion, always looking for the mean within each genus."[23] This passage implies a taxonomic approach to knowledge, and conforms to the Platonic notion that there are template-ideas for the various classes of object existing in the world: for the class or "genus" of chairs, there is one Idea of the Chair from which all existing chairs are derived, and so on. Like Plato also, Galen grants this class-idea the epithet of "beauty," thus aligning aesthetics with ontology: that which has unchanging truth and reality as Idea is also the "most beautiful." What Galen has done in this passage is to graft this Platonic understanding of the Ideas onto an Aristotelian notion of the way we arrive at universals or class-ideas through repeated experience of diverse objects of a certain sort. In Plato's transcendent epistemology, sensory experience of worldly objects may help to prompt the recollection of their Ideas, but those Ideas cannot be *derived* from sensory experience.[24] In Aristotle's empirical epistemology, by contrast, the mind derives universals or class-ideas directly from sensory experience. This happens through a process called *korismos* or "separation," later translated by medieval scholastic philosophers as "abstraction." Abstraction describes a mental process of "pulling away" (the etymological meaning of the word abstract) perceived features of objects. Certain objects resemble each other and the mind abstracts the differences from these objects to consider only their resemblance, as for example when we derive a general idea of the color "red" from multiple individual objects possessing that color by ignoring the type, material, shape, texture, size, and so forth of the objects. For Galen, this process can be used to derive general ideas not only of simple qualities like red and softness, but also of more complex classes of objects such as those of man, cow, horse, and lion. To discover the universal idea of man, multiple individual men are compared, all of their differences are eliminated or abstracted—variations in skin color, hairstyle, physical build, and so forth—and only that which is common to every individual in the entire class is retained. The idea thus derived can be considered "ideal" precisely because it eliminates everything that changes or varies from individual to individual, retaining only that which, being common to all, can be considered the essence of the class.

By defining the ideal as the "mean within each genus," Galen seems furthermore to infer that individual existing objects deviate more or less symmetrically from the Idea from which they were derived: some people's noses are unusually large, others' are unusually small; these extremes are abstracted or averaged and the median or mean is the ideal.[25] The abstractive process is thus the inverse of the Zeuxian selective process, arriving at the ideal by eliminating or attenuating imperfections rather than by collecting piecemeal instances of perfection, achieving the ideal through a process of distillation rather than of aggregation. Through abstraction, then, the mind is able to generate ideal knowledge of classes of objects out of an empirical experience that shows only highly varied and imperfect instances of those objects.

In his treatise *De statua*, Alberti also explicitly equates the concept of ideal beauty with the mean or median form of a family of objects. Noting that appearances differ from individual to individual in such a way that "no voice or nose or similar part resembles any other among all the rest of the people," Alberti asserts nonetheless that "each [individual] is like the rest of its kind" in some way as well. There is diversity in individual appearances, but at the same time a unity is apparent amid this diversity that "remains always constant and unchangeable in relation to the species" or class to which the individual belongs.[26] While the bulk of *De statua* is concerned with outlining a system of precise measurement by means of which the sculptor can accurately copy the "live model," toward the end of the treatise Alberti emends his process to derive what he calls the "perfect beauty" of the class of man in general:

> I took on the task of recording the *dimensiones* of man. I proceeded accordingly to measure and record in writing, not simply the beauty found in this or that body, but, as far as possible, that perfect beauty distributed by Nature, as it were

> in fixed proportions, among many bodies. . . . [So we] chose many bodies, considered to be the most beautiful by those who know, and took from each and all their *dimensiones*, which we then compared one with another, and leaving out of account the extremes on both sides, we took the mean figures validated by the majority of the *exempeda* [measurements].[27]

Here again "perfect beauty" is derived from an abstractive or generalizing process: a number of individual models are "compared," the extremes are abstracted or "left out," and the average or "mean" is derived. The class-idea and perfect beauty of any given type of object can thus be discovered by generalizing or averaging multiple objects of that type. Some individual men are fat and some are thin; a blacksmith is highly developed in the upper body, a marathon runner is leaner, and so on. The ideal form of man is the average of all of these variations. While we might intuitively balk at equating the ideal with the average, both Galen and Alberti explicitly do so, for their terms mean or average are used not to assess the qualitative value of the derived product, which both assert is the "highest beauty," but only to describe the quantitative process of arriving at that ideal.

Galen and Alberti offer relatively complete statements of the empirical process of abstraction or generalization, then, but to my knowledge these are isolated instances. Far more commonly cited in both of their periods were the processes of inspiration, imitation, and selection. By contrast, in the late-eighteenth century the process of abstraction was adopted as the core of classical art theory by many thinkers all across Europe. It was most prominently reintroduced into philosophical epistemology by John Locke and his followers in the late-seventeenth and eighteenth centuries, and most fully related to the classical project of idealization by Joshua Reynolds and the Professors of Painting at the British Royal Academy in the late-eighteenth and early-nineteenth centuries. It was also outlined at around the same time by French and German art theorists: briefly by Denis Diderot in his *Salon of 1767*; more extensively under the French *Encyclopédie* entries "abstraction," "idea," and "ideal"; clearly but somewhat dismissively by Immanuel Kant in his *Critique of Judgment* (1790); more thoroughly and with surprising implications by the Secretary of the French Academy Quatremère de Quincy in his *Essay on the Ideal* (1837). Many theorists of the time more or less systematically rejected the processes of imitation, inspiration, and selection as incoherent or even counterproductive, and advanced abstraction as the only cogent way of arriving at the true ideal. As we shall see in chapters 1 and 2, abstraction-theory essentially offered to these artists and theorists the potential for a *modern* classicism, one solidly founded on the new empirical epistemology of the Enlightenment.

From its advent, this new process entailed radical changes not only in the theory of classicism, but in its practice as well. Although many of them maintained a reverential respect for the Ancients and other past masters, the proponents of the new abstractive or generalizing process frequently came to very different conclusions than their forebears about the appearance of the ideal. In chapter 3, for example, we shall see that Joshua Reynolds cogently and repeatedly argued that the general ideal was best embodied by a broad, painterly brushwork. His argument has been almost completely overlooked in the scholarship, largely I believe because it so strongly contradicts our commonplace understanding of the classical style from Polykleitos to postmodernism as inevitably characterized by the linear precision of the Raphaelesque and Poussiniste paradigm. Reynolds's contemporaries were just as surprised, and some not a little dismayed, but the adjectives they used to describe the general ideal demand that we, too, question received notions about how ideal beauty was embodied in the British late-eighteenth century. Barry, Opie, Hazlitt, and others unequivocally characterize the abstract ideal as tending toward a "vague," "indeterminate," "unfinished," "muddy," "slovenly," "monotonous," and "insipid" appearance. Chapter 4 accordingly analyzes Reynolds's own works and the theory and practice of contemporary landscape painters Alexander Cozens and William Gilpin in relation to this painterly approach to ideal form. As we shall see, the potential of the new process radically to alter not only the theoretical and procedural basis of the classical project but also its end products is confirmed again and again throughout the nineteenth and early-twentieth centuries. Chapter 5 locates a paired theoretical and practical paradox within the generalizing process, the reductio ad absurdum that threatened to generalize things generically different and to obviate the formal coherence of mimetic representation. John Ruskin's fear that Reynolds's art theory would logically result in such monstrous apparitions as a pony-pig is confirmed by Richard Owen's extraordinarily odd Vertebrate Archetype, which its author achieved by means of generalization and celebrated as the Platonic Idea of the vertebrate subkingdom. The Symbolists Maurice Denis and Emile Bernard articulated a form of generalization-theory called "synthetism" that they claimed resulted in their radically schematic and "primitive" ideals of around 1890. Their argument is examined in chapter 6. Finally, in chapter 7 we shall see that Piet Mondrian took the classical abstractive process to its logical conclusion, affirming that not only the means but also the end of classicism is in abstraction.

1

The Epistemology of Classicism

ALTHOUGH THE PROCESS OF ABSTRACTING OR GENERALIZING towards the ideal was clearly described by Galen during the Ancient period and Alberti during the Renaissance, neither theorist elaborated or developed it beyond what I have cited. Galen provocatively asserts that Polykleitos used generalization to create his *Canon*, suggesting that the theory of generalization may have formed the substance of Polykleitos's lost treatise on art.[1] However, Galen himself refers to generalization only briefly, and only as an analogy to the relatively commonplace Ancient notion that ideal temperament and health consist in a perfect balance or medium of heat and cold, dryness and wetness. Alberti's reference to the process of generalization in *De statua* is similarly brief, and indeed Alberti confuses generalization with selection-theory, noting that in forming his table of proportions of perfect beauty he "imitated the artist at Croton [Zeuxis] who, when making the likeness of a goddess, chose all remarkable and elegant beauties of form from several of the most handsome maidens."[2] Although this confusion is somewhat justified by the fact that both generalization and selection derive the ideal from many individuals, the process of averaging those individuals and that of selecting isolated perfect parts are in fact fundamentally different. I do not intend by this remark to denigrate Alberti, but rather to emphasize, by contrast, the much more thorough and systematic development of generalization-theory in the late-eighteenth century, when many theorists clearly distinguished it from its sister processes of imitation, inspiration, and selection, and developed its broad range of implications for both the epistemological and technical practice of classicism.

Against Imitation

In the introduction to his *Salon of 1767*, Diderot asserted that "the arts have never, in any century or nation, attained a degree of perfection equal to that achieved in Greece."[3] In its commonplace formulation, of course, this is true because modern practice has strayed from Ancient example, and the solution is a more careful imitation of those prior models. For Diderot, however, it is precisely the imitation of Ancient models that has precluded modern excellence. His logic is this: while Ancient artists discovered and thus directly represented the ideal, the modern practice of imitating the works of the Ancients—and imitating the works of those who imitated the Ancients, and so on—has caused a gradual degradation of the ideal. When modern classicists imitate the Ancients, or worse yet imitate Poussin, who imitated Raphael, who imitated Michelangelo, who imitated the Ancients, more is lost than is gained. Each layer intervening between the source and the artist's product entails some corruption and misunderstanding: "At first [such imitators] remain slightly below the level of their model; little by little they become further removed from it; from the fourth remove of the portraitist or copyist, they lower themselves to the hundredth."[4] Ironically, then, for Diderot the venerable practice of imitation is worse than useless; it is counterproductive. Diderot's proposed solution to this problem of *n*th-degree degradation is literally iconoclastic: only "if all these models had been destroyed," he asserts, could contemporary French artists equal the Ancients, because only then would they, like the Ancients, have been forced to discover the ideal for themselves and know it directly, rather than indirectly and imperfectly through others.[5]

Significantly, Diderot's exposé of the degrading effects of imitation is not particularly novel. In its dedication to tracing the sources of antique "quotations" in neoclassical art—borrowings from the *Apollo Belvedere*, the *Medici Venus*, and so on—modern scholarship has often ignored the fact that the advice to imitate Antiquity is rarely given in latter-day classical art theory without immediate qualification. It was not the Romantics and modernists who established the deleterious effects of imitating others (thus triumphantly eviscerating the entirety of the classical discourse on art), but the classicists themselves. Both Bellori and Roger de Piles advocated an imitation of the Ancients, as we saw. However, both also insisted that the imitation of others' works is not an end in itself, but only a means "to guide us to the emended beauties of nature," a way "to know the purity of Nature,"[6] and both cautioned that there is great danger when the means is mistaken for the end. Bellori warned that "those who without knowing the truth follow common practice in everything create spectres instead of shapes; nor are they dissimilar from those who borrow from the genius and copy the ideas of others, creating works that are not natural children but bastards of nature, so that it seems as though they are wedded to the paintbrushes of their masters."[7] Similarly, de Piles immediately qualifies his advice to imitate Antiquity by defining imitation as something other than simple copying: "[The artist] must look upon the Antique as a Book to be translated into a different language, in which it is sufficient to convey the sense and the spirit without being slavishly confined to the words of the Original."[8]

Even at the height of the so-called neoclassical period of the late-eighteenth century, what was advocated was not the simple copying of prior models, but rather a looser understanding of imitation as emulation, an imitation of the *process* of the great artists of the past, and not of their products. British Academic theory, for example, explicitly described imitation as a way in which young artists can learn, not the ideal itself, but the proper way to approach nature and discover the ideal on their own. While Joshua Reynolds constantly advised his students to learn from the example of great artists, wherever he treats the issue of imitation explicitly he carefully distinguishes between the imitation of the process of past masters, which is laudable, and the imitation of their products, which is not. He approvingly cites the dictum of Edward Young in his *Conjectures on Original Composition* (1759): "He that imitates the Iliad . . . is not imitating Homer," and cautions, "It is not by laying up in the memory the particular details of any of the great works of art, that any man becomes a great artist, if he stops without making himself master of the general principles on which these works are conducted."[9] By simply copying past works the artist cannot hope to equal them—indeed, like Diderot, Reynolds insists that you thereby degrade your own work: "I wish you to profit, by the peculiar experience and personal talents of artists living and dead; you may derive lights, and catch hints from their practice; but the moment you turn them into models, you fall infinitely below them . . . and become bad copies of good painters, instead of excellent imitators of the great universal truth of things."[10] Reynolds's advice, then, is far from reducing latter-day classicism to a mere copying of prior artists' ideals. It is not so much in their products that these past masters provide a model, but in their process, the way they themselves approached the problem of discovering and rendering the ideal.

Reynolds's fellow Academicians were equally explicit in distinguishing between a superficial copying of past works and the true value of imitation in learning the process of past masters. James Barry, Professor of Painting at the British Royal Academy between 1782 and 1799, noted that "[The] remains of Grecian perfection are collected in academies and places of study; yet from the mere imitation of them but little can be expected. We must be able to investigate the *principles* upon which those statues were constructed, and adopt the same *mode of study* in our own pursuits, and imitation of nature, or we labour to no purpose [emphasis added]."[11] Similarly, John Opie (Professor of Painting, 1805–07) distinguishes between the false idea of imitation as "selecting some favourite figure, and using it on all occasions indiscriminately as a rule of proportion," and the true use of imitation as a route to the "re-discovery, in its fullest extent, of the *principle* on which [the works of the ancients] were formed."[12] Henry Fuseli (Professor of Painting, 1799–1805 and 1810–25) calls upon Ancient authority to make the same distinction. According to Eupompus, "such excellence as that of Phidias and Polycletus . . . is not obtained by the servile imitation of works, however perfect, without mounting to the *principle* which raised them to that height."[13] Even Quatremère de Quincy, the secrétaire perpétuel of the French Académie des Beaux-Arts between 1816 and 1839 and for many scholars the "incarnation of the despotic academician," was careful to qualify his advice to imitate other artists.[14] In his *Histoire de la vie et des ouvrages de Raphaël*, for example, Quatremère asserts that while Raphael profited from seeing Michelangelo's work, he directly borrowed "neither his style, nor his ideas, nor his forms and his compositions," but only learned from him "the secret of a grander manner of seeing and of execution." Quatremère likens this form of imitation to "the way in which one borrows from the fire, from which one takes heat without removing anything from the hearth that produces it."[15]

It has been necessary to multiply these citations because the scholarship is so dominated by the notion that latter-day classicists allocated both consequence and significance to their works simply by regurgitating half-digested prior models.[16] In part our reductive understanding of classical imitation-theory is due to the understandable urge of modernist artists and theorists to make the sharpest possible distinction between their own practice and the Academic classical practice with which they were so often at odds. Reducing the Academy to a locus for perpetuating slavish conformity and arrogating all originality and artistic engagement to themselves was a convenient way of setting the new art in high and sympathetic relief. But the reiteration of these claims by subsequent art-historical scholarship, as in the commonplace heroic narrative of the maverick modernist struggling against the moribund dogmas of the Academy, is more pernicious. Such stories lead both to an inaccurate assessment of the nature of modernist originality and, of course, to a caricatured understanding of the Academic classical tradition. Even Rensselaer Lee, in his outstanding study *Ut Pictura Poesis*, cannot resist echoing modernist platitudes, thus ironically consolidating the superiority of modernism in the middle of his treatment of classicism. Although he notes that Ludovico Dolce's advice to imitate "the beautiful marble and bronze figures of the antique Masters" was balanced by "less precarious" advice to "improve upon nature with means drawn from nature herself," Lee still finds it necessary to remark that

> the advice to follow the antique, or perhaps an exemplary modern like Raphael who had shown the way to its successful imitation, always tended to become a dogmatic counsel to abide by an artificial and forever invariable canon of beauty. And, if accepted in any sense literally, such counsel could only result in that uninspired traditionalism against which the Romantic Movement in the name of individual expression and a fresh interest in particular nature would finally revolt.

Such a passage uncritically validates the Romantic rhetoric of renewed engagement with nature, human experience, and art itself, and reinforces the notion that classical theory and practice was such that "only the deeper understanding of a Poussin could save [it] from empty formalism."[17]

Although it would be willfully myopic to deny that imitation—even in its narrowest sense—was practiced by late-eighteenth- and nineteenth-century classicists, the process of imitation cannot be used to make hard-and-fast theoretical or practical distinctions between classical and modernist practice. In its looser sense as a way of finding solutions to formal or semiotic problems, imitation has been practiced to a certain extent by *all* artists. The genealogy of Jackson Pollock's highly "original" flung and poured paint, for example, has been traced to Navajo sand-painting, to Surrealist automatism, to psychoanalytic techniques, and so on. Even in its more restrictive sense of a wholesale borrowing of figures or form, imitation is perhaps only slightly less rife in the modernist tradition than it is in the classical. Is the evident influence of Japanese prints or so-called "primitive" art on many modernist artists somehow less a matter of imitation than that of Antique statues on latter-day classicists? Like the Academicians cited above, the Realist Gustave Courbet confessed to studying past art but repudiated any mere copying of it: "I have studied the art of the ancients and moderns without any dogmatic or preconceived ideas. I have not tried to imitate the former or to copy the latter." And if scholarship finds it difficult to reconcile Academic assertions of this looser sense of imitation with some rather obvious borrowings in certain Academic works, the same difficulty should obtain in reconciling Courbet's aim "to record the manners, ideas and aspect of the age as I myself saw them" with his wholesale lifting of the composition and poses of his work *The Meeting* (1854) from a popular woodcut of a Wandering Jew.[18] In neither the Academic nor the modernist case is it helpful to cry hypocrisy at examples such as these. Borrowing is useful for many reasons, as for example to overlay new shades of meaning onto old ideas or to put the viewer in a proper frame of mind to understand a work—even if, as in Manet's *Olympia* or Reynolds's *Master Crewe as Henry VIII*, the aim is to undermine that frame of mind.[19]

Since latter-day classical theorists explicitly

argued that the proper function of imitation is to rediscover the *process* of past classicists, their method of approach to the problem of discovering and rendering the ideal, then the next logical question is this: by what process or processes did these past artists work? The entire tradition of idealization in art cannot be reduced to the imitation of prior artists' ideals: how did the Ancients, who, as Diderot noted, "had no antiquities," discover the ideal?[20] If all of the Ancient models had been destroyed, how could the modern classicist originate ideal works? By the late-eighteenth century, as we saw, there were two long-established theories of "original" classical practice, one based on a fundamentally transcendent epistemology that conceived of the artist as a sort of visionary capable of penetrating to the Platonic Ideas by means of inspired enthusiasm, and another, more empirical process embodied in the equally venerable Zeuxian method of selection from dispersed natural beauties. While both of these processes avoid the problem of *n*th-degree degradation and "uninspired traditionalism," both were also widely repudiated in late-eighteenth century Academic theory.

Against Inspiration

As we saw in the introduction, transcendent versions of classical process are characterized by their reliance on an otherworldly source for knowledge of the ideal. The artist either acts as a channel or conduit from the gods (inspiration) or attempts to recollect innate ideas received beforehand in the supercelestial place (unforgetting). In addition to avoiding at least one degree of degradation of the ideal (the artist's work is a copy of an idea received directly from its source, rather than a copy of a copy [of a copy . . .] of that idea), notions of transcendent process had considerable attractions for classical artists and theorists on social and economic fronts as well. The high ontological status of the Platonic Idea established the high value of an art that aspired to its direct representation, as opposed to a merely naturalistic art that copied the corrupted and everchanging appearances of the phenomenal world. The ability of the artist to transcend the lower reality of worldly objects for the higher reality of the Ideas similarly consolidated the social status of the artist, especially at a time when artists were attempting to raise the rank of their discipline from that of a mere mechanical trade to that of a liberal art, a labor of the higher intellect rather than merely one of the hands and senses. We should thus take serious note when classical theorists explicitly reject the transcendent version of classical process, for in so doing they sacrificed a neat rhetoric with a long and prestigious genealogy that clearly established the superlative philosophical and social status of their practice.

Joshua Reynolds was one such theorist.[21] In his third Discourse, he unequivocally asserted that "ideal perfection and beauty are not to be sought in the heavens, but upon the earth. They are about us, and upon every side of us."[22] Compare a statement by Reynolds's contemporary, the radical skeptic and empiricist David Hume:

> *There is a God within us*, says OVID, *who breathes that divine fire, by which we are animated.* Poets, in all ages, have advanced this claim to inspiration. There is not, however, any thing supernatural in the case. Their fire is not kindled from heaven. It only runs along the earth; is caught from one breast to another; and burns brightest, where the materials are best prepared, and most happily disposed.[23]

Eighteenth-century empirical philosophy can in general be characterized as a redescription of the origin, nature, and extent of human knowledge based upon a conscientious rejection of any transcendent epistemology. What Locke and Hume attempted in philosophy, Reynolds attempted in classical art theory.[24] Although he recognized the rhetorical and social value of the transcendent discourse on art—and indeed although throughout his writings he is concerned with enhancing the social status of artists—Reynolds nonetheless dismisses that discourse:

> Those who have undertaken to write on our art, and have represented it as a kind of *inspiration*, as a *gift* bestowed upon peculiar favourites at their birth, seem to insure a much more favorable disposition from their readers. . . .
>
> . . . The untaught mind finds a vast gulph between its own powers, and those works of complicated art, which it is utterly unable to fathom; and it supposes that such a void can be passed only by supernatural powers.
>
> And, as for artists themselves, it is by no means their interest to undeceive such judges, however conscious they may be of the very natural means by which their extraordinary powers were acquired.[25]

Throughout classical art theory, the problem is to explain how the artist can traverse the "gulph" that Plato and others had described between the contingency and deformity of phenomenal nature and the absolute truth and beauty of the ideal. For transcendent classical art theory, such a gulf can be traversed only with the aid of divine intervention, Michelangelo's "grace." Reynolds preserves that gulf and the ability of the artist to span it—preserves, then, the superlative philosophical status of classical art and the superior social status of the classical artist—but at the same time he replaces the postulate of "supernatural powers" with an assertion of the artist's "very natural means." The entire discourse of transcendent art theory is dismissed as the fabrication of awestruck critics: "It is very natural for those who are unacquainted with the *cause* of any thing extraordinary, to be astonished at the *effect,* and to consider it as a kind of magick. They, who never observed the gradation by which art is acquired; who see only what is the full result of long labour and application of an infinite number and infinite variety of acts, are apt to conclude from their entire inability to do the same at once, that it . . . can be done by those only, who have some gift of the nature of inspiration bestowed upon them [Reynolds's emphases]."[26] Thus although he occasionally uses epithets that imply that artists have transcendent powers—referring in the fifteenth Discourse to the "divine energy of [Michelangelo's] mind," for example—Reynolds uses such language only to signal the superlative philosophical status of idealizing art, not to suggest divine intervention in the process of formulating the ideal.[27] Indeed, in the same Discourse, Reynolds asserts that Michelangelo himself rejected the transcendent discourse on art:

> [Michelangelo] appears not to have had the least conception that his art was to be acquired by any other means than by great labour; and yet he, of all men that ever lived, might make the greatest pretensions to the efficacy of native genius and inspiration. . . . He was conscious that the great excellence to which he arrived was gained by dint of labour, and was unwilling to have it thought that any transcendent skill, however natural its effects might seem, could be purchased at a cheaper price than he had paid for it.[28]

As we saw in the introduction, Michelangelo did indeed make "pretensions" to native genius and inspiration, but despite his tremendous regard for the Renaissance master, Reynolds cannot endorse transcendent methods.

By framing classical art as the product of "an infinite number and infinite variety of acts"—cause-and-effect acts, which are therefore potentially susceptible to the scientific methods that were having great success in the field of natural philosophy—Reynolds displaces classical process from its vertical (transcendent) axis to a more horizontal (worldly) axis. He was clearly aware that this secularization of classical process threatened by implication to demote the status of the artwork. How can the final effect of a horizontally articulated chain of cause-and-effect actions achieve the state of transcendence that every step of its process denies?[29] Some note of this difficulty is clear in Reynolds's third Discourse. Exploring the problem of achieving the "idea of the perfect state of nature, which the Artist calls Ideal Beauty," Reynolds remarks that "this is the idea which has acquired, and which seems to have a right to the epithet of *divine*; as it may be said to preside, like a supreme judge, over all the productions of nature; appearing to be possessed of the will and intentions of the Creator, as far as they regard the external form of living beings."[30] We should note the numerous qualifications to this "divinity": it "*seems* to have a right to the epithet"; it "*may be said* to preside;" it "*appears* to be possessed of the will and intentions of the Creator," at least as regards "external form." Reynolds admits that the use of such epithets is useful as a pedagogical device—"a student by such praise may have his attention roused, and a desire excited, of running in this great career"—but such praise is metaphoric, and is dangerous when taken literally:

> It is possible that what has been said to excite, may only serve to deter [the student]. He examines his own mind, and perceives there nothing of that divine inspiration, with which, he is told, so many others have been favoured. He never travelled to heaven to gather new ideas; and he finds himself possessed of no other qualifications than what mere common observation and a plain understanding can confer.[31]

Reynolds thus unequivocally rejects the transcendent classical discourse, which endows the artist with supernatural powers, in favor of an entirely normative and empirical discourse founded on "common observation and a plain understanding." Somehow, with no other qualifications, the artist should be able to arrive at the ideal.

In his *Salon of 1767*, Diderot similarly borrows some of the rhetoric of Platonic transcendence to describe the ontological aspirations of the classical artist to "raise [his works] to the second order" (as a direct representation of the Idea), rather than remaining on the "third order" (a copy of a copy of the Idea; that is, a copy of natural objects).[32] As for Reynolds, however, such language is only figurative. It is designed to preserve the high status of classical art and its artist, and should not be taken to imply that the artist has supernatural powers. The editor of the *Encyclopédie* could not give credence to any transcendent version of artistic process. In a theoretical gloss explaining Diderot's terminology, his publisher Grimm explains that the modern empirical notion of the "general idea" (see below) replaces the older Platonic notion of the "first type":

> To get a good handle on this very abstract theory, we must recall that what our modern Plato here calls the 'general idea,' was by the old Plato called 'the truth' or 'the first type.' This type, this truth, existed, the old Plato says, in the understanding of God; and the *fantasmata*, the forms, which our philosopher calls 'the individual thing,' were so many emanations of these first types, of these truths existing in the understanding of God. Thus the truth, the type, the general idea, does not exist in nature. The old Plato would tell you that it exists in the divine understanding, the modern Plato would say that it's an ideal being.[33]

The "general idea" is the modern empirical equivalent of the Platonic Idea; it differs, however, in that the general idea does not exist exclusively "in the divine understanding," but is "an ideal being"—the word "ideal" is here to be taken in its etymological sense as a product of the (human) mind: an empirical idea, and not a transcendent one.

In his "Recherches philosophiques sur l'origine et la nature du beau," Diderot makes a further objection to transcendent doctrine: the Platonic theory of beauty tells us only "what [beauty] is not, but does not tell anything of what it is."[34] This problem is indeed endemic to transcendent classical art theory, which almost invariably concentrates on repudiating worldly beauty rather than describing ideal beauty or explaining how to achieve it. In his First Ennead, for example, Plotinus directly addressed the question of how to visualize the ideal: "But what must we do? How lies the path? How come to vision of the inaccessible Beauty, dwelling as if in consecrated precincts, apart from the common ways where all may see, even the profane?" How indeed? "He that has the strength, let him arise and withdraw into himself, foregoing all that is known by the eyes. . . . [A]ll this order of things you must set aside and refuse to see: you must close the eyes and call instead upon another vision which is to be waked within you, a vision, the birth-right of all, which few turn to use."[35] As Diderot suggests, although Plotinus claims here directly to confront the question of how to discover the ideal, his answer is more concerned with rejecting the apparent beauty of "profane" vision than it is in showing how, exactly, to attain transcendent vision. Because transcendent processes by definition depend upon supernatural events or sources, they are not susceptible to the cause-and-effect explanation of the natural sciences, the only kind of explanation that could satisfy Diderot. Ultimately it is to read transcendent art theory against the grain to seek out concrete formulas for visualizing ideal beauty and producing works of art. Such visions are ineffable; they are dependent on divine inspiration and not on human powers, and are therefore not susceptible to reasoned explanation. Both Plotinus and Plato are concerned more with truth than with beauty, and while for both, as for Keats, "Beauty is Truth, and Truth Beauty," they do not mind sacrificing the formal viability of Beauty to preserve the ontological superiority of Truth.

It would clearly be ahistorical to extend these objections to the point of evacuating all transcendent process from the history of idealizing art theory and practice, as Reynolds does. Transcendent discourses have been given credence throughout history. Indeed, artists in particular are still described, at least in popular and metaphoric discourse, as endowed with certain "gifts" or an innate "vision" that they strive to convey. Whether we choose a transcendent or empirical explanation of superlative art is ultimately, I believe, a matter of prejudice, or even faith: faith in grace or faith that empirical science will eventually explain the apparently ineffable. However, Reynolds's and Diderot's observations do accurately point out a crucial distinction between transcendent and empirical classical theory: for the latter, the process of visualizing ideal beauty should be predicated only on the data of the senses and should be explicable throughout as the causal events of a purely normative mental activity.

Against Selection

The rejection of the transcendent discourse on art leaves the idealizing artist with considerable theoretical difficulties. The aspiration of all idealizing art is to render a transcendent perfection that is nowhere directly available on earth. There is a neat reciprocity in proposing a transcendent process to achieve this product, and indeed we may question whether a transcendent product is at all possible without a transcendent process. However, in addition to the basically Platonic tradition of transcendent classicism, there was an equally venerable empirical tradition, focused mainly on the notion of "selection," as we saw. Although "nature has not refined to perfection any single object in all its parts," Zeuxis rendered ideal beauty by selecting the most perfect parts of the most beautiful maidens of Croton.[36] With this process, it seems, the artist relies only on empirical data and normative mental processes, but is able to achieve a model of beauty that surpasses its source material.

Although the idea of selection was a commonplace of classical art theory for centuries, many theorists in the late-eighteenth century noted its fundamental incoherence on both practical and theoretical levels. In his *Salon of 1767*, Diderot contrasts the pursuit of the *beau idéal* to portraiture, the imitation of a particular individual model. Addressing a fictive artist-friend, Diderot "broaches matters of the technique of [the artist's] craft," asking, "If you'd selected as a model the most beautiful woman known to you, and had rendered with the utmost care all her facial charms, would you think you'd represented beauty? If you answer me positively, the youngest of your students will refute you, and tell you that you'd produced a portrait."[37] For Diderot, individuals are corrupted both "at the point of origin" (that is, through what we would today call genetics) and "through circumstantial necessity" (that is, through the deforming effects of "daily, habitual functions").[38] Thus the ideal woman could occur on earth only if she were both born perfect and subsequently preserved from all the worldly functions and passions that would deform her features. This is manifestly impossible, and sufficient to disqualify portraiture from any pretense at representing ideal beauty: "it is impossible to imagine . . . an equilibrium so rigorous and continuously maintained that nothing would have gone awry, be it on the side of excess or on that of absence."[39] Of course, Zeuxis had also rejected the idea of merely copying an individual model, but Diderot extends his critique of the "portraitic" method to the selective process as well. Worldly passions and functions will affect not only the "integral mass" of the individual but also the "separate parts,"[40] and therefore even a selective imitation is still in the portraitic mode: "if there's a portrait of a face, then there's a portrait of an eye, there's a portrait of a neck, of a throat, of a stomach, of a foot, of a hand, of a big toe, of a fingernail, for what is a portrait if not the depiction of a being in all its individuality?"[41] Selection is only a more piecemeal type of portraiture—a portraiture of parts rather than of the whole—and thus selection still results only in the individual, not in the ideal. Selection-theory is incoherent because perfect parts cannot subsist in this imperfect world any more than perfect wholes can, and thus for Diderot "there is not, nor could there be, either an entire subsisting animal nor a portion of a subsisting animal which, strictly speaking, you could take as a primary model."[42]

In his *Essai sur l'idéal* (1837), Quatremère de Quincy agrees with Diderot that the "ideal style . . . cannot be understood as being the superficial imitation of a collection of parts of the human body."[43] Significantly, for Quatremère, unlike Diderot (whose rejection of selection-theory remains purely theoretical), the process of selection is formally catastrophic as well as philosophically incoherent. Lysippus did not, in fact, counsel artists to "copy in detail an arm from one, a leg or foot from another, a torso from another, and so on." Such a process would not be "physically practicable."[44] How could the artist unify the representation? What would in fact result from any "joining of dispersed individual beauties"[45] would be a formal disaster, a "masterpiece of discordance."[46] Although Quatremère acknowledges the widespread acceptance of the Zeuxian method as a mode of classical process, he ultimately dismisses selection as only "a metaphor employed by art theory" that could not have been employed by artists themselves:[47] "it is nothing but a clever method, employed by the writer, to cause the reader to imagine a comprehensive perfect beauty." The ancient writer, *qua* writer, had to take recourse in this rhetorical device "in order to make the mind understand what he could not show to the eyes."[48]

Both Diderot and Quatremère note an even more fundamental problem with selection-theory. Asked how he makes a statue of a beautiful woman, Diderot's artist-friend replies: "I have a great number [of women] undress for me; all of them have some parts that are beautiful and others that are misshapen; I take from each of them whatever is beautiful." Diderot, unsatisfied, but this time allowing for the sake of argument that perfect parts may exist in this world, probes further: "And how do you recognize these parts?—Why by comparison with the antique, which I've studied closely.—And if the antique had not existed, how would you proceed? You do not respond."[49] Diderot's probing has apparently confounded his interlocutor; indeed, to my knowledge selection-theory had never addressed the question of *how the artist knows what to select*. Quatremère similarly notes that the selection of one part over another demands some external criterion, and asks, "On what should [the artist's] preference be founded? What is the basis of the choice?"[50] One possible answer to that question, that we simply know a beautiful part when we see it, fails to distinguish between the *beau* and the *beau idéal*, that is, between the subjective beauty of individual taste and the universal beauty of classical aspiration. Diderot accordingly asks how true (classical) beauty can be distinguished from that which is "judged beautiful in accordance with a popular opinion confronting the artist at his birth and that shapes his judgment."[51] A second answer to that question, that while we may not be born with innate ideas of perfect beauty, we are endowed with a special "sixth sense" that allows us to recognize it (as Thomas Hutcheson suggested, for example), is mere sleight-of-hand, grounding selection-theory in a deferred form of transcendent art theory.[52] A third answer, that the artist selects that which conforms to antique models of the ideal, basically grounds selection-theory in imitation, and is susceptible to the fundamental objection that Diderot raised about the process of imitation: how did the Ancients, who "had no antiquities," select ideal beauty from natural deformity?[53] Diderot thus asserts, "It's an old wives' tale, my friend, that in order to formulate the statue, real or imagined, that the ancients called the canon and that I call the ideal model or true line, they scoured nature, borrowing from her the most beautiful portions of an infinity of individuals, from which they constituted a whole. How would they have recognized the beauty of those portions?"[54] Selection-theory is philosophically incoherent, formally disastrous, and ultimately does not answer the question of how to discover the ideal; it only displaces it.

Abstraction and Generalization

Having rejected imitation, inspiration and selection, Diderot asserts that the true method of idealization, that which was practiced by the Ancients and that which should be adopted by modern artists, is a fourth process: abstraction. Answering his own question, Diderot says that the Ancients managed "to rise to the true ideal model of beauty" simply by means of "effacing the changes and deformities worked by corrupting nature, either at the point of origin or through circumstantial necessity."[55] For Diderot, the means whereby the Greeks and subsequent "true" classicists derived ideal beauty from empirical deformity was by simply "effacing" or abstracting those deformities. At almost exactly the same time, Reynolds also asserted that in order to formulate "Ideal Beauty," the artist must "distinguish the accidental deficiencies, excrescences, and deformities of things, from their general figures," thereby making out "an abstract idea of their forms more perfect than any one original."[56] We shall examine his art theory more thoroughly in chapters 2 and 3. Similarly, for Quatremère de Quincy the ideal is to be formulated through "the power of ideating, or generalizing in abstraction,"[57] as opposed to the merely "portraitic" process of imitating the life-model in contemporary Academic art:

> We know that the modern works of which I have spoken, and to which we have given the name 'academic,' proceed according to a principle of imitation that I call 'particular' or 'individual,' and thus their style is the opposite of the style of the ideal. It is consequently natural to conclude that the antique works, where the 'ideal style' dominates, must have been the result of an opposite principle; that which we must call 'abstract' or 'generalizing.'[58]

Quatremère defines the process of generalization as follows: "To generalize, in the sense of this theory, is to bring as much of the object as is possible to the simplicity of its principle, to the moral unity of its nature—or, what means the same thing, to bring the object to its highest significant value, by disengaging it of its accessories."[59] Generalization achieves the "highest significant value" of the object by a process of abstraction, by "disengaging it of its accessories." Quatremère constantly uses the terms "abstrait," "abstraction," "générale" and "généraliser" to describe classical process and products.[60] Throughout his *Essai sur l'idéal*, Quatremère distinguishes between a "particularized and minute way of seeing" and a "generalized way of seeing."[61] He accordingly describes Greek art as marked by this abstraction: the Greek image of man evinces a process of "privation" and a "systematic negligence;"[62] it is "purified," "purged of all its accidental minutiae" to its "elementary type,"[63] with "few details, large divisions, and above all simplicity."[64]

The process of abstraction can be conceptually separated from those cited above. Abstraction is the inverse of selection-theory, arriving at the ideal by eliminating imperfections rather than by collecting piecemeal instances of perfection. Because Diderot was so aware that selection-theory begs the question of what to select, he felt it necessary to account for how abstraction knows what to "efface." He thus describes a gradual realization and refinement of the abstractive process in ancient Greece, admitting only one starting postulate: that the largest, most obvious deformities are easily recognized because of their singularity and extremity.

> [The Greeks] began to develop a sensitivity to these great changes, to the most extreme deformities and the most intense suffering. This was the first step, one that really affected only the general mass of the animal system, or a few of its main parts. With the passage of time, in an advance which was slow, tentative, painfully groping . . . the recasting was effected on lesser parts, and then on still lesser parts, and after these on the very smallest ones, such as fingernails, eyelids, eyelashes, and hair.[65]

Thus for the ungrounded, additive practice of selecting beautiful parts, Diderot substitutes a gradually refined, subtractive process of abstracting the deformed. The very deformed is easily recognized; and once the Ancients discovered the general principle of abstraction, it was gradually applied to smaller and less obviously deformed parts; and by this means the Greeks slowly derived a model of ideal perfection.

The notion of abstraction can also be distinguished from the neoclassical process of imitation and the Neoplatonic process of inspiration. Clearly no consultation of prior artistic models is necessary, and as Diderot asserts, abstraction-theory can thus resolve the question of how the Ancients discovered the ideal. Abstraction also does not rely on any transcendent knowledge, but only on ordinary perception and the normative mental functions of comparison and elimination. In these respects the process of abstraction resolves a major problem with both the imitative and the transcendent routes to the ideal: the utter passivity of the artist relative to the model. In both transcendent and neoclassical processes the artist receives the ideal from an authoritative outside source, and thus is open to charges of not truly knowing the ideal. Although subsequent classical art theorists borrowed Plato's notion of inspiration as the origin of their knowledge of the ideal, in so doing they also inherited Plato's own scorn, for Socrates' apparent compliment to Ion in calling rhapsodic and poetic activity a direct channeling from the gods was actually backhanded. Ion is too slow witted to realize Socrates' implication that he is an idiot, only a mouthpiece for a message he does not understand (*Ion* 533c–535a). Reynolds explicitly makes this point by ridiculing the common figuring of inspiration as a poet writing directly from the dictation of a winged genius:

> To understand literally these metaphors or ideas expressed in poetical language, seems to be equally absurd as to conclude, that because painters sometimes represent poets writing from the dictates of a little winged boy or genius, that this same genius did really inform him in a whisper what he was to write; and that he is himself but a mere machine, unconscious of the operations of his own mind.[66]

For Reynolds, the notion of inspiration does not convey any status to the artist; quite the reverse, for the inspired type of "genius" is literally external to the artist, an attribute of God and not of the painter. The inspired artist is like a machine responding to the beck and call of an external mind, and thus the artist's own ability remains purely mechanical, like that of any other craftsperson. Imitation-theory is subject to the same objection. Diderot calls those who copy the Antique "servile, almost stupid imitators of their predecessors" who "have but an incomplete notion" of the ideal.[67] Once again, genius resides outside of the artist, this time in prior artists. With generalization, by contrast, classical artists do not copy a prior ideal—one that preexisted their work and their minds—but actually derive it for themselves, actively transforming the rude chaos of accidents and deviations that is the phenomenal world into a higher reality, a higher truth, and a higher beauty. With generalization, the artist *originates* ideal beauty, rather than passively copying it.

Selection-theory similarly appears to offer an original classicism, and is like generalization-theory in that it is also empirical, predicated on the ordinary perception of nature and the operation of normative mental faculties. Indeed, many empirical classical theorists of the late-eighteenth century and beyond continue to refer to selection as a valuable tool in formulating ideal beauty. However, selection and the venerable Zeuxis myth are probed, taken less literally, and where they are preserved, new qualifications are introduced. In his article "Idéal" for the *Encyclopédie*, François-Jean de Chastellux makes the conventional distinction between the "imitative" as a "vulgar and narrow mode that consists only in copying that which is under the eyes," and the "ideal," which designates "the highest point of perfection that can be attained." The process of selection, or what Chastellux denominates "le choix de la belle nature," is explicitly opposed to the process of abstraction or the "research for abstract and ideal beauty," and indeed as for Diderot selection emerges as a sub-operation of the imitative mode, and not of the ideal mode.

> [There is] no one even a little acquainted with the fine arts who can believe with the masses that the choice of *la belle nature* suffices to . . . give birth to a model of beauty such as the *Apollo Belvedere*. . . . When Zeuxis assembled the most beautiful women of Croton to copy the particular and local beauties that each one of them eminently possessed, he only made simple studies. It was no doubt with the aid of abstraction that he succeeded in painting a perfect figure.[68]

Quatremère de Quincy took more pains than Diderot or Chastellux to preserve selection in the idealizing process and the integrity of the Zeuxian myth as its paradigm, but he glossed that myth with the proviso "to consult is not necessarily to imitate, still less to copy the separate parts."[69] As an artistic process, Quatremère knows, selection is incoherent unless there is a valid criterion guiding selection: "In effect, if [the artist] gives preference to a part on the body of one model instead of another, he decides on this preference by comparing this or that part to a *type intérieur* that he possesses."[70] Although Quatremère borrows the notion of the *type intérieur* from Cicero's transcendent art theory, he argues that this *type* is not an innate or transcendent idea, but rather an empirical idea: it is "a collection of acquired knowledge," an image that the artist's "studies and observations have allowed him to acquire."[71] He even argues (wrongly, I believe) that Cicero never meant his *type intérieur* in the Platonic sense.[72] For Quatremère, the *type intérieur* is in fact what contemporaneous empirical philosophy called the "general idea," formed in the mind through abstraction: "This is the true *type général*, the true exemplar to which we can compare each part of the particular model."[73] Selection-theory is cogent only when grounded in generalization-theory.

Relatedly, Henry Fuseli notes that only by consulting a prior "homogenous" idea could Zeuxis have avoided another problem with selection-theory, the discordance of any work formed by aggregate selection:

> Fancy [is] not [able] to compose an ideal form by mixing up a mass of promiscuous beauties; for, unless you consulted what was homogenous and what was possible in Nature, you have hatched only a monster: this, we suppose, was understood by Zeuxis when he collected the beauties of Agrigentum to compose a perfect female.[74]

For Fuseli, two criteria must guide the selection and aggregation of perfect parts: possibility and homogeneity. The "possible" is of course the traditional criterion of Aristotelian poetics, and will preclude the sort of monstrous results that could easily result from a random selection of parts. More significant for my purposes is Fuseli's mobilization of the criterion of "homogeneity," literally "sameness" within a type or "genus." The process of abstraction achieves homogeneity in exactly this sense, for the artist eliminates all that differs from individual to individual within a class, retaining only that which is common to all of its members. Inasmuch as Chastellux, Fuseli, and Quatremère allow selection to inform the process of the idealizing artist, then, they do so only when the criterion for selection is predicated on prior knowledge of the "abstract" or "general" idea.

Such a concerted and systematic assault on imitation, inspiration, and selection—hitherto the three main theoretical pillars of the classical tradition—could have been raised only if these theorists felt secure in the epistemological cogency of the new method of idealization through abstraction and generalization. What, then, are "general ideas"? How does the process of "abstraction" arrive at them, and how do they instantiate the ideal and resolve the problematics of classical art? To answer these questions, we must turn to the empirical epistemology of John Locke and his followers such as David Hume and Etienne Bonnot, abbé de Condillac. In empirical epistemology, human knowledge of all sorts—including knowledge of what the classicist calls the ideal—must ultimately be derived from sensory data as modified by normative mental faculties. A cursory "map" of the eighteenth-century empiricist's mind will serve to indicate the terrain through which sense-ideas must pass and the processes they must undergo in order to become ideal knowledge.

Abstraction and Empirical Epistemology

The eighteenth-century empiricist's model of the mind was largely materialist. Ideas were thought to enter the mind through the physical stimulus of perception as "sense-impressions" and to be stored there in fluid sacs of "animal spirits" or at the nodes of a network of nervous fibers. In turn, perceived and stored ideas were thought to be connected in the mind by the stimulation of certain of these sacs or nodes, causing the animal spirits to flow from one sac to another, or causing a distribution of tensions in the network of nervous fibers, making up "trains of thought."[75] Mental functions were accordingly described as ways of organizing these trains into controlled groupings depending on need.

At this level of analysis, there are only two basic mental functions: the additive connection of ideas by stimulating the flow of animal spirits, and the subtractive division of ideas by denying that flow. The first thing a mind must do is to *discern* a given idea or sense-impression from its constantly changing perceptual matrix, effectively by subtracting out the context and retaining only a more limited unit, such as a view of a single object at one moment in time, or even more simply, that of a particular color or of a particular texture. The latter were called "simple ideas," the fundamental unit of empirical epistemology.[76] Once a smaller unit-idea has been discerned, the mind can perform one of two operations, presided over by the two master faculties of eighteenth-century faculty psychology: it can put ideas together through the additive faculty of imagination or "wit," or separate them through the subtractive faculty of "judgment," as John Locke described in his highly influential *Essay Concerning Human Understanding* (1690):

> Wit l[ies] most in the assemblage of *Ideas*, and putting those together with quickness and variety, wherein can be found any resemblance or congruity, thereby to make up pleasant Pictures, and agreeable Visions in the Fancy: *Judgment*, on the contrary, lies quite on the other side, in separating carefully, one from another, *Ideas*, wherein can be found the least difference, thereby to avoid being misled by Similitude, and by affinity to take one thing for another.[77]

This restriction of mental operation to adding and subtracting, comparing and distinguishing ideas is a commonplace of eighteenth-century empirical epistemology. Even the most complex mental operations were reduced to these two basic operations.

Also a commonplace is the qualitative distinction that Locke makes between wit and judgment. Although it creates "pleasant pictures" through its additive operation, wit "misleads"; it is the subtractive faculty of judgment that carries the burden of finding truth. A major part of the qualitative distinction between wit and judgment is due to the fact that the additive wit was largely theorized as a reflexive function of the mind, one not necessarily controlled by the thinking subject. A branch of epistemology called "associationism" outlined the ways in which ideas were reflexively—and often perniciously—connected in trains of thought. Initially formulated by Thomas Hobbes in his epistemological and political treatise *Leviathan* (1651), associationism took on increasing importance in both the epistemological and aesthetic theory of the subsequent century, as Walter Jackson Bate has noted:

> The psychological criticism of this period was either determined or, more often, strongly colored by the doctrine of 'the association of ideas'; it may be questioned, indeed, whether any philosophical or psychological doctrine has since permeated critical thought in so great a degree as did that of the association of ideas at this time.[78]

Martin Kallich has traced the extensive influence of associationism from its roots in empirical epistemology to its popular application by such critics as Isaac Watts, George Turnbull, Henry Home (Lord Kames), James Beattie, Alexander Gerard, Archibald Alison, and Francis Jeffrey.[79] For our purposes, it is most important to remark that the doctrine of associationism essentially multiplied the traditional problem of classicism, for not only is nature bewilderingly diverse, misshapen, and contingent, the viewer's mind adds to this diversity and contingency through its own reflexive associative deflections.

Implicitly in Hobbes and Locke, and more explicitly in David Hume, the principles governing the association of ideas were reduced to two: ideas are reflexively connected if they entered the mind at around the same time (the principle of contiguity), or if they are similar to each other in some way (the principle of resemblance). As Hume noted in his *Treatise of Human Nature* (1739–40):

> 'Tis plain, that in the course of our thinking, and in the constant revolution of our ideas, our imagination runs easily from one idea to any other that *resembles* it, and that this quality alone is to the fancy a sufficient bond and association. 'Tis likewise evident, that as the senses, in changing their objects, are necessitated to . . . take them as they lie *contiguous* to each other, the imagination must by long custom acquire the same method of thinking, and run along the parts of space and time in conceiving its objects [Hume's italics].[80]

Crucially, neither one of these associative principles has any necessary correlation with truth or natural law. Resemblance is a particularly slippery and subjective concept, clearly, and while certain contiguous ideas, such as fire and heat, do seem to be naturally and necessarily connected, making the associative leap from one to the other valid, by far the majority of contiguous ideas are not, such as fire and hearth or fire and the teakettle. Although as we shall see in chapter 2, a *repeated* contiguity of certain ideas or sense-impressions does begin to authorize certain associations as natural, this is not always the case, and indeed often results in a confusion of natural law with local custom.

The reflexive association of ideas by the wit or imagination, then, is not conducive to the acquisition of valid and objective knowledge. As should be clear by now, the possibility of reason given this model of mind will be heavily predicated on the ability to *subtract* and *distinguish* ideas—hence Locke's promotion of the subtractive judgment over the additive wit. Immediate sensory data forms a constantly changing flow of perceptions from which the mind must be able to discern specific individual objects and "simple ideas," effectively by subtracting out the contextual ideas with which they are associated in original perceptions. In turn, each perception and each simple idea reflexively calls up other ideas with which it was previously contiguous and to which it is related by resemblance, further contributing to the white noise of the mind. From these associations, the rational mind must eliminate merely coincidental contiguities (a *madeleine* and Sunday mornings in Combray) and irrelevant resemblances (a *madeleine* and a *coquille Saint-Jacques*), and validate only those contiguities and resemblances that are authorized by natural law. The associations in Proust between pastries and crustaceans, and pastries and childhood are perhaps aesthetically pleasing and biographically authentic, but they are surely not ontologically authorized. Locke's French follower Etienne Bonnot, abbé de Condillac gives a particularly vertiginous picture of the rapidity and density of these reflexive associations. Immediate sensory data forms

> a sequence of fundamental ideas. . . . Out of each idea will rise other series of ideas that form chains. . . . We could even note that, as the chain lengthens, it subdivides into different chains, such that the farther we get from the first set, the more the chains multiply. One fundamental idea is linked to two or three others; each of these to an equal number, or maybe even more, and so on.[81]

This description holds for *one* set of connections, arising from one sensory experience. Since sensory data is continually being displaced by new impressions, even this account underrates the rapid and cacophonous associative deflections occurring in time.

Such is the chaos and density of these associative deflections, and such is their fundamental irrationality, that for Hobbes, Locke, and Condillac (among others), the ungoverned association of ideas is both a symptom and a cause of madness. In *Leviathan*, Hobbes noted that while "fancy" or associative wit can please,

> without steadiness and direction to some end, a great fancy is one kind of madness, such as they have, that entering into any discourse, are snatched from their purpose by everything that comes in their thought, into so many and so long digressions and parentheses that they utterly lose themselves.[82]

For Locke as well, "*mad Men*" are those who, "having joined together *Ideas* very wrongly, they mistake them for truths." This creates a "disorderly jumbling" in the stock of ideas in the mind,[83] which, Locke elsewhere notes, "gives Sence [sic] to *Jargon*, Demonstration to Absurdities, and Consistency to Nonsense, and is the foundation of the greatest, I had almost said, of all the Errors in the World."[84] Similarly, although Condillac reduces all mental operation to the association of ideas,[85] and although he notes that an individual who is not able to associate ideas "will be absolutely incapable of reflection; he will be an imbecile [*imbécille*]," he also asserts that the individual in whom the association of ideas is too rapid and strong "will have too much memory and too much imagination. . . . He will only barely be able to reflect, he will be a madman [*fou*]."[86] For eighteenth-century empirical epistemology, then, extramental nature is bewilderingly complex and contingent, and the reflexive tendency of the mind is to contribute further to this complexity and contingency by its own subjective associations. Without some subtractive force to restrain this "disorderly jumbling," the mind sinks into madness under the weight of its constantly multiplying and subdividing *chaînes* and *chaînons* of associative thought.

Laurence Sterne's novel *The Life and Opinions of Tristram Shandy*, published in installments between 1759 and 1767, playfully embodies the "associationist crisis" of eighteenth-century empirical epistemology. While that novel clearly demonstrates the fecundity of associationism as an aesthetic process, it also (and more to the point for my purposes here) demonstrates its ruinous effect on what the eighteenth century conceived as the rational pursuit of knowledge. The very first chapter cites rampant associationist digression as the creative device behind the text:

> . . . you have all, I dare say, heard of the animal spirits, and how they are transfused from father to son &c. &c.—and a great deal to that purpose:—Well, you may take my word, that nine parts in ten of a man's sense or his nonsense, his successes and miscarriages in this world depend upon their motions and activity, and the different tracts and trains you put them into, so that when they are once set a-going, whether right or wrong, 'tis not a halfpenny matter,—away they go cluttering like hey-go-mad; and by treading the same steps over and over again, they presently make a road of it, as plain and smooth as a garden-walk, which, when they are once used to, the Devil himself sometimes shall not be able to drive them off it.[87]

Constantly distracted by the digressive tracts and trains taken by his own animal spirits, the narrator Tristram doesn't even manage to get to the time of his birth until the fourth book of his autobiography. Like the cited passage—which is all one sentence—the text acts as an index of the "disorderly jumbling" of Tristram's mind.

Significantly, the confusion and distraction of that mind is specifically located in a Lockean crisis of associationism. The last phrase of the above citation directly paraphrases a passage from Locke's *Essay*:

> Custom settles habits of Thinking in the Understanding . . . which seems to be but Trains of Motion in the Animal Spirits, which once set a going continue on in the same steps they have been used to, which by often treading are worn into a smooth path, and the Motion in it becomes easy and as it were Natural.[88]

There is a dangerous similarity between the "as it were Natural" connections of ideas that are the result of mere "custom" (repeated contiguity) and Locke's just previous (but largely unexplored) assertion that "Some of our *Ideas* have a natural Correspondence and Connexion one with another."[89] Tristram's "animal spirits"—and hence his text—have been set a-going through a particularly "unhappy association of ideas." His father had formed the habit of winding the clock on the same night of the month that he made love to his wife. As a result of her husband's odd association of these actions in the dubious category "family concernments," Tristram's "poor mother could never hear the said clock wound up,—but the thoughts of some other things unavoidably popped into her head—& *vice versa*."[90] At the climax of Mr. Shandy's lovemaking, then, Mrs. Shandy interrupts with the apparently unrelated question, "Pray, my dear . . . have you not forgot to wind the clock?"[91] Mr. Shandy is startled, and as a result, the "animal spirits" that were to conduct Tristram's preembryonic "homunculus" to its place of reception were "scattered and dispersed." The homunculus arrived at its destination "ruffled beyond description,—and . . . in this sad and disordered state of nerves, he had laid down a prey to sudden starts, or a series of melancholy dreams and fancies for nine long, long months together."[92] Again, the problem is related to Locke's pedagogy, where dire results were said to attend the improper association of ideas, and it was accordingly the responsibility of parents and educators "diligently to watch, and carefully to prevent the undue Connexion of *Ideas* in the Minds of young People."[93] This startlingly disjunctive association, inculcated at such an unfortunately formative moment, resulted in Tristram's own permanent state of distraction and hence in his digressive style.

Tristram Shandy is of course a fictional text, but the knowledge of the nature and dangers of associationism that it relies on establishes at once the logical extreme of and the general cultural knowledge of the associationist problem. The issue is one of "distraction" and the fundamental tendency of the mind to make multiple, subjective, and indeed irrational leaps when the additive "wit" is uncontrolled by the subtractive "judgment." It is in direct relation to the associationist problem that we should understand the need for "generalization" and "abstraction," both in philosophical epistemology and in classical art.

That need is predicated first of all on the overabundance and fundamental particularity of sensory data and "simple ideas." As Locke noted:

> The natural tendency of the Mind being toward Knowledge; and finding that, if it should proceed by, and dwell upon only particular Things, its Progress would be very slow, and its Work endless: Therefore to shorten its way to Knowledge, and make each Perception the more comprehensive; the first Thing it does, as the Foundation of the easier enlarging its Knowledge, either by Contemplation of the things themselves, that it would know; or conference with others about them, is to bind them into Bundles, and rank them so into sorts, that what Knowledge it gets of any of them, it may thereby with assurance extend to all of that sort; and so advance by larger steps in that, which is its great Business, Knowledge. This, as I have elsewhere shewed, is the Reason, why we collect Things under comprehensive *Ideas*, with Names annexed to them into *Genera* and *Species*; *i.e.* into kinds, and sorts.[94]

The "particular" ideas of sensation are variously grouped and ranked into more comprehensive ideas; it is only thus that the mind can attain knowledge of horses in general in lieu of the particular habits and form of every individual horse. As Locke notes, by means of this "bundling," various levels of inductive knowledge can be reached. Figure 3 shows a graphic representation of how the mind can impose a structure of general categories on its ideas, a structure corresponding to the general order of nature that underlies the particular perceived instances. The mind at its most basic level consists of a disorderly jumble of current sense-impressions and associationist deflections through prior sense-impressions and simple ideas with which those impressions have some connection. The duty of the mind is to reform that chaotic jumble of ideas into a rational taxonomic pyramid of knowledge, first by discerning distinct unit ideas (individual objects or simple ideas) from the complex and ever-changing impressions received by the senses, then by regrouping similar ideas into bundles and ranks that have a natural relation to one another, presided over (as we shall see) by "general ideas" that represent the distilled essence of all the individual ideas or entities falling under a given class, excluding any adventitious associations formed through merely coincidental contiguity and trivial resemblances. The categories "species, genus, family," and so on, familiar currently from the binomial taxonomy of the eighteenth-century Swedish naturalist Carl von Linnaeus, were used by Locke to rank and sort ideas as well. The red of a particular piece of cloth is a simple idea; it is part of the "species" red, which is part of the "genus" color, which is part of the "family" quality, and so on.

For Locke, the mind will refer to these "general ideas" in the pursuit of knowledge, rather than to any given particular idea or to an exhaustive survey of all similar particular ideas stored in the memory. Now the question becomes this: how does the mind form the "general

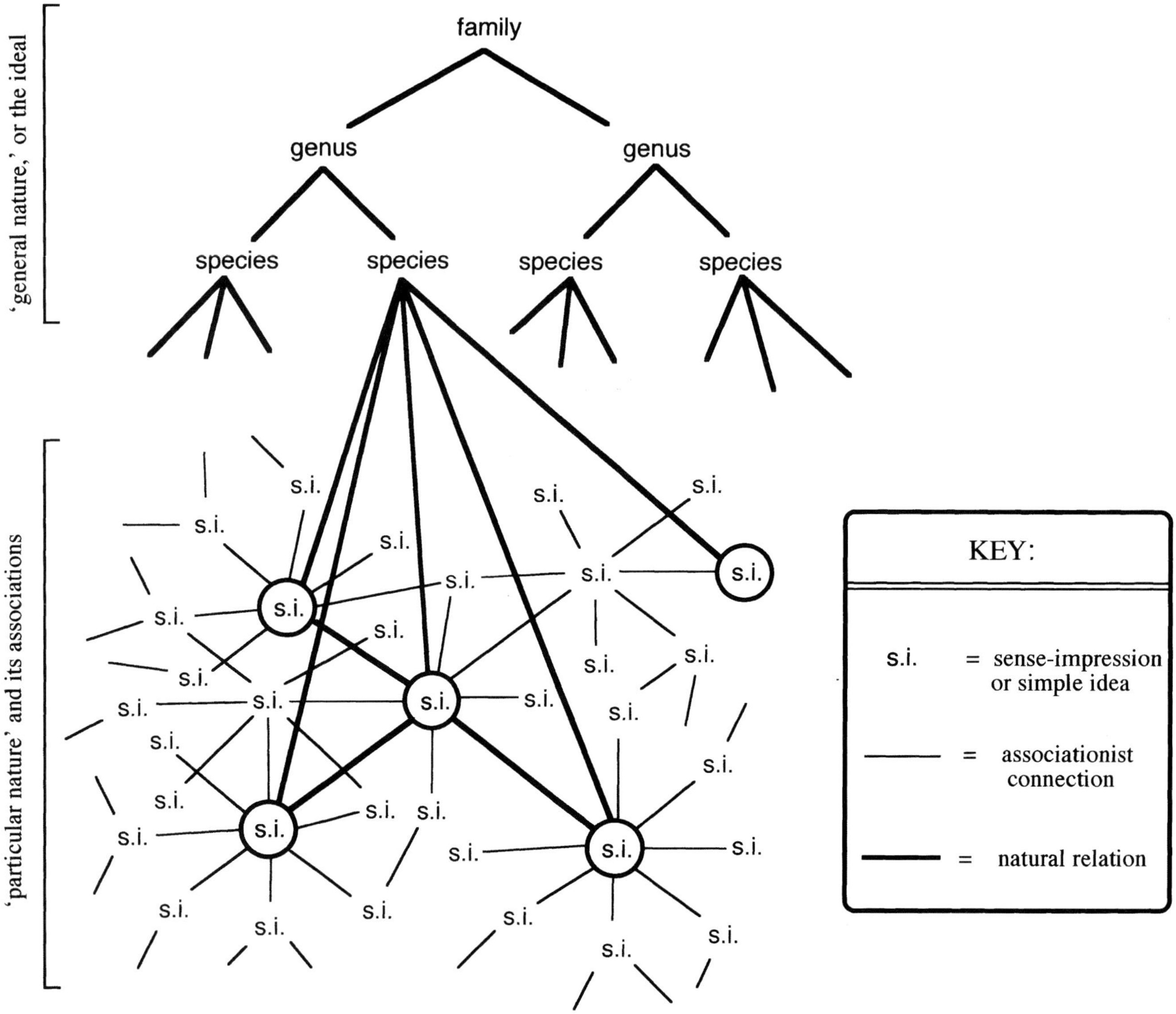

3. Tree diagram of sense-impressions to general ideas.

ideas" that are the ambassadors of a bundle of similar "particular ideas"? For Locke, general ideas of any taxonomic level are formed through a process called "abstraction." Although the context is part of Locke's consideration of language, the following passage shows the relation between abstraction and the general ideas that are necessary to broaden empirical knowledge, and gives us an idea of how the function of abstraction operates on the data of the senses:

> The use of Words then being to stand as outward Marks of our internal *Ideas*, and those *Ideas* being taken from particular things, if every particular *Idea* that we take in, would have a distinct Name, Names must be endless. To prevent this, the Mind makes the particular *Ideas*, received from particular Objects, to become general; which is done by considering them as they are in the Mind such Appearances, separate from all other Existences, and the circumstances of real Existence, as Time, Place, or any other concomitant *Ideas*. This is called *ABSTRACTION*, whereby *Ideas* taken from particular Beings, become general Representatives of all of the same kind, and their Names general Names, applicable to whatever exists conformable to such abstract *Ideas* [Locke's italics].[95]

The generalization of ideas occurs by "separating" or "abstracting" from those ideas "all other Existences" with which they occurred in particular contexts, "all the circumstances of real Existence," such as the marks or attributes that localize the idea as an individual existent in time and space, and "any other concomitant ideas" such as will arise through associationism. Even though its primary aim is (additively) to "bundle" similar ideas under the aegis of a representative type, the formation of the general idea is founded on a process of *subtraction*—the abstraction of contextual ideas, accidental and contingent qualities, and subjective associative deflections.

The eighth volume of Diderot's *Encyclopédie*, issued just two years before his *Salon de 1767*, contains an extensive discussion of general ideas and the process of abstraction under the entry "Idea" that, because of its clarity and obvious relevance to the idealizing project, is worth excerpting at some length:

> If I imagine a real being, and I retain all the qualities that are particular to that being, then the idea that I have is a singular idea; but if, discarding all these particular ideas, I retain only the qualities of that being that are common to all those of the same species, I form a universal, general idea.
>
> Our first ideas are obviously singular. I first have a particular idea of my father and of my wet nurse; I subsequently observe other beings who resemble this father, this woman, in terms of form, of language, and other qualities. I remark that resemblance, I give it my attention, I subtract from it the qualities by which my father and my wet nurse are distinguished from those others; and so I form an idea in which all these beings partake equally. . . . I thus form a general idea; that is, I discard from many singular ideas that which is particular to each, and I retain only that which is common to all. This sort of idea thus owes its birth to *abstraction*. . . .
>
> In observing the resemblance between general ideas, one comes to form ideas more general yet; thus one constructs a sort of ladder or pyramid that mounts by degrees, from the individual to the idea of all, the most general idea.[96]

The *Encyclopédie*, like Locke, goes on to discuss the prevalence and necessity of general ideas in language:

> Who could imagine and retain proper names for all the things that we know? Where would this multitude of singular names end? It is true that our understanding is founded on particular existences, but they only become useful as general conceptions of things, ranged under certain species, and designated by a given name.[97]

We are not concerned here with the names used to mark such general or abstract ideas. The name is arbitrary, as Locke recognized. There is no motivation obtaining between signifier (word) and signified (general idea) in verbal language, and therefore there is no motivation obtaining between the signifier (word) and the referent (general nature, or the ideal). The case is otherwise for the visual arts, where there can be conformity between the signifier (visual representation) and the signified (idea) inasmuch as the signified is itself visual, and therefore between the signifier (visual representation) and the referent (the ideal). Along these lines it is significant that Locke notes that abstract or general ideas are formed as clear and distinct "Appearances" in the mind: "Such precise, naked Appearances in the Mind . . . the Understanding lays up (with Names commonly annexed to them) as the Standards to rank real Existences into sorts, as they agree with these Patterns."[98] The "general idea" formed by the process of "abstraction" serves both to control associationism and to order nature into its essential classes, and is stored as a distinct image in the mind.

This, then, is what Reynolds, Diderot, and Quatremère mean by equating the classical ideal with the "general idea" and citing the process of "abstraction" as the way to formulate that idea. The abstractive capacity of judgment is mobilized both to distill the accidental and contingent particularity of empirical nature down to its underlying essence, and to eliminate the reflexive and largely subjective deflections of the associative imagination, retaining only those portions of perceptual data and only those associated ideas that are universally valid, authorized by natural law. It is in the art theory of Joshua Reynolds and the British Royal Academy that the notion of abstraction and generalization are most thoroughly explored, with a wide array of implications for both the theory and the practice of classical art.

2
Classicism and Generalization

Reynolds subjected classical art theory to the new empirical epistemology in his first published theoretical statements, a series of letters written in 1759 to Samuel Johnson's *The Idler*. Explicitly equating "beauty" with the "general idea," and "deformity" with the "particular," Reynolds wrote: "If it has been proved that the Painter, by attending to the invariable and general ideas of Nature, produces beauty, he must, by regarding minute particularities, and accidental discriminations, deviate from the universal rule, and pollute his canvas with deformity."[1] Johnson would have been predisposed to embrace this formulation, for it mirrors Imlac's ideas about poetic process in Johnson's novel *Rasselas* of the same year:

> "The business of a poet," said Imlac, "is to examine, not the individual, but the species; to remark general properties and large appearances: he does not number the streaks of the tulip, or describe the different shades in the verdure of the forest. . . . He must divest himself of the prejudices of his age or country; he must consider right and wrong in their abstracted and invariable state; he must disregard present laws and opinions, and rise to general and transcendental truths, which will always be the same."[2]

On one level, these statements are commonplaces of classical aesthetic theory. Both restate the Aristotelian distinction between history, which deals merely with "singulars" or "the thing that has happened," and poetry or art, which deals with "universals" or "what is possible as being probable or necessary."[3] What is novel here is Johnson's and Reynolds's usage of the terms "general" and "abstract" to describe the goal of classical art, and it is the nature and effects of this redescription that is the subject of this study.[4]

Like Diderot and Quatremère de Quincy, Reynolds misleadingly suggests that there was nothing novel about the notion of generalizing or abstracting towards the ideal. In his annotations to Charles du Fresnoy's *Art of Painting*, Reynolds attempts rather disjunctively to conform du Fresnoy's mid-seventeenth-century art theory to the eighteenth-century discourse of abstractive generalization. In lines 51 to 54 of the poem, du Fresnoy makes a commonplace declaration of the need to imitate the Ancients in order to depict the true beauty of nature:

> 'Tis Painting's first chief business to explore
> What lovelier forms in nature's boundless store,
> Are best to art and ancient taste allied,
> For ancient taste those forms has best applied.

Reynolds's gloss approves du Fresnoy's assertion that art entails "a knowledge of what is beautiful in nature," and eventually concurs, "to facilitate the acquisition of this ideal beauty, the Artist is recommended to a studious examination of ancient sculpture," but in between these classical commonplaces Reynolds interjects a process of generalization that is nowhere espoused in du Fresnoy's poem: "There is an absolute necessity for the Painter to generalize his notions; to paint particulars is not to paint nature, it is only to paint circumstances. When the Artist has conceived in his imagination the image of perfect beauty, or the abstract idea of forms, he may be said to be admitted into the great Council of Nature, and to 'Trace Beauty's beam to its eternal spring / And pure to man the fire celestial bring.'"[5] Although in his fifteenth and last Discourse, Reynolds claims with pride to have "in no part of [his Discourses], lent [his] assistance to foster *newly-hatched unfledged* opinions [Reynolds's italics]," as his use of the terms "abstract" and "generalize" suggests, his theory of classicism is in fact radically reconfigured to conform to the framework of eighteenth-century empirical epistemology.[6]

For Reynolds, what is "deformed in nature" is "what is particular and uncommon," and therefore the artist must "get above all singular forms, local customs, particularities, and detail of every kind" in order to achieve "ideal perfection and beauty":

> All the objects which are exhibited to our view by nature, upon close examination will be found to have their blemishes and defects. The most beautiful forms have something about them like weakness, minuteness, or imperfection. But it is not every eye that perceives these blemishes. It must be an eye long used to the contemplation and comparison of these forms; and which, by a long habit of observing what any set of objects of the same kind have in common, has acquired the power of discerning what each wants in particular. This long laborious comparison should be the first study of the painter, who aims at the greatest style. By this means, he acquires a just idea of beautiful forms, he corrects nature by herself, her imperfect state by her more perfect. His eye being enabled to distinguish the accidental deficiencies, excrescences, and deformities of things, from their general figures, he makes out an abstract idea of their forms more perfect than any one original; and what may seem a paradox, he learns to design naturally by drawing his figures unlike any one object. This idea of the perfect state of nature, which the Artist calls Ideal Beauty, is the great leading principle, by which works of genius are conducted.[7]

I quote this passage at length because of the density with which Reynolds deploys the new terms and processes of empirical epistemology and the seamlessness with which he conforms these terms to the commonplaces of classical art theory. As is usual in classical theory, nature is filled with blemishes and imperfections, a long way from "Ideal Beauty." As is usual in specifically empirical classical theory, the ideal must nonetheless be derived from that imperfect source: the artist must learn to "correct nature by herself" rather than rely on Platonic Ideas or past art. Intricately entwined with these commonplaces is Reynolds's solution to this problem, described in the terminology of a distinctly Lockean epistemology. Through a "long laborious comparison" of a "set of objects of the same kind," the artist gradually learns to "distinguish the accidental deficiencies, excrescences, and deformities of things," and determines what those objects "have in common." This process determines an "abstract idea" or "general figure," which, Reynolds explicitly asserts, is equivalent to the "Ideal Beauty" of classical aspiration.

In practice, Reynolds's espoused method involves two distinct but related processes. The first is an elimination of "accidents," that is, features that are unnecessary to the object or class of object. Such accidents are recognized by their rarity of occurrence. For example, in a survey of a number of human bodies, the artist will come to realize that features such as warts, birthmarks, freckles, jowls, supernumerary or missing fingers and so forth are relatively uncommon; and where they do occur, they occur in different places. Such a lack of uniformity reveals that these features are merely accidental to the human body, and should thus be entirely eliminated or abstracted. In the course of comparison, however, other features can be identified that are common to all individuals within a class, but which vary in form. With very rare exceptions, all human beings have noses, but the shape and size of the nose will vary considerably (within certain definite limits). With such features, a generalizing process is applied that identifies the average of all of those variations as the ideal. Reynolds explicitly called the ideal "that central form, if I may so express it, from which every deviation is deformity," thus more closely than Diderot or Quatremère de Quincy mirroring Galen's and Alberti's assertion that the ideal is an "average" or "mean" of all the particular deviations of individual nature.[8] In his 1759 *Idler* essays, Reynolds compared the variations of such features to "pendulums vibrating in different directions over one central point," and identified the center of that oscillation as the ideal: "To instance a particular part of a feature; the line that forms the ridge of the nose is beautiful when it is straight; this then is the central form, which is oftener found than either concave, convex, or any other irregular form that shall be proposed."[9]

Reynolds used the theory of abstraction and generalization to redescribe the epistemological, social, and ultimately economic value of classicism (or what he called "Grand Manner" art). The "instruction" of classical art consists not only in its display of exemplary narratives, but also in its display of general ideas. By representing these abstract or general ideas, classicism performs a valuable sorting function in the spectator's mind, subduing the contingency and multiplicity of his or her ideas, and taming the mad, disjunctive metonymic and metaphoric deflections of associationism. This epistemological consideration gives a new urgency to the commonplace distinction between classical practice and the naturalistic practice of copying phenomenal nature. A merely naturalistic art is worse than trivial for Reynolds; it is epistemologically dangerous inasmuch as it "divides" and "distracts" the mind—a potential that, as we have seen, was in eighteenth-century epistemology a root of "madness":

> [The painter should not] waste a moment upon those smaller objects which only serve to catch the sense, to *divide* the attention.[10]

> The subject selected [by the artist] . . . should be kept unembarrassed with whatever may any way serve to *divide* the attention of the spectator.[11]

> The mind is apt to be *distracted* by a multiplicity of objects; and that scale of perfection, which I wish always to be preserved, is in the greatest danger of being totally disordered, or even inverted.[12]

> We must take care that the eye be not *perplexed and distracted* by a confusion of equal parts.[13]

> To prevent the eye from being *distracted and confused* by a multiplicity of objects of equal magnitude, those objects . . . must be disposed in large masses and groups properly varied and contrasted.[14]

> The detail of particulars, which does not assist the expression of the main characteristick, is worse than useless, it is mischievous, as it *dissipates* the attention, and draws it from the principal point.[15]

We should pay particular attention to the language Reynolds uses to make this point, for what may seem at first to be a critical commonplace is implicitly linked to the associationist problem of late eighteenth-century empirical philosophy and art criticism. Reason is commonly metaphorized as a straight, clear discursive path or train of ideas. The words I have marked with italics indicate forks, detours, or mergers—associative divisions, deflections, and comminglings in the train of ideas. The "distracted" mind is drawn away from the point (<L DIS+ *trahere*, to draw); the "perplexed" mind simultaneously entertains multiple incompatible points (<L PER+ *plectere*, to braid); the "confused" mind links or fuses two or more distinct points (<L CON+ *fundere*, to pour), and so on.

In contrast to this distractive and perplexing multiplicity, the classical style is above all characterized by *unity* and *simplicity*. Unity and simplicity are also commonplace characteristics of classical art, but crucially, for Reynolds these are not only aesthetic qualities, but also epistemological ones. Just as the representation of "particular nature" distracts and perplexes the mind, classical or Grand Manner art has the capacity to "fashion and consolidate" our ideas, as Reynolds notes in a consideration of imitation that we shall further explore below:

> The addition of other men's judgment is so far from weakening our own, as is the opinion of many, that it will fashion and consolidate those ideas of excellence which lay in embryo, feeble, ill-shaped, and confused, but which are finished and put in order by the authority and practice of those, whose works may be said to have been consecrated by having stood the test of ages.[16]

Again, Reynolds's language is particularly significant within the context of empirical epistemology: ideas "in embryo" tend to be "feeble, ill-shaped and confused" and must be "finished and put in order." The empirical mind in its raw state consists of a "stock of ideas" of particular nature, loosely (and often perniciously) organized into confused groupings and sprawling chains by the association of ideas. These ideas must be "fashioned and consolidated" in order to constitute valid knowledge. The main agent of this consolidation, for Reynolds as for Locke, is the subtractive "judgment," which performs the function of carefully distinguishing among the connections formed by original contiguity and the faculty of wit. The faculty of judgment discerns unitary ideas, rejects certain contiguous associations as the result of mere coincidence, and rejects certain associations formed through resemblance as mere fancy, thus forming an idea of the general species of object, or the general principle of the act. Accordingly, Reynolds explicitly considers the contemplation of great art to be an "addition of other men's judgment" to our own, an aid to our own process of controlling our associations and generalizing our ideas.

Reynolds's assertion of the capacity of great art to aid its spectators' minds—to foster their judgment, to fashion and consolidate their ideas, to elevate their considerations from the merely local and particular to the universal and general—ultimately amounts to a social and economic justification of patronage. The "taste" exhibited by such patronage is not founded on the je ne sais quoi, an ineffable and vaporous personal quality, but on the solid foundation of the new empirical epistemology. Although presumably anyone can *profit* from an art of general ideas, the ability to *appreciate* the general is not innate or universal, but "presupposes in the spectator, a cultivated and prepared artificial state of mind." Hence the social display of classical taste is a display of a well-formed mind.[17]

Social historians of eighteenth-century art have further linked this display to established social and economic hierarchies: the capacity to appreciate the general and abstract indicates an ability to transcend the material and factional considerations of the manual trades. In his *Life of Sir Joshua Reynolds*, James Northcote transcribes a "fragment written in [Reynolds's] own hand" that best illustrates this point:

> Josiah Tucker, Dean of Gloucester, at a meeting of the Society for the Encouragement of Arts, Manufactures, and Commerce, said, that he thought a pin-maker was a more useful and valuable member of society than Raffaelle. This is an observation of a very narrow mind; a mind that is confined to the mere object of commerce, that sees with a microscopic eye but a part of the great machine of the economy of life, and thinks that small part which he sees to be the whole.[18]

The concern to elevate the "liberal" artist above the "mechanical" tradesperson is frequently evident in Reynolds's *Discourses*. Here Josiah Tucker's failure to concede that point indicates his inability to see the whole "economy of life" rather than just his own narrow economic interests.[19] The capacity to appreciate the general, in art as in life, is especially reserved to "gentlemen" who by their abundance of money and lack of profession are released from the petty exigencies of material and economic life: the display of taste for the general is a display of social status as well as a well-formed mind.

Generalization from the Customary to the Universal

Reynolds repeatedly and unequivocally equated the empirical "general idea" with the classical ideal, "the idea of the perfect state of nature, which the Artist calls Ideal Beauty."[20] Indeed, he called the Lockean "general idea of nature" the "presiding principle" of his Discourses.[21] However, there is a major philosophical problem with that equation that requires a somewhat lengthy—but worthwhile—digression. We may concede the necessity of generalizing our ideas, and we may find in abstraction and averaging a cogent method for doing so, but does the "general idea" carry the ontological status attributed to the classical ideal? In other words, what guarantees the conformity of our general ideas with the transcendent and universal truth and beauty of classical aspiration? We saw Reynolds, like Galen and Alberti, assert that the "central form" of a class of objects is the "truth of nature" and the "highest beauty," but what if such ideas are merely human conventions, useful for workaday knowledge and for communication, but devoid of any higher ontological significance? Accepting this notion is tantamount to denying the possibility of knowing the ideal at all, or at least to demoting it from its status of metaphysical reality to the status of a simple human custom.

As John Barrell has noted, Reynolds repeatedly advances an argument that would seem to imply that his theory of beauty was indeed merely a matter of local custom, not of universal truth. Reynolds first advances the argument that beauty arises from custom in his 1759 letters to *The Idler*:

> Among the various reasons why we prefer one part of [nature's] works to another, the most general, I believe, is habit and custom. . . . [C]ustom alone determines our preference of the colour of the Europeans to the Ethiopians, and they, for the same reason, prefer their own colour to ours.
>
> . . . [I]t may be inferred [from this], that the works of Nature, if we compare one species with another, are all equally beautiful; and that preference is given from custom, or some association of ideas.[22]

Judgments of beauty are mere "custom," not universal; and they accordingly differ by region and race and are guided by local and subjective associations, not by universal and objective judgment.[23] To extend this grounding of beauty and truth in custom to its logical conclusions, as we tend to do today, is to limit "beauty" to preference, and "truth" to prejudice, utterly dissociated from any higher aesthetic or ontological status.

Barrell has taken such statements to indicate a shift in Reynolds's thinking towards a newer "discourse of custom" and away from the older "discourse of the universal" that is undoubtedly more characteristic of classical art theory before Reynolds. "In his early addresses to the

Academy," Barrell argues, Reynolds defined the Academic project in terms of a discourse of "civic humanism," in which "we become citizens of the republic of taste by overcoming the customs, prejudices and interests which conceal from us our true identity, as that may be imagined to be based on the universal and permanent principles of human nature." Reynolds's form of argument "changes tack" in the "later addresses," for Barrell:

> He slackens his efforts to define a civic art, and a "universal" republic of taste constituted on the uniformity of human nature in "all ages and at all times," and begins to consider whether the dignity of his art, and the security of the state, might not better be defended in the discourse of custom. . . . In these discourses, he begins, accordingly, to advocate an art which would address itself to a national community, a nation state, different in character from other states . . . a result of the history, the customs, and of whatever else constituted the national character of the British.[24]

I agree with Barrell's assertion that Reynolds played back and forth between the customary and the universal in his *Discourses*. But I do not concur that the *Discourses* show evidence of a change in Reynolds's thinking on this issue. As we saw, Reynolds fully stated the "discourse of custom" already in 1759—nine years before the delivery of his first Discourse—and Barrell himself qualifies this change of tack between the "earlier" and "later addresses" into near nothingness: the "first six discourses" *and* the "ninth and tenth" support the universalizing tendency, while the "seventh and eighth discourses" and the "thirteenth and fourteenth" advance the discourse of custom. Furthermore, Barrell notes that "[Reynolds's] conversion to the discourse of the customary is never complete," and can actually be found bolstering the universalizing discourse "where it seems appropriate or convenient" to Reynolds.[25]

If there is a gyroscopic shifting between these apparently different discourses in Reynolds's theory, it is because Reynolds believed that he had reconciled them; that he had formulated a method whereby the artist begins in the merely customary but nonetheless ends in (or at least rises towards) the universal. Indeed, this reconciliation was essential not only to Reynolds's art theory, but also to the entire epistemological project of the Enlightenment. We have seen that the empirical mind begins with the chaos of particular nature, which is further perplexed by the promiscuous couplings of associationism. As with the clock-coitus confusion in Mrs. Shandy's mind, these associations are frequently the result of mere custom, in Hume's formulation the "constant conjunction" of certain contiguous ideas or perceptions. Yet even for a conscientious skeptic like Hume, there is a possibility of formulating valid knowledge out of this chaos. In an essay on "The Rise and Progress of the Arts and Sciences," Hume makes a distinction between chance and cause on the approach to a "real science": "What depends upon a few persons is, in a great measure, to be ascribed to chance, or secret and unknown causes: What arises from a great number, may often be accounted for by determinate and known causes."[26] This recognition of the subjective, psychological foundation of the notion of causality is, of course, consistent with Hume's earlier treatment of the cause-and-effect relation in his *Treatise*: causality can only be recognized by the constant conjunction (an associationist phenomenon, proper to the subject and not the object) of two perceived events occurring contiguously in time. Hume notes that such a constant conjunction of ideas, occurring in a single or only a few minds, is not sufficient to extrapolate a general, universally valid law. A second level of confirmation is necessary: the confirmation of a "great number" of other observers who have performed the same experiment or who have seen the same association. In other words, the rise from the merely contingent (the individual and subjective) and customary (the collective but possibly only local and circumstantial) to the truly scientific (the universal and objective) is achieved through *repetition*. By implication, the very same principles underscore the customary as the universal: they differ not in *type*, but merely in *degree*, the amount of repetition and confirmation. The merely customary will eventually be revealed as such by its extinction, while the universal truth will remain operative. Hume applies this reasoning to the arts in his consideration "Of the Standard of Taste." The foundation of certainty in the arts "is the same with that of all the practical sciences, experience; nor are they any thing but general observations, concerning what has been universally found to please in all countries and in all ages."[27] The universalizing discourse is the same as the discourse of custom for eighteenth-century empirical epistemology, at least in its foundation and method. The customary simply localizes a lesser or provisional degree of the universal, one confined to a narrow temporal or geographic extension.

Reynolds makes this point most clearly in the seventh Discourse, precisely where he most strongly states Barrell's discourse of custom:

> In proportion as these [customary] prejudices are known to be generally diffused, or long received, the taste which conforms to them approaches nearer to certainty, and to a sort of resemblance to real science, even where opinions are found to be no better than prejudices. And since they deserve, on account of their duration and extent, to be considered as really true, they become capable of no small degree of stability and determination by their permanent and uniform nature.[28]

We should note the many different ways in which Reynolds was able to word these two means of proportioning truth to temporal and geographic extension: long received and generally diffused, duration and extent, permanent and uniform. Indeed, this is the very move performed by the function of abstraction, which as Locke noted consists in considering ideas separate from the adventitious circumstances of time and place.[29] Hence Johnson, although antagonistic to many of Hume's conclusions, substantially agrees with his method of approach to truth: the artist "must consider right and wrong in their abstracted and invariable state; he must disregard present laws and opinions, and rise to general and transcendental truths, which will always be the same."[30] Through the abstraction of the customary circumstances of time and place, we can approach (what deserves to be considered) "real science" and "really true." Reynolds accordingly advises his students that

> a knowledge of the disposition and character of the human mind can be acquired only by experience: a great deal will be learned, I admit, by a habit of examining what passes in our bosoms, what are our own motives of action, and of what kind of sentiments we are conscious on any occasion. . . . This examination will contribute to suggest to us matters of enquiry; but we can never be sure that our own sensations are true and right, till they are confirmed by more extensive observation. One man opposing another determines nothing; but a general union of minds, like a general combination of the forces of all mankind, makes a strength that is irresistible.[31]

The process of generalization does not divide an absolute truth from an absolute falsehood, but rather defines a *gradual approach* to greater and greater truth by abstracting the contingent circumstances of time and place as soon as they become evident. As an empirical process, generalization necessarily begins with a purely subjective examination of "what passes in our bosoms." It advances from there to the more widely accepted truths or customs of a particular time and place, and gradually rises ever "nearer to certainty" by repeated experience and consultation with others.

Reynolds uses this reasoning to describe the way in which the classical artist can transcend mere custom. There is a crucial difference between the "genuine habits of nature" and "those of fashion," and the artist must therefore "endeavour to separate simple chaste nature, from those adventitious, those affected and forced airs or actions, with which she is loaded by modern education."[32] In the epistemological context of British empiricism, this is no easy feat, for peculiarly British eighteenth-century customs such as fashions or gestures are constantly repeated in the viewer's experience, reinforcing their associative connection and therefore their appearance of being "genuine habits of nature." The solution to this problem is simple: the viewer must range more widely in experience, and take note of the very different fashions of other people with other customs. In the seventh Discourse, Reynolds imagines a meeting between a fashionable European and an equally fashionable Cherokee. The former has "cut off his beard, and put false hair on his head, or bound up his own natural hair in regular hard knots . . . and after having rendered them immoveable by the help of the fat of hogs, has covered the whole with flour." The latter has "bestowed as much time at his toilet, and laid on with equal care and attention his yellow and red oker on particular parts of his forehead or cheeks, as he judges most becoming." Relieved of its derogatory tone, this image would probably seem to his audience to invite a contrast between European civility and Cherokee barbarity, but Reynolds does not draw this facile conclusion.[33] Instead he says, "whoever of these two despises the other for this attention to the fashion of his country, which ever first feels himself provoked to laugh, is the barbarian."[34] The encounter with other fashions and customs should provoke introspection, and not ridicule or condemnation. Ideally both the European and the Cherokee should realize from this encounter that what they had hitherto thought to be indispensable accouterments to male beauty are in fact adventitious customs. Following Reynolds's abstractive route to the ideal, the merely customary annihilates itself in confrontation with other customs: the Cherokee's face paint and the European's wig are found not to be universal, and should therefore be eliminated by each.

The use of wigs and face paint are examples of entirely adventitious customs, ones that are highly local in time and space, and ones that can easily be eliminated or abstracted. However, there are other ideas or customs that are widely diffused in time and space, but which vary considerably in their particular forms. Reynolds considers an example of such customs that begins to demonstrate a second level of challenge in determining and rendering general ideas in art: showing respect. In Reynolds's experience, all cultures seem to have a system of social ranking that requires submissive gestures, but particular manifestations of submission vary considerably. It is only "a matter of custom" whether a given culture shows respect by "bowing the body, kneeling, prostration, pulling off the upper part of our dress [i.e. the hat], or taking away the lower [the shoes]." However, Reynolds insists that underlying those variable customs is a single "general idea" that can be discovered by comparing them all and reducing them to their fundamental commonality: "The general idea of shewing respect is by making yourself less."[35] This is indeed an adequate epistemological solution to the challenge of discovering the general idea of showing respect across cultures—but crucially, it is not an adequate aesthetic solution. How can the artist represent a show of respect without choosing one or another mode of self-lessening? This is indeed a concession to custom, but it is only an aesthetic concession, not a philosophical concession. The practical constraints of the visual arts, which tend toward concrete representation, require the artist to represent a particular custom (removing the hat or kneeling), even though he or she can clearly conceive the underlying universal. This practical consideration helps to account for Reynolds's occasional concessions to the customary in his art and in his theory, even when his philosophy tends always to privilege the universal.

Thus in considering customs, a distinction must be made between the entirely adventitious, like wigs and face paint, which should be abstracted, and the particular or customary manifestations of a universal rule, like bowing or removal of the shoes, which should be generalized were possible toward their higher truth. There is also frequently some difficulty in making the distinction between which of these two operations to apply, as is particularly evident in Reynolds's consideration of fashion in clothing. On one hand, clothing of some sort is worn by all people, but on the other hand its particular form varies so greatly that there does not seem to be any general rule. Reynolds accordingly equivocates, but he does so in a reasoned manner that preserves the overall logic of generalization. In several places in the seventh Discourse, he asserts that all fashion is "equally distant from nature,"[36] a matter for the mechanical art of tailors and not for the liberal art of painters.[37] Significantly, Reynolds applies this logic even to Ancient drapery and ornaments, thus using the logic of generalization to annihilate an important aspect of neoclassical practice. It is only his period's "veneration" for Ancient Greece and Rome that causes its "approbation of every ornament and every custom that belonged to them, even to the fashion of their dress." If all fashion is equally distant from nature, then a togate sculpture is no more ideal than the "fantastick dress" of Van Dyck portraiture. Reynolds explicitly asserts that both are considered excellent simply by "association": the association of Van Dyck dress with excellence in portraiture, and the association of Greco-Roman fashions with "the pleasure and knowledge which they have afforded us" through their art and philosophy.[38] Logically, then, clothing should be entirely abstracted from idealizing representation.

In the same discourse, however, Reynolds directly contradicts himself, arguing that there is such a thing as a "general dress" underlying all of the varieties of fashion. While the "component parts of dress are continually changing from great to little, from short to long," the "general form still remains: it is still the same general dress which is comparatively fixed, though on a very slender foundation."[39] And this general dress, Reynolds later suggests, is indeed best manifested in the fashion of the Ancients. Since both of these arguments occur in the same Discourse, Reynolds must have felt there was no major contradiction between them. And indeed, if we follow Reynolds's notion that idealization is a process, an approach to the ideal, there is no contradiction. Ancient dress is more ideal because it has greater "simplicity" than modern or Van Dyck dress, the encumbrance of which in "whimsical capricious forms" essentially means that there is *more to abstract* in modern fashion than in the ancient.[40] Although this argument reinstates neoclassical practice, we should note that it does so based, not on a neoclassical argument from dogmatic authority, but on the discourse of abstraction. Ancient drapery is still a particular and customary type of clothing, not universal, but its lesser degree of adventitious ornamentation makes it more ideal, *comparatively* speaking, than modern dress. This is again the sliding scale of idealization that Reynolds everywhere mobilizes with respect to his espoused process. There is no sharp distinction between the customary and the universal. There are only greater or lesser degrees of particularity and universality articulated on one hand by the approach, where possible, to the general or "central form," and on the other hand by the degree of abstraction of the merely accidental.

Reynolds advances another argument in favor of a judicious concession to custom that does not contradict his overall thesis of generalization. Because custom is definable as a practice that is diffused across time and space, as opposed to an individual eccentricity or idiosyncrasy, customary practice can safely be considered a form or degree of truth. Truth can be known only by its geographic and temporal diffusion, and even adventitious customs manifest such diffusion. However, Reynolds everywhere asserts that the "apparent truth" of customs is only a "secondary truth that comes from conformity to general prejudice and opinion."[41] "Real truth" must necessarily be "uniform," and indeed is known by its uniformity across time and space. Secondary truths, such as those of fashion, are "variable," and therefore must be called only "truth by sufferance, or truth by courtesy." Although secondary truths are allowable in painting because art must please as well as instruct, crucially, for Reynolds, such customary truths are only a matter of pleasure, and not of instruction, which is the province of those more general ideas that abstract viewers from the circumstances of their time and place.[42]

Reynolds's seventh Discourse thus does concede that the "apparent or secondary truths [that proceed] from local and temporary prejudices, fancies, fashions, or accidental connexion of ideas" are an important part of painting. However, he does not allow them to substitute for or even compete with the larger "general habits of nature; the result of which is an idea of perfect beauty." Although the "secondary truths" of custom "deserve and require the attention of the artist" because they "have still their foundation, however slender, in the fabrick of our minds," Reynolds concludes that they require attention only in proportion to their generality, "in proportion to their stability or duration, or as their influence is more or less extensive."[43]

Most current thought would continue to doubt the validity of generalization-theory on two grounds, one philosophical and one social. The latter, social objection can be formulated as follows: were a truth to be discovered by abstraction or generalization as universal, it would as likely be the result of intellectual or actual colonialism as the real existence of a "Great Family of Man." The artists, scientists, and historians who investigate the geographic and temporal diffusion of a custom are inevitably prejudiced, and will mistake or can indeed only understand geographically and temporally Other customs according to the paradigms of their own prejudices; or, alternatively, the appearance of a general uniformity may simply be a result of the diffusion of a local custom enforced by an economic and political hegemony. I have no desire to negate this objection: it is valid, and there is considerable tenacity as well as superfluity in Reynolds's and other theorists' assertions that the man (inevitably a man) who is best able to generalize his ideas and thus act for the general good of the nation and of humankind is a "gentleman."

The philosophical objection to generalization-theory is this: as Karl Popper and many others would insist, the generalizing process could never arrive at the absolute ideal, for just as no amount of repetition can give absolute certainty that the same experiment performed tomorrow will have the same results, no breadth of consultation or consent will ever be universal. Such a goal is neither possible as a purely practical matter, nor is it theoretically possible, for who knows what future generations will recognize as merely customary and contingent in today's ideal? Locke and Hume also recognized this objection: our certainty that the sun will rise tomorrow is founded only on our past experience, and it is neither self-evident nor demonstrable that past experience is a certain indicator of future events. Along these lines it is significant that Reynolds is surprisingly modest in his claims for the generalizing process. By means of cross-geographic and cross-temporal consultation, the artist "approaches nearer to certainty" and to a "sort of resemblance to real science." The end results have "no small degree of stability and determination," but are only a degree nonetheless; they are sufficiently broad that they "deserve, on account of their duration and extent, to be considered as really true," but Reynolds does not assert their absolute truth.[44] Reynolds's ideal is not the dogmatic and absolute ideal of Neoplatonic philosophy, then, but this once again establishes his relatively thorough internalization of contemporaneous epistemology. Reynolds's is a theory of *idealization*, not of the ideal; he defines a process, and not a product. In fact, Reynolds's notion of art as an *approach* to the ideal, both in the sense of a method and in the sense of a gradual advance, is perhaps the most fruitful as well as the most characteristic feature of his "modern" classicism, as we shall see.

Generalization and Imitation

At this point, Reynolds's continuing insistence on the utility of imitation becomes clear from two different angles, both arising out of his equation of the classical ideal with the general idea. First, just as classical art helps the general audience to "fashion and consolidate" their ideas, it helps the tyro artist in the same way. In his third Discourse, Reynolds notes that "the investigation of this [central] form, I grant, is painful, and I know but of one method of shortening the road; this is, by a careful study of the works of the ancient sculptors; who, being indefatigable in the school of nature, have left models of that perfect form behind them." Imitation is thus useful because the "central form" is more nearly approximated in Ancient art than it is in particular nature. Note that this argument subsumes the neoclassical practice of imitation to the overall logic of generalization: imitation is of value only as a means of discovering the central form. Note as well that imitation is *only* a short cut, not the sine qua non of classicism for Reynolds. The Ancients themselves, who had no prior models, prove this: "If industry carried them thus far, may not you also hope for the same reward from the same labour? We have the same school opened to us, that was opened to them; for nature denies her instructions to none, who desire to become her pupils."[45] While Reynolds does reassert the value and even necessity of the imitative or neoclassical process throughout his Discourses, these assertions are always qualified and even, in several important ways, radically different from the commonplace scholarly understanding of that process.

As we saw in chapter 1, imitation is not simply borrowing for Reynolds and the British Royal Academy. Although Reynolds asserts that "the study of other masters, which I here call imitation, may be extended throughout our whole lives,"[46] he specifically disavows what he calls a "*pasticcio*" process except for young students:

> It would certainly be no improper method of forming the mind of a young Artist, to begin with such exercises as the Italians call a *Pasticcio* composition of the different excellencies which are dispersed in all other works of the same kind. It is not supposed that he is to stop here, but that he is to acquire by this means the art of selecting, first what is truly excellent in Art, and then what is still more excellent in Nature.[47]

Those acquainted with the scholarship on latter-day classical art will know to what extent the works of even professional artists are reduced to a pastiche of borrowings from prior sources, as though this alone sufficiently accounts for the process of the artist as well as the meaning and authority of the work.[48] Reynolds, however, explicitly notes that the *pasticcio* process is only a pedagogical exercise restricted to the "young artist." The utility of this exercise is a corollary to the overarching utility of classical art: just as classical art will "fashion and consolidate" the ideas of the general audience, the study of past classical art is useful in "*forming the mind* of a young artist [emphasis added]"—and, we should note, the ultimate application of that mind is not to recycle prior ideas, but to discover "what is still more excellent in Nature."

Accordingly, Reynolds determines the moment at which students are released from this obligation to imitate others as the moment in which their minds are properly formed. And this, significantly, is in turn defined as the moment in which they can trust their own "judgments." Reynolds divides the study of art into "three distinct periods."[49] Only the first period is technically artistic, in which the artist learns "the rudiments; including a facility of drawing any object that presents itself, a tolerable readiness in the management of colours, and an acquaintance with the most simple and obvious rules of composition." The second and third stages are the domain of epistemology. In the second stage, the student should "collect subjects for expression; to amass a stock of ideas, to be combined and varied as occasion may require." The amassing of a "stock of ideas" is best achieved, not in nature, but in past art, among the "perfections which lie scattered among various masters," simply because past (classical) art better embodies the truth of nature than does individual nature herself. Accordingly, it is during this second, imitative stage that the crucial "general idea" of nature is formed in the student's mind: more "sublime and general instructions" are achieved, and the varied perfections "are now united into one general idea, which is henceforth to regulate his taste, and enlarge his imagination." Significantly, in this second, mind-forming stage the student "must still be afraid of trusting his own judgment," while in the third stage, the student may "confid[e] now in his own judgment." Again, what seems to be a commonplace phrase has special resonance in eighteenth-century epistemology: it is the faculty of judgment that carries the burden of forming the rational mind by imposing a superstructure of general ideas on the confusion and diversity of particular nature. After the judgment has been formed in the second stage, "the third and last period emancipates the Student from subjection to any authority, but what he shall himself judge to be supported by reason." The judgment being trained, the artist's own reason may be trusted to make valid connections among properly general ideas and continue the classical project. Thus, as Reynolds asserts again and again, the true purpose of imitation is not to amass forms and motifs, but rather "to form a *mind* [Reynolds's italics]," a mind informed by general ideas and by the principles of abstraction and generalization, and thus a mind "to which all nature is then laid open, and which may be said to possess the key of her inexhaustible riches."[50]

In this way, Reynolds is able to reinforce the commonplace classical insistence on imitation, but using contemporary epistemology to do so. So far, however, imitation remains largely within the tradition of past classical art theory. Although Reynolds gives it a less restrictive definition than is usually allowed in the scholarship, imitation retains its fundamental quality of an appeal to prior authority: trust past masters, for it is in them that general ideas are to be found. But from another angle—the second angle that I alluded to above—Reynolds's consideration of the utility of imitation is entirely novel, tending not toward a retrogressive conformity to past art, but a progressive advance of classicism beyond the achievements of past art. Recall that the determination of any idea or practice as "universal" and not merely customary depends upon its diffusion in time and space. Just as the encounter between a Cherokee and a European aids in the abstraction of the peculiar customs of each, the practice of consulting past art embodies the process of discovering what aspects of present practice are merely a matter of temporary custom, and what aspects are universal. A single, solipsistic mind can already generalize its ideas to a certain extent as that mind contemplates multiple objects of the same sort, identifying the contingent and accidental by its relative rarity. We remain within the confines of direct experience with nature, the foundation and ultimate justification of all empirical science, but nonetheless we begin to approach the universal. However, so far the process would result only in a very limited, geographically and temporally local ideal: a late eighteenth-century British ideal for Reynolds, a quattrocento Italian ideal for Alberti, a fifth-century B.C.E. Greek ideal for Polykleitos, and so on. How is this local and temporal restriction to be transcended? Presuming that Reynolds, Alberti, and Polykleitos all mobilized a valid process of generalization grounded in actual observation, a more universal ideal can be achieved simply by combining their efforts, and those of other classicists past and present, local and foreign. Still the process is founded only on the specific, directly observed data of individual nature, but it becomes ever more universal and certain as "a general combination of minds . . . makes a strength that is irresistible." Imitation, the neoclassical process, is preserved within the process of generalization as a means of increasing the duration and extent of the artist's ideas.

It is for this reason that Reynolds advises students to range widely in their imitations:

> In the study of our Art, as in the study of all Arts, something is the result of *our own* observations of Nature; something, and that not a little, the effect

> of the example of those who have studied the same nature before us, and who have cultivated before us the same Art, with diligence and success. The less we confine ourselves in the choice of those examples, the more advantage we shall derive from them; and the nearer we shall bring our performances to a correspondence with nature [Reynolds's italics].[51]

This advice makes little sense to the common understanding of classical imitation as an approach to the ideal as it is fixed in a few canonical works: Reynolds here explicitly adjures the student to imitate across a broad range of models. The paradox that the more extensive our imitation of others the "nearer we shall bring our performances to a correspondence with nature" is resolved by the understanding of nature as *general* nature, and imitation as a means of furthering the process of generalization. In other words, Reynolds has found in generalization-theory the ultimate epistemological ground for imitation-theory. For most classical theorists, imitation is regressive: Reynolds imitates Poussin who imitates Raphael who imitates Michelangelo who imitates the Antique, establishing a classical tradition entirely upon the basis of imitation, and grounding imitation only in an appeal to prior authority. This retrogressive appeal to authority would appear to be anathema to any empirical inquiry—mere hearsay rather than true science—but it does begin to make sense in the context of generalization-theory. For Reynolds, imitation is not regressive but progressive: the imitation of past art embodies the artist's consultation of multiple minds at multiple times and in multiple places. No longer does imitation problematically result in the *n*th-degree degradation of an ideal that was more perfect in the past. On the contrary, it has the potential to be constantly and progressively refined by each generation. While the theory of generalization loses the capacity to assert the *absolute* universality of its ideals, it gains the capacity to assert the *increased* universality of its ideals over those of past classicism.

Generalization and Social and Intellectual History

The classical project for Reynolds, Diderot, and Quatremère de Quincy is thus embodied in a *process*, not a product; the process of generalization, not the copying of an a priori ideal. The novelty of this formulation should be underscored. In all of the other three classical methods that we have considered, the ideal preexists the artist: in imitation, it is adopted from a few, privileged works; in inspiration it is transferred from God's mind; and in selection it is found preexistent, albeit dispersed, in nature, and furthermore is presumably recognized only by comparison to a preexistent idea of beauty. Accordingly, in these three processes the artist's task is to conform to that preexisting ideal as closely as possible. In generalization-theory, by contrast, the ideal is not a priori but a posteriori. What artists discover in the consultation with others' works is not the ideal itself, but the method of approaching it, and indeed the data for advancing beyond those prior ideals. This formulation effectively reverses the classical dynamic as it is usually described: classicism is not a retrospective project, a recovery of a lost ideal, but rather a continuing advance (with considerable difficulty) toward a future ideal. Indeed, because he recognized that the ideals of artists past and present are contingent and constantly subject to revision, Reynolds goes so far as to assert that the absolute ideal is unattainable:

> The mind is continually labouring to advance, step by step, through successive gradations of excellence, towards perfection, which is dimly seen, at a great though not hopeless distance, and which we must always follow because we never attain.[52]
>
> [T]he beauty of which we are in quest is general and intellectual; it is an idea that subsists only in the mind; the sight never beheld it, nor has the hand expressed it: it is an idea residing in the breast of the artist, which he is always labouring to impart, and which he dies at last without imparting; but which he is yet so far able to communicate as to raise the thoughts, and extend the views of the spectator.[53]

Although the philosophical and social place of Reynolds's classicism is preserved in its capacity to "raise the thoughts, and extend the views of the spectator," the ideal of any given artist or any given historical period is always only contingent, awaiting further refinement by subsequent artists, gradually rising through "successive gradations," providing a challenge to each generation of artists who, with new data and fresh observation, "dimly" see the possibility of further advancements. Generalization-theory is a *progressive* aesthetic, not a regressive aesthetic; it does not presume an a priori, "absolute" ideal, fixed in Ancient art or in a presumed "supercelestial place" and confirmed by the submission of latter-day artists to its predetermined contours, but a work in progress.

This progressive formulation of the classical project is of crucial importance both to the late-eighteenth century and to subsequent developments. In the late-eighteenth century, it is the very condition that made generalization-theory philosophically valid, especially in opposition to earlier models of reason such as those championed in Britain by the Cambridge Platonists of the seventeenth century. Ernst Cassirer describes a "characteristic change of meaning in the concept of reason" between the seventeenth century and the Enlightenment:

> In the great metaphysical systems of [the seventeenth] century—those of Descartes and Malebranche, of Spinoza and Leibniz—reason is the realm of the "eternal verities," of those truths held in common by the human and the divine mind. What we know through reason, we therefore behold "in God." Every act of reason means participation in the divine nature; it gives access to the intelligible world. The eighteenth century takes reason in a different and more modest sense. It is no longer the sum total of "innate ideas" given prior to all experience, which reveal the absolute essence of things. Reason is now looked upon rather as an acquisition than as a heritage. It is not the treasury of the mind in which the truth like a minted coin lies stored; it is rather the original intellectual force which guides the discovery and determination of the truth.[54]

In the older understanding of reason, the classical methods of transcendence and imitation made sense. If the "eternal verities" are like "minted coins," then the problem of classicism lies in the acquisition of these preexistent coins and their redeployment across the surface of the canvas. The mind and the canvas are both like the ground of a collage, a receptive medium on which this valuable coinage is collected and transferred. Just like Cassirer's pre-Enlightenment concept of reason, inspiration and borrowing, and to a certain extent selection as well, are all describable as the act of collecting a priori coins, whether those coins are found in God's mind, in past art, or piecemeal in nature.

By contrast, the Enlightenment's new concept of reason stresses not product, but process: the "intellectual force" that discovers the truth, not the individual nugget of truth. If the new classical ideal no longer preexists as a nugatory unit, but must be derived from experience by a certain process, always in a state of refinement, we should look for a corresponding emphasis on *verbs*—process words—rather than on nouns in generalization theory. Along these lines it is significant to remark that while the concept of the nugatory Platonic Idea dates back in the forms *idee*, *idea*, and *ideal* to at least the English fifteenth century, the verb form "to idealize," indicating the *process of discovering* the ideal, has its first historical usage (according to the *Oxford English Dictionary*) in the 1780s and '90s. Similarly, the first recorded usage of the verb form "to generalize" dates to 1751, in a particularly telling passage in Bolingbroke's *Essay on Human Knowledge*: "The mind . . . makes its utmost efforts to generalize its ideas," and again there is a great concentration of examples from the late-eighteenth and early-nineteenth centuries.[55] Even given the tremendous unlikelihood that the *OED* has indeed recorded the first written usage of the verbs "idealize" and "generalize," the abundance of references around the end of the eighteenth century indicates their currency during that period. It is my argument that the epistemological theory of the eighteenth century made such verbs necessary and relevant as indications that the "general" and "ideal" did not exist somewhere on their own in God's mind or passed from generation to generation, but were indeed to be arrived at through a human mental process. Reynolds's version of classicism is not to be read as a genealogical tree tracing a heritage backward to the Antique or to God, but rather as a stage in a progressive evolution toward a future ideal.

If both in its general notion of reason and in its specific understanding of epistemology the empirical philosophy of the late-eighteenth century made a reconsideration of classical art theory necessary, the same is true in the more practical realm of social history. In the first chapter of *The Discovery of Painting*, Iain Pears reviews a growing anxiety around the way in which social status was to be recognized and conveyed in the eighteenth century. The basic tenor of his citations and arguments is that an older method, which projected status through traditional symbols, such as a certain mode of dress or a certain code of behavior, became increasingly untenable throughout the century. Such symbols operated based on the recognition of certain visual insignia that were easily counterfeited. The "genteel mania of the age," together with an expanding market that made the deployment of such signs more readily available to the "unworthy" than was the case in the past, resulted in a dynamic widely recognized in bourgeois societies: the attempt to upgrade one's social class through conspicuous consumption and the deployment of symbols of a higher status.[56] Ann Bermingham has also traced this dynamic in the first chapter of her book *Landscape and Ideology*, reviewing contemporaneous etiquette books, which systematized and encoded gestures and poses with social and class meanings, and which were consulted by the practitioners of the English "conversation piece."[57]

Part of the response of the "higher circles" to this problem was to reformulate, again and again, the symbols and gestures of status. The result of this response is a rapid change in what we would recognize as "fashion." William Hazlitt later acidly defined this dynamic: "fashion is gentility running away from vulgarity, and afraid of being overtaken by it."[58] But the redefinition of the insignia of status only temporarily displaces the problem, it does not solve it; and furthermore even that temporary solution threatens the recognition of status symbols, which depend for their operation on the very conventionality that allows their appropriation by the unworthy. And the continual disavowal on the part of the higher circles of what they had previously accepted as inalienable symbols of greatness threatens, by implication, the validity of current symbols, and results in a dynamic of emulation in the "upper ranks" that is grotesquely similar to that practiced by the lower.

As David Solkin has noted, what was required in this context was a reformulation of the means whereby "greatness" could be conveyed. We will later explore Solkin's argument about the new appearance of greatness, but for the moment it is most significant to remark the fundamental shift in its theoretical basis. The older system of conveying greatness through discrete individual signs conforms to the older philosophical notion of reason as a deployment of nugatory "coins" of knowledge, and jibes well with the older classical method of imitation: once again, the greatness of a work of art (and its subject matter or sitter) is established by acquiring and distributing those coins. What Solkin, Bermingham, and Pears have noted is that this tactic, recognized by reading the work as a sort of "collage" of preexistent motifs, was socially as well as philosophically inept by the late-eighteenth century. Generalization was classicism's new basis for conveying greatness by approaching the depicted object to its general idea, conveyed through what we will explore as techniques of generalization. This solution was proffered as one that was philosophically and socially sound: one that resided not in a preexistent system of signs but rather, as Solkin underscores, in the *ability of the painter*, and which was therefore not available to mediocre talents or those who patronized them. In effect, the new way of conveying greatness in painting resides not in iconography but in style. An iconographic analysis of a work reveals the iconic signs whereby the sitter is aggrandized, tracing the deployment of the discrete, nugatory "coins" of worth across the surface of the painting: a certain type of lace or fabric, a sword, a gesture, and so on. These iconographic signs are easily available to imitation. The new basis of greatness will reside in the *style* of the work—not *what* is depicted, but *how* it is depicted: the act of generalization. It is within the terrain of style that we must trace the signs—now indexical rather than iconic signs—of greatness, as they reveal the painter's ability to approach the subject or sitter toward the crucial general ideal. In the next chapter, we shall examine the surface appearance of generalization; the signs of the painter's ability as embodied in certain techniques of generalization, and the way in which these signs were read as allocating value to works of art, to the artist who made them, to the patrons who purchased, sat for and appreciated them, and to the society populated by these paragons.

3
Techniques of Generalization

Did the theoretical changes outlined in the previous chapters result in a change in classical practice? On preliminary consideration, the answer is no. Although it is interesting that the period that is widely acknowledged to be the last significant gasp of the classical tradition saw a radical reformulation of its theoretical basis, that reformulation seems to have been designed to accommodate the established formal characteristics of classical art: "simplicity" and "unity." Similarly, although they lend a long and prestigious genealogy to that process, Diderot's and Quatremère's assertions that the Greeks and other prior classicists practiced generalization also seems to guarantee that latter-day generalizations should look similar to Greek and other past classical art. While the previous chapters effectively ground late eighteenth-century classicism in a specifically late eighteenth-century epistemology, the theory of generalization can easily be taken as a new gloss on an old formula, rather than as grounds for an entirely new practice.

Also militating against too great an insistence on the practical effects of generalization-theory is the fact that the scholarship has not signaled any marked change in late eighteenth-century classical style. The history paintings of Anton Raffael Mengs, Jacques-Louis David, Angelica Kauffmann, and Gavin Hamilton are well within the stylistic boundaries established by Michelangelo, Raphael, Annibale, and Poussin, and if the oeuvre of the chief theorist of generalization, Reynolds, transgresses those boundaries, the inevitable argument is that he did not practice what he preached. It seems that the debates between transcendent classicism and empirical classicism, and between selection and abstraction were only a matter of theory. After all, style consists of certain commonalities in formal features, and the matter of tracing differences in classical theory is purely academic if those differences do not translate into differences in practice.

There are two major problems with this argument, however. First, its logic is circular: if style consists in certain common formal features, then any significant difference in formal features means a new style—ergo any late eighteenth-century work that departs from our expectations of classical appearance is by definition not classical. We foreclose on the possibility that the new theory had any practical effects before we even investigate the evidence. Second, that argument leaves open what constitutes a "significant" change in formal practice, and presumes that the formal features that were visible to late eighteenth-century viewers will be equally visible to twenty-first-century viewers. This is an equally problematic assumption. Although the material composition and configuration of a given work of art is relatively stable (barring issues of preservation), its style is not, if style is to be interpreted (as I think it should) as *significant* formal features. This distinction between the material composition and configuration of a work of art—its pattern of brushwork, color, texture, and so on—and its style as "significant" formal features may seem to be sophistry, but it is in fact crucial for both the historical and the semantic dimensions of style. As long as style consists merely in the material evidence, the history of style will deny that there is any difference in what material features successive generations of viewers will notice in artworks and what significance they will attribute to what they see. Since the material composition of the works has not changed, we will believe that there is no difference between the work we see in the early twenty-first century and the work they saw in the late-eighteenth century; or to make the same point in a way that will seem more patently fallacious: we will believe we see style with late eighteenth-century eyes and eighteenth-century minds. Take the example of oral language in this regard. Given a purely materialist understanding of the senses, the sounds that the human ear can hear are more or less the same across history and culture, but the sounds that the ear and mind will *discern* are very different in the various languages. The Chinese speaker depends upon differences in short and long vowels for communication, and those differences are material and can be measured by the linguist's equipment, but the English speaker will literally not notice the difference. Can we presume that the case is any different for the eyes and the material facts of paintings?

Thus the study of style should wherever possible be informed by a conscious effort to interpret the material evidence based on contemporaneous theory and historical models of viewing. Heinrich Wölfflin's famous sorting of sixteenth and seventeenth-century Italian works based upon the differences he remarks between planar and diagonal recession; linear versus painterly rendering; absolute versus relative clarity and so on is not necessarily fallacious, but it relies on a dangerous assumption that his categories of difference, as formulated in the early twentieth century, informed the contemporary viewing of those works.

The purpose of this theoretical caveat will immediately become evident. A reading of contemporaneous theory and criticism will demonstrate that the process of generalization was both achieved and signified in the late eighteenth-century British Royal Academy by a broad, painterly facture. Thus painterliness of a certain sort constituted, and was recognized as, an approach to the ideal. This statement is counterintuitive both to the commonplace understanding of the classical style and to received notions about the significance of brushwork in art. As Wölfflin defined it, classicism is characterized by its "linearity," meaning both a confinement of internal form within clear, bounding contours and a disguising of the material facts of painterly application, in contrast to the Baroque tendency to compose in visible masses. This distinction between Renaissance classicism and the Baroque is almost universally carried by the scholarship into the distinction between eighteenth-century classicism and Romanticism—and thus any evidence of brushwork in classical art is overlooked or cited as proto-Romantic (or a holdover from the Rococo, or a crossover from the picturesque, and so on). Similarly, the significance of painterliness in art is inevitably located to distinctly nonclassical qualities: Rococo elegance, Romantic passion, picturesque atmospherics, and so on. In what follows I will attempt to elicit theoretical and, to the greatest extent possible, practical distinctions among these types of brushwork that will recognize the form and significance of the late eighteenth-century classical facture of generalization.

Techniques of Generalization

In at least four separate places in the *Discourses*, Reynolds disclaimed any pretense to giving specific technical advice.[1] He conceived of his lectures as an explication of the general principles underlying the more practical advice given by the students' professors. Despite these disclaimers, however, in his capacity as a critic and a "man of taste," Reynolds did treat some formal and technical matters in the *Discourses*. The gist of his advice is that the Grand Manner painter should concentrate on rendering the *whole*, rather than the *parts*.

The necessity of "wholeness" in art is from one angle predicated on the limitations of the medium: the painter, unlike the poet, "has but one sentence to utter, but one moment to exhibit," and therefore "what is done by Painting, must be done at one blow."[2] It is also predicated on expressive criteria, as conducive of an "effect of grandeur":

> It is impossible for a picture composed of so many parts to have that effect so indispensably necessary to grandeur, that of one complete whole. However contradictory it may be in geometry, it is true in taste, that many little things will not make a great one. The Sublime impresses the mind at once with one great idea; it is a single blow: the Elegant indeed may be produced by repetition; by an accumulation of many minute circumstances.[3]

For Reynolds, then, "wholeness" is proper to the visual arts and results in an effect of grandeur. Most importantly for my purposes, Reynolds's concept of the whole also has an epistemological dimension, as the previous chapter suggested: "smaller objects" serve to "divide the attention"; and therefore a painting "must be disposed in large masses and groups" in order "to prevent the eye from being distracted and confused."[4] A painting of the whole resolves the associationist problem of eighteenth-century epistemology.

What is the formal appearance of this counterassociationist whole? Reynolds suggests certain techniques that begin to define its form. In his *Life of Sir Joshua Reynolds*, James Northcote quotes a fragment written in Reynolds's hand that reads, "Look at the object from which you are painting, with your eye-lids half closed, which gives breadth to the object, and subdues all the little unimportant parts."[5] Reynolds's *Discourses* call upon a similar visual phenomenon in the form of a contrast between "contracted" and "dilated" vision:

> Excellence . . . will never be acquired by an artist, unless he has the habit of looking upon objects at large, and observing the effect which they have on the eye when it is dilated. At the same time I do not forget, that a Painter must have the power of contracting as well as dilating his sight . . . yet it is certain, that a nice discrimination of minute circumstances, and a punctilious delineation of them . . . never did confer on the Artist the character of Genius.[6]

Although in this passage the distinction is largely metaphoric, vision is literally dilated in the dark, and Reynolds accordingly remarks that "by candle-light, not only [do] objects appear more beautiful, but from their being in a great breadth of light and shadow, as well as having a greater breadth and uniformity of colour, nature appears in a higher style."[7] The technique of squinting or dilating the vision, then, suggests that a painting of the whole will be characterized by broad masses, relatively low-key and monotonous color, and a certain indistinctness in outline; and will be opposed to crisp, sharp edges, to fine distinctions in internal details, and to an overall linear, minute and multiplicitous appearance. Although these qualities contradict our usual understanding of the classical style, they clearly respond to the epistemological exigencies of late eighteenth-century classicism, particularly the fear that a minute and multiplicitous surface is a dangerous agent of distraction.

Already in the 1740s Reynolds painted a self-portrait that may contain a reference to this technique of dilated vision (figure 4). In this, the only self-portrait that depicts the artist in the act of painting, Reynolds shows himself shading his eyes with one hand, as though to stimulate the dilation of his vision. Because of the early date of this work (the above references to dilated vision date to the 1780s), this interpretation of the significance of the pose seems dubious. A connection to Rembrandt's many portraits with shaded eyes seems a more likely source and reference. But as the 1986 Reynolds exhibition catalog notes, there is no precedent in Rembrandt for this *active* shading of the eyes, as opposed to the incidental shade cast by the hat brim; and in Rembrandt the shading of the eyes is not associated with the activity of the artist, but rather with the psychology of the sitter.[8] The epistemological significance of shading the eyes is more certainly mobilized by Reynolds in his painting of *Justice*, which dates to 1778–79 (figure 5). In that work, the arm that holds up the scales on which the contrasting claims of the litigants are weighed casts a shadow across her eyes. As a change from the more traditional blindfold, the suggestion is perhaps that justice relies on empirical evidence. As a metaphor for the process of justice, the suggestion is perhaps the ability of judgment to weigh that empirical evidence based on broad, universal principles rather than minute, circumstantial details, just as the generalizing artist, with "dilated" vision, sizes up and sorts perceived objects without becoming lost in the welter of adventitious contingencies.

As the technique of dilated vision begins to suggest, for Reynolds a painterly approach is the most effective way to seize and convey this crucial whole. At the same time as the constitution of the surface in painterly masses contributes to the formal whole of the painting and its consequent effect of grandeur, the broad and sweeping application of paint serves to abstract the individual objects depicted in the work. In short, brushwork both unifies the painting and generalizes its constituent objects. Although this formulation strongly contradicts our usual understanding of classical art as "transparent" to higher reality, or workless, and seems to contradict Reynolds's own assertion that it is an "inferior artist [who] is unwilling that any part of his industry should be lost upon the spectator," we are neither theoretically nor practically justified in ignoring the painterly labor of late eighteenth-century classicism: to do so is to ignore both Reynolds's theory and his practice.[9] In his eleventh Discourse, Reynolds follows a chain of reasoning connecting the neatly finished (Wölfflin's "linear") surface both to a minute concentration on the parts (Wölfflin's "multiplicity") and to a *greater* technical labor on the part of the artist: "As [painting] is an art, [the ignorant] think they ought to be pleased in proportion as they see that art ostentatiously displayed; they will,

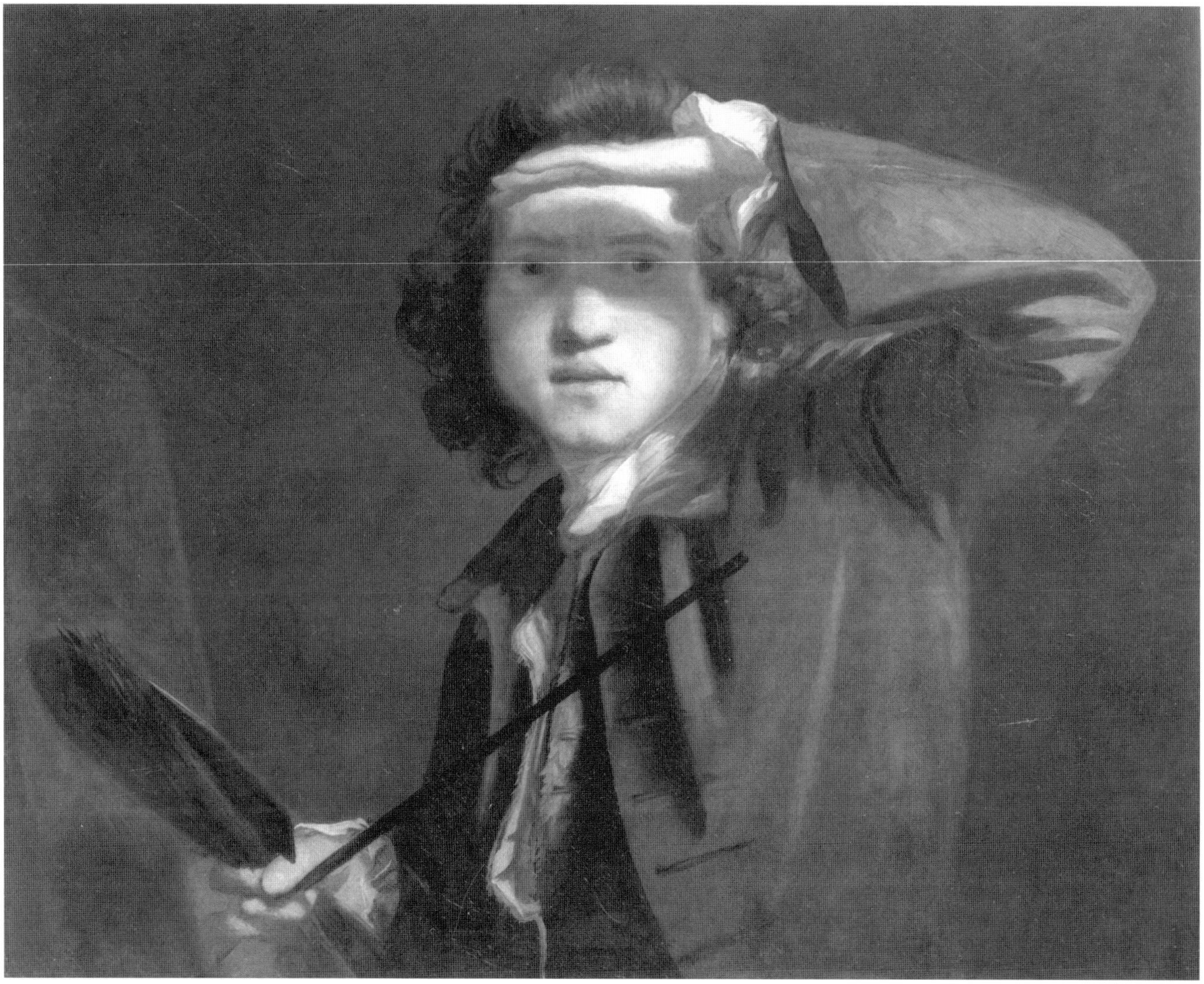

4. Joshua Reynolds, *Self-Portrait (Shading the Eyes)*, 1747–48. National Portrait Gallery, London.

from this supposition, prefer neatness, high-finishing, and gaudy colouring, to the truth, simplicity and unity of nature."[10] A high degree of finishing does not, for Reynolds, make the canvas transparent to its depicted objects; instead, it constitutes an ostentatious display of technique, and of technique directed toward a goal that is in fact contrary to general nature. The classical expression of the "truth, simplicity and unity of nature" is best performed not through a meticulous rendering, but through a "few well-chosen strokes":

> The pleasure we receive from imitation is not increased merely in proportion as it approaches to minute and detailed reality; we are pleased, on the contrary, by seeing ends accomplished by seemingly inadequate means . . .
>
> Carry this principle a step further. Suppose the effect of imitation to be fully compassed by means still more inadequate; let the power of a few well-chosen strokes, which supersede labour by judgment and direction, produce a complete impression of all that the mind demands in an object; we are charmed with such an unexpected happiness of execution.[11]

The visibility of these "few well-chosen strokes" does not indicate the manual labor of the painter, as is problematic in most antimechanic constructions of the high status of the artist, including those of the eighteenth century. Instead, these marks "*supersede* labour" (the manual labor of high finishing) in favor of mental "judgment." Recall the abstractive function of the judgment in eighteenth-century epistemology.

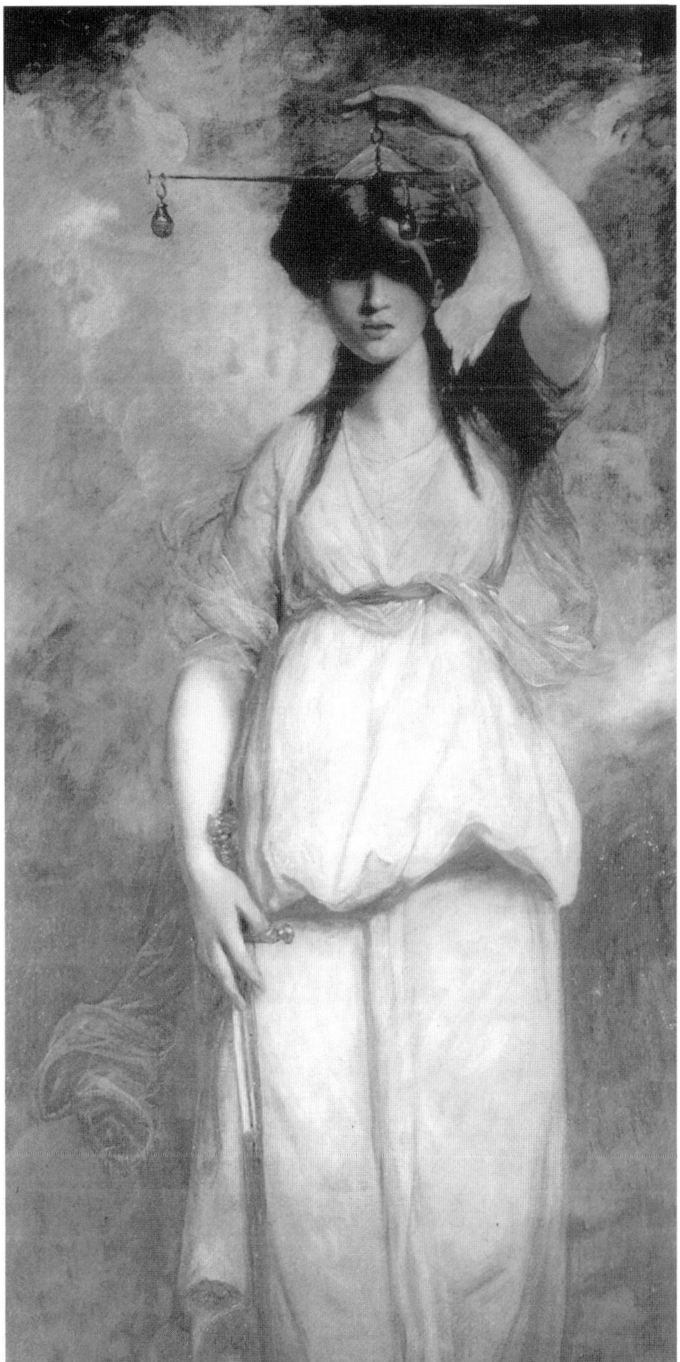

5. Joshua Reynolds, *Justice*, c. 1778–79. In a private collection.

The application of paint should in this case be seen, Reynolds is arguing, as a "directed" index of the mental faculty of judgment, as eliding the minute particularities of the depicted object. The continuous trajectory of a brushstroke can perform its own generalization of an object, for example, as the sweeping motion of the hand smoothes out the minute changes in the particular muscular constitution of an anatomical part, and as the stroke's continuous breadth and color elides small irregularities in a surface and simultaneously joins part to part to constitute a unified whole.

Emphatically, the "charm" and "happiness" of such painterly brushwork is not simply a delight in the technical skill of the artist—or rather, that skill is to be located not in manual dexterity but rather in dilated vision and mental "comprehension." Artists, with their "few well-chosen strokes," exhibit

> the habit of looking upon objects at large, and observing the effect which they have on the eye when it is dilated, and employed upon the whole, without seeing any one of the parts distinctly. It is by this that we obtain the ruling characteristick, and that we learn to imitate it by short and dexterous methods.
>
> . . . [G]reat fame does not proceed from [an artist's] works being more highly finished than those of other artists, or from a more minute attention to details, but from that enlarged comprehension which sees the whole object at once.[12]

Reynolds directly links these "short and dexterous methods" to the "enlarged comprehension" of the artist and the power of seeing the "whole"—epistemological skills, not mere technical skills. Even the word "comprehension" is carefully chosen to describe that epistemological skill: deriving from Latin COM + *prehendere*, to grasp or seize together, the word embodies the mental equivalent of seeing the whole, the unity amid multiplicity, through dilated vision. Reynolds repeatedly links painterly brushwork to such epistemological issues: "The great advantage of this idea of the whole is, that a greater quantity of *truth* may be said to be contained and expressed in a few lines or touches, than in the most laborious finishing of parts, where this is not regarded."[13] Where a minute and blended rendering displays only the technical skill of the artist (and results in a particularized and distracting work), a painterly rendering conveys the "*truth*, simplicity, and unity of nature."[14]

Reynolds elaborates on this capacity of generalizing brushwork to elicit and convey the general idea of the object in relation to a tree:

> I remember a Landscape-Painter in Rome, who was known by the name of STUDIO, from his patience in high finishing, in which he thought the whole excellence of art consisted; so that he once endeavoured, as he said, to represent every individual leaf on a tree. This picture I never saw; but I am very sure that an artist, who looked only at the general character of the species, the order of the branches, and the masses of the foliage, would in a few minutes produce a more true resemblance of trees, than this Painter in as many months.[15]

In this passage again, the truth of the object and a rapid execution of its general masses are closely linked. A painting that enumerated every individual leaf, every particular bend and fork of every branch in a given tree would at best—and with great manual labor—produce only a resemblance of an individual tree. By contrast, the painter who ignored these minutiae and concentrated only on the general—the "order of the branches" and the "masses of the foliage"—would produce a "more true resemblance of trees" in general (note the plural): the "general character of the species," not the individual member. "STUDIO" employs no significant mental power on his work: his "contracted" eye merely records exactly what is in front of it, and his hand merely copies what his eye sees, bypassing the mind entirely in a purely mechanical process. In Reynolds's espoused method, by contrast, the mind plays a central role. Viewed with a dilated eye, the particular tree acts only as a stimulus to recollect and further refine the general idea of the species formed by the painter's enlarged comprehension, and the painter's technique serves not only to embody but also to further abstract that idea. A painting of a tree by "STUDIO" would contribute nothing to the viewer's understanding beyond actually seeing a specific tree, where the painting that Reynolds describes manifests the "character of the species," thus providing viewers with a general idea under which they can subsume many particular instances past and future, "fashioning and consolidating" their ideas and elevating their minds from the contingent facts of individual nature to the universal truths of general nature. The painter exercises great epistemological labor in formulating this general idea—only a "long laborious comparison" can "distinguish the accidental deficiencies, excrescences, and deformities of things" and determine what those things all "have in common"[16]—but there is little executive labor: a "few lines or touches" will suffice to fix the general idea of the species, elevate the spectator's mind, and exhibit the elevation of the artist's own mind.

Reynolds repeatedly mobilized these criteria in his criticism of specific works, artists, and schools of painting. Style (the Grand Manner) is a more important, or at least more frequently cited, determinant of artistic quality in the *Discourses* than subject matter (history painting). In the eighth Discourse, Reynolds asked his listeners to perform a thought-experiment and "suppose a view of nature represented with all the truth of the *camera obscura*, and the same scene represented by a great Artist." Although the subject is the same, he notes, "how little and mean will the one appear in comparison of the other." The great artist, unlike the camera obscura, has the power of "elevating his style," and just previous, Reynolds had located the difference between "a higher and a lower style" in relation to the degree of "finish" exhibited in the work:

> If our judgements are to be directed by narrow, vulgar, untaught or rather ill-taught reason, we must prefer a portrait by Denner or any other high finisher, to those of Titian or Vandyck; and a landskip of Vanderhyde to those of Titian or Rubens; for they are certainly more exact representations of nature.[17]

"High finishing" is linked to "narrow, vulgar, untaught or rather ill-taught reason" (reason uninflected by proper judgment and generalization, I would extrapolate), and the "higher style" is here attributed not to Raphael, Michelangelo, or Poussin—the usual suspects when it comes to classical excellence—but to Titian, Van Dyck, and Rubens, all of whom are notable for their painterly facture. Indeed, whatever their merits, the paradigmatic classicists of the sixteenth and seventeenth centuries were taken to task by Reynolds for the lack of liquid breadth in their manners: Raphael "never was able to conquer perfectly that dryness, or even littleness of manner, which he inherited from [Perugino]"; Michelangelo is reprimanded for his "neglect of colouring" (the word "colouring" is opposed to "design" or drawing, and embraces brushwork in classical art theory); and Poussin is criticized for his "dry and hard" manner.[18]

A little, hard, and transparent rendering is especially evident in the work of Reynolds's younger contemporary, the American artist John Singleton Copley. In his *Boy with a Squirrel* (figure 6), for example, the capacity of oil paint and very small brushes to blend to a mirror-like finish and to mirror natural appearances has been exploited to very nearly the fullest power of the medium: every link in the squirrel's chain leash is not only rendered, but also modeled and highlighted, and it seems as though every individual hair on Pelham's head is painstakingly delineated. When Copley sent this work to England to be shown at the Society of Artists exhibition in the spring of 1766, he solicited advice from the artists there. Benjamin West reported to him that the work was criticized as being "to liney, which was judged to have arose from there being so much neetness [sic] in the lines."[19] Captain R. G. Bruce, a friend of Copley's, conveyed Reynolds's diplomatic opinion that "considering the Dissadvantages . . . you had laboured under, that *it was a very wonderfull Performance*," but that the work was characterized by "a little Hardness in the Drawing, Coldness in the Shades," and, most damning of all, "An over minuteness."[20] Of another portrait that Copley sent to the Society's exhibition of the following year, Reynolds was reported as objecting that "Each part of the Picture [is] Equell in Strenght of Coulering and finishing, Each Making to much a Picture of its silf, without the Due Subordanation to the Principle Parts, viz they head and hands [sic]."[21] Reynolds urged Copley to come to Europe "before your Manner and Taste were corrupted or fixed by working in your little way at Boston."[22] Although neither Reynolds nor West explains why Copley's "little way," "liney neetness," "hardness," "over minuteness," and lack of "Due Subordanation to the Principle Parts" is a problem beyond a matter of aesthetic taste, the language with which they criticize Copley's performance resonates with Reynolds's contrasts between the "portraitic" manner of depicting individual nature through a minutely transparent facture and the Grand Manner of depicting general nature through "a few, well-chosen strokes."

Interestingly, the smooth and linear surface of Copley's American manner is also characteristic of the most recognizable classicism of the eighteenth century, that of the German expatriate Anton Raffael Mengs and that of the French school after J. -L. David. Although

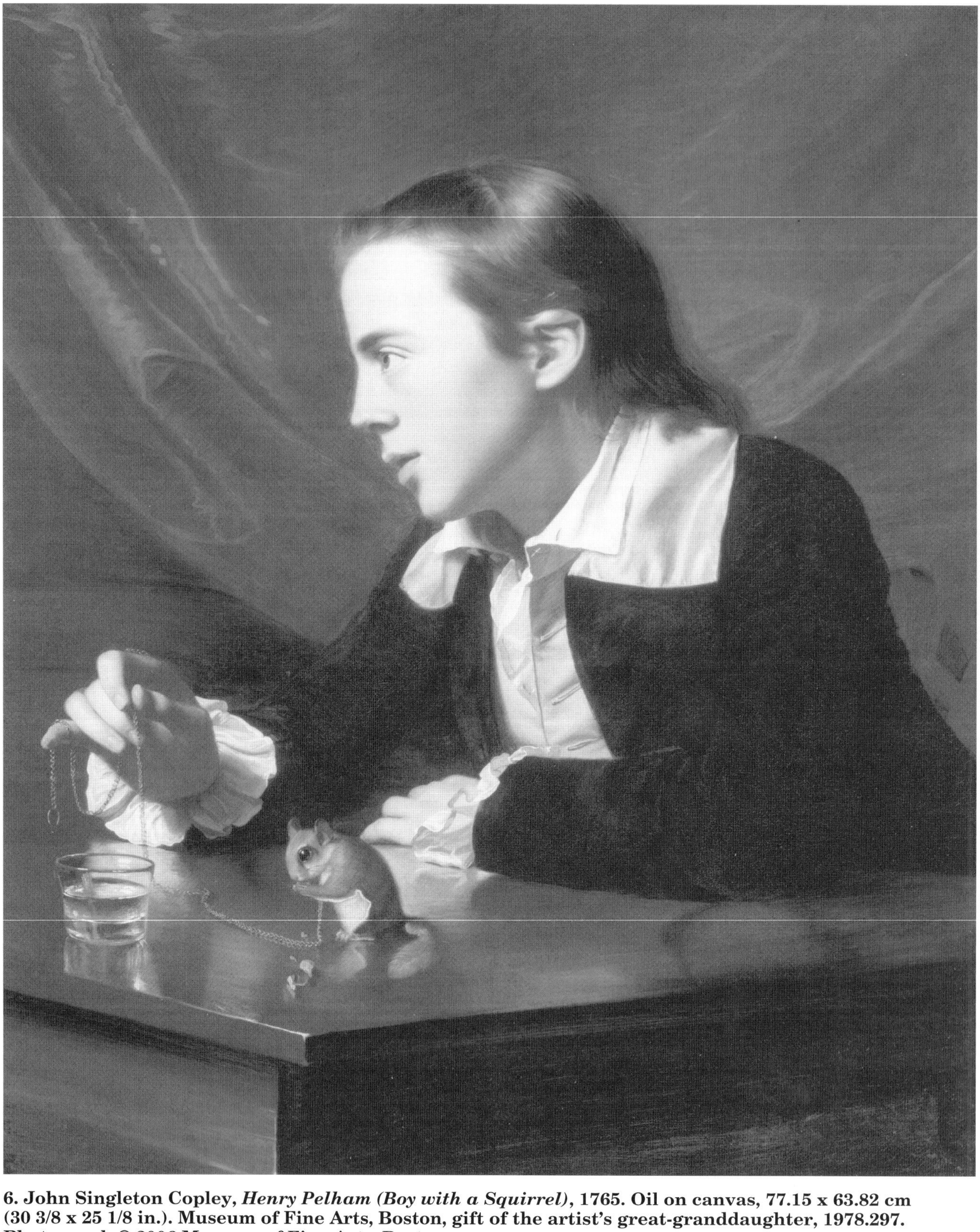

6. John Singleton Copley, *Henry Pelham (Boy with a Squirrel)*, 1765. Oil on canvas, 77.15 x 63.82 cm (30 3/8 x 25 1/8 in.). Museum of Fine Arts, Boston, gift of the artist's great-granddaughter, 1978.297. Photograph © 2006 Museum of Fine Arts, Boston.

Copley obviously departs from classical idealization in applying his style to painstakingly record the faults of his sitters—Henry Pelham's crushed left ear, for example—even the evidently flawless features of continental classicism were subject to criticism if the works exhibited a hard, linear style. For example, in his fourteenth Discourse, Reynolds castigates Anton Raffael Mengs and Pompeo Batoni, the best-known neoclassicists of their day, for a "routine of practice" that bears only a "superficial resemblance to the manner of the great men who went before them," and suggested that artists "looking for real and lasting reputation, must un-learn much of the common-place method so observable" in their works.[23] A hint of what Reynolds found so objectionable in the "routine" and "common-place" practice of these artists is recorded by Northcote, who reported that there was nothing that Reynolds "hated so much as a distinct outline, as you see it in Mengs and the French school."[24] The "liney" manner of the French classicists is further denigrated by William Hazlitt, who called the products of David and his pupils "execrable performances,"[25] and drew an explicit contrast between the French and English schools based upon handling: "The English seem generally to suppose, that, if they only leave out the subordinate parts, they are sure of the general result. The French, on the contrary, as idly imagine, that by attending to each separate part, they must infallibly arrive at a correct whole. . . . The French painters see only lines, and precise differences;—the English only general masses, and strong effects."[26] As we shall see, Hazlitt was as critical of Reynolds's painterly manner as he was of the French precise and linear manner, but his identification of the English notion that painting in "general masses" is designed to "leave out the subordinate parts" and thus achieve a "general result" reflects his understanding of Reynolds's painterly approach to ideal form. This manner is explicitly opposed to what the scholarship usually recognizes as the "common-place" of the classical style.

Critical Distinctions

With this entry of brushwork into the terrain of classicism, however, we should make careful distinctions in the sort of painterliness that is characteristic of generalization. It is a painterliness of *breadth* rather than a painterliness of depth, the more easily recognized sort of painterliness. A painterliness of depth is distinguished by a thickness and opacity of paint and by the visibility of individual strokes indexing the trajectory of the artist's hand. This type of painterliness is commonly conceived as an agent of expression: the motion of the hand is interpreted as indexing the "motion" of the artist's passions. As such, the painterliness of depth is perhaps more apposite to Romantic aesthetics, but it does have its cognate in the 1760s, as Mary Sheriff's analysis of Fragonard's *Portraits de fantaisie* suggests. Directly opposed to Reynolds's empirical construction of genius, a current of eighteenth-century French theories of the *homme de génie* linked genius to Platonic notions of enthusiasm and inspiration. The divine possession or "poetic fury" characteristic of artistic inspiration resulted in—and thus, Sheriff argues, could be signified by—a rapid, agitated brushwork that indexed the moving power of enthusiasm through the physical acts of the artist's gestures. The contemporaneous understanding of painterly *touche*, and gesture in general, as a "natural sign" put such a painterly practice in the realm of the transcendent, or at least the presocial. Fragonard's 1769 portrayal of *Inspiration* (figure 7) mobilizes this logic. Not only do the pose (which is similar to that of an Evangelist writing to the dictates of a higher power) and the dominant red-orange tone indicate the "fiery" genius and inspiration of the subject of the work, the very painterly rendering signifies Fragonard's own divine possession as he depicted the possessed.[27]

Reynolds's brushwork of generalization is both theoretically and practically different from the enthusiastic brushwork of Fragonard. Reynolds rejects the transcendent discourse of inspiration throughout his *Discourses*, citing brushwork as an agent of a purely empirical epistemology, as embodying the mental act of abstraction and generalization. And despite his characterization of this abstractive brushwork as "a few, well-chosen strokes," in Reynolds's own works we can see that he did not intend these strokes to remain distinct on the surface of the canvas as indexing discrete acts of the hand. At least in the final, most visible layer of his painting, Fragonard's brush is loaded, his paint is opaque and his facture is literally plastic: a stroke is laid on with considerable attack, and, once established, is not reinforced, corrected, or blended into the underlying surface or adjacent strokes. In this way the strokes retain their integrity as individual acts of a hand operating with uncanny speed and precision—and indeed, the discourse of inspired facture requires that this attack, precision, and speed be clearly legible in the work as the final act in a causal chain traceable to a divine source. Any evidence of deliberation or corrective overpainting would nullify the appearance of the artist's total abandonment to inspiration. Reynolds's brushwork of generalization, by contrast, is directional, but without any visible attack or insistence on the discrete act of the hand that laid it on, and it is reinforced again and again in a series of semitransparent strokes rather than in a single, vehement, opaque mark.[28] The effect is not only to direct attention away from the physical act of the hand that lays on the stroke, but also to enhance its generalizing qualities. An individual, opaque stroke retains distinct edges, particularizing contours and dividing the surface of the work. Repeated, semitransparent strokes blend together, reinforcing breadth but blurring contours, eliding minute distinctions in internal areas and unifying the overall surface of the painting.

Less easily distinguished from the brushwork of generalization is a brushwork of optical effect, such as critics had long located in Titian and the Venetian school. Reynolds himself seems to have had difficulty in making that distinction, as can be seen in his equivocation over Titian throughout the *Discourses*. For the most part, the Venetian painters are castigated for their "ornamental" manner, as opposed to the Grand Manner: "elegance is their principle object"; their works are epistemologically dangerous in that they show "more copiousness than choice, and more luxuriancy than judgment"; and they "seemed to be engrossed by the study of colours, to the neglect of the *ideal beauty of form* [Reynolds's italics]."[29] But Reynolds allows the Venetians merit in what would seem to be the most unlikely place: their brushwork. In the eleventh Discourse, Reynolds even locates Titian as the first practitioner of generalization through painterly brushwork:

> By a few strokes [Titian] knew how to mark the general image and character of whatever object he attempted; and produced, by this alone, a truer representation than his master Giovanni Bellino, or any of his predecessors, who finished every hair. . . .
>
> This manner was then new to the world, but that unshaken truth on which it is founded, has fixed it as a model to all succeeding Painters: and those who will examine into the artifice, will find it to consist in the power of generalising, and in the shortness and simplicity of the means employed.[30]

Titian's relatively painterly manner is seen as evidence of his "power of generalising," which renders the "general image and character" of the object in a "few strokes," and again this manner achieves a "truer representation" than a minute, hair-by-hair rendering. The fact that Reynolds locates Titian, and not Raphael or Michelangelo, as the first practitioner of the painterly route to the general is particularly interesting, for it hints again at the type of surface appearance such generalization should take, and clarifies Reynolds's problematic (or even, for some scholars, hypocritical) tendency toward a Venetian style.

However, Reynolds immediately qualifies his appreciation of Titian:

> We cannot entirely refuse to Titian the merit of attending to the general *form* of his object, as well as colour; but his deficiency lay, a deficiency at least when he is compared with Raffaelle, in not possessing the power, like him, of correcting the form of his model by any general idea of beauty in his own mind. . . . In his colouring he was large and general, as in his design he was minute and partial; in the one he was a Genius, in the other not much above a copier [of individual nature].[31]

This equivocation over Titian is due to the odd position that Reynolds's theory holds in the venerable "line versus color" debates. Reynolds's theory locates in color (here meaning brushwork and masses) qualities that are generally located to achievement in contour and line (*disegno*): the ideal or perfection of form. Consequently, he has to draw a very fine distinction in his criticism of Titian: the Venetian is granted the ability to generalize, but denied the achievement of general beauty. The suggestion, I believe, is that his brushwork effectively generalizes *only* the object immediately before him, and does even that with a lamentable concentration on its contingent appearance in a particular light. Titian fails to "correct" this individual model by a "general idea of beauty in his own mind"; that is, he fails to abstract from the given object's appearance the specific details

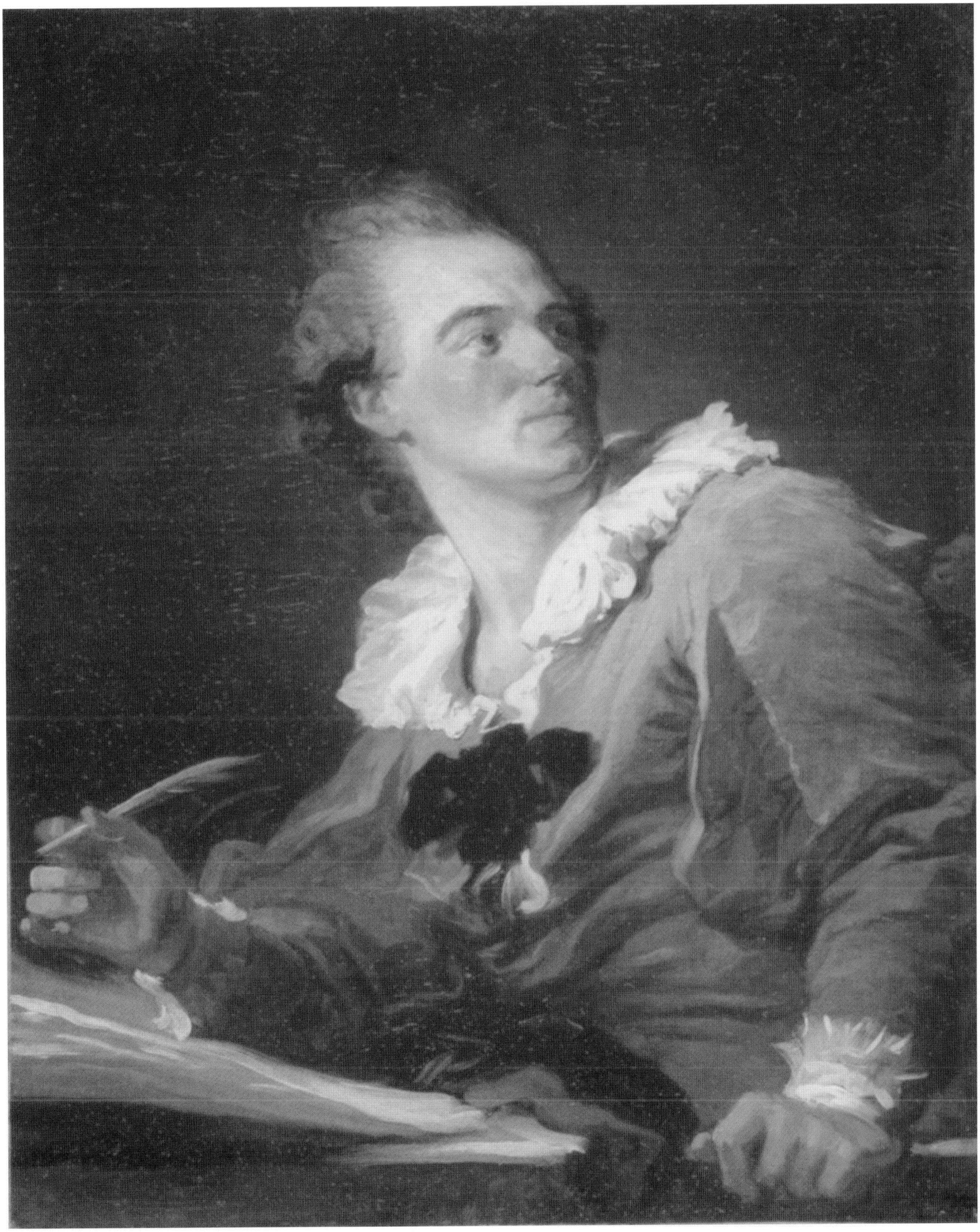

7. Jean-Honoré Fragonard, *Inspiration*, c. 1769. Louvre, Paris. Photo Credit: Réunion des Musées Nationaux/Art Resource, NY.

that multiple viewings of similar objects would have revealed as merely accidental, such as the effects of atmospheric lighting. His brushwork is thus promising, but it is mobilized for particular and optical effect rather than the higher goal of ideal beauty. Because the distinction is so fine, it does much to reconcile the apparent contradiction between Reynolds's theoretical advocacy of the Grand Manner and his own practical preference for the Venetian School. Art historians have introduced that contradiction themselves by picturing a Raphael or David when Reynolds says Grand Manner, instead of recognizing that for Reynolds, Grand Manner generalization is substantially closer (with important caveats) to the manner of the Venetians.

If the brushwork of generalization and that of the Venetians is similar, Reynolds can more explicitly differentiate his espoused manner from that of the Venetians in terms of color (in the sense now of hue). The "decorative" color harmonies of the Venetians were largely produced by what was at the time called "broken" and "transparent" color. Transparent color consists in highly diluted passages, such as glazes, that modify an underlying color but allow it to show through. Broken color signifies an apparently solid area of color that, on closer inspection, is revealed as composed of a variety of different tones—a technique later formalized by the Impressionists and Seurat, but informally practiced by Venetian artists and Rubénistes long before. François d'Aguilon, for example, described what he called the *compositio notionalis* of color in his *Opticorum* (1613), where the artist paints in "patches" of color that are so small as to "escape the eye," but converge as "sensory impressions in the eye so that for each combination of the colours a uniform colour is received."[32] The principle benefit of broken colors is that where compound colors mixed on the palette become dull and lifeless, purer colors mixed "in the eye" retain something more like the vitality of light. Venetian artists deployed broken and transparent color both for formal harmonies and for such optical effects. Titian, for example, would first *ébauche* his composition on canvas in a red earth and white lead monotone, and then add color in the form of broken, relatively opaque passages in the lit areas and more translucent passages in the shaded areas. "Received" color, color that is reflected from one surface to an adjacent one, was brushed opaquely over the translucent shadows once they were dry. This practice is obviously geared toward the more fugitive effects of light: color in painting consists in "accidental" effects overlying the tactile (modeled) surface captured in the initial *ébauche*. Furthermore, it is counterintuitive to the "truth" of the object represented. Broken color in particular denies the integrity of the local color of the object, rendering as a variety of tones what objectively appears to be a single color. As a technique for producing harmony or liveliness, broken color is a trick, requiring on the part of the artist a *conscious* suspension of considerations about the essential truth of the object, which is better described in consistent directional strokes, local color, and even pure chiaroscuro. In their subsequent visibility on the surface of the canvas, such passages call the spectator's attention not simply to the work of the artist (which all brushwork may be said to do), but to the "trickery" inherent in painting; or in other words, broken color calls attention not only to the craft but also to the craftiness of the painter.

Although Reynolds's practice of color was complex, and did include both transparent and received color, the theory of color that he endorsed in his *Discourses* differed sharply from Venetian practice. "Grandeur of effect" in color can be produced by two different means for Reynolds. These two means seem "entirely opposed to each other," but both can be characterized by their austere simplicity, as opposed to the decorative harmonies and complex trickery of the Venetians:

> One is, by reducing the colours to little more than chiaro oscuro, which was often the practice of the Bolognian schools; and the other, by making the colours very distinct and forcible, such as we see in those of Rome and Florence; but still, the presiding principle of both these manners is simplicity. Certainly, nothing can be more simple than monotony; and the distinct blue, red, and yellow colours which are seen in the draperies of the Roman and Florentine schools, though they have not that kind of harmony which is produced by a variety of broken and transparent colours, have that effect of grandeur which was intended.[33]

Transparent and broken colors can produce harmony, but not grandeur, and this difference adequately distinguishes the decorative Venetian manner from the classical Grand Manner despite the similarity of their brushwork. The second of Reynolds's two modes of simplifying color was long justified in classical art theory. The first printed recognition of the three subtractive (pigment) primaries dates to the mid-seventeenth-century Poussiniste circle, as Martin Kemp has noted.[34] Inasmuch as all other colors can be derived from mixtures of red, yellow, and blue pigments, those colors could be said to represent the distilled essence of all of the highly modified and accidental colors of nature. An instance of the general recognition of the ideal simplicity and grandeur of the subtractive primaries in the late-eighteenth century—their appropriateness to classical painting—is seen in François-André Vincent's *Zeuxis et les filles de Crotone* (1789, Louvre). This most famous moment in the mythology of classical art practice shows Zeuxis examining the maidens who were to serve as his models for Helen of Troy. Under the table against which Zeuxis leans is a paintbox with five colors: white, yellow, blue, red, and black. Five paintbrushes project with the same five colors as Zeuxis prepares to color in the *disegno* already rendered on his canvas. While the French school followed the Roman and Florentine Renaissance masters in choosing this method, the British school more commonly used the first, "monotonous" route to generalizing color, as Reynolds's assertion that nature appears in a "higher style" by candlelight already suggests and as we shall further explore below. The monotonous depiction of the object is also consistent with classical theory inasmuch as *all* color—local as well as atmospheric—can be conceived as an accidental feature of the substantial object, which is thus best rendered only in chiaroscuro.

Reynolds further clarifies his espoused method of generalization through broad brushwork in a set of distinctions between general marks and other types of marks with which they may be confused, such as "peculiar" marks, "unfinished" marks, and what I will call "unmotivated" marks. These distinctions would be entirely superfluous in any traditional understanding of classicism, where all facture is anathema, but they become necessary once brushwork becomes one of classicism's primary agents of idealization.

What Reynolds calls "peculiar" or "characteristical" marks are part of what we would call the individual style of the artist. They are marks deployed by the artist across all of their works regardless of the subject, and within individual works regardless of the object represented. As such they are informative about the artist rather than the depicted object, and are to be avoided: "Peculiar marks, I hold to be, generally, if not always, defects; however difficult it may be wholly to escape them."[35] Although Reynolds allows peculiar marks in the "inferior" styles—such as those of Thomas Gainsborough and Salvator Rosa—they are carefully distinguished from generalizing marks on an epistemological front:

> There is another style, which, though inferior to the [great style], has still great merit, because it shows that those who cultivated it were men of lively and vigorous imagination. This, which may be called the original or characteristical style, being less referred to any true architype [sic] existing either in general or particular nature, must be supported by the painter's consistency in the principles which he has assumed.[36]

A peculiar or "characteristical" style is not referable to general nature, nor even to particular nature, but rather to the artist, and specifically to what eighteenth-century epistemology marked as problematic for rationality: a "lively and vigorous imagination." While a characteristical painting, like a vigorous imagination, can please, it should not be taken too seriously and certainly should not be imitated, because "novelty and peculiarity being its only merit, when it ceases to be new, it ceases to have value."[37] Although a painting of peculiar marks has a sort of wholeness because "all the component parts . . . appear to hang well together, as if the whole proceeded from one mind,"[38] this is a wholeness that is predicated to the artist, rather than one reflecting the "truth, simplicity and unity of nature."

What Reynolds is effectively asserting with this distinction is that generalizing brushwork is to be considered *objective* rather than subjective, or more precisely that Grand Manner brushwork indexes the artist's universalizing "indifference," not his particularizing individuality. This is a difficult, but I believe practical distinction. A painting of peculiar marks will distribute a similar type of mark across the entire surface of the painting, rather than modify marks based on the object to be imitated. Gainsborough is indeed a good example of this practice. In his portrait of *Mrs. Richard Brinsley Sheridan* (figure 8), for example, the foliage, drapery and hair of the figure are all rendered in the same light, feathery brushwork.

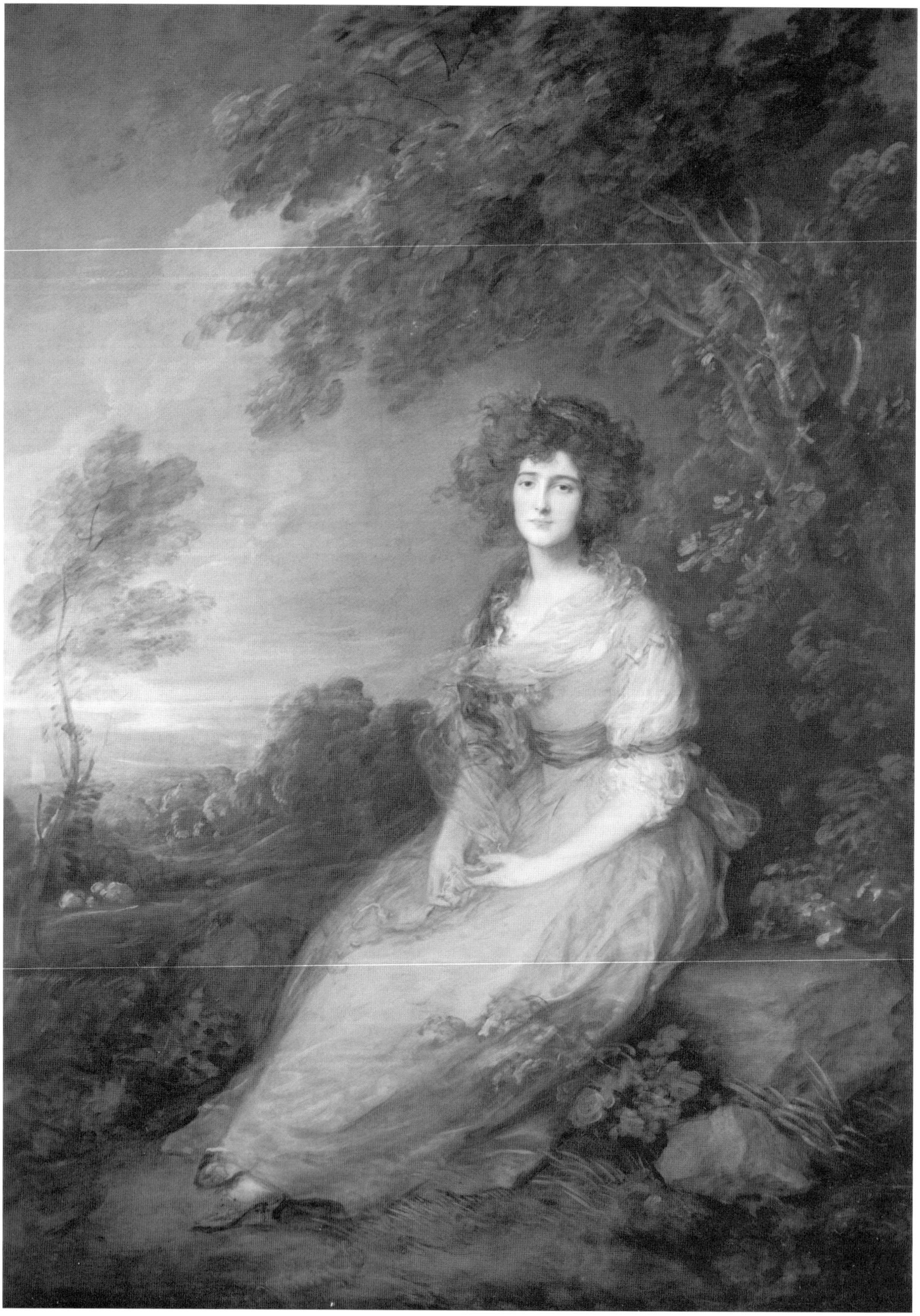

8. Thomas Gainsborough, *Mrs. Richard Brinsley Sheridan*, 1785–87. Andrew W. Mellon Collection, National Gallery of Art, Washington, DC. Image © Board of Trustees, National Gallery of Art, Washington.

John Hayes's catalog to the Tate Gallery's 1980 Gainsborough exhibition makes this point:

> The abandon of the hair, which curls right down to the waist, and of the gauze wrap that is intertwined with it, is matched by the sketchiness of the brushwork throughout the dress. More important, however, the character of the brushwork in the hair and costume is taken up in the foliage of the trees, so that trees and figure form a natural compositional flow and the sitter really seems to be enveloped by the landscape in which she is seated so much at her ease.[39]

Most analyses of Gainsborough's style make the same observation, although locating it to different purposes. Formalist art history sees it as a precocious achievement in the burgeoning modernist emphasis on the integrity of the overall surface, while social historians see Gainsborough's unification of figure and landscape as a means of "naturalizing" the land to the landowner.[40] Reynolds's point is that such consistency in brushwork across a variety of depicted objects is imposed by the "peculiar" artist, rather than derived from the nature of the depicted object.[41]

Another distinction that Reynolds found necessary within his method is that between painterliness as a mode of generalization and the painterliness of an unfinished artwork. Because Reynolds had so strongly condemned "high finishing" in painting, he realized that his method of generalization through brushwork tended to privilege unfinished works:

> I should be sorry, if what has been said should be understood to have any tendency to encourage that carelessness which leaves work in an unfinished state. I commend nothing for the want of exactness; I mean to point out that kind of exactness which is the best, and which is alone truly to be so esteemed.[42]

Again, this warning only makes sense if Reynolds's theory of the Grand Manner style was generally recognized as threatening to allow works whose brushwork was so broad as to appear "unfinished." On the same day as Reynolds made this distinction in his Discourse, the Royal Academy put it into critical practice. On December 10, 1782, John Hoppner was awarded the Gold Medal premium for History Painting. The General Assembly Minutes for that date read in part:

> Resolved/ That the President be desired to give Mr Hoppner the foll^g Reproof. The Academicians are of the opinion that tho there is that superiority in Your Picture, which intitles you to the Premium: They at the same time think that you have not exerted your self to the utmost & bestowed as much time on the Picture as it required compleatly to finish it. You are therefore desired before it is presented to his Majesty to finish it in a proper manner.[43]

This reproof acted as a reinforcement of the crucial (but doubtless somewhat difficult) distinction between proper painterly generalization and the mere lack of finish. Although due to press of time Hoppner could easily have submitted what he knew to be an unfinished work for the biennial premium awards, if the difference between finished and unfinished were clear, as it is in most scholarly understandings of the classical style, it is difficult to understand why Reynolds would find it necessary to draw that distinction publicly in his *Discourses*.

These distinctions between Venetian brushwork and generalizing brushwork; between peculiar marks and general marks; and between the general and the merely unfinished, are doubtless difficult to recognize in practice, but they are highly significant as discursive markers in a critical field arising when the generalizing capacity of painterly facture becomes an important tool in classical process. A further problem was recognized in passing by Reynolds and seems to have become urgent in the early nineteenth century; a problem that, though perhaps impossible to resolve, does demonstrate the widespread acceptance of Reynolds's new, painterly method of idealization. Reynolds's identification of brushwork as a *technique* of generalization allows the recognition of brushwork as a *sign* of generalization. Such recognition is doubtless crucial to an audience that might otherwise misinterpret the significance of Reynolds's brushwork, attributing it to more trivial goals or even sloppiness. But once identified as such, there is a risk that the signs of generalization can be mobilized without the proper motivation: a surface deployment of sloppy brushwork can substitute for the difficult epistemological process that should underwrite it. Reynolds attempted to resolve this problem in passing, insisting "I do not mean by dexterity a trick or mechanical habit, formed by guess, and established by custom; but that science, which, by a profound knowledge of ends and means, discovers the shortest and surest way to its own purpose."[44] Proper generalizing brushwork should be a science linking means (painterly breadth) to an end (the pursuit of the general ideal) and not a happy accident or a conventional sign. But invoking the need for properly motivated brushwork is a very different thing from defining the distinction between unmotivated and motivated brushwork. By the early nineteenth century, the surface deployment of signs of generalization had apparently become so commonplace in the Academy that a stronger insistence on proper motivation was required. In one of his lectures on painting, John Opie regretted that there were certain artists who, misunderstanding this new method of idealization,

> have even been so absurd as to think colouring, *chiaro scuro*, and all that contributes to illusion in painting, as beneath their attention; who, because they have heard that nature might be improved upon in some particulars, have fondly imagined that their compositions approached the heroic and poetical in proportion as they receded from nature and became muddy, tame, and monotonous in the effect.[45]

Opie's warning clearly indexes the widespread acceptance of Reynolds's method, for in what other theory of classicism does the goal of improving upon nature, of achieving the heroic grandeur and poetic generality of Aristotelian aspiration, threaten to devolve into the "muddy, tame, and monotonous"?

Critical Dissent

The interpretation of Reynolds's *Discourses* has changed remarkably over the two hundred and fifty or so years since their initial delivery. Although he correctly identifies Reynolds's major theme as that of generalizing toward the ideal, Robert Wark places greater emphasis on Reynolds's goal than on his process in his introduction to the standard edition of the *Discourses*. Thus he conflates Reynolds's theories with "a long and venerable tradition going back to Plato and Aristotle,"[46] asserts that "in this train of reasoning there is nothing that would in any way surprise Reynolds' contemporaries and predecessors," and concludes that "the *Discourses* are considered one of the most eloquent, as well as one of the last, presentations of the ideas that dominated European art criticism and theory from the mid-fifteenth to the mid-eighteenth century; they are regarded as a sort of coda in which the principal themes of the movement are given a final statement before another, or perhaps a variant, subject is developed."[47] As we have seen, there are important differences between Plato's transcendent approach to the universal and Aristotle's empirical approach, and much of Reynolds's theory and even vocabulary is incomprehensible before the Lockean empiricism of the eighteenth century. One of the major contentions of this study is that Reynolds stands, not at the endpoint of the classical tradition, but at a moment of reconception and revitalization—a revitalization the effects of which we will trace all the way to the early twentieth century. And far from mutely accepting Reynolds's formulation of the classical project, many of his contemporaries were indeed surprised and not a little dismayed by Reynolds's theories. Two appendices to Wark's edition of the *Discourses* record this surprise: William Blake's extensive marginal commentary to his copy of the 1798 edition of the *Discourses*, and William Hazlitt's critique of Reynolds's theory in essays written for *The Champion* between 1814 and 1815. Significantly, both consider Reynolds to be a radical revisionist rather than a conserver of tradition, and both single out Reynolds's painterly method of generalization as a particularly dangerous innovation.

William Blake's marginal commentary to his copy of Reynolds's *Discourses* is a major source for his art theory. Although it is perhaps unfair to assume that Blake would have been able thoroughly to express his own theory of art in direct reference to another's theory and in the limited space left in the margins and layout of another's book, a coherent cluster of ideas does emerge that is a neat opposite to Reynolds's empirical discourse of painterly generalization: Blake adhered to the transcendent classical discourse and asserted the linear precision of the ideal. He virulently rejected empirical observation as the origin of the artist's ideas, contending that empiricism promoted an overly sensual and indeed atheistic aesthetic that was inconsistent with art's divine aims. For Blake, "Bacon's Philosophy has Ruin'd England. Bacon is only Epicurus over again;" "Such is the End of Epicurean or Newtonian Philosophy: it is Atheism."[48] Blake required the more overt and immediate presence of the divine in art and in human affairs than did most Enlightenment thinkers. He therefore replaced Reynolds's highly mediated empirical process with what Reynolds (and Locke) had explicitly rejected, innate ideas:

> Reynolds Thinks that Man Learns all that he knows. I say on the Contrary that Man Brings All that he has or can have Into the World with him. Man is Born Like a Garden ready Planted & Sown. This World is too poor to produce one Seed.[49]

Blake was especially disturbed by Reynolds's attempts to dismiss the transcendent classical discourse on art as mere critical rhetoric: "The Ancients did not mean to Impose when they affirm'd their belief in Vision & Revelation. Plato was in Earnest: Milton was in Earnest. They believ'd that God did Visit Man Really & Truly."[50] Blake, then, reasserts "Spiritual Perception," and not materialist empiricism, as the origin of the artist's idea:

> Burke's Treatise on the Sublime & Beautiful is founded on the Opinions of Newton & Locke; on this Treatise Reynolds has grounded many of his assertions in all his Discourses. I read Burke's Treatise when very Young; at the same time I read Locke on Human Understanding & Bacon's Advancement of Learning; on Every one of these Books I wrote my Opinions, & on looking them over find that my Notes on Reynolds in this book are exactly similar. I felt the Same Contempt & Abhorrence then that I do now. They mock Inspiration & Vision. Inspiration & Vision was then, and now is, & I hope will always Remain, my Element, my Eternal Dwelling place; how can I hear it Contemned without returning Scorn for Scorn?[51]

Blake, then, recognized the close links between Reynolds's art theory and Locke's philosophy, and he repudiated this empiricization of the discourse of ideal beauty:

> Knowledge of Ideal Beauty is Not to be Acquired. It is Born with us. Innate Ideas are in Every Man, Born with him; they are truly Himself. The Man who says we have No Innate Ideas must be a Fool & Knave, Having No Conscience or Innate Science.[52]

Interestingly, then, Blake viewed his theory as a return to tradition as opposed to Reynolds's empirical revisionism. With telling precision, Blake rejects all of what I have identified as the novel features of British Academic classicism. Singling out Reynolds's assertion that "There is a rule, obtained out of general nature, to contradict which is to fall into deformity," Blake asks, "What is General Nature? is there Such a Thing? what is General Knowledge? is there such a Thing? Strictly Speaking All Knowledge is Particular."[53] Together, I assume, with the particular and distinct ideas of sensation that are of this world (and are irrelevant to Blake's art), there are particular innate ideas, which are providentially clear and distinct:

> The Man who asserts that there is no Such Thing as Softness in Art, & that every thing in Art is Definite & Determinate, has not been told this by Practise, but by Inspiration & Vision, because Vision is Determinate & Perfect, & he Copies That without Fatigue, Every thing being Definite & determinate.[54]

Blake advances this assertion in direct opposition to what current scholarship has failed to recognize, the Academy's painterly approach to the ideal. Thus where Reynolds, as a corrective to the tendency of idealization toward the "muddy," asserts that "every thing shall be carefully and distinctly expressed, as if the painter knew, with correctness and precision, the exact form and character of whatever is introduced into the picture," Blake perceptively glosses, "Excellent, & Contrary to his usual Opinions!"—although Blake would doubtless object to the circumspection that makes Reynolds say, "*as if* the painter knew . . . the exact form" of the object.[55] Unlike the British Royal Academicians, who tended to posit an approach to the ideal, for Blake the ideal is fully revealed and fully determinate in innate spiritual perception.

Hazlitt's essays on Reynolds's *Discourses* concentrate on six major points that he considered "either wrong in themselves, or liable to misconception and abuse." Point one relates to the imitation of others, which Hazlitt gives an overly restrictive definition and an overly central place in Reynolds's theory. I have attempted to mitigate the causes of his concern above (see chapters 1 and 2). The five remaining points all relate to Reynolds's novel discourse of abstraction and generalization:

> 2. That the great style in painting depends on leaving out the details of particular objects.

> 3. That the essence of portrait consists in giving the general character, rather than the individual likeness.
> 4. That the essence of history consists in abstracting from individuality of character and expression as much as possible.
> 5. That beauty or ideal perfection consists in a central form.
> 6. That to imitate [particular] nature is a very inferior object in art.[56]

Hazlitt was in a better historical position than current scholars to determine exactly what was novel about Reynolds's version of the classical project, and, like Blake, with telling precision he picks out the most novel aspects of that theory in terms of both vocabulary and process: "leaving out the details," rendering the "general" rather than the "individual," and "abstracting . . . individuality" in favor of the "central form." One of his major disputes with this abstractive and generalizing process, significantly, is the perilous connection that Reynolds had drawn between sloppy brushwork and the ideal. Hazlitt protests that "if the rule here objected to,—that the careful imitation of the parts injures the effect of the whole,—be at once admitted, slovenliness would become another name for genius, and the most unfinished performances would necessarily be the best."[57] Hazlitt's proposed corrective is a critical distinction between "execution" and "daubing":

> Sir Joshua seems, indeed, to deny that Titian finished much. . . . It is true that [Titian] availed himself, in a considerable degree, of what is called *execution*, to facilitate his imitation of nature, but it was to facilitate, not to supersede it. . . . We do not object to execution: it saves labour, and shews a mastery both of hand and eye. But then there is nothing more distinct than execution and *daubing*. . . . Leave out all regard to the details, reduce the whole into crude unvarying masses, and it becomes totally useless; for these can be given just as well without execution as with it.[58]

Hazlitt, then, uses the motivation problem to discredit Reynolds's painterly process of generalization. By identifying painterliness as a technique and therefore a sign of idealization, Reynolds had inadvertently given status to unqualified daubers. Ironically, Hazlitt subjects Opie, who had attempted to make the same correction, to this criticism.

> The late Mr. Opie proceeded entirely on this principle . . . he never finished any of the parts, thinking them beneath the attention of a great man. He went over the whole head the second day as he had done the day before, and therefore made no progress. The picture at last, having neither the lightness of a sketch, nor the accuracy of a finished work, looked course [sic], laboured, and heavy.[59]

Although Hazlitt's distinction between "execution" and "daubing" is no more enlightening than Reynolds's own distinction between proper generalization and "a trick or mechanical habit, formed by guess, and established by custom," it again establishes an extreme toward which Reynolds's method was widely perceived as tending. We can use this extreme, this tendency toward the "unfinished," the "muddy, tame and monotonous," the "coarse, labored and heavy," the "crude unvarying masses" of the dauber, as critical guideposts in analyzing late eighteenth-century British classicism.

4
The Practice of Generalization

With the previous chapter's understanding of the relation between generalization and brushwork, Reynolds's own painterly practice comes into sharper focus (although this is perhaps the wrong metaphor). Many scholars have remarked on some apparent contradictions between Reynolds's theory and his practice, especially inasmuch as he advocated Grand Manner history painting but practiced a rather elegant portraiture. There was certainly very little market in late eighteenth-century Britain for history painting, but Reynolds annexed his preferred genre to the Grand Manner by stating that the "lower" subjects can be improved by "borrowing from the grand." In most scholarship, this is taken to mean that the portraitist should use the iconographic accouterments of Grand Manner history painting, deploying here a Greek column and there a Roman oratorical pose. Reynolds certainly aggrandized his sitters in this way, but he did so in another way as well, one commonly overlooked in the scholarship. "If a portrait-painter is desirous to raise and improve his subject," Reynolds asserts, "he has no other means than by approaching it to a general idea." The approach to the general idea is achieved in two ways. One, which I have already considered, is by changing the sitter's clothing "from a temporary fashion to one more permanent" (see chapter 2, "Generalization from the Customary to the Universal"). The second is by abstracting the "minute breaks and peculiarities in the face," thereby approaching the sitter's features toward the central form.[1] If there is any consistency between Reynolds's theory and practice, then, we should look to the surfaces of Reynolds's portraiture for the paint that signifies and enacts this abstraction.

Portraiture and the Ideal

An apposite *locus* for this search is Reynolds's *Commodore Augustus Keppel* of 1752 (figure 10), which many scholars have described as a sort of pictorial manifesto announcing Reynolds's arrival on the London scene after his Grand Tour.[2] The similarity of the *Keppel* to Alan Ramsay's *Norman, Twenty-second Chief of Macleod* (figure 9) is immediately evident both in the general composition of a centralized figure on a shore with a steep cliff rising to the left, and in the pose of the figures, which echoes that of the *Apollo Belvedere* and executes a gesture of confident command. However, there is a marked difference in style. As David Solkin notes, whereas Ramsay's portrait is an "isolated figure defined against a more or less neutral and unimportant background," Reynolds achieves a "high degree of pictorial unity." Solkin defers this unity to Reynolds's "exposure to Italian art (and in this case to Tintoretto in particular)," thus complementing Reynolds's borrowing of the pose with a borrowing of the style.[3] But the detection of borrowing does not resolve questions of iconography or style; in fact, it begs the question of what significance the latter-day artist attributed to the techniques or motifs he or she adopted (or adapted). In the previous chapter I followed Reynolds's argument connecting Venetian brushwork to "the power of generalising." Where Ramsay's *Macleod* inhabits a crystalline atmosphere that sharply outlines his figure on every side, the contours in Reynolds's *Keppel* are soft and diffused, as though observed through a slight squint; and whereas in Ramsay's work the brushwork is minute and carefully blended to show every pocket and protuberance in Macleod's face and every Tartan square as modified by the precise, linear folds of the drapery, Keppel's clothing, face, and hands are rendered in sweeping strokes that describe only broad, general masses.

These two methods of handling could be said to embody two different modes of idealization. Macleod's cheek is unblemished because Ramsay painstakingly renders it as such:

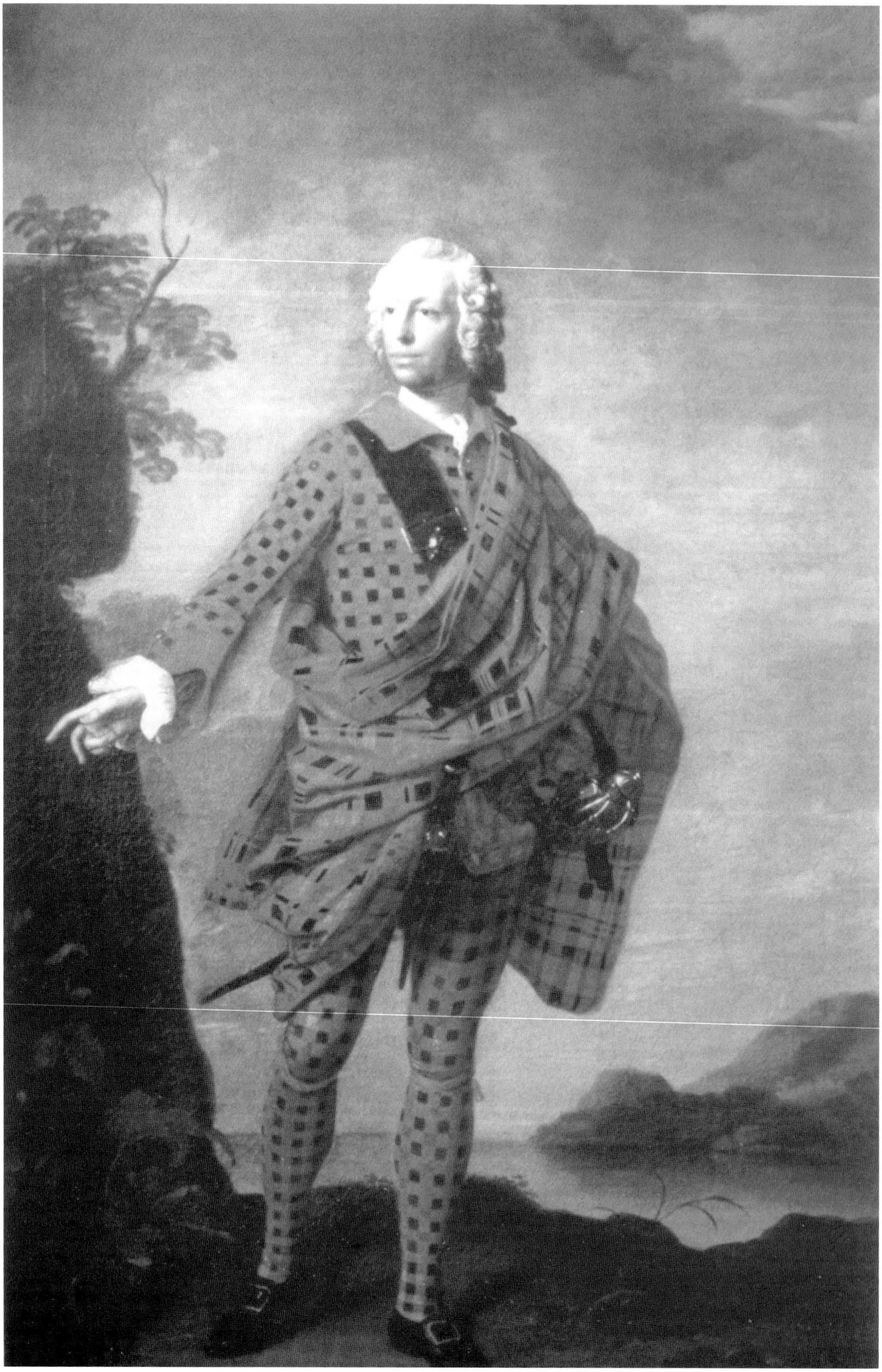

9. Alan Ramsay, *Norman, Twenty-second Chief of Macleod*, 1747. Collection of John Macleod, Dunvegan Castle, Isle of Skye, Scotland.

by eliminating the evidence of his brushwork, the smooth and blended surface of Ramsay's painting is made identical with the surface of Macleod's flesh. If Ramsay's *Macleod* is idealized, then, it is idealized in a fundamentally naturalistic way: by eliminating all traces of the handiwork of the artist, the perfection is implied to be resident in the sitter, and the artist simply mirrors that perfection in his glossy finish. In Reynolds's *Keppel*, by contrast, a screen of brushwork mediates both between the artist and the sitter and between the sitter and the viewer. Keppel's cheek is unblemished because Reynolds's broad, painterly brushwork prohibits his attention to any of his sitter's minute flaws and peculiarities. Reynolds's idealization, then, is actively displayed. His means of idealization resides in his practice; by showing his work, idealization becomes an attribute of Reynolds's dilated vision and enlarged comprehension—in brief, his ability to generalize, made visible in painterly brushwork. An analogy may help to clarify this distinction. The facial and figural distortions of Quentin Massys's *Old Woman (The Queen of Tunis)* are rendered in a relatively tight, transparent manner, in effect assuring the viewer that those distortions are resident in the woman Massys depicts. By contrast, the distortions of Willem de Kooning's *Woman* paintings are enacted through the very brushwork used to describe his subjects, and thus the viewer is conscious of the work not (only) as a deformed woman, but (also) as a woman deformed by de Kooning. In the terminology of Peircean semiotics, the Massys is (or pretends to be) only an icon of deformity, while the de Kooning *Women* are indices of deformation, or more precisely indices of a deformation that discovers the inner deformity of the individual or type. The same distinction applies to the two modes of idealization: Ramsay's work is an icon of Macleod's ideality; Reynolds's work is both an icon of Keppel's discovered ideality and an index of the act of generalization that discovers that ideality.

If in his practice as in his theory Reynolds's brushwork is an index of generalization, we can clarify something that Solkin identifies as problematic, which amounts to a further contradiction between Reynolds's theory and his practice. Solkin identifies the "high degree of pictorial unity" in Reynolds's *Keppel* as Reynolds's solution to the problem outlined in chapter 2 above: the propensity of the "unworthy" to borrow any isolated, reiterable signs of greatness. In the *Keppel*, Solkin asserts, Reynolds ties up the "greatness" of the sitter in the whole appearance of the work, rather than in the distribution of isolated signs across a compartmentalized surface. While the sharp linear definition of Ramsay's *Macleod* easily allows a borrowing of its parts—the old head can be razored off and a new head grafted in its place, and so on—Reynolds's *Keppel* cannot be borrowed without reperforming the entire surface, so tightly bound are all the parts into the overall pictorial unity of the work. But Solkin considers Reynolds's painterly style only as a way of negating the ability of "unworthy" painters and patrons to borrow the pictorial signs of greatness. Reynolds's theory of approaching the individual to the universal Solkin considers to be a "fantasy of transcendent art" that was "willingly embraced" by his clientele because it offered a way out of a "world foundering in the quicksands of fashion."[4] In a modified "Emperor's New Clothes" story, Reynolds's patrons believed Reynolds had clothed them in greatness because the *Discourses* advertised Reynolds's ineffable ability to do so, because they wanted to believe it, and because they believed that their contemporaries believed it. I am arguing that what Solkin identifies as pictorial unity in the *Keppel* is precisely the "whole" of which Reynolds spoke in his *Discourses*: the broad, monotonous, painterly rendering that generalizes the individual, approaching his or her appearance to the universal, and thus making their greatness permanently legible to their contemporaries and to future generations. In Solkin's analysis, Reynolds's practice was grounded only in convention, a collective belief that, although it was unfounded, allowed a certain form of communication. It is my contention that Reynolds coherently grounded his practice, at least within the intellectual discourse of his moment. Far from taking recourse in the ineffable, Reynolds carefully explained the epistemological cogency of his method in accord with the best modern experts, and even identified the techniques by which generalization could be achieved and thus the pictorial signs by which it could be identified. Two of the main contradictions that scholars have discovered between Reynolds's theory and his practice thus resolve one another: it is Reynolds's "Venetian" brushwork, acting as an index of generalization, that raised his portraitic practice towards the high aspirations that he advocated.

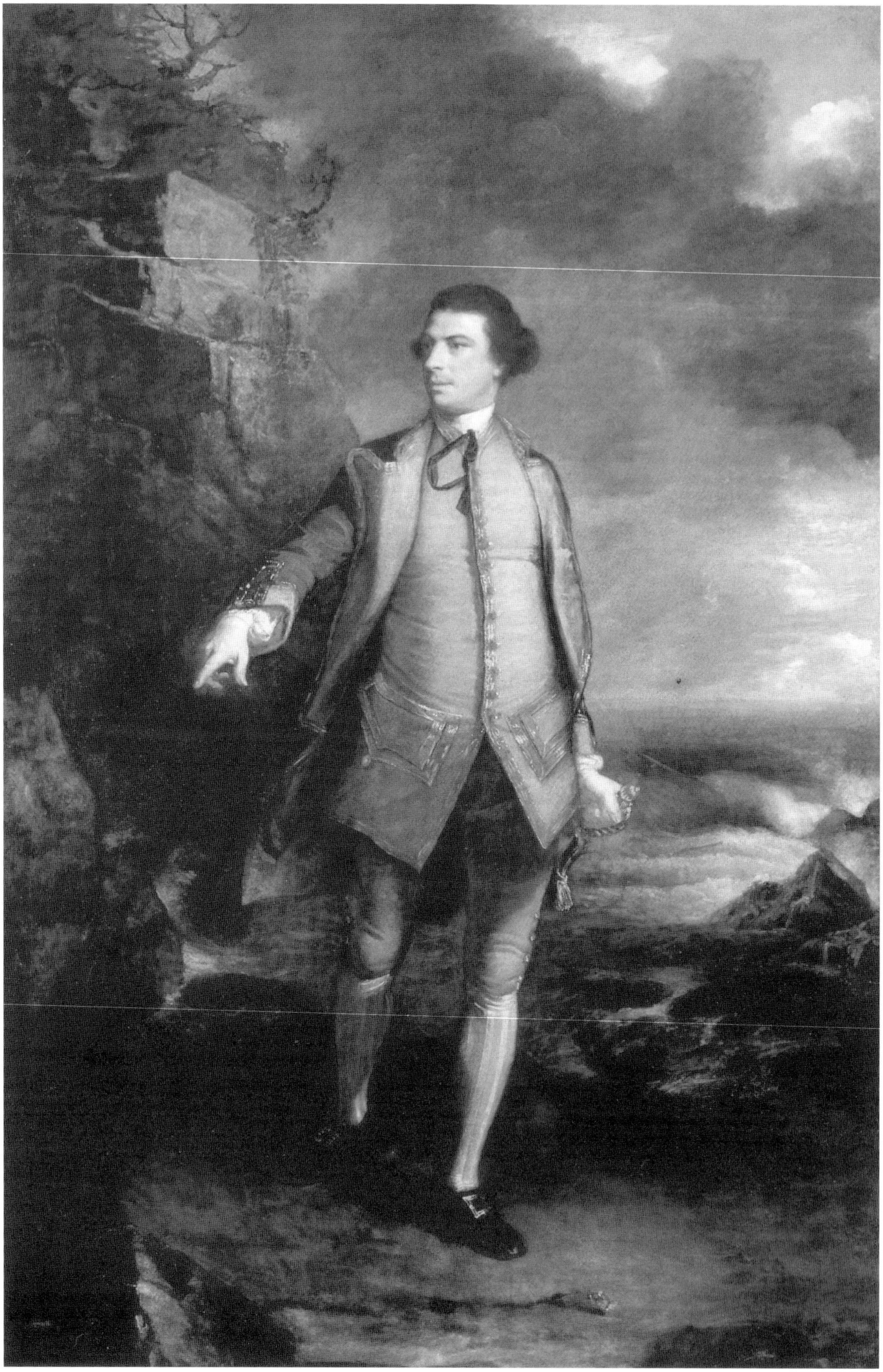

10. Joshua Reynolds, *Commodore Augustus Keppel*, c. 1752. © National Maritime Museum, London.

Of course, many aspects of the *Keppel* still obviously conform more to local than to universalizing criteria: Keppel's hairstyle, body type, face, and clothing are still largely individual to the sitter or to mid-century fashion. Portraiture almost by definition prohibits too great of an approach to the "general idea," where all individual, temporal, and geographic variations meld into a common central form. As Reynolds notes, "It is very difficult to ennoble the character of a countenance but at the expense of the likeness, which is what is most generally required by such as sit to the painter."[5] However, it is one of the main virtues of Reynolds's formulation of classical art theory that idealization, understood as generalization, operates on a *sliding scale*. The vast gulf between the real and the ideal of Platonic theory is replaced with a gradual approach to the ideal through degrees of generalization and abstraction. In Reynolds's notion of Grand Manner portraiture, the artist engages in an implicit compromise with the sitter along the sliding scale of idealization. The sitter is modified towards the universal and the central form in order to demonstrate that which is beautiful, true, and good about the individual; but at the same time enough likeness and enough customs are maintained to ensure that the viewers of the work will allocate that ideality to the sitter and to his or her society. Although theoretically the closer the portrait approaches to the central form the more universal *ethos* and ideality is conveyed, sitters may prize their individuality and the status symbols of their own time more than they do those of all time, and the portraitist who fails to acquiesce to the sitter's demands will fail professionally. Practical social and economic considerations thus constrain portraiture from too great an approach to the central form.

Reynolds notes another important reason why the artist should make judicious concessions to local and temporary custom, even when he or she can clearly see the underlying universal:

> Whoever would reform a nation, supposing a bad taste to prevail in it, will not accomplish his purpose by going directly against the stream of their prejudices. Men's minds must be prepared to receive what is new to them. Reformation is a work of time. A national taste, however wrong it may be, cannot be totally changed at once; we must yield a little to the prepossession which has taken hold on the mind, and we may then bring people to adopt what would offend them, if endeavoured to be introduced by violence.[6]

Not only economic interests, but also an altruistic intent to reform will sometimes require a strategy of concessions to the individual and to the local custom. Grand Manner portraiture, in other words, is a valuable, albeit modest, first step toward the overall goal of leading a recalcitrant public toward a higher ideal.

Allegorical Figures and the Ideal

As we saw in chapter 1 and shall more thoroughly explore in the next chapter, the sliding scale of generalization is articulated in eighteenth-century Academic theory as a sort of taxonomic pyramid of referential classes. At the bottom of the pyramid is the unmodified data of reality, where individual differences prevail; and at the top is the absolute ideal, where all such differences are elided into a common form. Significantly, however, between these two levels—between the individual and the universal, the real and the ideal—there is a gradual continuum defined by the variable application of the generalizing process: again, Reynolds's theory of classicism is a theory of idealization, not of the ideal. Individual peculiarities and actions can be generalized toward regional types; various regional types can be generalized toward a more universal human character, and so on. Although none of these levels is strictly speaking the absolute ideal, any taxonomic level beyond the individual carries a measure of ideality proportionate to the breadth of the artist's comparative generalization. Interestingly, not only portraiture but also history painting rarely if ever requires great heights in this referential pyramid or sliding scale of idealization. History painting normally depicts what the late-eighteenth century called "characters," figures instancing a particular expression or human type in relation to the painting's narrative. Inasmuch as the characters of history painting are, for the purposes of the narrative, older or younger, embodiments of grace, strength, or speed, or evincing a certain emotion, they are not fully ideal.

Probably the closest that Reynolds came to the absolute ideal of classical aspiration was not in his history paintings, but in his single allegorical figures, especially his *Theory* and his

Virtues. Not only are these works released from the exigencies of likeness to a particular sitter, they also are among the few mature works by Reynolds that were fully painted by him, and thus more fully responsible to his own ideas.[7] In a consideration of Ancient sculpture, Reynolds noted the relevance of the concept of the ideal in such allegorical figures, which, he claims,

> are distinguished by their *insignia* more than by any variety of form or beauty. Take from Apollo his Lyre, from Bacchus his Thirsus and Vineleaves, and from Meleagar the Boar's Head, and there will remain little or no difference in their characters. In a Juno, Minerva, or Flora, the idea of the artist seems to have gone no further than representing perfect beauty, and afterwards adding the proper attributes, with a total indifference to which they gave them.[8]

Although this argument is unconvincing based on past evidence (Apollo and Bacchus do not share the same body type in most representations), it suggests that Reynolds considered it possible to relegate issues of character to subsidiary iconographic attributes, thus preserving the figure as exclusively the province of the ideal.

Of his own allegorical figures, Reynolds's *Theory* (figure 11), painted for the coved ceiling of the Royal Academy Library in its original location in Somerset House, is perhaps the closest to demonstrating this idea. The library's collection of original and translated books of art theory was a necessary aspect of the student's education in the principles of art, and the figure's characterization as Theory, painted by the chief theorist of the British Royal Academy, was a natural place for Reynolds to demonstrate his own ideas in practical application. Joseph Baretti's official *Guide through the Royal Academy* (1781) describes the work as follows:

> The Center-Painting represents *The Theory of the Art* under the form of an elegant and majestick Female, seated in the clouds, and looking upwards, as contemplating the Heavens. She holds in one hand the Compass, in the other a Label, on which this sentence is written:
>
> *Theory is the Knowledge of what is truly Nature*. This Picture is the work of *Sir Joshua Reynolds*; a noble Specimen of that elegance of taste, strength of imagination, spirit and brilliancy of colouring, for which he has been so often and so justly celebrated [Baretti's italics].[9]

Baretti's description misreads the work, interestingly because he attempts to conform it to *past* classical theory rather than to Reynolds's own. Seated in the clouds and looking farther upward, the figure certainly signifies lofty aspirations, but to suggest that for Reynolds theory is a contemplation of "the Heavens" implies a notion of transcendence in the *Theory* that Reynolds specifically disavowed in his theory. More egregious is Baretti's citation of a "Compass" in Theory's hand that does not exist. It is possible that the figure's headband, which seems to emerge from her left hand and crooked pinkie, suggested a compass to Baretti, but his expectation was informed more by past theory than current observation. Ripa's *Iconologia* includes a compass as an appropriate attribute of Theory, but in this case Reynolds did not follow past practice. Instead, the allegorical character of the work is conveyed exclusively by the label she holds in her right hand. As a label, it is at once a more understandable and a more obviously "added" attribute of the accompanying figure, which therefore can stand as the embodiment, and not just an arbitrary symbol, of the allegorical message.

The sentence on the label is of course a reference to Reynolds's distinction between particular nature and general nature, the first of which is merely contingent and the second of which is "truly nature." In his seventh Discourse, Reynolds identified "two errors" that he found to be "most prevalent" and "most injurious" to artists, one of which is "that of taking particular living objects for nature."[10] For Reynolds,

> the first idea that occurs in the consideration of what is fixed in art, or in taste, is that presiding principle of which I have so frequently spoken in former discourses,—the general idea of nature. . . . This general idea therefore ought to be called Nature, and nothing else, correctly speaking, has a right to that name.[11]

As an embodiment of this theory, the work conforms closely to the formal appearance of a "general idea" as we were above able to elicit it from Reynolds's technical advice. It is composed of only two basic colors, the reddish-brown hues of the flesh, hair, label, and sky, and the blue hues of the drapery, headband, and clouds. The two colors are only very moderately carried into each other's zones, as in the reflected blue on the outside of the right

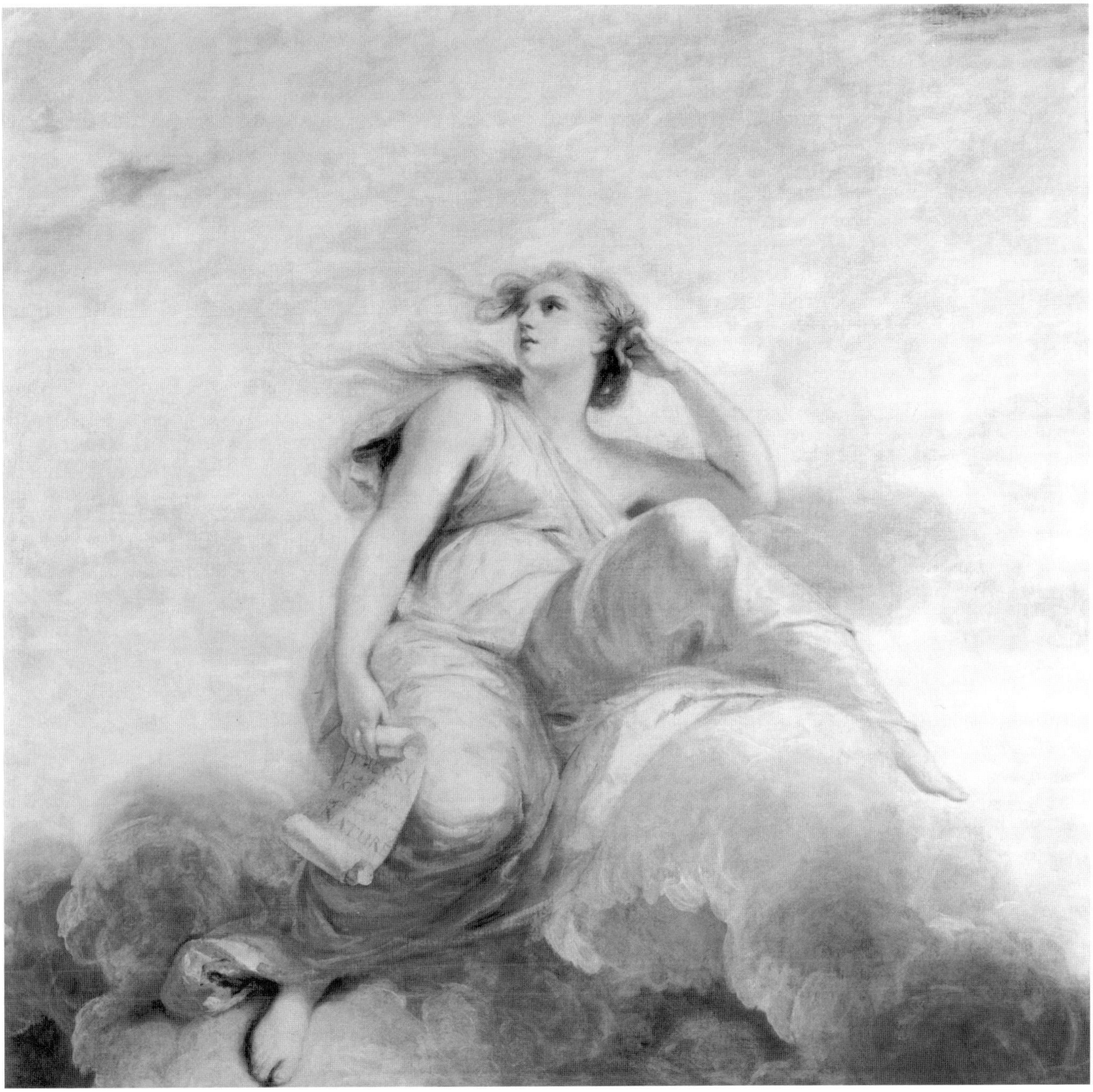

11. Joshua Reynolds, *Theory*, 1779. Royal Academy of Arts, London.

shoulder and the brown shadows on the drapery between the thighs and on the inside right of the torso. This simple, duotonous color scheme is applied in thin, sweeping, semitransparent strokes that generalize contours by their continuous trajectory and by blurring, only rarely allowing any opaque buildup of impasto or any abrupt juxtaposition of dark and light values such as would sharply define a line or edge: the whole work appears as though viewed through a slight squint that has generalized color, contour, and value into large masses. A certain opacity and thickness of paint is allowed in the clouds and hem of the drapery; and there also Reynolds's brushwork is the most obviously visible as it simulates their respective textures, but the figure's flesh is laid on almost like a wash in repeated, dilute, directional strokes that screen out internal details such as creases, wrinkles, abrupt bony protuberances, body hair, or of course any obvious imperfections. The breadth of Reynolds's brush simply does not allow him to render such minute particulars; nor does it allow the spectator to consider them. It is my argument, then, that Reynolds's omission of any conventional insignia from this work, such as Theory's usual compass, was part of his attempt to convey the allegorical character of the work through style rather than iconography. Where traditional allegorical figures are purely conventional, relying on agreed and artificial symbols to carry their meaning, Reynolds's *Theory* aspires to naturalize its meaning. The purpose of the work is to demonstrate that "theory" is the knowledge of what is "truly nature," and Reynolds's *Theory* is not a symbol but an instance of that theory: the *Theory* is the general idea of woman rather than a portrait of a specific individual; and the general idea is that which is truly nature.

Similar techniques inform Reynolds's depictions of the three Christian and four Cardinal Virtues, studies for the painted windows of the chapel at New College, Oxford (see figures 12 and 13). Reynolds was asked only for drawings for the design of the windows (Thomas Jervais did the actual painting on glass), but instead he produced full-scale finished paintings on canvas. Rationalizing this multiplication of his labor, Reynolds explained to William Mason that "he had been so long in the use of the pallet [sic] and brushes, that he found it easier to him to paint them to drawing. 'Jervas [sic], the painter on glass', says [Reynolds], 'will have a better original to copy; and I suppose persons hereafter may be found to purchase my paintings.'"[12] The third, mercenary reason was only partially successful. The Duke of Rutland bought the Nativity in 1784 for 1,200 guineas, but the Virtues remained in Reynolds's estate until they were sold to the Earl of Normanton in 1821 for 3,565 pounds. Divided by seven, that makes over 500 pounds (over 475 guineas) per Virtue, where Reynolds generally charged only 200 guineas for a whole length even at the height of his fame in the 1780s.[13] The significance of the works to Rutland and Normanton must have been great, and the prices they were willing to pay for their opinions are at least a partial gauge to the contemporaneous value of their taste.

The first two reasons for Reynolds's production of full-scale paintings rather than drawings are equally significant, if more difficult to evaluate. Reynolds "found it easier to paint" the studies because indeed he was not in the habit of making drawings. According to contemporary witnesses and contrary to standard Academic procedure, Reynolds would begin his work directly on canvas, without any preparatory underdrawing.[14] This practice is particularly significant given Reynolds's theory of brushwork, his wish to see in broad, painterly masses rather than in precise linear boundaries, and his reluctance even in finished paintings conclusively to fix contours or edges. Similarly, since it was not Reynolds but Jervais who was to execute the actual glass paintings, and if, as I am suggesting, the brushwork is of some significance, it would be necessary for Reynolds to give the executor an "original" that demonstrated this technique, rather than a linear sketch. And indeed, although here the figures are relatively traditional in their standardized iconography (a broken column and lion for *Fortitude* and a sword and scales for *Justice*, for example), and although their characters are relatively marked (*Fortitude* is a stern matron with a contracted brow and somber color scheme; *Justice* is a more youthful *ingénue* with parted lips and a pastel color scheme), their style once again conforms to Reynolds's rather novel theory of idealization. They are articulated in a relatively monotonous color range, with blurred contours and construction in large, painterly masses with broad, thin, directional brushwork.

More telling than a twenty-first-century description of the works is one from the late-eighteenth century. Written in 1782, Thomas Warton's *Verses on Sir Joshua Reynolds's Painted Window at New-College Oxford* demonstrates a thorough knowledge of Reynolds's theory. The theme of the poem is that its narrator, previously "enraptur'd" by the "capricious . . . maze" of Gothic taste, gradually becomes reconciled to classical simplicity by contemplating Reynolds's work. This theme is highly relevant not only to the contest between neoclassical and Gothic taste, between the empirical and transcendent routes to truth, and probably between Church of England and Catholic doctrines, but also to the contest that Reynolds outlined between classical art and associationism. While at first the narrator resists the reformation of his mind ("Ah, stay thy treacherous hand, forebear to trace / Those faultless forms of elegance and grace!"), he later acquiesces:

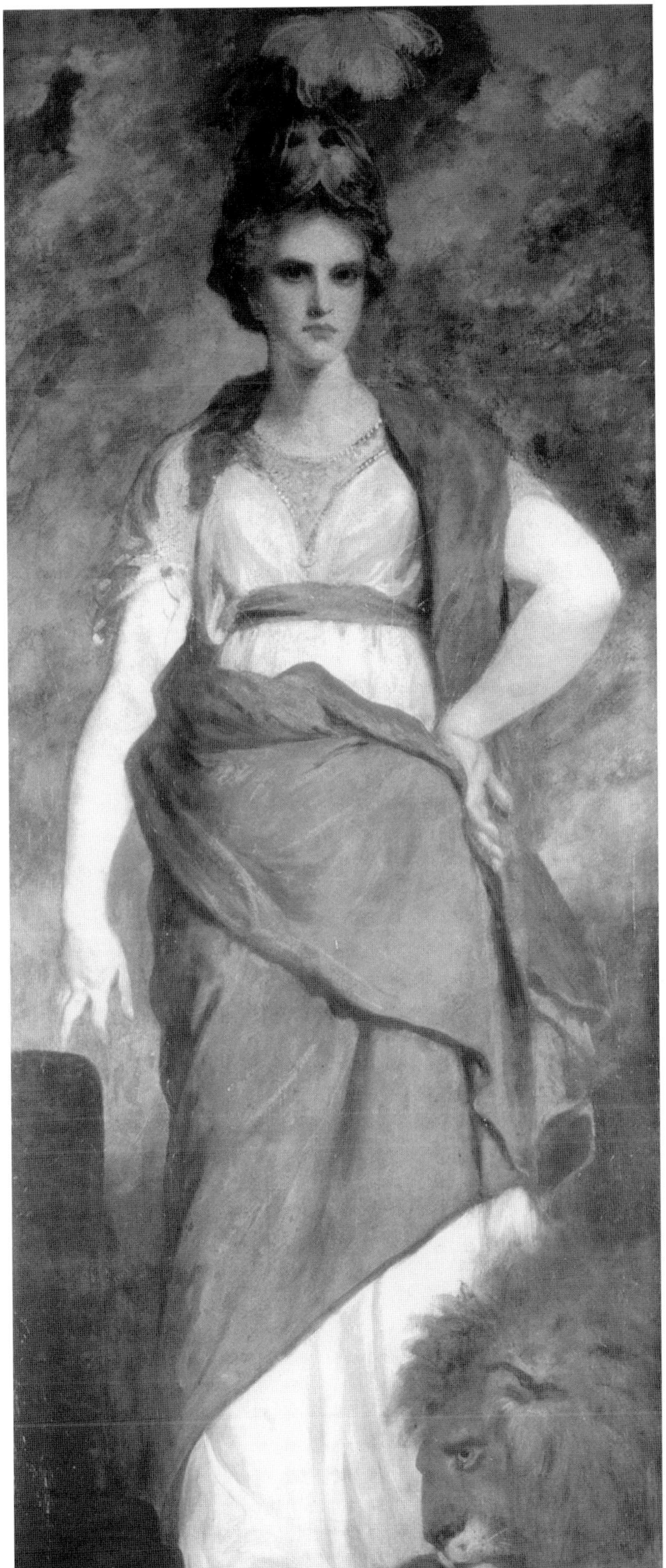

12. Joshua Reynolds, *Fortitude*, c. 1778–79. In a private collection.

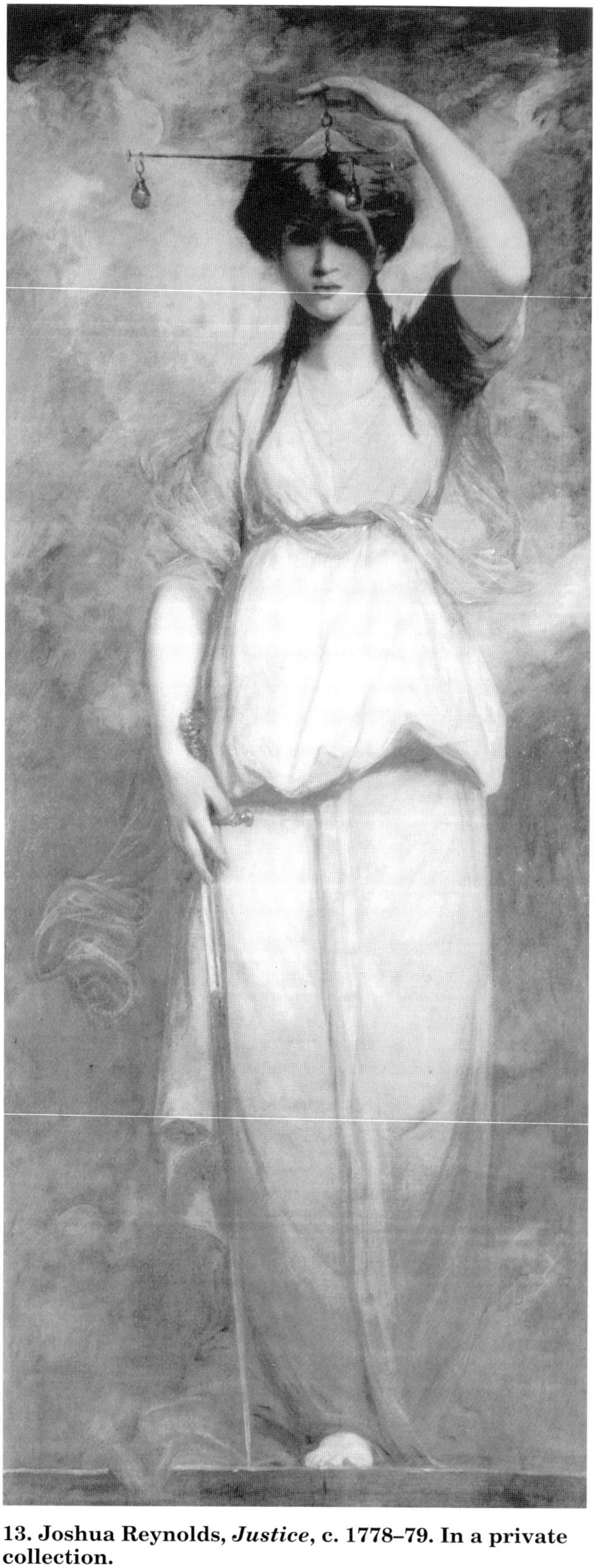

13. Joshua Reynolds, *Justice*, c. 1778–79. In a private collection.

No more the matchless skill I call unkind
That strives to disenchant my cheated mind.
For when again I view thy chaste Design,
The just proportion, and the genuin [sic] line . . .
Sudden, the sombrous imagery is fled,
Which late my visionary rapture fed:
Thy powerful hand has broke the Gothic chain,
And brought my bosom back to truth again:
To truth, by no peculiar taste confin'd,
Whose universal pattern strikes mankind;
To truth, whose bold and unresisted aim
Checks frail caprice, and fashion's fickle claim;
To truth, whose charms deception's magic quell,
And bind coy Fancy in a stronger spell.[15]

The last three couplets directly dramatize classicism's contest against associationism: the "universal" and "true" are arrayed against, and overwhelm, the "peculiar," "capricious," "fashionable," "fickle," and "deceptive." Reynolds's "chaste design" "bind[s] coy fancy"—and we will recall the erratically additive function of the fancy in eighteenth-century epistemology. Warton clearly echoes what Reynolds cited as the goal of classical art: to "fashion and consolidate" the stock of ideas in the viewer's mind.[16]

The main agent of this reform, significantly, is not the iconographic program of the work, for all its Christian themes. Indeed, the iconographic program is barely mentioned in the poem.[17] Although scholars usually look to subject matter for classical "instruction," here Warton cites the style of the works, and specifically their brushwork, as the main agent of reform. The first lines already contain reference to the artist's "hand" (although again the narrator is at first reluctant to submit to its reform):

Ah, stay thy treacherous *hand*, forbear to *trace*
Those faultless forms of elegance and grace!
Ah, cease to *spread* the bright transparent *mass*,
With *Titian's pencil*, o'er the speaking glass!
Nor steal, by *strokes of art with truth combin'd*,
The fond illusions of my wayward mind!
[emphasis added]

Toward the end of the poem Warton returns again to the brushwork:

Behold, [Beauty] *prints* upon the crystal plain [sic],
With her own energy, th'expressive *stain*!
The mighty Master *spreads* his mimic *toil*
More *wide* . . .
While in the warm enamel Nature lives [emphasis added].[18]

Particularly the phrase "strokes of art with truth combin'd" suggests a direct reference to Reynolds's painterly project of classical reform. Reynolds's letter of appreciation for the poem is also significant: "It is not much to say that your Verses are by far the best that ever my name was concerned in. I am sorry therefore that my name was not hitched in in the body of the Poem, if the title page should be lost it will appear to be addressd to Mr Jervais."[19] Warton's poetic tribute is inept exactly where it is most apt. Indeed it was Jervais's hand that executed the painted glass versions of the works.

Caricature and the Ideal

A brief mention of caricature at this point is of direct relevance to the discourse of generalization as its complement and its opposite. A typical definition of the technique of caricature is this, found in the *Penguin Dictionary of Art*: "to seize upon some trait of appearance . . . and to exaggerate it, but not so much as to lose likeness."[20] The word itself derives from the Italian *caricare*, to load. But exactly what features should be exaggerated? An exaggeration of all the features would result only in a larger representation, so there must be a choice involved; a choice that the phrase "some trait" fails to specify. A second problem: exaggeration in caricature must be understood not only as making larger, but can include an exaggeration by way of diminution as well: the projection of the chin may be reduced at the same time as that of the nose is increased. Only by understanding caricature relative to classicism, and specifically in relation to generalization and the central form, can we resolve both of these problems. A caricature will exaggerate precisely those aspects of the real that the idealized or classical representation will eliminate or attenuate. In the Grand Manner portrait, as we saw, the artist will eliminate or attenuate that which is "peculiar" or deviant from the central form: if the sitter has an unusually large nose, the artist will tactfully reduce its prominence; if a receding chin, the artist will increase its prominence. The technique of personal caricature is exactly the opposite, or more precisely the complement of idealization in this respect. Where idealization reduces deviations from the central form, caricature exaggerates those deviations: the slightly prominent nose will be enlarged to grotesque proportions, and the slightly receding chin will disappear into the neckline. The formula for the production of caricature, then, is this: caricature equals real minus ideal times "x." The function "real minus ideal" determines what individual traits deviate from the central form, and "x," the caricature factor, exaggerates those deviations: a slight caricature will have a small value for "x," and an extreme caricature will have a large value.

In a comparison between a caricature of Thomas Bentley by the eighteenth-century Italian caricaturist Pier Leone Ghezzi (figure 14) and a typical classicizing figure from Flaxman's illustrations to *The Iliad* (figure 15, just left of center), we can see the formula at work. In the caricature, the size of Bentley's nose is exaggerated relative to Flaxman's figure. Following the formula "caricature equals real minus ideal times 'x'," then, when Ghezzi mentally subtracted the ideal nose from Bentley's actual nose, there was a positive value left over: Bentley's nose was too large. The multiplication by "x" or the caricature factor exaggerated that superfluity. Conversely, when Ghezzi subtracted the ideal calves from Bentley's, he came up with a negative value: Bentley's calves were too thin. Again the caricature factor was applied, but this time multiplied a negative, resulting in an exaggeration by way of diminution.

Because the technique of caricature can be reduced to this mathematical operation, caricatures can be generated by computers as well as by artists. In a recent clinical trial, which tested subjects for the speed with which they recognized representations, the subjects were shown three images of Arnold Schwarzenegger: a "veridical" or unmodified photograph; and two others, which the researchers called the "caricature" and the "anti-caricature" (figure 16).[21] In order to produce these latter two images, the researchers had to generate a fourth, the face on the right, which is an average of the faces of eighty-nine male celebrities—or in other words, an approach to what Reynolds would call the "central form" of the (turn-of-the-century American celebrity) male face. Its departure from the Greek archetype and its lack of conspicuous beauty may trouble us, but this is what Reynolds's process explicitly identified as the ideal. The Schwarzenegger caricature, then, was generated by a fifteen percent exaggeration of all of Arnold's features that deviated from this central form (the caricature factor, then, was 1.15). Although it is not named as such, the "anti-caricature" is what Reynolds would call a Grand Manner portrait of Arnold, and was produced in exact mirror to the caricature: all of the features that deviated from the central form were *reduced* by fifteen percent (the caricature factor, or rather anti-caricature or idealizing factor, was .85). In fact, we can now see that the formula for the production of the Grand Manner portrait is identical to that of the personal caricature: "real minus ideal times 'x'," but in a Grand Manner portrait "x" will have a value of less than one while in a caricature "x" will have a value greater than one.

William Hazlitt recognized the tight complementarity of classicism and caricature along these lines. Considering Reynolds's advice that when the portraitist wishes to improve his sitter, he "has no other means than by approaching it to a general idea,"[22] Hazlitt objects:

> Portraits of this kind . . . have been elevated by ignorance and affectation, to the dignified rank of historical portrait. But in fact they are merely *caricature transposed*: that is, as the caricaturist makes a mouth wider than it really is, so the painter of *flattering likeness* (as they are termed) makes it not so wide, by a process just as mechanical, and more insipid [Hazlitt's italics].[23]

Hazlitt uses this complementarity to discredit the "flattering likeness" by association. But once again he is acute in recognizing the nature of idealization in Reynolds's Royal Academy: it is a "process" (Hazlitt derisively calls it "mechanical") that is based on eliminating or attenuating peculiarities toward the central form.

Although they are nominally opposites, then, the personal caricature and the Grand Manner portrait are tightly bound together across the central form of the classical ideal. It is doubtless because of this complementarity that caricature and classicism are so often found together historically, especially in the period under consideration here, when classicism was thoroughly associated with the idea of a central form. The decades between 1760 and 1830 were simultaneously the Golden Age of British classicism, presided over by Reynolds and the Royal Academy, and the Golden Age of British caricature, presided over by James Gillray, Thomas Rowlandson, and the Cruikshanks.

In the next chapter we shall further examine the approach to the ideal in the human figure, the traditional subject matter of classicism,

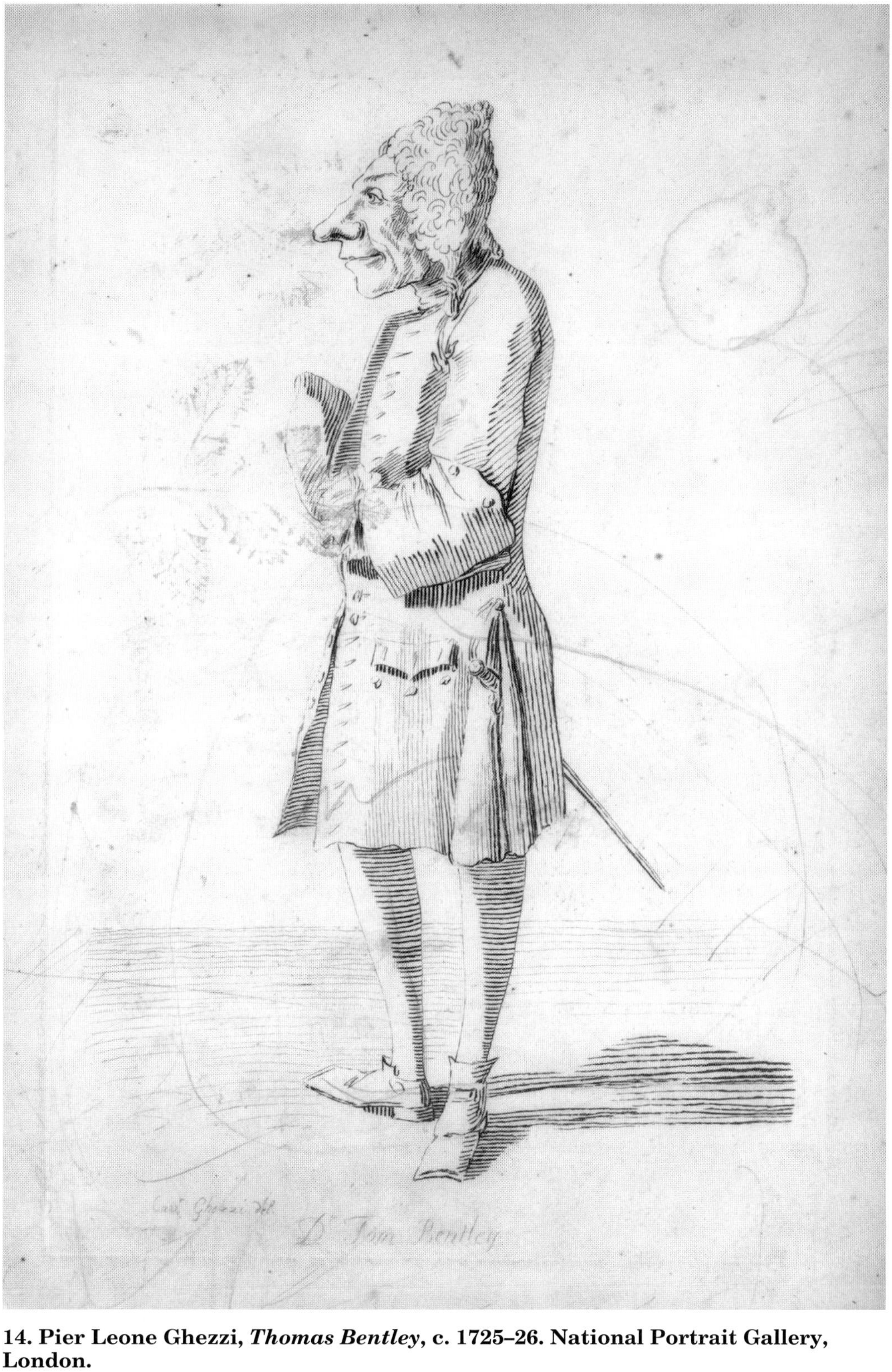

14. Pier Leone Ghezzi, *Thomas Bentley*, c. 1725–26. National Portrait Gallery, London.

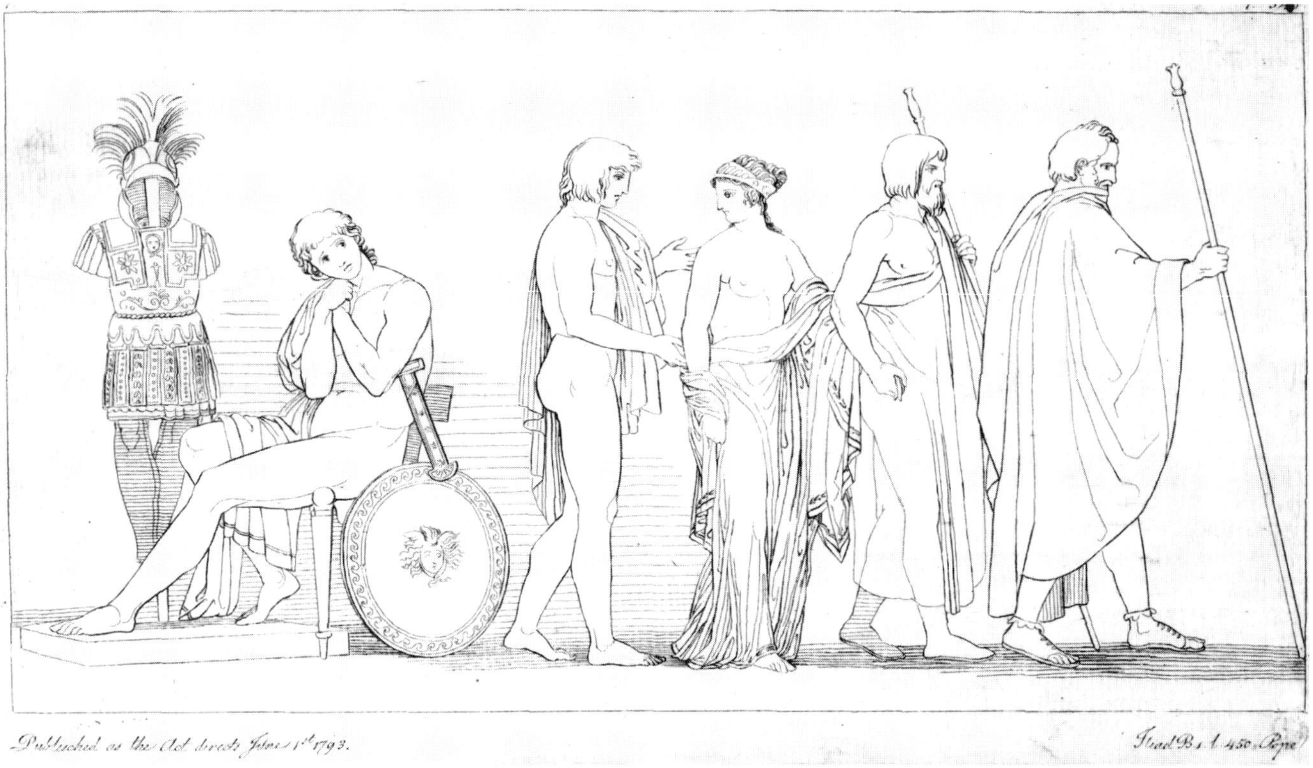

15. John Flaxman, *The Departure of Briseis from the Tent of Achilles*, from *The Iliad of Homer, Engraved by Thomas Piroli from the Compositions of John Flaxman, Sculptor* (Rome, 1793). Beinecke Rare Book and Manuscript Library, Yale University.

but I wish here to indicate that generalization-theory can be applied to *any* subject matter. Any object can be idealized inasmuch as it can be abstracted from its individual appearance toward the general idea of its class. Although the phrase "classical landscape" is most commonly used in the scholarship to refer to a landscape that conforms to certain standardized (Claudean) compositional paradigms, in the late eighteenth-century understanding of classicism as an approach to the general ideal, the classical landscape is one in which objects and compositions are generalized toward class-ideas, rather than being rendered as particular individuals.

Picturesque and General Landscape

In a draft prospectus for his book of engravings of *English Landscape Scenery* (1832), John Constable considered marketing his work under the aegis of classicism:

> It is surely to be regretted that the scenes with which we are surrounded—abounding as they do in Grandeur, and every description of pastoral beauty, and endeared as they are to us by the most powerful associations—should be either overlooked, or else rejected as unsuited to the Classical style. But why should not subjects purely English be made the vehicle of General Landscape? —and, when embodied by its highest principles, and at the same time original—and consequently classical art.[24]

As a strategy for attracting an audience to his book by annexing his works to the elevated aesthetic aims of classicism, this passage is perhaps understandable (despite its syntax toward the end). As a document in the history of ideas of classicism, however, it is puzzling: in what way can the "powerful associations" of "purely English" landscape painting be reconciled with the "Classical style," even in a rough draft? Surely the purely English is the terrain of Realism and powerful associations are the terrain of Romanticism, and both are categorically different from classicism? Although history painting is its favored genre, we may allow that there is such a thing as a classical landscape, based on the precedents established by Claude Lorraine and

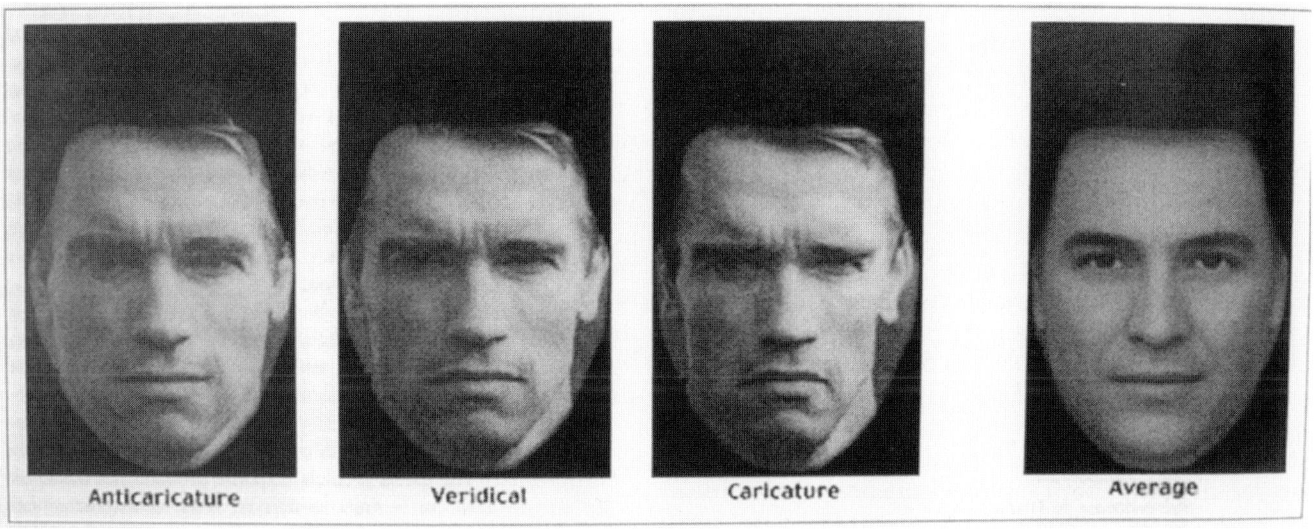

16. ***Examples of the three image types—anticaricatured, veridical, and caricatured faces—and the average face.*** **Kieran Lee, Graham Byatt, and Gillian Rhodes, "Caricature Effects, Distinctiveness, and Identification: Testing the Face-Space Framework,"** ***Psychological Science*** **11, no. 5 (2000), fig. 1. Blackwell Publishing.**

Nicolas Poussin. But then surely it is conformity to their precedent, and not "originality," that constitutes the classical style of landscape? If we distend the definition of originality, which was indeed in flux as Constable wrote, we can create a liminal space where the original and the classical coincide, but in what understanding of either term can the classicism of a work be a *consequence* of its originality, as Constable specifically suggests?

This is the first time we have seen the term classicism used to refer to the discourse I have singled out, and it is significant that Constable's usage conforms to that which I have attempted to maintain throughout this study: the classical is here linked not to history painting or past masters, not to the antique or the Italianate, not to stylistic conventions or a compositional formula, but to the "General." Constable's draft prospectus is incoherent only if classicism is conflated with *neo*classicism, the route to the ideal through the imitation of past masters. Constable, who was a student at the Royal Academy in the late 1790s and early 1800s, did not reflexively associate the classical with the neoclassical. In his *Lectures on Landscape*, delivered just after the publication of *English Landscape Scenery*, Constable ridicules the "absurdity of imitation" characterizing landscape artists like "Wootton, who painted country gentlemen in their wigs and jockey caps, and placed them in Italian landscapes resembling Gaspar Poussin [Gaspar Dughet], except in truth and force."[25] To import the compositional formulae of past masters and the furniture of Italian scenery into English landscape painting is absurd, contrary both to the truth of nature and to the force of the work. It is easy to extract statements from Constable's writings that announce his rejection of neoclassicism, but Constable did not so unequivocally reject the classical tradition as the Royal Academy defined it. Even in his oft-cited 1802 letter to his friend John Dunthorne, Constable maintained a great respect for the classical tradition. The letter as it is usually excerpted seems to take the form of a personal manifesto of release from the classical Grand Manner and the Academic theory of imitation:

> For the last two years I have been running after pictures, and seeking the truth at second hand. I have not endeavoured to represent nature with the same elevation of mind with which I set out, but have rather tried to make my performances look like the work of other men. . . . I shall return to Bergholt, where I shall endeavour to get a pure and unaffected manner of representing the scenes that may employ me. There is little or nothing in the [Academy] exhibition worth looking up to. *There is room enough for a natural painter.*

The rejection of neoclassicism, of "seeking the truth at second hand," is unequivocal, and it is easy to read in this "return to Bergholt" (the region of his childhood) and in his aim to be a "natural painter" Constable's thoroughgoing rejection of the Academic classical tradition in favor of a more personal and naturalistic style; a style more attuned to the Romantic and Realist tendencies of the age than the stale dogmas of the Academy.[26] Immediately preceding this manifesto of release, however, Constable writes: "I am just returned from a visit to Sir George Beaumont's pictures with a deep conviction of the truth of Sir Joshua Reynolds' observation, that 'there is no easy way of becoming a good painter.'"[27] While the individual performances of the Academy are rejected, its principles and its pantheon are not: Claude's *Hagar and the Angel* in Beaumont's collection and Reynolds's theories directly inspired Constable's rejection of "second hand" imitation. The odd notion that his work can be "original—and consequently classical art" is fully responsible to Reynolds's own distinction between "bad copies of good painters" and "excellent imitators of the great universal truth of things:"[28] the former rely too dogmatically on "seeking the truth at second hand" while the latter seek the truth at its origin, in empirical nature.

Thus Constable's question is cogent within the discourse of classicism propounded at the British Royal Academy: "why should not subjects purely English be made the vehicle of General Landscape?" If previous British landscape painting—that of John Wootton and Richard Wilson, for example—had "overlooked" British scenery and foundered in secondhand imitation and awkward amalgamations of the Italianate and the English, Constable could legitimately aim to apply the generalizing process to the English landscape, rather than force its conformity to prior classical models. And indeed, in this sense Constable's classicism would be a direct consequence of his "originality," not only because Constable would be seeking the truth of (English) nature firsthand at its empirical origin; but even in a modernist understanding of the term as "that which has never before been done." Even if it were only liminally classical in itself—resulting in a regional ideal of England rather than fully universal ideal of all nature—to fix the "character" of the English landscape (or even of Suffolk County), as Claude had done for the Italian, would be a valuable contribution to the classical project as a whole, and would provide the necessary data for future artists who could transcend the several ideals of the regional locales for a yet more comprehensive generalization.

With these theoretical indications, and considering Constable's famously painterly manner, it is perhaps tempting to reexamine Constable as a classicist in Reynolds's understanding of that tradition, but to my mind this would be a forced interpretation. In the final prospectus for *English Landscape Scenery*, the references to the classical and the general are dropped, and in the printed introduction to his book, Constable more convincingly argues that his aim was to

> direct attention to the sources of one of [art's] most efficient principles, the 'CHIAR'OSCURO OF NATURE,' to mark the influence of light and shadow upon landscape . . . to arrest the more abrupt and transient appearances . . . to characterize the scenery of England; the effects of light and shadow being transcripts only of such as occurred at the time of being taken.[29]

The qualities of Constable's painterliness are much more cogently defended as a heightened naturalism, a concentration on the "transient appearances" of particular nature in specific atmospheric conditions, rather than on the enduring essence of general nature.

However, Constable's draft prospectus does direct our attention away from the red herring of the Claudean paradigm and toward what could legitimately be considered the classical style of landscape in the British Academic understanding of that tradition. Although we tend reflexively to associate classical "instruction" with the didactic narratives of exemplary human behavior in history painting, we should recall that the representation of general ideas was itself considered a valuable instruction; a way to control the chaotic deflections of the associationist mind, and to teach the universal order of nature that underlies its distractive and perplexing multiplicity. Reynolds himself used the example of a tree to explain his painterly approach to generalization, as we saw: rather than enumerate every leaf like the Academic painter "STUDIO," Reynolds insists, "an artist, who looked only at the general character of the species, the order of the branches, and the masses of the foliage, would in a few minutes produce a more true resemblance of trees, than this painter in as many months."[30] Truth is found not only in the iconography and the narrative, but also in the general idea.

Gilpin and "Picturesque Beauty"

In his 1772 Lakes Tour sketchbook, William Gilpin labeled a drawing "The general idea of Keswick-lake" (figure 17). Although Gilpin associated his practice with the "picturesque," and although the picturesque is often opposed to the classical, this opposition is again based on a restrictive understanding of the classical landscape as more or less rigidly conforming to Claudean compositional formulae and Italianate subjects. Such are the landscapes of, for example, Richard Wilson and his students—but as Constable reminds us, this is not original classicism. Although Gilpin's *Keswick Lake* also exhibits the careful framing and compositional balance characteristic of the Claudean neoclassical landscape, it began in the empirical observation of "particular nature" and ended (Gilpin asserts) in a "general idea," and indeed Gilpin's process of deriving what he called "Picturesque Beauty" from the English landscape conforms closely to the epistemology and techniques of classical generalization.

Gilpin describes the technical aspects of his process in the third of his *Three Essays* (1792), "The Art of Sketching Landscapes." The first step is to "fix your point of view" and discern "how to reduce it properly within the compass of your paper."[31] These considerations serve to determine the overall composition of the work, and it is here that Gilpin's practice is most obviously classical in the commonplace understanding of the term. As Malcolm Andrews has noted, Gilpin's idea of the properly "picturesque" landscape "has a decidedly classical or neoclassical foundation in its strong compositional emphasis, its respect for the *beau idéal*, and its predominantly Claudean idiom."[32] Accordingly, the *Keswick Lake* is carefully framed and just off-center enough to prevent an overly formal symmetry. Twin bushes close the composition on either side and the space is divided like a stage set into three "skreens" at left, right, and center. An annotation to the right-hand screen remarks that the "mountain line" is "bad," and Gilpin seems accordingly to have corrected the problem by raising the height of the hills on that side. As Gilpin remarks, it is relatively rare that the picturesque tourist is "fortunate enough to fall in with" whole compositions; "oftener we find only beautiful *parts*," and so "we examine what would amend the composition; how little is wanting to reduce it to the rules of our art."[33] In this case, the "rules of art" seem to consist in certain a priori notions of composition; rules that in their conformity to the established Claudean idiom are perhaps not inappropriately called neoclassical.

Another problem with the view that Gilpin remarks in his annotations is its "broken" quality in places. While the left-hand screen is "the most beautiful part," the right-hand screen is "very much broken" and the middle screen is "too much broken." These annotations seem to contradict Gilpin's overall definition of the picturesque as characterized by roughness, as opposed to the "smooth" of the classical/beautiful. In the *Three Essays*, Gilpin notes that a "piece of Palladian architecture" may be pleasing in its symmetry, proportion, and propriety, but introduced into a picture it "ceases to please."

> Should we wish to give it picturesque beauty, we must use the mallet, instead of the chissel [sic]: we must beat down one half of it, deface the other, and throw the mutilated members around in heaps. In short, from a *smooth* building we must turn it into a *rough* ruin.

Where the youthful face is beautiful, the "forehead furrowed with wrinkles," the "prominent cheek-bone," and in general the "*rough* touches of age" are picturesque. The human body at rest is beautiful, but "the more its *smooth surface* is *ruffled*," the more it is picturesque, and so on.[34] According to these examples, the more "broken" parts of the view of Keswick Lake should be the more picturesque, and the picturesque should once again be the very antithesis of the classical—indeed, it is explicitly described as a mutilated Palladianism and a ravaged youth. But elsewhere in Gilpin's theory, the picturesque is described in an almost directly contrary manner. For example, he advises picturesque tourists to use what was called a Claude Glass, a tinted, convex mirror, as a way of transforming nature into the picturesque, because "in the minute exhibitions of the convex-mirror, composition, forms, and colours are brought closer together; and the eye examines the general effect, the forms of the objects, and the beauty of the tints, in one complex view [italics removed]."[35] In addition to framing the image, bringing the diffusion of the attention and the peripheral vision into a smaller purview discontinuous with its context, Gilpin notes that in the Claude Glass, "forms and colours are brought closer together," presumably because

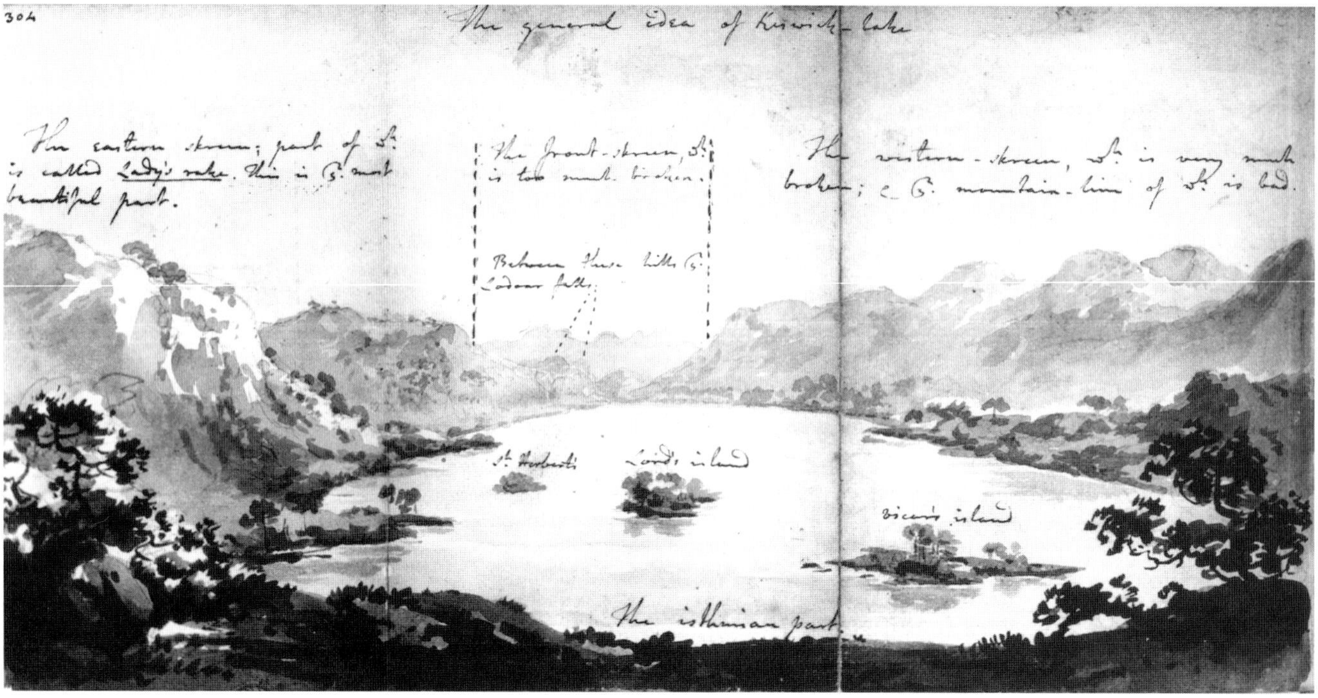

17. William Gilpin, *The general idea of Keswick-lake*, from his MS Lakes tour notebook, 1772. The Bodleian Library, University of Oxford MS. Eng. Misc. e. 488/3, drawing between fols. 303 and 304.

the tinting subdues the variety of colors and the range of values—somewhat the same effect as squinting. Carefully framed, small enough to see the whole at once, and suitably muted, the Claude Glass generalizes nature. So on one hand, the properly picturesque is the rough and ruffled, and on the other hand it is the muted and general: how can both be true?

Both are true because for Gilpin, the picturesque does not consist in any fixed formal value, but in a process of compensation for extremes. When Gilpin describes the picturesque as "rough," it is a roughening of what once was smooth and symmetrical (Palladian architecture, the youthful face); and when Gilpin describes the salubrious unifying effects of the Claude Glass, it is a unification of the variety of particular nature. Gilpin's picturesque is best described in the form of a dialectic: where the smooth regularity of Palladian architecture requires correction by way of a mallet, the broken irregularity of Keswick Lake requires correction by way of Claude; each form of extreme soliciting its opposite by way of compensation.

The dialectic process of Gilpin's picturesque is best demonstrated in two contrasting illustrations in the *Three Essays* (figures 18 and 19), which illustrate the following passage:

> In *landscape-painting* smooth objects would produce no composition at all. In a mountain-scene what composition could arise from the corner of a smooth knoll coming forward on one side, intersected by a smooth knoll on the other; with a smooth plain perhaps in the middle, and a smooth mountain in the distance[?] The very idea is disgusting. Picturesque composition consists in uniting in one whole a variety of parts; and these parts can be obtained only from rough objects. If the smooth mountains, and plains were broken by different objects, the composition might be good, on a supposition the great lines of it were so before.[36]

Picturesque compositions are not found simply in "a variety of parts," but in "*uniting in one whole*" that variety of parts. Thus while the picturesque and the beautiful are again contrasted as the "rough" and the "smooth," the picturesque version of the composition is good only "on a supposition the great lines of it were so before." While the picturesque abhors monotony, it is predicated on an underlying monotonous form. Although Gilpin does not explicitly mark it as such, with his earlier close association between the "smooth" and the "beautiful" it is strongly implied that figure 18 represents the eighteenth-century "beautiful" in landscape, and again, it is a beauty that is so

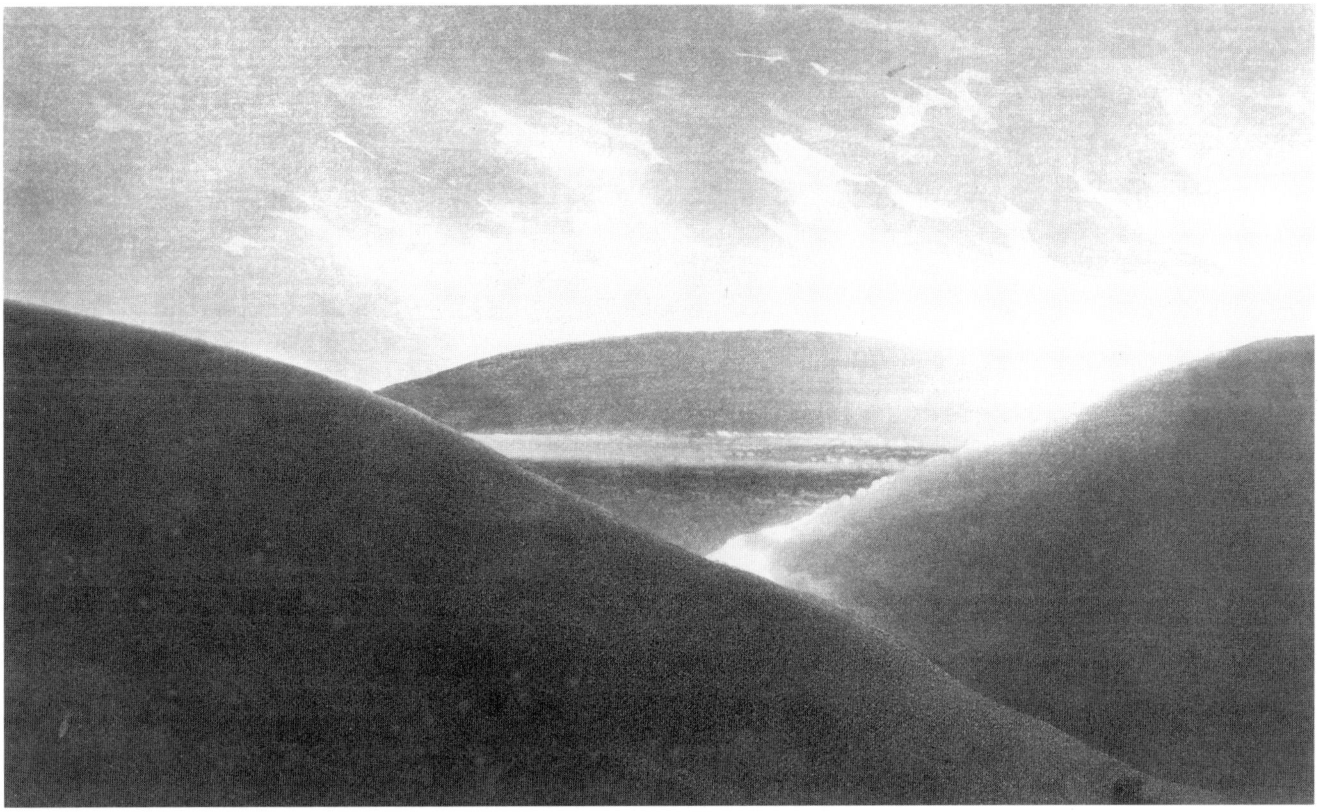

18. William Gilpin, untitled "non-picturesque" landscape, from *Three Essays: On Picturesque Beauty; on Picturesque Travel; and on Sketching Landscape* (London: R. Blamire, 1792), plate between pp. 18 and 19. Beinecke Rare Book and Manuscript Library, Yale University.

tame, monotonous, and insipid that it strongly requires the corrective of variety.

To return to Gilpin's "general idea of Keswick-lake," then, just as in Gilpin's picturesque the monotonous and insipid must be "broken by different objects," so the variegated and particular must be unified. Accordingly, the central screen of Keswick Lake, which was "too much broken" in nature, is rendered by Gilpin as single wash of almost completely unvaried tone. Like Reynolds, Gilpin focuses his technical advice on the propensity of certain media for rapid, elisive mark making that is conducive to seizing the general or characteristic:

> In sketching, black-lead is the first instrument commonly used. Nothing glides so volubly over paper, and executes an idea so quickly. . . . The virtue of these hasty, black-lead sketches consists in catching readily the *characteristic features* of a scene. Light and shade are not attended to. It is enough if you express *general shapes*; and their relations . . . A few lines drawn on the spot, will do this [Gilpin's italics].[37]

The hasty, voluble gliding of the instrument is convenient for catching the "general shapes" and "characteristic features" of the scene. Gilpin suggests reinforcing especially the foreground of the drawing later with a pen in order to avoid "confounding distances," and for this again he recommends a reed pen, "which runs more freely over paper" than the common pen.[38] Finally, washes may be applied when the artist has the space and equipment available, and as we can see in the drawing of Keswick Lake, such washes are to be applied with similar rapidity with an eye to the large masses.

Although it is tempting to see this execution in relation to an increasing liberation of art from its objects, Gilpin explicitly denies that the "facility of execution" is only about execution. He asks, "Is the smart touch of a pencil [paintbrush] the grand desideratum of painting? Does [the artist] discover nothing in *picturesque objects*, but qualities, which admit of being *rendered with spirit*? I should not vindicate him, if he did [Gilpin's italics]." Rather than merely devolve on "the graces of art," the facility of

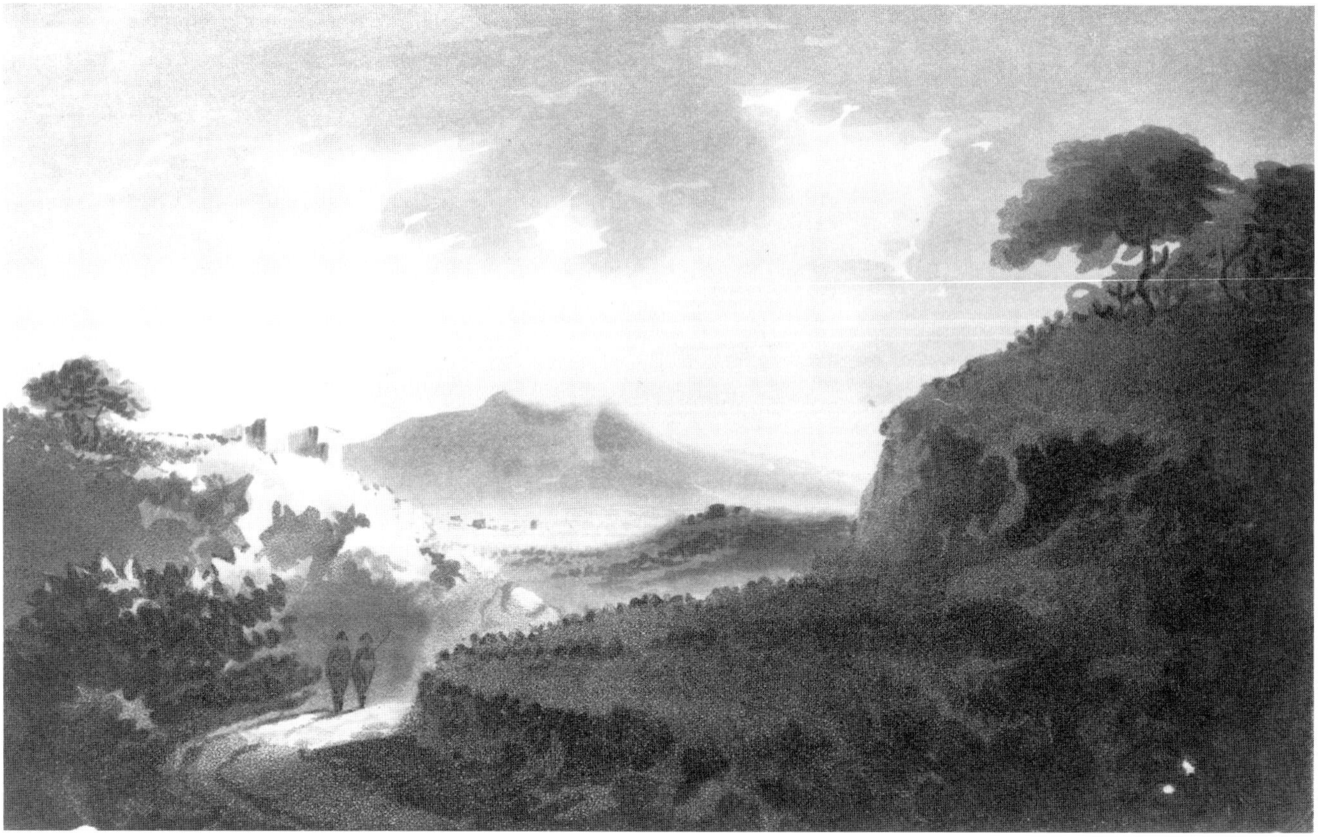

19. William Gilpin, untitled "picturesque" landscape, from *Three Essays: On Picturesque Beauty; on Picturesque Travel; and on Sketching Landscape* (London: R. Blamire, 1792), plate between pp. 18 and 19. Beinecke Rare Book and Manuscript Library, Yale University.

picturesque execution must be motivated by the object whose "characteristic" it is seizing. In a footnote Gilpin clarifies

> A stroke may be called *free*, when there is no appearance of constraint. It is *bold*, when a part is given for the whole, which it cannot fail of suggesting. This is the laconism of genius. But sometimes it may be free, and yet suggest only how easily a line, which means nothing, may be executed. Such a stroke is not *bold*, but *impudent*.[39]

Like Reynolds, Gilpin insists that the proper mark must be motivated by the object that it is describing, and that the "laconism of genius" consists in an abbreviated mark making that characterizes the object and comprehends the whole with rapid facility.

Although Gilpin labels his drawing "The general idea of Keswick-lake," and although it is marked by the executive qualities that we have seen were associated with generalization in the late-eighteenth century, we may question whether Gilpin had any notion of the epistemological implications of the phrase "general idea." Is this just a colloquialism and the work's execution just a matter of artistic shorthand appropriate to a sketch, or did Gilpin really mean to have generalized the landscape and its objects with this execution? Although he does not directly connect his technical advice to these epistemological issues, Gilpin explicitly notes the epistemological advantages of picturesque tourism. In addition to the aesthetic pleasure to be obtained:

> Our next amusement arises from inlarging [sic] and correcting our general stock of ideas. The variety of nature is such, that *new objects*, and new combinations of them, are continually adding something to our fund, and inlarging our collection: while the *same kind of object* occurring frequently, it is seen under various shapes; and makes us, if I may so speak, more learned in nature. We get it more by heart. He who has seen only one oak-tree, has no compleat idea of an oak in general: but he who has examined thousands of oak-trees, must have seen that beautiful plant in

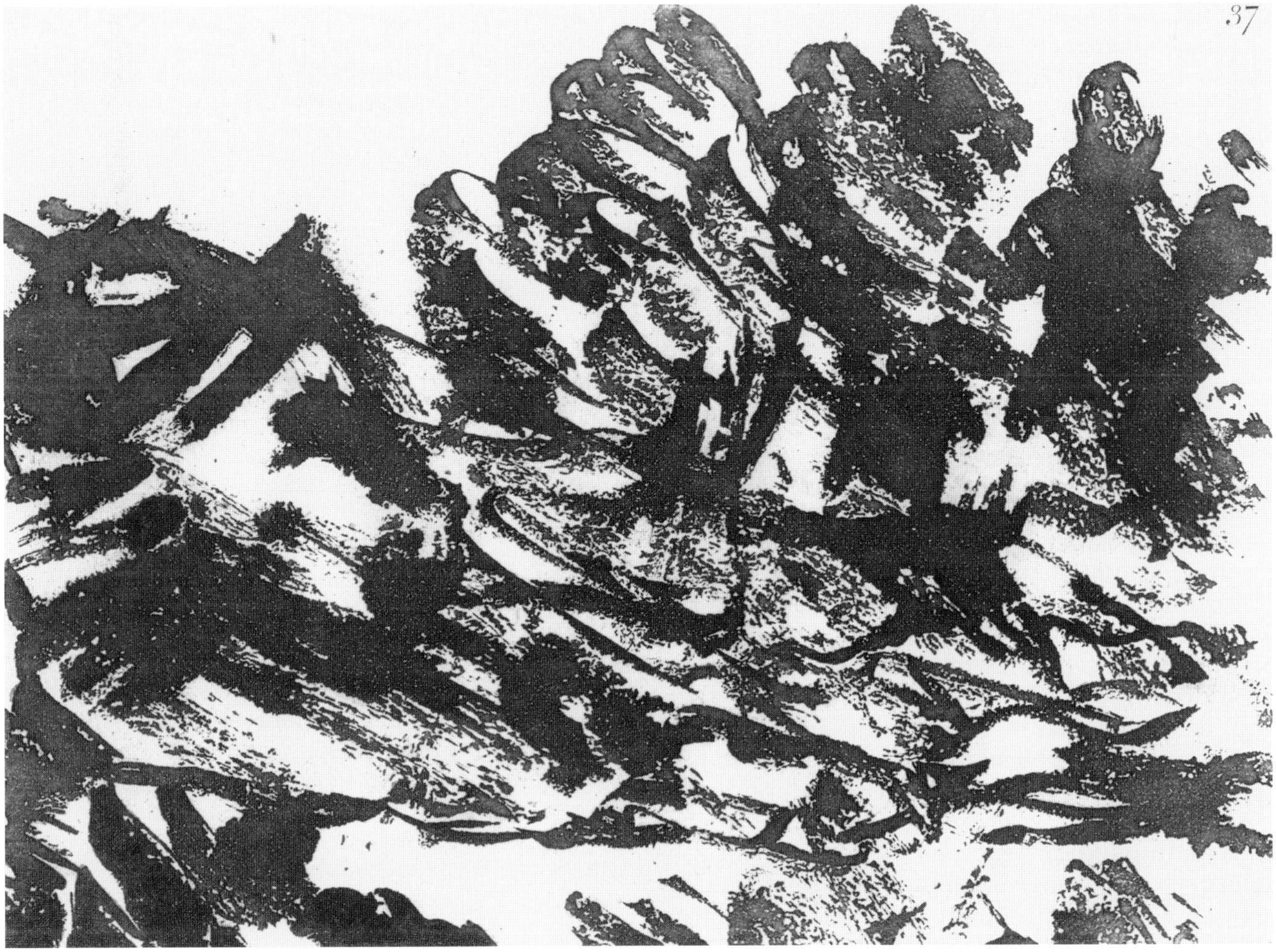

20. Alexander Cozens, *A Blot*, from *A New Method of Assisting the Invention in Drawing Original Compositions of Landscape* (London: J. Dixwell, 1785), plate 37. Beinecke Rare Book and Manuscript Library, Yale University.

all its varieties; and obtains a full, and compleat idea of it [Gilpin's italics].[40]

Thus the object of the picturesque is not only the sensuous pleasure of finding "beauty of every kind, which either art, or nature can produce,"[41] but also the epistemological advantage of "inlarging and correcting" our "stock of ideas." The enlargement of our stock of ideas very simply entails experiencing new objects; and the correction involves generalization: by seeing a given type of object such as an oak tree again and again in all its varieties, the viewer is enabled to formulate a "compleat idea of an oak in general," and thus and become "more learned in nature." Although it is perhaps easier to see the broad, painterly masses of Gilpin's "general idea of Keswick-lake" in terms of traditional optical effect—establishing the various grounds and unifying the light and atmosphere or "keeping" of the work—we have seen that for Reynolds a broad rendering simultaneously performs both functions. Gilpin's correction of Keswick Lake consists not only in conforming it to an established Claudean type, but also in reforming the particularity of the scene and its constituent objects into general ideas rendered in broad masses.

The Blot and the Ideal

A further instance of the application of classical generalization to the objects of the landscape and their disposition in composition can be found in the art and theory of Alexander Cozens.[42] In 1771 (reprinted 1786), Cozens published a treatise on *The Shape, Skeleton and*

Foliage of Thirty-two Species of Trees for the Use of Painting and Drawing. Just as Reynolds had noted that the painter of trees who looked to the "general character of the species, the order of the branches, and the masses of the foliage" is closer to the truth than the leaf enumerator,[43] and just as Gilpin noted the benefit of seeing many oak trees in order to obtain a "compleat idea" of the species, Cozens's treatment of trees aims to fix the general ideas of the various species in relation to their "shape, skeleton and foliage." Even more interesting is his 1785 *New Method of Assisting the Invention in Drawing Original Compositions of Landscape*, which in addition to sorting the various "species" of landscape composition into sixteen basic types, proposes as its "new method" to base landscape compositions on a gestural, hasty "blot," in thick, opaque black ink on white paper (figure 20), which could later be elaborated into a finished drawing (figure 21). Cozens describes the making of the blot as follows: "Take a camel's hair brush, as large as can be conveniently used, dip it in a mixture of drawing ink and water . . . and with the swiftest hand make all possible variety of shapes and strokes upon your paper."[44] This is certainly an unusual process and an unusual product for its time. Twentieth-century scholarship has tended to displace Cozens's method and his blots to almost any other context than the British eighteenth century. Cozens's radical blots seem to leap out of their historical moment towards the Baroque, Romanticism, Abstract Expressionism, and even to the "Other" hemisphere of the Orient.[45] Once again this displacement is due to a restrictive understanding of eighteenth-century art in general, and of picturesque and even classical art theory in specific. Cozens outlines the utility of his "new method" in specific relation to the epistemology of his day, and even his products are clearly anticipated in contemporaneous art theory.

As in Reynolds's *Discourses*, epistemological issues are given a central place in Cozens's explanation of the art of blotting. Cozens claims that blotting solves three major problems to which "bad, or indifferently good" artistic productions may be attributed:

1. To the deficiency of a stock of ideas originally laid up in the mind, from which might be selected such as suit any particular occasion;
2. To an incapacity of distinguishing and connecting ideas so treasured up;
3. To a want of facility, or quickness, in execution; so that the composition, how perfect soever in conception, grows faint and dies away before the hand of the artist can fix it upon the paper, or canvas.[46]

The first and second problems are completely epistemological; only the third is technical (and even there it is related to a problem of "conception"). The three periods of artistic pedagogy outlined in Reynolds's second Discourse confront nearly identical issues.[47] For both theorists, art must be created not only by a hand with certain executive skills, but by a mind possessed of a "stock of ideas" which it is capable of "distinguishing" and "connecting," and from which might be "selected" such as "suit any particular occasion." In chapter 1 I sketched contemporaneous epistemology to demonstrate how the mind "stocks" ideas through perception and memory and "connects and distinguishes" (adds and subtracts) them through imagination and judgment. The particular problem in this epistemological system is to be able to distinguish between ideas that, as Locke put it, are "ally'd by Nature" and those that are only allied by the caprices of ungoverned associationism. Cozens specifically notes the capacity of his method not only to "increase the original stock of picturesque ideas" but also to "enable the practitioner to distinguish those [ideas] which are capable of being connected, from those which seem not naturally related."[48] Indeed, Cozens asserts that blotting is "extremely conducive to the acquisition of a theory," which "is, in fact, the art of seeing properly."[49] Cozens clearly shares his model of mind with Reynolds and contemporary empirical epistemologists, and he claims that his method resolves what his contemporaries had identified as the major problem for achieving a rational mind and a rational art.

This is possible because the technique of blotting subdues the contingent, particular details of particular nature. In fact, far from being original or unique to Cozens, blotting had long been used by the eighteenth century as a way of eliminating distractive excess—only in literature rather than the visual arts. From its literal meaning as "to make writing invisible, by covering it with ink" (Johnson's definition), the word passed into metaphoric usage meaning

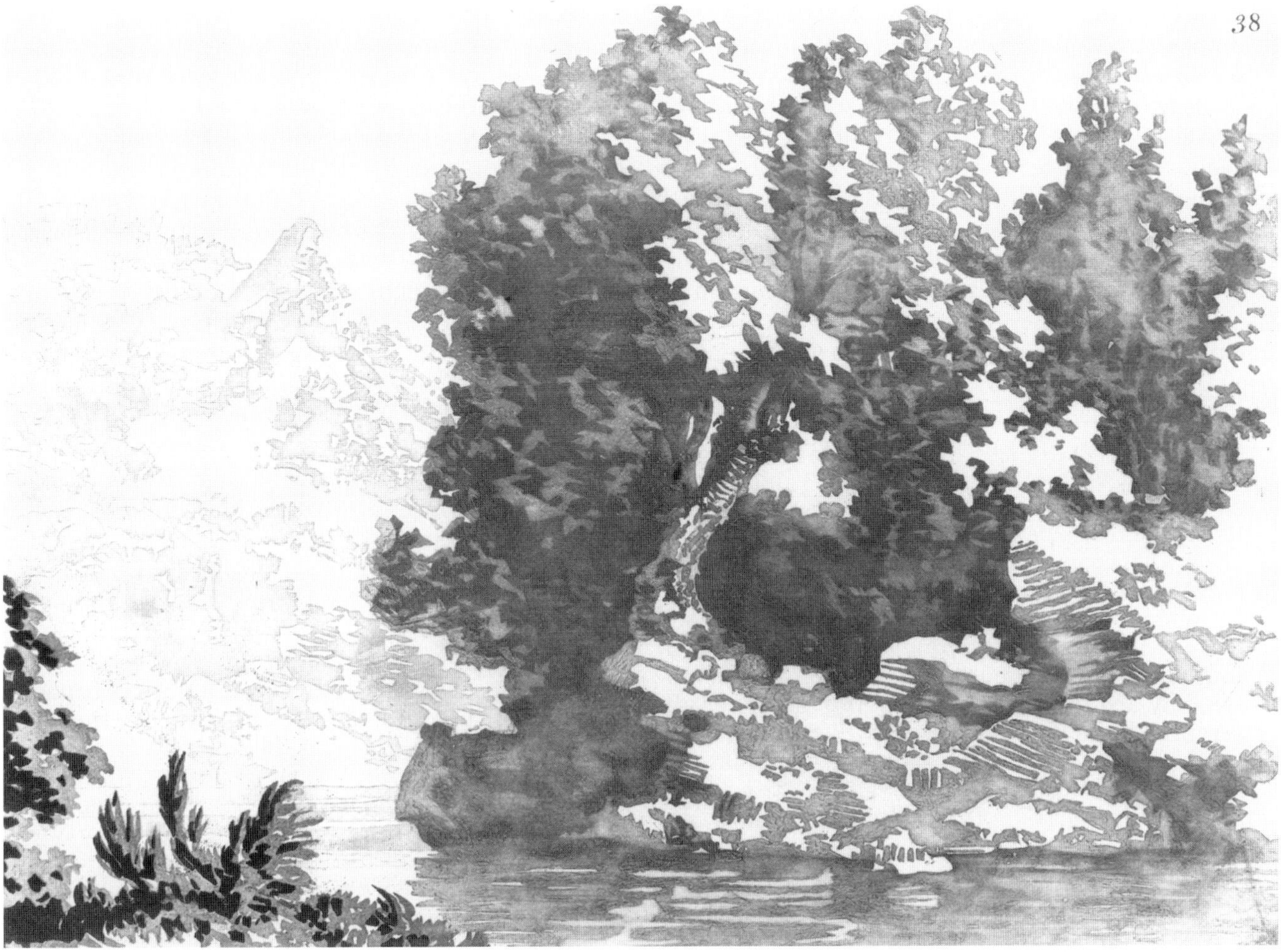

21. Alexander Cozens, *A print, representing a sketch made out with a brush, from the preceding blot*, from *A New Method of Assisting the Invention in Drawing Original Compositions of Landscape* (London: J. Dixwell, 1785), plate 38. Beinecke Rare Book and Manuscript Library, Yale University.

any correction by means of elimination. Johnson illustrated the usage of the term with a significant example from Alexander Pope: "Even copious Dryden wanted, or forgot, The last and greatest art, the art to *blot*."[50] One of the examples of this metaphoric usage of the term in the *Oxford English Dictionary* (expanded here to give context) is from Jonathan Swift's "Author's Apology" to a new edition of his *Tale of a Tub*:

> He [Swift] was then a young Gentleman much in the World, and wrote to the Tast of those who were like himself; therefore, in order to allure them, he gave a Liberty to his Pen, which might not suit with maturer Years, or graver Characters, and which he could have easily corrected with a very few Blots, had he been Master of his Papers, for a Year or two before their Publication.[51]

Similarly, Oliver Goldsmith, in the "Preface" to his *History of England* (a condensation of four previous histories), uses the trope of blotting as a synonym for abridgment: "The business of abridging the works of others has hitherto fallen to the lot of very dull men; and the art of blotting, which an eminent critic calls the most difficult of all others, has been usually practiced by those who found themselves unable to write." With his "blotting" of the history of England, Goldsmith hopes to avoid the common problem of abridgments that "have effectually embarrassed [that is, overloaded or obstructed] that road which they labored to shorten."[52] The metaphor seems curiously inapt, since to "embarrass" a road is not necessarily to fail to shorten it. However, inasmuch as improper blotting leaves irrelevancies and eliminates unifying themes, the shortest road is open to infinite associative distraction. Blotting, then, was a recognized technique for distilling the essence of a subject by subduing the "copious."

It is interesting that all three of the above passages take blotting to be a difficult act—indeed, the "very few blots" that Swift's *Tale of a Tub* required would have taken "a year or two" to effect. This difficulty is because proper blotting is mobilized by the (subtractive) judgment, a faculty that, unlike the immediate action of the associative fancy or imagination, is only developed in "maturer years" through long mental labor. Cozens describes how his method of blotting in the visual arts effectively manages to achieve in an instant what is normally a long and difficult epistemological labor:

> It may be remarked, that there is to be discerned, in all whole compositions of nature, a gradation of parts, which may be divided into several classes; for instance, the class of the smaller parts, the class of those of larger dimensions, and so on to the largest. The curious spectator of landscape insensibly acquires a habit of taking notice, or observing all the parts of nature, which is strengthened by exercise. It may be perceived, that the application of this notice in youth is directed to the smaller parts . . . from which it is gradually transferred to the larger as we approach to age, at which time we generally take notice of whole compositions. By the means of this propensity we lay up a store of ideas in the memory, from whence the imagination selects those which are best adapted to the nature of her operations. All the particular parts of each object may not be preserved in the memory, yet general ideas of the whole may be thrown as it were into the repository, and there retained.[53]

What Cozens is describing is the formation of the rational mind, which starts with "particular" ideas of the "smaller parts" (toward which the mind of youth is naturally directed), and progressively forms more comprehensive ideas of "wholes," for example gradually relating and subsuming the minutiae of leaves to the general pattern of their forms and growth on a branch, then the pattern of branches to the general form of the tree, and so on. Reynolds implies the same gradual attainment of an ability to discern the "whole" as the artist's "judgment" is formed. For Reynolds, the judgment is most quickly formed by the contemplation of past classical art, in which students can both see ready-made general ideas and discover the principles for deriving general ideas for themselves. Cozens's "new method" offers even more immediate gratification, for the blots that fix the "general ideas of the whole" require no special epistemological or executive ability whatsoever.

The epistemological value of the blot is that by fixing the whole, the subsequent elaboration of the blot into a finished landscape drawing is assured of being properly generalized—that is, of being "whole" both in the sense of a unified composition and in the sense of subduing distracting particularity to general forms. After the blot is made, the artist lays a sheet of semitransparent paper over it, on which the ink-wash landscape drawing is to be made. At this stage, artists can draw upon their "particular ideas" of nature in order to transform the gestural, unmeaning shapes of the blot into landscape elements. Consistent with eighteenth-century epistemology, Cozens does not consider this aspect of his method problematic:

> On the foregoing principles, very few can have reason to suspect in themselves a want of capacity sufficient to apply the use of blotting to the practice of drawing, nor can they be totally ignorant of the parts of composition in nature, for as they are previously prepared with ideas of parts, as before proved, so [blotting] affords an opportunity of calling them forth. . . . Previous ideas, however acquired (of which every person is possessed more or less) will assist the imagination in the use of blotting.[54]

The elaboration of the blot into a drawing is not problematic because it requires only "particular ideas," not those difficult "general ideas." Looking through the semitransparent paper at the blot, the artist projects the particular ideas that are stored in the memory onto its general form, elaborating its painterly masses into hills, foliage, rocks, trees, and so on.

At the same time as the mind's particular ideas serve to embellish the general form of the blot, the blot's general form serves to abstract those particular ideas. For this reason, the blot must be made with broad strokes, and "the attention of the performer must be employed on the whole, or the general form of the composition, and upon this only; whilst the subordinate parts are left to the casual motion of the hand and the brush." There is always the danger that, in making a blot, "the person blotting is inclined to direct his thoughts to the object, or particular parts, which constitute the scene or subject, as well as to the general disposition of the whole." In itself, this "superabundance of design" is not bad, but Cozens cautions that the drawing later to be made from such a blot must be done "with judgment"—that is, the performer has in this case destroyed the very purpose of blotting, which is to serve the subtractive function of the judgment (or rather, to eliminate its necessity).[55] Blotting is an immediate, if slightly surreptitious, way to generalize the landscape. Cozens even asserts that blotting embodies "the art of seeing properly," and that its practice serves not only to assist the "invention" in composing landscapes in the studio, but, once its principles have been internalized, "will always conduct the artist in copying nature with taste and propriety . . . In short, whoever has been used to compose landscapes by blotting, can also draw from nature with practice. But he cannot arrive at a power of composing by invention, by the means of drawing views from nature, without a much greater degree of time and practice."[56] The artist trained in blotting will learn to project blots onto nature, screening out particularities in favor of the general and subordinating the parts to one whole.

Although Cozens's blots appear surprising, then, they are thoroughly justified by Cozens from within contemporaneous epistemology. They deal with and aim to resolve the same problems as those dealt with by Academic art at the time, and they even use one of the techniques of generalization described by Reynolds: broad, painterly brushwork. Indeed, Academic descriptions of the generalizing process as tending toward the "muddy, tame, and monotonous," the "vague and indeterminate," the "crude and unvarying masses" of the "dauber" actually perfectly describe Cozens's blots. Because his subject matter was the more allowing genre of landscape, and because the blots are only preliminary stages toward a finished composition, Cozens was able more fully to embody the late eighteenth-century ideal in landscape.

5
Reductio ad Absurdum

In the first volume of *Modern Painters* (1843), published some fifty years after the death of Reynolds, John Ruskin protests against the continuing ascendancy of generalization-theory in the British discourse on art. Objecting to "a maxim which is in everybody's mouth . . . [that] 'General truths are more important than particular ones,'" Ruskin formulates a coherent, but refined, argument: everything that can be predicated of more than one object is a general truth, but only those general truths are important that are particular to the subject concerned. In the statement "all men in China eat," the subject "all men in China" and the predicate "eat" are general, and the statement is true, but it is an unimportant truth, because the same predicate applies to all men outside China as well. By contrast, the statement "all men in China are opium-eaters" is important because the predicate "are opium-eaters" is particular to the subject "all men in China" (the example is Ruskin's, not mine).[1] In his review of *Modern Painters*, John Eagles, art critic for *Blackwood's Edinburgh Magazine* and a champion of Reynolds's ideas, called this passage "a little needless display of logic," and largely ignored it. Both Eagles and George Darley, art critic for *The Athenaeum*, assumed that by emphasizing the particular Ruskin was promoting a completely indiscriminate naturalism, and both reiterated the standard defense of the general against the particular. Darley complained that Ruskin's aesthetic would reduce landscape painting to a "Denner-like portraiture of the earth's face," and Eagles reminded Ruskin that in imitating nature "there may be many particulars that are best sunk." As an antidote to the particularized imitation of modern painters, both critics called upon the authority of the Ancients, who "took a broader, deeper, higher view of their art; they neglected particular traits, and gave only general features."[2]

In the preface to the second edition of *Modern Painters* (1844), Ruskin strengthened his argument against "that constantly enunciated dogma of the parrot-critic, that the features of nature must be 'generalized,'" this time expressing his concerns with a less demanding logic and a greater urgency of tone: "Generalized! As if it were possible to generalize things generically different." Responding directly to Darley, Ruskin gives a rather surreal example:

> If there were a creature in the foreground of a picture of which he could not decide whether it were a pony or a pig, the *Athenaeum* critic would perhaps affirm it to be a generalization of pony and pig . . . But *I* should call it simple bad drawing . . . There is no grandeur, no beauty of any sort or kind, nothing but destruction, disorganization, and ruin, to be obtained by the violation of natural distinctions. The elements of brutes can only mix in corruption [Ruskin's italics].[3]

While he begins by dismissing the hypothetical pony-pig on aesthetic grounds, as an example of "bad drawing," for Ruskin the notion of generalization is more pernicious because it violates "natural distinctions," wreaking havoc on the natural order of things.

Here we can consolidate a connection between classicism and taxonomy, the classification of things, which has been implicit throughout this study. While the etymology of the term classicism is usually traced to the notion of an object or artwork being "of the first class," and therefore worthy of imitation, that definition begs the question of what constitutes first class. The more fundamental issue is not one of relative ranking but of classification in general. Classicism requires a classification of individual objects into their various sorts and kinds, for the quest for the ideal ultimately demands that the artist should depict the *class-idea* of the object rather than one of the individual members of that class. For Reynolds, it is the "lower painter" who will "exhibit the minute discriminations, which distinguish one object of the same species from another"; the Grand Manner painter will "represent in every one of his figures the character of its species."[4] Similarly, "an History-Painter paints man in general; a Portrait-Painter, a particular man, and consequently a defective model."[5] Classicism can practically be defined by this attempt to depict the class-idea of the object rather than any of its individual members, and by its assertion that this class-idea or ideal is what constitutes enduring beauty and true reality. Hence the questions for classicism are the same as those for taxonomy: what defines a real or natural class of object, and how can we know the class-idea?

Although on the basis of his rather extreme example Ruskin's objection seems to be merely rhetorical, it was not. In fact, it singles out the major methodological weakness of generalization-theory: defining the scope of generalization. The first step in Reynolds's process involves comparing of "a set of objects of the same kind," which begs the question, what is the "kind" of a given object?[6] Ponies and pigs share the taxonomic class *mammalia*, but is this a natural distinction, and is a generic mammal a suitable subject for classical representation? We shall look largely to contemporary art theory and natural history for responses to this question, but since as we shall see theological issues become strongly implicated I should first note that the Bible is equivocal on the question of what constitute natural distinctions in the order of things. In the King James version, God created organisms "after their kind," a phrase that confirms the presence of natural classes of organism, but does not specify the taxonomic level of those classes. The word "kind" is ambiguous, and is used in Genesis to refer at once to taxa as specific as "great whales" and as general as "winged fowl" and "everything that creepeth upon the earth" (Gen. 1:21–25). Thus even given the postulate of creation, the question of what constituted a natural (that is, divinely ordained) class of objects or organisms was left to the ingenuity of theologians, artists, and natural historians.

Generic Differences 1: The Problem of "Character"

Ruskin's example of the pony-pig is extreme in part for rhetorical emphasis, for the difficulty of visualizing a general class of objects or organisms increases proportionate to the scope of the class. Where the human nose, for instance, shares a basic form and thus an averaging of all noses would still end in a recognizable human nose, a mammal nose, midway between that of a pony and a pig (and an aardvark, a whale, and a platypus) would resemble none of them, but in theory should referentially comprehend all. We shall return to the problem of generic differences among animals and plants below, but the usual subject matter of classicism is, of course, the human figure, which would seem to be of a suitable scope for generalization. However, long before Ruskin's objection theorists both within the Academy and without discovered an ineluctable variety in the human form that seemed to be insusceptible to generalization. An examination of this issue will reveal four things. First, Ruskin's objection did not blindside the Academic position with a devastating blow from an unexpected quarter, but was in fact a common matter of debate in the eighty or so years preceding the publication of *Modern Painters*. Second, the general consensus arising out of that debate was that the generalizing process, and therefore the scope of idealizing art practice, was limited to the category of "character," at least in the representation of humankind. The category of character can be defined as a sort of subspecies of the human kind, a division of the diverse aspects of human physical and moral potential into its various avatars of power, grace, charity, authority, and so forth. The difficulty, in art as in life, is comprehending all of these various perfections in one individual. And finally, while some theorists saw the generic limits of character as the "end of art," in the sense of its highest possible achievement, others took this limitation as a challenge to surpass the Ancients and perform yet higher generalizations.

In his essays on Reynolds's Discourses, written for *The Champion* between 1814 and 1815, William Hazlitt stated the characteristic objection to generalization-theory. Castigating Reynolds's theory of the ideal as being that of "shadowy middle forms, made up of an abstraction of all others," Hazlitt asks, "Where shall we stop in the easy down-hill pass of effeminate, unmeaning insipidity?" An artist following Reynolds's principle of generalization even within the limited scope of the human form would

> confound all difference of sex or passion. . . . In representing a Grecian marriage he will refine on his favourite principles till it will be possible to transpose the features of the bridegroom and the bride without the least violation of propriety; all the women will be like the men; and all like one another, all equally young, blooming, smiling, elegant, and insipid. On Sir Joshua's theory of the *beau ideal*, Mr. Westall's pictures are perhaps the best that ever were painted, and on any other theory, the worst; for they exhibit an absolute negation of all expression, character, and discrimination of form and colour.[7]

This is the same objection as that embodied in Ruskin's pony-pig, but transposed a few steps down the taxonomic hierarchy.[8] Here we can see the dual aesthetic and ontological nature of the objection. The quest for the ideal form of the human figure will necessarily result in homogeneity; a homogeneity that Hazlitt objects to on two grounds. First, inasmuch as it abstracts all the variations of "character" and "expression" from the human form, the resulting representation will be "insipid," bland and nondescript. Second, in generalizing all such variations into one central form, the representation will "violate propriety" by generalizing things generically different.

The logical structure of both Ruskin's and Hazlitt's objections to generalization-theory is a form of the reductio ad absurdum argument, in which an opponent's position is taken to such an extreme that it reveals an internal contradiction or at least becomes absurd, contrary to common sense. George Berkeley was perhaps the first to mobilize this type of argument against generalization-theory. Protesting against John Locke's notion of abstraction in the formation of general ideas, Berkeley wrote in his *Principles of Human Knowledge* (1710):

> As the mind frames to itself the abstract ideas of qualities or modes [such as red or softness], so does it, by the same precision or mental separation, attain abstract ideas of the more compound beings. . . . For example, the mind having observed that Peter, James, and John, resemble each other, in certain common agreements of shape and other qualities, [it] leaves out of the complex or compounded idea it has of Peter, James, and any other particular man, that which is peculiar to each, retaining only what is common to all; and so makes an abstract idea wherein all the particulars equally partake. . . . And after this manner it is said we come by the abstract idea of *man*, or, if you please, humanity or human nature; wherein it is true, there is included colour, because there is no man but has some colour, but then it can be neither white, nor black, nor any particular colour; because there is no one particular colour wherein all men partake. So likewise there is included stature, but then it is neither tall stature nor low stature, nor yet middle stature, but something abstracted from all of these. And so of the rest. . . .
>
> Whether others have this wonderful faculty of *abstracting their ideas*, they best can tell.[9]

How can the general idea simultaneously represent *no* particular quality—no particular color, no particular height—and yet be referentially adequate to or "bundle" *all* particular qualities? This is indeed an internal contradiction.

The reductio ad absurdum argument is especially apposite to the discourse of generalization, for the paradox becomes evident as its practitioner literally "reduces" or abstracts details from the mimetic object. Up to a certain point that process does not seem to entail any absurdity or contradiction. Abstracting away obvious blemishes such as moles and wrinkles while preserving much of the likeness of the individual seems to be unproblematic, and thus the relatively low degree of idealization necessary for Grand Manner portraiture is still possible. Berkeley's objection lies in the linkage of the process of abstraction (the elimination of "accidents") to generalization (an increase in the referential capacity of the idea or representation). For Berkeley, the process of abstraction cannot increase the referential scope of the representation or mental image: because the qualities are inevitably particular (height, skin color, and so on), the reference must remain particular, and not general. Reynolds might counter that Berkeley's examples of height and colour both admit of infinite gradations within certain definite limits, and thus can be averaged to, say, a middle brown colour and a mean height. Although Reynolds clearly consulted only European racial characteristics in deriving ideals such as his *Theory* and *Justice*, his theory at least would confirm a more miscegenous "central form" as closer to the true ideal. Berkeley's objection still stands, however: such a color and height would still be particular, not general; and thus for him would refer to only those individuals of that particular height and skin color, rather than successfully "bundling" the entire range of human variations. The implication for art is that the *Doryphoros* cannot successfully embody the general idea of man, but will only appear as a portrait of a particular individual whom we have never seen. General reference may be possible in words because of the arbitrary nature of the signifier, but is impossible in art and even in the imagination because the signifier (the mental or pictorial image) is always particular and (Berkeley tacitly assumes) is isomorphic with the referent.[10]

In his *Treatise of Human Nature* (1739–40), David Hume called Berkeley's objection "one of the greatest and most valuable discoveries that has been made of late years in the republic of letters," concluding that

> abstract ideas are therefore in themselves individual, however much they may become general in their representation. The image in the mind is only that of a particular object, tho' the application of it in our reasoning be the same, as if it were universal.

For Hume, so-called "general ideas" are not in fact unitary images, as Locke had posited, but only a way of describing a mental process of "surveying" a number of individual ideas. Upon hearing a term like "man," which can be applied to many individuals, we do not "draw" a general idea in the imagination, but merely "keep ourselves in a readiness to survey any [individual ideas], as we may be prompted by a present design or necessity." Because it is virtually impossible to survey all acquired mental images to which the term man may be applied, "we abridge that work by a more partial consideration, and find but few inconveniences to arise in our reasoning from that abridgment." Hume gives the example of a triangle: when the word is mentioned as a general idea, we may "form the idea of a particular equilateral [triangle] to conform to it," and up to a certain point we reason from that specific image. If, in the course of such reasoning, the mind should "assert, *that the three angles of a triangle are equal to each other*," then we rapidly survey other mental images to which the term triangle may be applied, and "the other individuals of a scalenum and isosceles, which we overlook'd at first, immediately crowd in upon us, and make us perceive the falsehood of this proposition."[11]

Berkeley's and Hume's objection to unitary general ideas is founded on a dubious premise: the notion that general ideas are pictorial. This premise courts the "homunculus fallacy," for a pictorial general idea would require a resident homunculus in the mind that in turn perceives such ideas, like a spectator at a theater (prompting the question, what is the nature of that faculty's perception? and so on).[12] The reductio ad absurdum can be resolved by current computationalist theories of mind: a general idea like "triangle" does not appear as an image, but as a set of criteria that the mind rapidly surveys: is it a three sided figure? (yes/no); do its sides consist of straight lines? (yes/no). Other visual qualities that an individual triangle must have, but which are not common to all triangles, such as color and size, are simply ignored as irrelevant. Similarly, in current biological taxonomy, classes like "mammal" are defined, not by a common overall form, but by isolated common characteristics: warm-bloodedness, vertebrate structure, and lactation, none of which are easily susceptible to satisfactory visual representation. However, the notion that general ideas are pictorial was tacitly assumed in eighteenth-century and much nineteenth-century philosophy, and the computationalist theory is not an option for the classical artist, who must not only conceive but also picture and indeed depict general ideas.

Hazlitt's criticism of Reynolds's process of generalization essentially grounds this philosophical question in an immediate, common sense example: any artist who attempted to depict the ideal of the human species as a whole would either have to eliminate (that is, abstract) characteristic gender distinctions or average (generalize) those distinctions. Either solution would "violate propriety" by creating a sexless or androgynous figure that is nowhere authorized in empirical nature (or rather is by social consensus considered "monstrous" where it does appear in empirical nature). Hazlitt also expresses an aesthetic objection to generalization that we shall see is common: insofar as the artist abstracts all of the modifications of the individual that result from and in turn serve to indicate a specific power or personality, the resulting representation will be "insipid," bland and nondescript. Hazlitt's solution to both problems is to limit the scope of artistic representation to the taxonomic category of "character": a proper representation will have "a marked and decided character, and not a character of indifference."[13] Character for Hazlitt is a specific mental and physical disposition, such as melancholy or vivaciousness, which can be depicted with precision inasmuch as it marks the countenance and bearing of the human figure, and which will convey a strong impression to the viewer. Hazlitt even cites one of Reynolds's own works as a salutary example: a portrait of Samuel Johnson in one of his characteristic fits of concentrated convulsion. The "sluggishness of outward appearance," the "want of quickness and versatility," the "absorption of faculty, and look of purblind reflection" evident in the portrait were altogether "characteristic of [Johnson's] mind," and to have abstracted or attenuated these characteristics would also have eliminated the work's value.[14] Any attempt to abstract the representation of its characteristic personality will result in insipidity, and any attempt to generalize characters, such as femininity and masculinity, will violate propriety.

Kant's philosophy of the ideal has an interesting relation to generalization-theory in this respect, although his approach is from a different direction. In his *Critique of Judgment*, Kant recognizes as a component of the ideal of beauty "the image on which nature's technic was, as it were, intentionally based, and to which only the kind as a whole but no individual by itself is adequate." The ideal of beauty can be considered the equivalent of the template from which all individual members of a given class are derived. Kant notes that this class-idea "would be suitable as the universal standard for judging each individual of that species aesthetically," and furthermore allows that "this idea and its proportions can be exhibited as an aesthetic idea fully *in concreto* in a model image."[15] In a psychological explanation of "how . . . we arrive at such an ideal of beauty," Kant rehearses the discourse of generalization: "the imagination projects, as it were, one image onto another, and from the congruence of most images of the same kind it arrives at an average that serves as the common standard for all of them." Externalizing this exercise in "an analogy from optics," Kant suggests that if a thousand transparent images of men were projected onto the same screen,

> in the space where most of the images are united, and within the outline where the area is illuminated by the color applied most heavily, there the *average size* emerges, equally distant in both height and breadth from the outermost bounds of the tallest and shortest stature; and that is the stature for a beautiful man [Kant's italics].[16]

As we follow his argument to this point, then, Kant's theory seems to be very much the same as that of Reynolds: the ideal of beauty is the central form within a species of objects. Kant notes that "a Negro's standard of beauty of the [human] figure necessarily differs from that of a white man, that of a Chinese from that of a European" because the constituent images of this averaging process will be different in each race's experience. However, this does not disqualify the process from theoretically arriving at a comprehensive ideal of the human species as a whole, presuming a hypothetical world-traveler. Kant calls this idea

> the image for the entire kind, hovering between all the singular and multiply varied intuitions of the individuals, the image that nature used as the archetype on which it based its productions within any one species, but which it does not seem to have attained completely in any individual.

He suggests this process informed both Polykleitos's *Doryphoros* and Myron's *Heifer*, and thus Kant appears to have repaired the loss of Polykleitos's treatise on art and resolved the problem of the ideal in both the imagination and in art through generalization-theory.[17]

However, for Kant this "standard idea" is only one component of the ideal of beauty, which must also include a "rational idea" involving the "purposes of humanity."[18] While the standard idea is an "indispensable condition of all beauty," it is "by no means the entire *archetype of beauty*" for it contains no "expression of the *moral* [Kant's italics]."[19] Through this insistence on a moral component in the ideal of beauty, Kant's treatment of generalization entails the suite of objections we are considering here. In a footnote, Kant remarks that because the "standard idea" of beauty "contains nothing characteristic," that is, nothing of the moral character or purpose of humankind, it "conveys nothing" and indeed will usually be taken to "indicate that inwardly too the person is only mediocre." Character entails a marking of the countenance, and "if none of the mental predispositions stands out beyond the proportion that is required for someone to constitute merely a person free from defects, then we must not expect in him any degree of what we call *genius*." Although he does not recite the reductio ad absurdum argument, then, Kant's theory of the ideal seems also to be limited to the characteristic. Interestingly, Kant also makes the complementary observation that if "what is characteristic . . . is exaggerated, i.e. if it offends against the standard idea (of the purposiveness of the kind) itself, then it is called *caricature*."[20] Generalization is caught between the Scylla of insipidity and the Charybdis of caricature.

Although these arguments against generalization-theory are damning, they in fact only reiterate the problems and conclusions reached by the Academicians themselves, including Reynolds. In several places throughout his Discourses, Reynolds explicitly considers the problem of defining a comprehensive ideal in the face of ineluctable generic differences in age, gender, race, and especially character. Recognizing the considerable variety in Ancient depictions of male ideality, Reynolds remarks:

> I must add further, that though the most perfect forms of each of the general divisions of the human figure are ideal, and superior to any individual form of that class; yet the highest perfection of the human figure is not to be found in any one of them. It is not in the Hercules, nor in the Gladiator, nor in the Apollo; but in that form which is taken from them all, and which partakes equally of the activity of the Gladiator, of the delicacy of the Apollo, and of the muscular strength of the Hercules. For perfect beauty in any species must combine all the characters which are beautiful in that species.[21]

The pendulum of human variation is not singular but plural, oscillating around the various characters of activity, delicacy, strength, and so on. The central forms of these several oscillations have been fixed in the Greco-Roman representations of the gods who personified those characters. In this respect Reynolds is in substantial agreement with past classical theory. In his "Idea of the Painter, Sculptor and Architect" (1672), Bellori had allowed that

> the Idea is not one beauty; its forms are various—strong, noble, joyful, delicate, of any age and both sexes. We do not . . . praise with Paris on lovely Mount Ida only soft Venus, or extol the tender Bacchus in the gardens of Nyssa, but we also admire in the wearying games of Maenalos and Delos the quiver-bearing Apollo and Diana the huntress. The beauty of Jupiter in Olympia and of Juno in Samos, as well as of Hercules in Lindos and Cupids in Thespiae, was certainly different again. Thus different forms conform with different people.[22]

But unlike Bellori, Reynolds preserves the possibility that all of these various types of beauty could at least theoretically be combined into a "perfect beauty" that "partakes equally" of them all. The process of generalization allows and even demands this move, for just as a variety of individuals can be generalized to a given character, so a variety of different characters can theoretically be generalized to a higher type. But therein lies the difficulty. Considering the problem of combining characters in art, Reynolds cites Pliny, who "observes, that in a statue of Paris, by Euphranor, you might discover at the same time three different characters; the dignity of a Judge of the Goddesses, the Lover of Helen, and the conqueror of Achilles." Such a pretense is ridiculous: "A statue in which you endeavour to unite stately dignity, youthful elegance, and stern valour, must surely possess none of these to any eminent degree." Thus on one hand the "highest perfection of the human figure" must "combine all the characters which are beautiful in that species," but on the other hand any attempt to do so is deluded. The problem is not merely with that specific instance (that particular statue of Paris), but is endemic to generalization:

> From hence it appears, that there is much difficulty as well as danger, in an endeavour to concentrate in a single subject those various powers, which, rising from different points, naturally move in different directions. The summit of excellence seems to be an assemblage of contrary qualities, but mixed, in such proportions, that no one part is found to counteract the other. How hard this is to be attained in every art, those only know, who have made the greatest progress in their respective professions.[23]

How can the artist maintain the robust strength of a Hercules (figure 22) while at the same time adding the gracile delicacy of an Apollo (figure 23)? One character seems to counteract the other, and thus the attempt to combine characters in an advance toward the comprehensive ideal even of just the male of the species is extraordinarily difficult.

Reynolds's solution to this problem, like Hazlitt's, was to subdivide the human species into several subordinate classes of "character," but he differs from Hazlitt in defining each of these classes as an aspect of or approach to a more comprehensive ideal. The process of generalization can be variably applied toward class-ideas

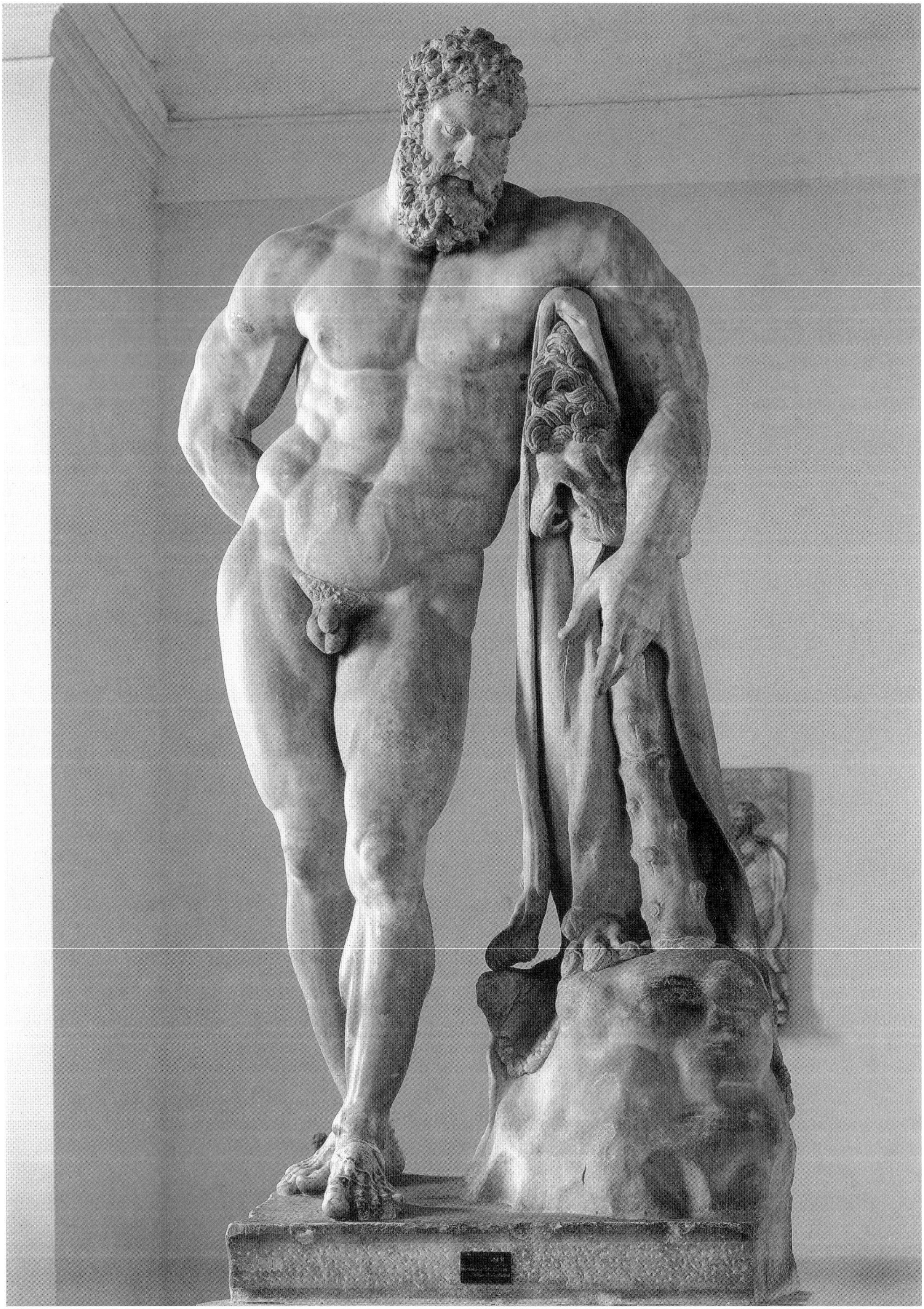

22. *Hercules Farnese*, Roman copy of the first century BCE after a Greek original of the fifth century BCE. Museo Archeologico Nazionale, Naples. Photo Credit: Scala/Art Resource, NY.

of increasing referential scope. Although the absolute ideal of humankind is to be found in the "one general form" that "belongs to the human kind at large," within that comprehensive ideal of the species there are various subordinate or constituent ideals of character, race, age, and (presumably) gender. Directly following his analogy of the pendulum in the *Idler* essays, Reynolds noted that if an Ethiopian artist "were to paint the Goddess of Beauty . . . he would represent her black, with thick lips, flat nose, and woolly hair." Since he had just professed that the straight nose is the central form, there is an implicit assertion that the European (and especially Greek) ideal is closer to the true ideal, but rather than forcing conformity to a single ideal, Reynolds subdivides the very concept of the ideal, allowing that the beauties of the "black and white nations" must "be considered as different kinds, or at least a different species of the same kind," and noting that any comparison between different species is invidious.[24] Similarly, the "forms of childhood and age differ exceedingly," but still "there is a common form in childhood, and a common form in age, which is the more perfect, as it is more remote from all peculiarities." This fragmentation of the ideal according to character, race, age, and so on will necessarily demote the ontological status of the representation, which increases in proportion to its taxonomic scope, but it preserves the validity of classicism as the representation of a class-idea, and of generalization as a process for determining that class-idea, for "still none of [these subdivisions] is the representation of an individual, but of a class."[25]

The professors of painting at the Royal Academy followed Reynolds in fragmenting the human species into several subordinate distinctions and remarking the difficulty of subsuming this variety to a homogeneous universality. James Barry described "pure simple beauty or perfection" as an idea that excludes all of the characteristic emendations of the human form but at the same time comprehends all of these characters: "Pure simple beauty or perfection, being equally adapted to all the several animal destinations proper to its species, is therefore equally removed from the several classes of character, which so evidently define and manifest their peculiar powers." Like Reynolds, then, Barry allows that there is such a thing as "pure simple beauty" that combines all of the various perfections of the several characters of beauty. But how can this postulated "simple beauty" be at once "equally adapted" to all characters and "equally removed" from all characters? Barry concludes that a comprehensive or simple beauty must necessarily be "vague and indeterminate, as it indicates no particular expression of the body or mind."[26] While character is formally viable because it is determinate, simple beauty is not—and he suggests that the pure ideal is simply too vague to be depicted in art. John Opie explicitly comes to that conclusion. After asserting that "the highest and ultimate exertion of human genius" consists in "getting above individual imitation" and "rising from the species to the genus," Opie warns,

> Hitherto shalt thou go, and no further—every step in every direction from this pole of truth is alike retrograde—for, to generalize beyond the boundaries of character, to compose figures of no specific age, sex, or destination, with no predominant quality or particular end to be answered in their construction, is to violate propriety, destroy interest, and lose the very essence of beauty in contemptible nothingness and insipidity.[27]

Opie's conclusion is the same as Barry's and Reynolds's, and for that matter Hazlitt's. The "character" of the figure as determined by its "destination" or "end" in the narrative is the proper goal of idealization. Any attempt to depict a higher ideal will "violate propriety" both formally, by ending in "contemptible nothingness and insipidity," and ontologically, by confounding natural distinctions of age, sex, and character.

The immediate implication of this debate, explicitly confessed by Reynolds, Barry, and Opie, is that no artist, including the Ancients, had yet achieved even the relatively limited ideal of the male human figure. A more distant implication, which Reynolds did not admit but the German philosopher G. W. F. Hegel did, is that the problem of character prescribes a definite limit to the classical project. Both implications rely on a contrast between the monotheistic Christian concept of God and the polytheistic Ancient concept. For Barry, the Ancients could not even conceive of the absolute ideal of humankind because their religion divided the various characters of human perfection among as many distinct gods: the ideal of strength in Hercules, the ideal of grace in Apollo, the ideal of majesty in Jupiter, and so on. Ancient polytheism was thus

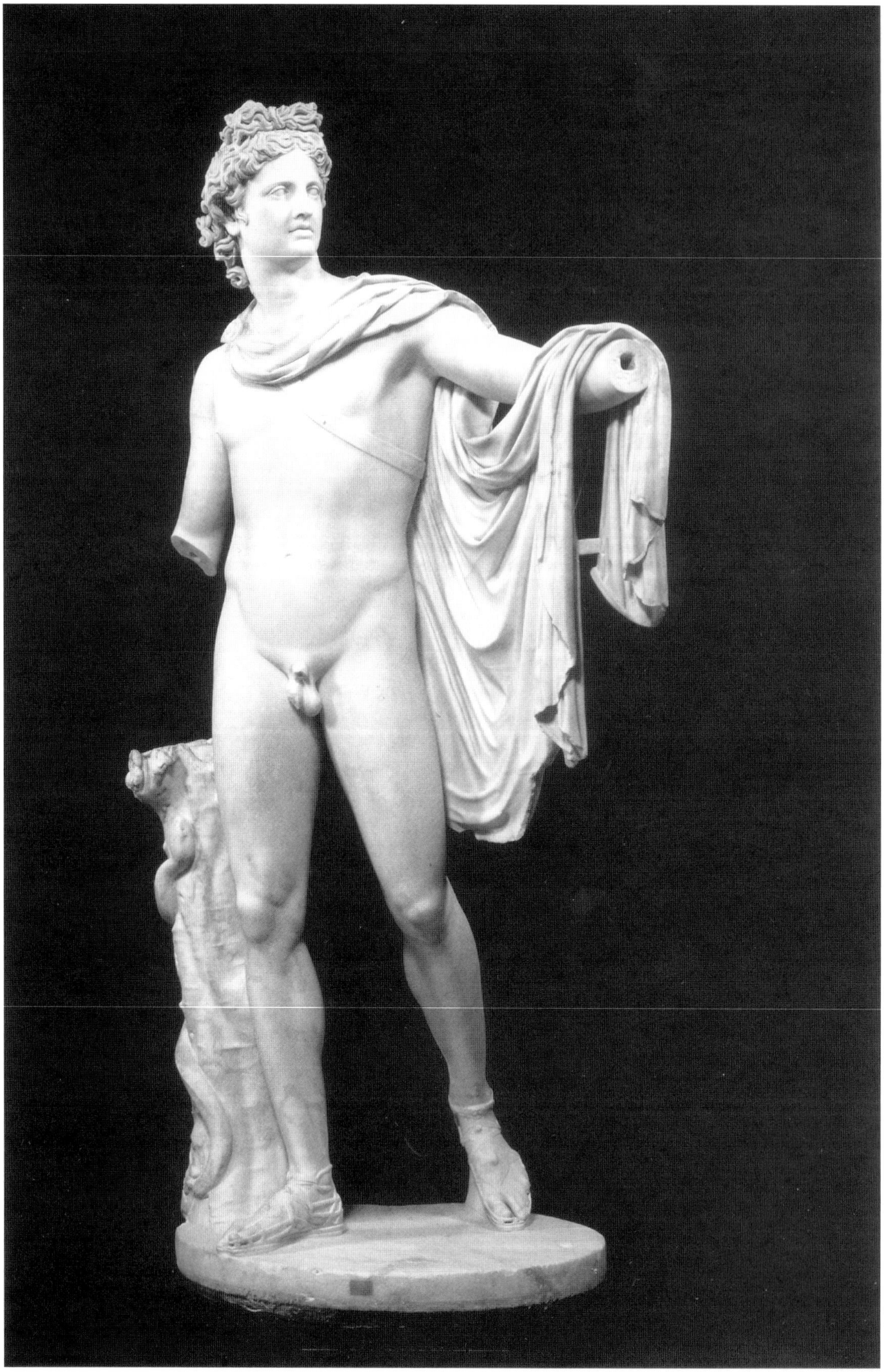

23. *Apollo Belvedere*, Roman copy after a Greek original, c. 350–320 BCE. Museo Pio Clementino, Vatican Museums. Photo Credit: Scala/Art Resource, NY.

conducive only to the limited ideals of the various branches of character:

> The characters and forms of their several deities were copied after the abstract idea of whatever was found to be most majestic, most beautiful, graceful, or interesting in human nature. Their artists had a fair opportunity of introducing as much aptness and perfection, as such a system of Polytheism was capable of receiving. To obtain this, they were necessarily led into the most attentive investigation of general nature, for the culling out all those several perfections, male and female, that were particularly adapted to each walk of character. This is the *ideal* of art . . . [Barry's emphasis].[28]

Although Barry calls Ancient productions the "ideal of art" (because they are "abstract ideas" resulting from an "investigation of general nature"), he clearly states that the Ancients achieved not the absolute ideal of the species as a whole, nor even those of the two genders of the species, but only those limited and "several" perfections of character: majesty, beauty, grace, and so on. This is all the ontological height that their polytheistic mindset was "capable of receiving." The various statues of Greek and Roman gods and goddesses were accordingly described, not as absolute ideals, but as marked by those several subordinate character-ideals: for Opie, the Ancients "produced those concentrated, dephlegmated, and highly rectified personifications of strength, activity, beauty, majesty, wisdom, and enthusiasm, which astonish and enchant us, under the names of the Hercules Farnese, the Venus, the fighting Gladiator, the Jupiter, and the Apollo [italics removed]."[29] Similarly, although unlike Barry he asserted that in their god Jupiter the Ancients possessed the idea of a comprehensive (male) ideal, Reynolds also denies that Ancient art ever successfully depicted that ideal:

> Art has its boundaries, though Imagination has none. We can easily, like the Ancients, suppose a Jupiter to be possessed of all those powers and perfections which the subordinate Deities were endowed with separately. Yet, when they employed their art to represent him, they confined his character to majesty alone.[30]

There is a distant potential for advancing beyond the several character-ideals personified by the Ancient gods, but so far at least the reductio ad absurdum has precluded its achievement. The definition of this potential is, I would argue, a major reason for Reynolds's assertion in the ninth Discourse that classical art had not yet achieved its aim or end. Although scholarship commonly assumes that the classical style was an achieved aesthetic, whose procedure was primarily confined to the reiteration of the absolute perfection of Ancient and other prior models, for Reynolds, perfection in art is "an idea that subsists only in the mind; the sight never beheld it, nor has the hand expressed it. . . . The mind is continually labouring to advance, step by step, through successive gradations of excellence, towards perfection, which is dimly seen, at a great though not hopeless distance, and which we must always follow because we never can attain."[31]

Reynolds, then, implicitly held out the possibility of a future classicist who could transcend the confines of character and expand the boundaries of art to include higher class-ideas than those achieved by the Ancients. With exactly the same problem in mind, however, Hegel pronounced the end of classicism and therefore the end of (visual) art. Art, for Hegel, is defined as the "sensuous manifestation of the Idea," a definition that contains two crucial criteria. First, in its vocation as manifesting the Idea, art is ultimately responsible to the human Geist (mind/spirit), which in turn evolves the Idea into greater and greater comprehensiveness and truth. Second, art is a fundamentally *sensuous* means of grasping Idea, which necessarily limits its potential. Geist has had three basic historical modes of grasping Idea: art, religion, and philosophy, which amount to three different epistemologies: art deals with Idea through sensuous means, in concrete form; religion through pictorial means, in the imagination; and philosophy through purely abstract means, by means of reason. Thus art "shares the vocation" of grasping Idea with religion and philosophy, "but in a special way, namely by displaying even the highest [reality] sensuously, bringing it thereby nearer to the senses, to feeling, and to nature's mode of appearance."[32]

The paradox for art is immediately evident. Although for Hegel, "art has above all to make the Divine the center of its representations," the divine is ultimately not susceptible to sensuous or even imaginative representation. "The Divine, explicitly regarded as unity and universality, is essentially only present to thinking and, as in itself imageless, is not susceptible of being imaged and shaped by imagination." What saves art, and indeed makes it appropriate to an early phase in the development of Geist, is that the Idea was not revealed to humanity immediately as "unity and universality" insusceptible to sensuous form, but as "split and broken up into a multitude of independent and self-reposing gods, as in the polytheistic vision of Greek art."[33] "Polytheism is absolutely essential to the principle of classical art, and it would be a foolish undertaking to propose to shape in plastic beauty the one god of sublimity and pantheism or that of absolute religion [i.e. Christianity] which apprehends God as spiritual and purely inner personality."[34] In its early unfolding, Geist's polytheistic grasp of Idea is available to sensuous representation, and thus art is its proper epistemology. The gods typify human "pathos," "pathos in concrete activity is the human character"; and therefore for Hegel as for the British Academicians, "character is the proper centre of the ideal artistic representation."[35] However, where Reynolds preserved the possibility that a progressive classicism would eventually transcend character, for Hegel the sensuous nature of art makes this manifestly impossible:

> For precisely on account of its form, art is limited to a specific content. Only one sphere and stage of truth is capable of being represented in the element of art. In order to be a genuine content for art, such truth must in virtue of its own specific character be able to go forth into [the sphere of] sense and remain adequate to itself there. This is the case, for example, with the gods of Greece. On the other hand, there is a deeper comprehension of truth which is no longer so akin and friendly to sense as to be capable of appropriate adoption and expression in this medium. The Christian view of truth is of this kind, and, above all, the spirit of our world today, or, more particularly, of our religion and the development of our reason, appears as beyond the stage at which art is the supreme mode of our knowledge of the Absolute.[36]

The "end of (visual) art" for Hegel is the point at which art is no longer capable of representing the evolving Idea, and is determined by much the same conditions that caused the British Academicians to remark a limitation of the classical project: the problem of formulating a "comprehensive" truth that would not violate the necessarily sensual "determinacy" of artistic representation.

Generic Differences 2: Glacial Buttercups and Park Oaks

It is perhaps fortunate that artists are very rarely required to depict an absolute ideal of "pure, simple beauty or perfection." Even the highest genre of art, history painting, usually requires only characters, figures instancing some specific power or passion in relation to the narrative. Ironically, the case is otherwise for the lesser genres and for the minor accouterments of history painting, especially the minerals, plants, and animal staffage of the landscape background. Reynolds and other classicists felt little theoretical and even less formal compunction about performing more radical generalizations and rising to higher ideals outside of the human figure. Indeed, Ruskin's protest against generalization is specifically directed against "the remarks of historical painters on landscape. . . . Accustomed themselves to treat their backgrounds slightly and boldly . . . they naturally lose sight of the peculiar and intrinsic beauties of things which to them are injurious, unless subordinate. Hence the frequent advice given by Reynolds and others, to neglect *specific* form in landscape, and treat its materials in large masses, aiming only at general truths; the flexibility of foliage, but not its kind; the rigidity of rock, but not its mineral character [Ruskin's italics]." Ruskin clarifies his criteria for landscape elements in a contrast between the backgrounds of Poussin's *Jupiter's Nourishment* (figure 24) and Reynolds's *Holy Family* (figure 25). "Owing to the utter neglect of all botanical detail," Ruskin argues, Reynolds's work "has lost every atom of ideal character," whereas Poussin's,

> in which every vine leaf is drawn with consummate skill and untiring diligence, produces not only a tree group of the most perfect grace and beauty, but one which, in its pure and simple truth, belongs to every age of nature, and adapts itself to the history of all time.[37]

The formal differences between the two works are immediately evident, and confirm what Ruskin recognized and current scholarship has largely overlooked: Reynolds's was a painterly approach to the ideal. Unlike Poussin, Reynolds renders his vegetation in "large masses" that, following his theory, generalize "tree," "shrub," and "grass" rather than copying an exact individual or even indicating a particular species.

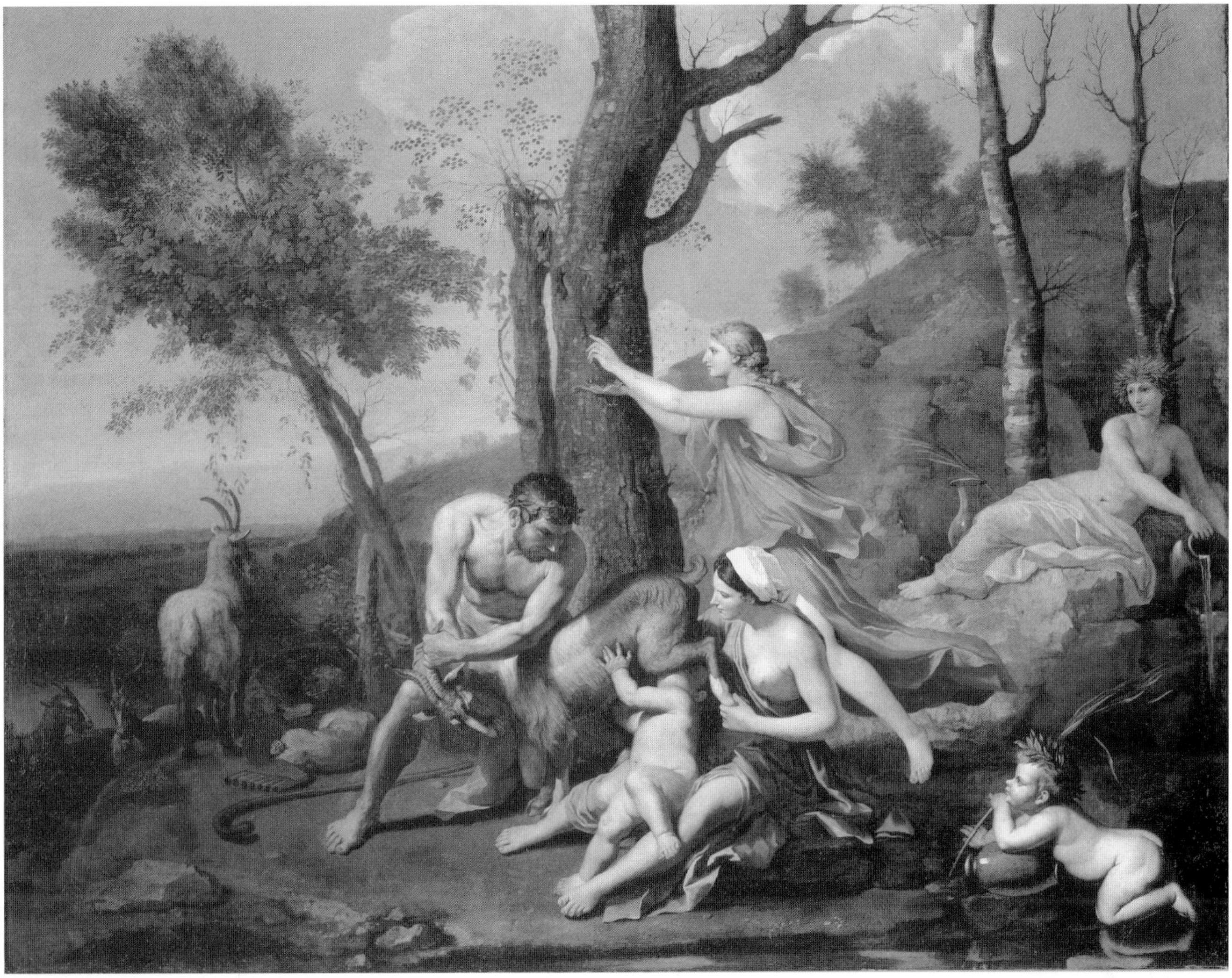

24. Nicolas Poussin, *Jupiter's Nourishment*, 1636–37. Dulwich Picture Gallery, London. Photo Credit: Erich Lessing/Art Resource, NY.

It seems that the limits of generalization apply only to humankind; other objects can be generalized without compunction to very broad taxa indeed. The artist should always rise from the individual to the species, allowing the "lower painter . . . to exhibit the minute discriminations, which distinguish one object of the same species from another."[38] Indeed, wherever possible the artist should rise from the species to the genus: the representation of drapery should be "neither woollen, nor linen, nor silk, sattin or velvet: it is drapery; it is nothing more."[39]

Ruskin does not object a priori to a painterly handling, as his extensive defense of the later Turner clearly establishes. He is as derisive as Reynolds of the "numbered hairs and mapped wrinkles of Denner," and allows that great art treats its objects in "a manly, broad, and impressive manner." Nor, despite Darley's contention, does Ruskin object to the representation of the object as a class rather than an individual, and the consequent abstraction of the "meaner beauties which are accidentally peculiar to the object, and yet not specifically characteristic of it."[40] Ruskin's objection to Reynolds's theory and practice lies in the extreme scope he allowed to the generalization of landscape elements. Interpreting the notion of generalization literally as an idealization toward the biological genus of the object, Ruskin limits the scope of idealization, in landscape as in the human figure, to "specific character":

> The true ideal of landscape is precisely the same as that of the human form; it is the expression of the specific—not the individual, but the specific—

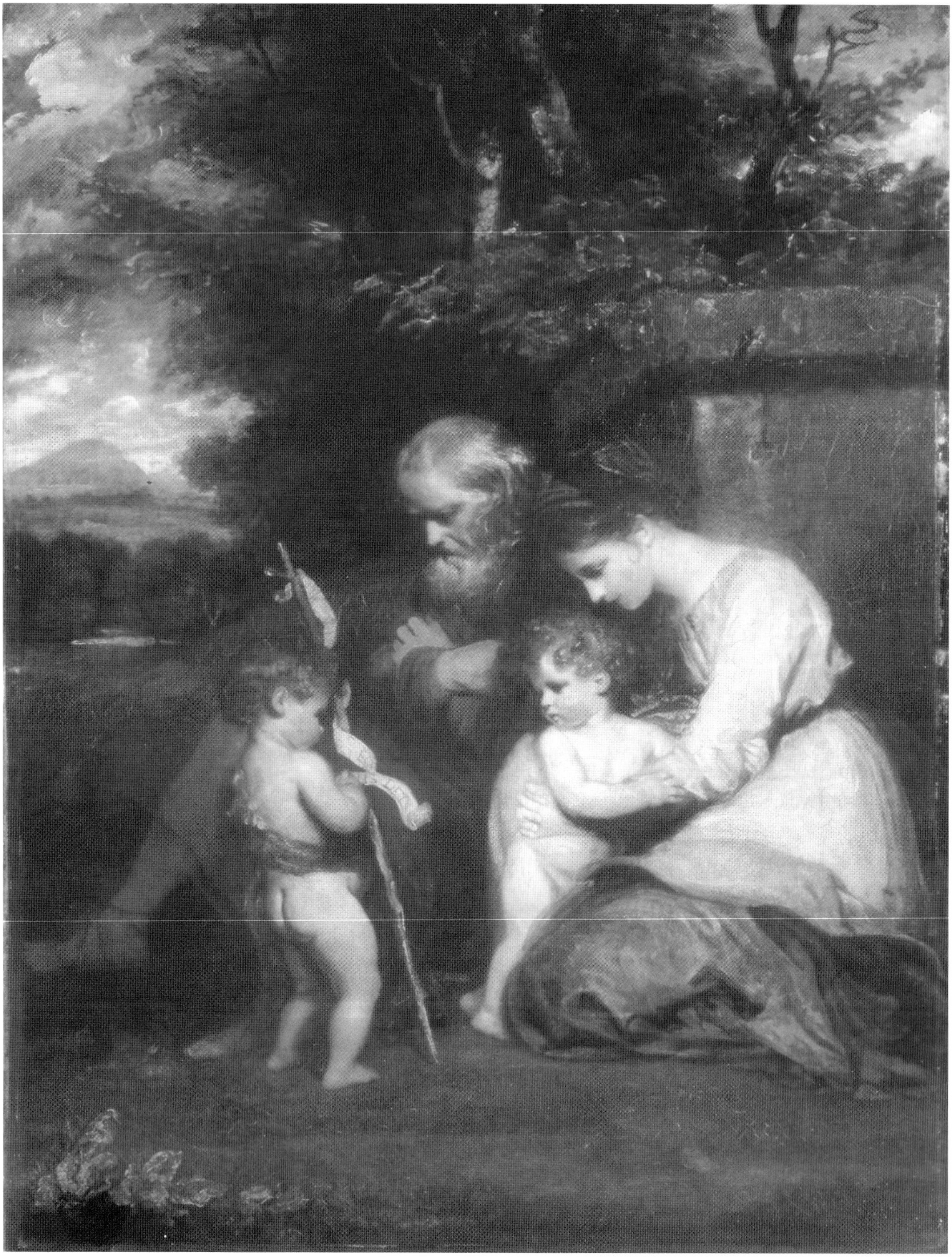

25. Joshua Reynolds, *Holy Family with the Infant St. John*, 1788–89. Presented by the British Institution, 1830. Tate Gallery, London. Photo Credit: Tate Gallery, London/Art Resource, NY.

> characters of every object, in their perfection. There is an ideal form of every herb, flower, and tree, it is that form to which every individual of the species has a tendency to arrive, freed from the influence of accident or disease.[41]

Despite his tirade against generalization, Ruskin does not, in the end, reject it, but limits it:

> That generalization then is right, true, and noble, which is based on the knowledge of the distinctions and observance of the relations of individual kinds. That generalization is wrong, false, and contemptible, which is based on ignorance of the one, and disturbance of the other. It is indeed no generalization, but confusion and chaos.[42]

For Ruskin, generalization is not in itself wrong, but the Royal Academy had taken it too far, violating "natural distinctions" by overgeneralizing the landscape:

> It is just as impossible to generalize granite and slate, as it is to generalize a man and a cow. An animal must be either one animal or another animal: it cannot be a general animal, or it is no animal; and so a rock must be either one rock or another rock; it cannot be a general rock, or it is no rock.[43]

We have returned to, and can now refine, one of our original questions: what constitutes the natural "type" or "kind" of a given object or organism? The Academicians Barry and Opie largely used their common sense and aesthetic sensibilities in answering this question. "Character" seemed to be a logical limit for generalization in humankind because it maintained intuitive or social notions of generic distinctions (such as those of gender), and expectations of the proper formal qualities of art (that is, a certain minimum degree of determinacy and finish). In plants and animals, where those constraints of common sense and those aesthetic norms were less imperative, a greater degree of generalization was permissible. Reynolds concurred with this plan in practice, but ultimately hedged on the question in theory. By defining a gradated scale of perfection in which the representation increases in ideality proportionate to its taxonomic scope, Reynolds ultimately admitted no absolute or "natural" distinctions, but only apparent distinctions that a progressive classicism would gradually resolve into higher and higher ideals.

Ruskin's intervention in generalization-theory and his broad philosophical difference with the Royal Academicians can now be stated with precision. Ruskin enunciated the exact limits of generalization based not on common sense or vague aesthetic criteria but upon a firm methodological basis: the class of the object is determined by its *function* in a divinely ordained ecological and moral economy. The beauty of the object is explicitly defined in *Modern Painters II* as "the appearance of felicitous fulfilment of function in living things":[44]

> Taking it for granted that every creature of God is in some way good, and has a duty and specific operation providentially accessory to the wellbeing of all, we are to look, in this faith, to that employment and nature of each, and to derive pleasure from their entire perfection and fitness for the duty they have to do, and in their entire fulfilment of it; and so we are to take pleasure and find beauty in the magnificent binding together of the jaws of the ichthyosaurus for catching and holding, and in the adaptation of the lion for springing, and of the locust for destroying, and of the lark for singing, and in every creature for the doing of that which God has made it to do.[45]

Properly assessed by this criterion of ecological function in a great, designed economy of life, every object is beautiful. The only ugliness in nature occurs when the object is displaced from its ecology and forced to perform unnatural functions, "when the creature is either unfaithful to itself, or is afflicted by circumstances unnatural and malignant to its being, and for the contending with which it was neither fitted nor ordained."[46] What is lost in Reynolds's attempt to depict a "tree-in-general," that is, an ideal tree for all times and all places, is precisely what constitutes its beauty for Ruskin: the tree's function in a particular ecology according to its ordained duty. The natural order of things does not consist in a family of forms abstracted from circumstantial contingencies, but in the articulation of that order according to each object's and organism's specific function in an ordained economy of life.

This determination of the beauty of an object or organism according to its ecological function is what constitutes that object's "vital beauty" for Ruskin. Not only does disregarding the object's function eliminate its vital beauty, it also (and perhaps even more dangerously) eliminates what Ruskin called the object's "typical beauty." Typical beauty is defined as "that external quality of bodies . . . which . . . may be shown to be in some sort typical of the Divine attributes."[47] Thus overlapping the ecological function of organisms is a moral function: organisms (and other created objects) have been designed for the instruction of humankind as well as their role in an economy of life. The flower *Soldanella alpina* is found in small breaks in mountain snow, "a slender, pensive, fragile flower, whose small, dark, purple, fringed bell hangs down and shudders over the icy cleft that it has cloven, as if partly wondering at its own recent grave, and partly dying of very fatigue after its hard won victory." This personification of the *Soldanella* is not merely poetic license; it articulates the "typical beauty" of that flower, whose emergence from its own recent grave (implicitly) symbolizes or typifies the Resurrection, and whose tenacity in the face of adversity more generally offers to us "an image of moral purpose and achievement."[48] If we were to displace the *Soldanella* from its alpine ecology, even with the apparently laudable intent of improving its lot by placing it in the more salubrious climate of a greenhouse, we would improve its fate but destroy its special character.[49]

Ruskin also gives an example of two oak trees that clearly demonstrates how his "functionalist" idea of beauty differs from Reynolds's. He first describes the "ideal . . . of the park oak," which would closely approximate the normative classical ideal of the species: "full size, united terminal curve, equal and symmetrical range of branches on either side." This is the oak growing under "fortunate conditions," where it can achieve its perfect form exclusive of any ecological conditions that might hinder it, and hence is a classical ideal in the traditional sense. But parks are not natural creations; they are human creations, and they therefore alter the divinely ordained order of things. Ruskin gives the counterexample of a "wild oak," which "may be anything, gnarled, and leaning, and shattered, and rock-encumbered." Clearly for Reynolds this would violate the ideal of the oak, for its "misfortunes" in the matter of climate and soil are accidental, and have prevented its normative growth. However, for Ruskin the wild oak is "more ideal than the [park oak], in so far as by its efforts and struggles, more of its nature—enduring power, patience in waiting for, and ingenuity in obtaining what it needs,—is brought out, and so more of the essence of oak exhibited, than under more fortunate conditions."[50] Similarly, the *Ranunculus glacialis* or glacial buttercup

> might perhaps by cultivation be blanched from its wan and corpselike paleness to purer white, and won to more branched and lofty development of its ragged leaves. But the ideal of the plant is to be found only in the last, loose stones of the moraine, alone there; wet with the cold, unkindly drip of the glacier water, and trembling as the loose and steep dust to which it clings yields ever and anon, and shudders and crumbles away from about its root.[51]

Ruskin's will to personify and sympathize with objects and organisms is more than just a pathetic fallacy or Victorian sentimentality; it is intimately connected with his notion of ontology and taxonomy, the natural order of things. His frequent and sustained sentimental or moral readings of natural objects is intended to evince their very function or purpose, and with that purpose the truth and beauty of those objects: the true reality and beauty of an object lies not in the object-in-itself, but in its "vital" connection to its environment and its "typical" symbolism of Divine attributes.

To relate this notion to Ruskin's earlier observation that to constitute an "important" truth, the predicate must be particular to the subject, what Ruskin is asserting is that the most important truths of any given class of object or organism are the features that distinguish that class from all other classes, rather than what all members of that class have in common (the typical assertion of generalization-theory). Those distinctive features are the predicates that should be strongly marked or foregrounded in the representation, and are defined by the ecological and moral function of the object. While all *Soldanella alpina* have a stem, leaves, petals, and so forth, these are relatively unimportant truths for Ruskin, since they are also true of all other flowers. What constitutes the truth and beauty of the *Soldanella alpina* are those particular features that demonstrate its ecological niche in the alpine snows, and that typify Divine attributes. For most generalization-theory, the reverse would be the case: the more general the predicate, the more important its truth.

Form and Function

George Landow has related Ruskin's notion of "typical beauty" to a longstanding tradition of typological symbolism in which the Old Testament is read for anticipations of Christ, and has traced the pervasive influence of this "habit of mind" throughout Victorian art and literature.[52] Beverly Seaton has more specifically traced a tradition of "natural typology" in Victorian flower books (including Ruskin's own primer on flowers, *Proserpina*), whose writers "looked on nature as they did on scriptures . . . [for] guidance in their moral lives [and] prophecy concerning sacramental or revealed religion."[53] We can in the same way trace the intellectual genealogy of Ruskin's notion of "vital beauty," which he undoubtedly developed out of his extensive studies in the professional science of the day, and especially through his association with William Buckland, Professor of Geology at Oxford. Ruskin studied with Buckland in the 1830s and continued to associate with him during the period when he was writing the first two volumes of *Modern Painters* through his membership in the Geological Society, of which Buckland was a founding member and twice president.

One overall effect of the functionalist doctrine of early nineteenth-century natural science is the same as that of typological symbolism—a revelation of the divine through the study of nature—but here that revelation takes the more orthodox (for the time) scientific form of an argument from design rather than direct symbolism or allegorical parables. A seminal text for the functionalist creed was William Paley's *Natural Theology* of 1802, which popularized and consolidated the view of nature as showing evidence of divine creation and divine order in the providential adaptation of each species to its particular function. A typical argument of functionalist "natural theology" was to consider an organism that at first sight appears awkward and ugly in form, and to reveal the reverse by demonstrating the perfection of its design for its ordained function. Considering the Megatherium or giant ground sloth as an instance of "egregious apparent monstrosity," for example, Buckland demonstrated that features "that at first sight appear imperfectly contrived . . . become intelligible when viewed in their relations to one another, and to the functions of the animal in which they occur"—in the case of the sloth, digging up and feeding on roots.[54] For Buckland, such functional perfection despite formal monstrosity reveals that "the frame and mechanism of every animal . . . were framed and fashioned by the same Almighty hand, and were designed and contrived by the same Almighty mind."[55] That Ruskin was directly thinking of his mentor Buckland when he was formulating his concept of "vital beauty" in the second volume of *Modern Painters* is established by one of his more esoteric examples, that we are to "find beauty in the magnificent binding together of the jaws of the ichthyosaurus for catching and holding" (cited above). Buckland had devoted an entire chapter to the newly discovered ichthyosaurus in his 1836 treatise *Geology and Mineralogy Considered with Reference to Natural Theology*, concluding from his analysis of the "perfect appointment" of the features of the fishlike reptile that we "cannot but recognize throughout them all, the workings of one and the same eternal principle of Wisdom and intelligence, presiding from first to last over the total fabric of Creation."[56] The functionalist creed, then, allowed Ruskin to unite his scientific and religious interests and simultaneously to enunciate the exact focus of artistic representation on those features that exhibit the underlying functional ontology of nature.

There was a rival school of natural history, however, that sought the beauty and truth of organisms in their form or structure rather than their function: transcendental morphology.[57] In the debate between these two schools we find replayed, once again, the same arguments about the nature of generic differences and the precise limits of generalization. Like the functionalists, the transcendental morphologists believed that God had created the world, and that a scientific exploration of the natural order of things would reveal God's creative ideas, but the two schools differed in their understandings of the *nature* of God's ideas. A brief detour through Aristotelian causal theory will help to distinguish the two schools. According to Aristotle, there are four types of cause that inform anything that has being: the *material* cause, which includes all of the matter of which the object is made (the bronze of a bell); the *efficient* cause, which includes all of the actions performed on that matter by its maker (melting, casting, and so on);

the *formal* cause, which is the idea according to which the object was made (the blueprint or plan of the bell); and the *final* cause, which is the purpose or function for which the object was made (ringing).[58] While the two schools agreed on the material and efficient causes of natural objects, they assigned different priority to the formal and final causes. For the functionalists, as we have seen, the final cause is the most crucial informing factor of creation: God created each organism with its predetermined function in mind, and thus the formal cause (or blueprint) is predicated on the final cause (the function or purpose of the organism). For the transcendental morphologists, however, the functionalist interpretation lost sight of or ignored some tremendous formal similarities between organisms and parts of organisms that have completely different functions. In 1753, Georges-Louis Leclerc, comte de Buffon considered the similarity of the horse's hoof and the human fingernail:

> One will judge if this hidden resemblance is not more remarkable than the apparent differences, if this constant conformity and this plan [*dessein*] followed from man to the quadrupeds, from quadrupeds to cetaceans [marine mammals], from cetaceans to birds, from birds to reptiles, from reptiles to fishes, etc. . . . does not imply that in creating animals, the Supreme Being desired to employ only one idea, and at the same time to vary it in all possible manners, so that man might equally admire the magnificence of the execution and the simplicity of the plan.[59]

There are evident formal similarities in creation that run across differences in function; indeed, human fingernails seem to be vestigial (or incipient), and largely nonfunctional, traces of a common morphological feature that in grazing mammals serves the function of protective covering (hooves) and in predatory mammals serves the function of rending their prey (claws). Functionalism cannot explain any morphological features that serve no significant ecological function (such as human fingernails); nor can it explain why some very different functions (such as those of the horse's hooves and the lion's claws) are performed by very similar morphological features. The postulate of the transcendental morphologists, then, is that underlying the adaptive, functional diversity of creation there is "one idea," as Buffon put it, or a "unity of plan," as it was more commonly termed, predicated on a purely formal cause, the variations of which are to be attributed to functionalism only as a secondary cause.

In Britain, this distinction between the functionalists and the transcendental morphologists was articulated as a difference between "analogous" and "homologous" morphological features. Richard Owen defined the terminological distinction in the 1840s, and it has been generally accepted in the biological literature.[60] For Owen, an "analogous" part is "a part or organ in one animal which has the same function as another part or organ in a different animal," where a "homologous" part is "the same organ in different animals under every variety of form and function."[61] The legs of lobsters and llamas are analogous, since they perform the same locomotive function; but they are not homologous, for articulates (such as lobsters) and vertebrates (such as llamas) derive their skeletons from "distinct systems."[62] By contrast, Owen argued, the forelimbs of humans, bats, horses, and whales are all homologous, demonstrating that all belong to the same natural class. Although the forelimbs of humans are used for object manipulation, those of bats for flying, those of horses for walking, and those of whales for swimming, Owen saw a fundamental structural identity underlying those functional differences. Following the French transcendental morphologist Etienne Geoffroy Saint-Hilaire, Owen located structural homologies not in the exact visual resemblance between organs or bones but in their "number and relations."[63] That is, while there are clear visual differences between the humerus of the human, the bat, the horse, and the whale, they are homologous features inasmuch as they take the same place in the structure of all of those animals as the bone mediating between the shoulder girdle on one side and the radius and ulna on the other.

In natural history, the distinction between functional analogies and structural homologies (before and after Owen's terminological distinction) allowed the transcendental morphologists to isolate the formal cause (God's blueprint for creation) from the final cause (the adaptation of that formal blueprint to various functions), and ultimately to demonstrate the priority of the former. A key argument took place in France between the functionalist Georges Cuvier and the transcendental morphologist Geoffroy over the structure of the gills in fishes (the "operculum"). In his analysis of the skulls of fishes and mammals, Cuvier had determined the operculum to be unique to fish, which to his mind offered a proof of the functionalist hypothesis: God created those bones to order for the fishes' breathing function in their ordained environment, and did not need to include them in humans or horses since their environments do not require gills. Geoffroy reexamined the evidence, however, and discovered a homology between the fishes' operculum and some bones left out of Cuvier's own analysis of the mammalian skull. The bones of the mammalian inner ear, Geoffroy asserted, were of the same number and relations to surrounding bones as those found in fishes' gills. Not only did this discovery draw a much closer parallel between the fish-plan and the mammal-plan, it also transcended functional differentia, for the same bones that in fish are dedicated to breathing are in mammals dedicated to hearing.[64] Now the evidence seemed strongly to support the morphological hypothesis, for it was apparent that the Creator did indeed use the same basic plan, the same bones in the same sequence, over and over, and the modification of that plan to suit particular functions was only a secondary consideration.

The rivalry between these two schools of natural history was constant in the decades before Darwin, several times reaching the public forum. In 1830, when Geoffroy championed two young naturalists who claimed to have discovered structural homologies between the apparently very different taxa of mollusks (e.g., clams and oysters) and articulates (e.g., insects and lobsters), Cuvier met Geoffroy in a series of highly publicized debates. On the day that news of France's July Revolution reached Weimar, Goethe was reported to have exclaimed to a friend, "Now, what do you think of this great event? The volcano has come to an eruption; everything is in flames." Goethe's friend naturally assumed that he was referring to the overthrow of Charles X, and Goethe had to clarify that he was more interested in the debates between Cuvier and Geoffroy.[65] In England, William Buckland and Richard Owen both adhered to the functionalist position in the 1830s, but in the course of the 1840s Owen gradually converted to transcendental morphology. What is most significant for the purposes of this study is that the debate between the functionalists and the transcendental morphologists exactly parallels the debate about "character" within the Academy and the later debate between Ruskin and the Academics. Ruskin, like the functionalists, had sought the beauty and truth of the tree in relation to the specific ecological function of each type of tree, and ignored or sidelined the evident formal and structural similarities that all trees share despite those functional differences. The tendency of functionalism is thus toward a limited and highly fragmented taxonomy. Reynolds, by contrast, sought a "unity of plan" for all trees, and demoted the evident differences between species of trees, like that between individual trees, to a secondary (and largely dispensable) consideration. Such a project allows a much broader taxonomy of fewer basic classes. Similarly, the inter-Academic debate about the relation of character to the ideal divided between a functionalist view of the human frame as modified to perform certain actions (Herculean feats of strength, Apollonian feats of grace), and the possibility of finding a "unity of plan" within the human frame exclusive of (and/or equally adapted to) all such specialized functions. James Barry most clearly exemplifies the dual ontologies of this debate. Barry begins his Academic lecture on design by reconfirming Reynolds's contention that the great artist finds his designs in "*abstract or general nature*" and that "individuals of every species" tend toward "a certain point or form" that is "the standard of each species." However, he denies that every deviation from this central form is necessarily a degree of deformity. For Barry, there are two types of deviation from the central form: "first, deviations indicating a more peculiar adaptation to certain characters of advantage and utility, such as strength, agility, and so forth," and second, deviations "visibly indicating the contrary, as being useless, cumbersome, or deficient." The second alone is to be considered a "deformity"; the first types "exhibit the *abstract* or *ideal* perfection in the several classes or species of *character*."[66] Thus Barry explicitly defines character as a sort of "functional deviation" from the species type. To this extent he effectively conforms to the functionalist view. However, at the same time, Barry still held that character was indeed a deviation from a more fundamental taxon, and still maintained the higher ideal of "simple beauty" defined by its abstraction from any particular power or function. Thus Barry, like the transcendental morphologists, presumed an a priori region of ontology that transcended the contingent circumstances of earthly function.

As we saw, the reductio ad absurdum seemed to have blocked the attempt to represent the absolute ideal of the human species, but the transcendental morphologists finally solved the problems facing the quest for class-ideas of broad scope. During the 1840s—precisely the time during which Ruskin was composing the first volumes of *Modern Painters*—the transcendental morphologists reached their greatest influence in Britain and, using generalization-theory, resolved the reductio ad absurdum and achieved by 1848 what Ruskin had derided and Reynolds had (implicitly) predicted: a coherent and determinate generalization of a pony and a pig.

Richard Owen's *Archetype*

Although Geoffroy held the *concept* of a "unity of plan" that would generalize all vertebrates (and even all of the animal kingdom), he was content only to trace various specific homologies, and did not attempt to generalize these homologies into a coherent visual model. Following Geoffroy's and his own work in identifying such homologies, Richard Owen felt by the late 1840s that the quantity and precision of these discoveries had become "so great . . . as to imperatively press upon the thinking mind the consideration of the more general condition upon which the existence of special homology depends."[67] By combining all of the specific instances of homology discovered within a given class, the "thinking mind" could recreate God's own blueprint for that class as a clear and distinct visual model or "archetypal exemplar."[68] Owen's method, like that of the generalizers, involved a close comparison of multiple individuals within a class, most famously the entire vertebrate subkingdom. He trumped Berkeley, Hazlitt, and Ruskin and resolved a number of the most obvious objections to generalization-theory by the simple expedient of entirely eliminating the skin—feathers or fur; white, brown, or red; all these features vary by function and should thus be abstracted (a more comfortable proposition in scientific anatomy than in art, to be sure). That which is common to all vertebrates is, after all, the vertebrate skeletal system.

Owen illustrated God's blueprint for the entire vertebrate class in a foldout plate accompanying his 1848 book *On the Archetype and Homologies of the Vertebrate Skeleton* (figures 26 and 27). The *Vertebrate Archetype* occupies the upper right portion of the plate, and consists essentially of a series of vertebrae with attached ribs. For Owen, the Archetype itself consists of a single unit, the vertebra, repeated with modifications along the length of the body. The ribs and other projections (such as limbs) develop out of the spiny protuberances of the vertebrae. Following the "vertebrate theory of the skull," adopted by Owen from earlier morphologists such as Lorenz Oken and Goethe himself, the head itself is still incipient, consisting of four anterior vertebrae that bulge slightly to incorporate the swelling of the spinal nerves that will become the brain. The sensory organs are similarly incipient, and are indicated by means of external schemas for eye, nose, and ear, with diagrammatic arrows designating the vertebral cavities in which they will develop. The limbs are still almost entirely the same structure as the ribs, but in the posterior vertebra of the head, for example, the rib that will become the humerus is numbered to identify it with the corresponding bones in developed animals.

Something of the ontological charge of this visual representation of the Vertebrate Archetype is conveyed in a review of Owen's works by W. J. Broderip (and in fact coauthored by Owen himself) in the *Quarterly Review* of 1853:

> Here the *Vertebrate Archetype*, so often accepted for the mere verbal and vague indication of a more or less inchoate abstraction—is placed bodily before our eyes in the same 'picture language' as that by which the type-skeletons of the fish, the reptile, the bird, and the beast are distinctly represented in one comprehensive field. By a careful examination of this plate alone, we venture to say, any one intelligently desirous to comprehend the structure of the bony frame-work of Man and the lower animals, would learn more, and more easily, than from any previous work on Comparative Osteology.[69]

This passage not only indicates the great scientific advantage of Owen's Archetype, but read in the context of (especially) British considerations of the ideal, it virtually declares that Archetype to be the solution to the problem outlined above: that as a generalization increases in taxonomic scope, it approaches the "vague" and "inchoate," becoming insusceptible to "picture language." Here, finally, is the direct and determinate representation of an ideal of such comprehensive

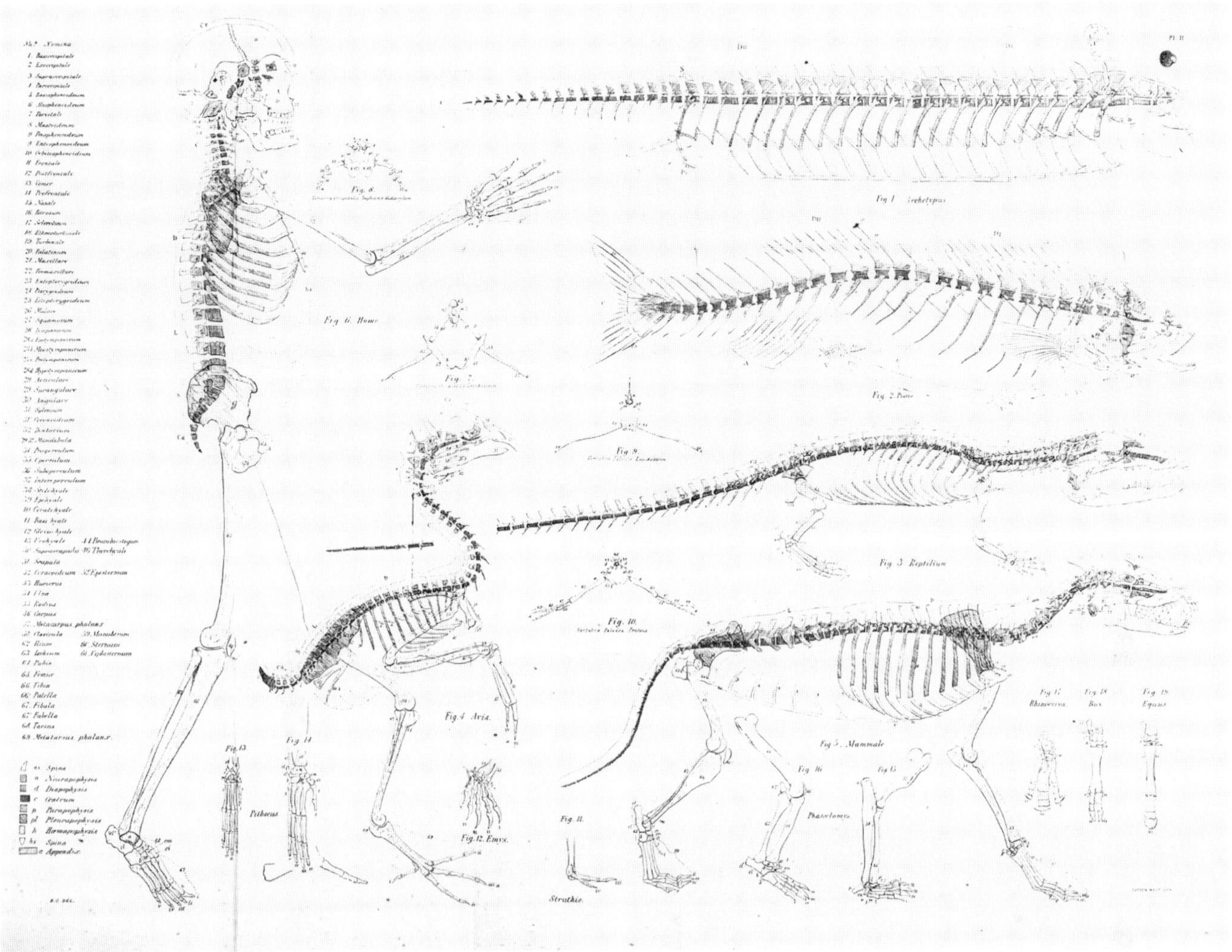

26. Richard Owen, foldout plate accompanying *On the Archetype and Homologies of the Vertebrate Skeleton* (London: R. and J. E. Taylor, 1848). Yale University, Harvey Cushing/John Hay Whitney Medical Library.

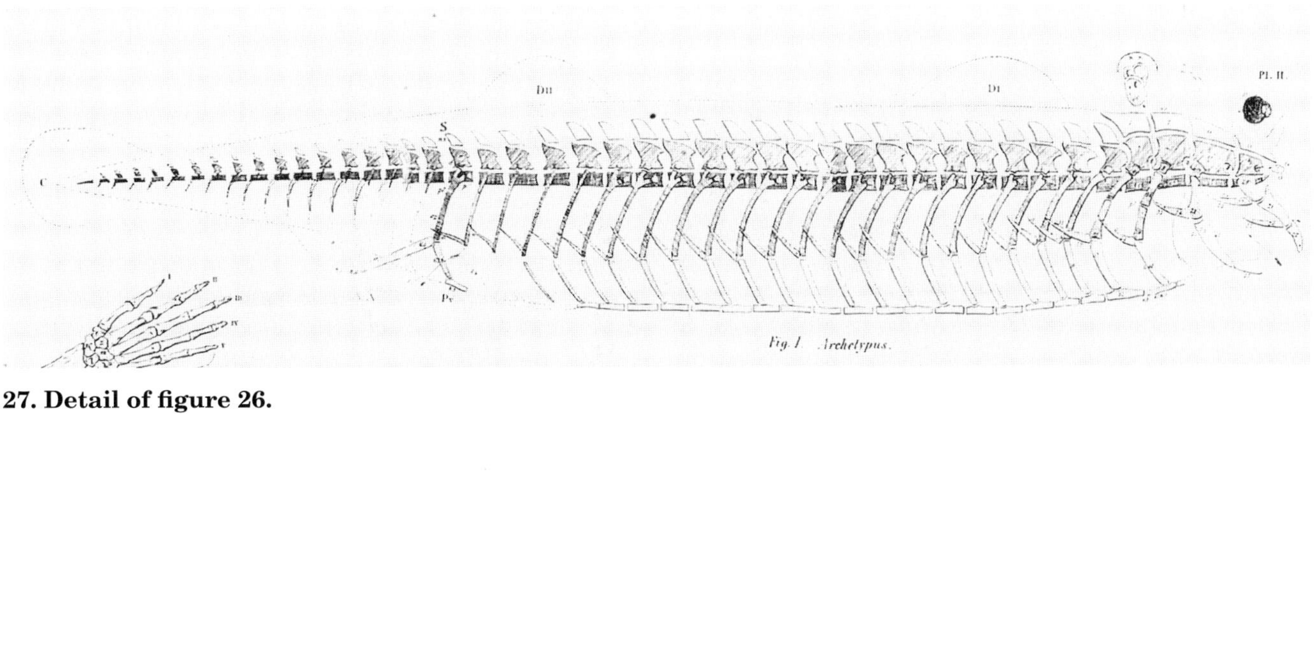

27. Detail of figure 26.

taxonomic scope, and at the same time such precise sensual determinacy, that it manages to generalize a pony and a pig—and the entire human species in all of its characteristic variety as well.

Before we can elevate Owen above Raphael in the classical pantheon, however, we must consider the plate further. The other five illustrations demonstrate the major "modifications" of the Archetype, exemplified in actual, existing animals, that are "characteristic of the four great divisions of the vertebrate subkingdom, viz. fishes, reptiles, birds, mammals, and of man."[70] Read clockwise in a sort of Great Chain of Being, these five subtypes show an increasing departure from the Archetype, from the fish skeleton, which most closely resembles it, to the human skeleton, which differs from it the most. In Owen's scheme, two morphological "forces" are at work in each existing organism and class of organism, corresponding to the two Aristotelian causes outlined above: the "polarizing force," or formal cause, which tends toward "vegetative" repetition (that is, the simplest possible repetition of the ideal vertebra), and the "special organizing force," or final cause, which adapts the archetype to a specialized ecological function. The Archetype is constituted by pure formal cause or polarizing force; the fish is slightly modified by special organizing forces to suit its ecology, the reptile is more modified, and so on to "Man," who is called "the highest and most modified of all organic forms, in which the dominion of the controlling and specially adapting force over the lower tendency to type and vegetative repetition is manifested in the strongest characters."[71] This observation brings up a tricky point: where, exactly, is the ideal in this plate? On one hand, we could identify the ideal as the human skeleton, the "highest" possible modification of the Vertebrate Archetype. In this view, the Archetype is reduced to a primitive, underdeveloped state of unrealized potential. On the other hand, however, following the discourse of generalization, the Archetype itself is the ideal, for no matter how salubrious or spiritual are the modifications of the human skeleton, they remain only relative and contingent (function based) modifications away from its comprehensive generality.

This very contradiction is raised, and not resolved, by Owen himself. In his treatise *On the Archetype*, Owen identified the "platonic idea" not with the "polarizing force" that tends toward the archetypal form, but with his functionalist "specific organizing principle," which is the main cause of adaptive variation away from the Archetype:

> The platonic idea or specific organizing principle or force would seem to be in antagonism with the general polarizing force, and to subdue and mould it in subserviency to the exigencies of the resulting specific form. The extent to which the operation of the polarizing or vegetative-repetition-force is so subdued in the organization of a specific animal form becomes an index of the grade of such species, and is directly as its ascent in the scale of being. The lineaments of the common archetype are obscured in the same degree.[72]

Owen here equates the Platonic Idea with the forces causing the functional *modification* of the Archetype, resulting in plans of ascending perfection culminating in man, and demotes the Archetype itself, and the polarizing force it embodies, to the status of something "antagonistic" to and holding back the development of such unfolding ideality.

This hypothesis is consistent with the general assumption that man is God's highest achievement, but Owen was evidently of two minds. The following year, in his lectures *On the Nature of Limbs* (1849), Owen identified the general homologies embodied in the Archetype as signifying

> that essential character of a part which belongs to it in its relation to a predetermined pattern, answering to the "idea" of the Archetypal World in the Platonic cosmogony, which archetype or primal pattern is the basis supporting all the modifications of such part for specific powers and actions in all animals possessing it, and to which archetypal form we come, in the course of our comparison of those modifications, finally to reduce the subject.[73]

As Nicolaas Rupke has noted, this is a direct contradiction of Owen's earlier use of the Platonic Idea: now the Idea is associated not with man, but directly with the Archetype as the "primal pattern" underlying all subsequent functional modifications.[74] Since an exploration of Owen's clearly confused understanding of Platonic cosmogony would be of little profit, I would draw two conclusions from this equivocation. First, it can be accounted for by the fact that the lecture *On the Nature of Limbs* was delivered before a nonspecialist "general audience," for whom (and perhaps for Owen as well) a direct correlation between the Aristotelian "formal cause" and the Platonic Idea was a desirable simplification. Indeed, such a correlation lends even greater prestige to Owen's discovery of the Archetype. Second, Owen's equivocation reveals a tendency of generalization-theory that may be troubling but should not be explained away: the elimination of specialized features necessarily entails a corresponding loss of specialized powers, and thus the ideal will be "vegetative" in an almost literal sense in proportion to its abstract generality. We have already encountered this tendency of generalization-theory: it is substantially the same conclusion as that which pronounces the ideal to be "insipid" because of its lack of characteristic personality, and "vague" because of its lack of determinate form. It is indeed the contradiction embodied in the reductio ad absurdum endemic to generalization-theory, and anticipated in the dual meanings of the term "abstraction," which describes both the process of arriving at the ideal through an elimination of specialized features, and its final formal appearance.

6

Symbolism and Classicism

Symbolism is frequently cited in the scholarship as the first unequivocal manifestation of "modernist" art, whether because its privileging of the artist's subjectivity over reality seems to anticipate modern expressionism, because its relative flatness seems to anticipate Greenbergian formalism, because its embrace of the "primitive" is a clear repudiation of the Western tradition, or simply because its radical formal distortions seem to anticipate and authorize the increasing license taken by twentieth-century art (see figures 29 and 30 below). For Maurice Denis, however, Symbolism was also a form of classicism. Notwithstanding the "formal excesses and theoretical paradoxes" of the Symbolist movement, Denis claims, "starting around 1890 it was easy for the attentive observer to disentangle the heralds of a classical reaction."[1] It is the intent of this chapter to take up Denis's suggestion and examine Symbolist art and art theory for signs of classicism. Clearly such an undertaking cannot be based on an understanding of classicism as an imitation of the Ancients; nor on Raphaelesque or Poussiniste formal standards such as linearity, planarity, balance, and so on; nor yet on an overall tone of emotional restraint such as Winckelmann's "noble simplicity and quiet grandeur." Denis's suggestion is cogent, though, when we define classicism as a quest for the ideal, and especially as a quest for the ideal through an epistemological process of generalization resulting in a radical simplification of form.

I should state at the outset, however, that Denis is correct: it is a matter of "disentangling" classicism in this sense from an extremely heterogeneous aggregate of theories and practices. Within the hodgepodge of Symbolist theory, and even within Denis's own writings, it is also possible to disentangle strands relating to formalism, to primitivism, to personal expression, to transcendent classicism, and so on, and Symbolist art can easily be described as manifesting those tendencies as well. It is not my intent to diminish these aspects of Symbolism, but rather to underscore yet another aspect of its complex and multifaceted discourse.

The Ideal in Symbolist Art Theory

Amid the cacophony of diverse calls for a new art in the late nineteenth century one of the clearest is the call for a return to higher ontological values and more enduring artworks than those of literary Naturalism and pictorial Impressionism. One of the ways in which the advocates of Symbolism sought to define and promote the young movement was by severely restricting the aims and achievements of its predecessors and competitors. Both Naturalism and Impressionism were to a large extent dismissed by the Symbolists and their apologists as objective in the most trivial sense of the term, as accumulations of facts that could lead only to an endless sequence of ontologically insignificant and immediately outdated descriptions of nature.

This dismissal of mere factuality and the complementary call for higher ontological values is especially legible in the first critical champion of the Symbolist painters, Albert Aurier. Aurier wrote in his 1891 essay on Gauguin:

> It is becoming evident that in literature today we are witnessing the death throes of naturalism and the beginnings of an idealist, even mystical reaction. It would be astounding if the plastic arts did not manifest a tendency toward a similar evolution. [Gauguin's *Vision after the Sermon*] . . . sufficiently demonstrates, I believe, that this tendency exists, and it is understandable that the painters engaged with this new project should wish to relieve themselves of that absurd label "impressionism," which implies, I must repeat, a project that is directly contradictory to theirs.[2]

For Aurier, Impressionism is only "a type of realism . . . the faithful translation of a sensation, of an *exclusively sensorial impression, with nothing beyond* [Aurier's italics]."[3] Art should be something more than this.

The next year, in his article "Les peintres symbolistes," Aurier broadens his critique to include, not just the immediately prior movements in the arts, but an indictment of virtually the entire century: "The nineteenth century, after having proclaimed for eighty years, in its infantile enthusiasm, the omnipotence of observation and of scientific deduction, after having affirmed that no mystery could survive its lenses and its scalpels, seems finally to realize the vanity of its efforts, the puerility of its boasts."[4] Until recently, the century of Cuvier and Comte had been exclusively "materialistic, industrial, utilitarian," and correspondingly, Aurier notes, "the word *ideal* inspired laughter as a ridiculous and senseless utterance that would soon be classified in the dictionaries as a disused archaism."[5] In an unfinished *Essai sur une nouvelle méthode de critique*, Aurier traces the ruinous effects of this philosophical stance in the scientific art theory of Hippolyte Taine. So far, Aurier laments, "the goal of the nineteenth century has been to introduce science everywhere, even where it is least appropriate."[6] Taine is the best example of this tendency: "The doctrine of M. Taine, as we know, is based on the idea that a work of art is an essentially relative and contingent phenomenon; that [it] does not exist in itself, and that its only value is to bear witness to the physiological state of a people at a given time."[7] In his *Philosophie de l'art* (1865–69), Taine had explicitly rejected any attempt to subsume art to a homogenous and prescriptive norm, and instead articulated a relativist description of the different schools of art that had emerged in various historical periods and geographic regions.[8] The ineluctable variety of art is, for Taine, largely governed by "climate," understood both as the physical climate that determines the geographic types, and the moral (or social) climate that determines the historical manners of those types. The Flemish type, for example, is formed by "alluvions," the humid deposits of soil at the mouths of its rivers:

> From this single word is born an infinity of particularities that compose the whole way of being of the region, not only the physical make-up in itself, but also the spirit and the moral and physical qualities of its inhabitants and their works.[9]

In a causal chain starting at the fertile soil and humid environment of the alluvial plains and ending at the physical and moral character of the Flemish people, Taine writes,

> We could say that in this country, the water makes the grass, the grass makes the beast, who makes the cheese, the butter and the meat; which, together with the beer, make the inhabitant. In effect, from this rich and fatty life and from the influence of the humid air, you see the birth of the Flemish temperament.[10]

Rubens is revealed as the paradigmatic interpreter of Flemish character because in works such as his *Kermesse* we find that alluvial character more concentrated than it is in real life. While this notion that art distills and concentrates character seems similar to the classical theories we have been exploring, the crucial difference is that for Taine, "character" is not an absolute or predetermined element, but is determined by the milieu; it is relative to the changes of historical circumstances and of environment, and thus carries none of the essentializing implications usually ascribed to the classical ideal. For Reynolds, once the alluvial characteristics of the Flemish people had been shown to be dependent merely upon the contingent circumstances of their particular environment, those characteristics should be eliminated; for Taine, however, it is precisely those characteristics that should be seized.[11]

The historical and climatic relativism of Taine is typical of certain branches of nineteenth-century thought, and even prompted some critics to redefine the notions of the ideal and of beauty. In 1863, Jules-Antoine Castagnary, champion of the Realists, declared:

> The Ideal is not a revelation from on high, set up before humanity, which must ever approach but can never attain it; the Ideal is the free product of the conscience of each and every person placed in contact with external realities, and thus an individual concept varying from artist to artist.
>
> The Beautiful is not a reality which exists outside man . . . the Beautiful is an abstract word, an abbreviation, under the label of which we group a mass of different phenomena which act in a certain way on our organs and our intelligence; consequently, it is an individual or collective concept which varies, in a given society, from age to age, and, within a particular age, from man to man.[12]

Castagnary's relativist notion of the ideal and of beauty would, of course, make the traditionally classical project of discovering the ideal indistinguishable from the Realist project of documenting contemporaneous social conditions, or even from the Romantic project of expressing the artist's individual "temperament."

In direct contrast to such relativism, Aurier based his evaluation of art and the artist on their ability to transcend the conditions of their milieu and "renvoler vers le ciel":

> Yes, it is unhappily true that [artists] absorb the influence of their milieus, more or less, and despite their desires, when it is their duty to distance and abstract themselves from it. They are somewhat like swans, who have fallen by chance into a quagmire and who attempt to fly back to the sky, but whose wings have been soiled by the mud of the swamp.[13]

For Aurier, then, "*The value of a work of art is inversely proportional to the influence of milieus that it exhibits* [Aurier's italics]."[14] This aspect of Symbolist theory and criticism closely parallels an aspect of classical art theory as we have explored it. Some of the terms and the stylistic attributes have changed, but essentially ideas of positivism and relativism replace ideas of particular nature and of custom, and the faults of the Realists and Impressionists replace the analogous faults of Denner or the Dutch genre artists. The Symbolists are credited with a revival of the "ideal" in art, as opposed to the merely actual and contingent.

Logically following this broad distinction there arises the traditional problem of classical art theory: how can the artist conceive and render the ideal when the senses offer only a mass of adventitious deformities? Here again the Symbolist debate closely parallels that of classicism: it is divided between transcendent and empirical routes to the ideal. Aurier, for example, was largely an advocate of transcendence in an almost doctrinaire Neoplatonic sense.[15] Artists are set apart from the bulk of humanity by their dual soul—"âme d'homme et âme d'artiste"—the former of which is temporal and the latter eternal. This dualism accounts for Aurier's distinction between the "réaliste" art of the Impressionists and the "idéiste" art of the Symbolists, and the attempt of the latter to transcend the conditions of their milieu forces the "idéistes" to a position outside of their temporal and geographic moment: they are "Les Isolés."[16] Similarly, Sâr Péladan saw his group Rose+Croix as artists by virtue of their capacity for transcendent vision, asserting that, "To produce a masterpiece, it is necessary to have glimpsed the divine," and that "a work, like a being, has no other excellence than the sustained vision of the divine."[17] It is only by virtue of a transcendent faculty (the artist's soul) that transcendent art (the ideal) is possible.

The Swiss Symbolist Ferdinand Hödler agreed that the "mission of the artist" is "to express the eternal element of nature, beauty, to bring out nature's essential beauty," and even cites "Plato's definition of beauty as the resplendence of truth," but in direct contrast to such transcendent theories he asserts that Plato

> means that we must open our eyes and look at nature. If a man starts with nothing, he can do nothing. In executing a work of art, the artist borrows elements from the existing world in which he lives. The most imaginative [artist] is guided by nature, the great source of information that stimulates our imagination. The more one penetrates the spirit of nature, the more completely one can convey it.[18]

Although he cites Plato, Hödler stresses that the necessary starting point of even "the most imaginative" artist is "the existing world in which he lives." Indeed, the citation from Plato that "beauty [is] the resplendence of truth" does *not* necessarily imply that "we must open our eyes and look at nature," as Hödler insists; the passage only establishes that Hödler, unlike Plato, has an empirically oriented idea of beauty and truth.

Much of the scholarship that has explored these issues in relation to Symbolism has concentrated on the transcendent route to the ideal, and it is true that many Symbolist artists and theorists leaned toward that route. There are many cogent and even imperative reasons for this tendency. First, the notion of transcendent abilities still (or again) carried a certain cachet in the late-nineteenth century: it was one of the easiest ways to define the unique privilege of the artist in society, even if (as for Aurier) that privilege increasingly placed the artist outside of society rather than within it. Second, the Symbolists' virulent rejection of "mere" naturalism made suggestions of transcendent art processes more cogent: empiricist processes, which necessarily start from a direct study of nature, would seem like equivocation when most Symbolist theories begin with a strong rejection of naturalism. Third, in terms of intellectual history it is easier to maintain an absolute disjunction between the actual and the ideal than it is to argue the derivation of the ideal from the actual. The critical and philosophical literature maintaining such a disjunction is more plentiful, has a longer as well as a broader genealogy (see the Eastern mystical traditions, for example), and has a more powerful rhetoric. By the late-nineteenth century, furthermore, empiricism had for many Symbolists been discredited as tending either toward skepticism or toward positivism, and in either case as incompatible with an aspiration to ideal knowledge. Thus the desire to define their own privilege, to disassociate their work from mere naturalism, and to associate their work with high ontological values in a powerful epistemological tradition made notions of transcendent processes much easier to mobilize than empirical processes.

Mark Cheetham has explored the transcendent aspect of Symbolist theory in his study *The Rhetoric of Purity*. One of the overall aims of that book is to demonstrate a theoretical genealogy of abstract (nonrepresentational) art that can be traced back as far as Plotinus. His description particularly of Gauguin's practice is a neat opposite to the (alleged) Impressionist optical-record practice of art: Symbolist artists should ignore sensory data, should literally close their eyes to nature and concentrate on recollecting the innate Platonic Idea. The motifs that Cheetham cites—the closed eyes, painting from memory as opposed to the motif, and the notion of memory as *aletheai*, an "unforgetting" of the Platonic Idea—are indeed significant to certain facets of the movement. However, there is one elision in Cheetham's text that demonstrates a willful neglect of other routes to the ideal propounded by artists of the time. A citation from Emile Bernard is selected and decontextualized to emphasize the nonempirical nature of Bernard's process. Cheetham's Bernard says:

> "We must simplify [reality] in order to disclose its meaning . . . I had two ways to achieve this. . . . The second way . . . consisted in relying on conception and memory and in disengaging myself from all direct contact [with nature]. . . . [This] was an act of my will signifying through analogous means my sensibility, my imagination, and my soul" [Cheetham's ellipses and interpolations].[19]

The passage as cited has a very transcendent sound to it, although two questions should immediately arise. First, and most obviously, what was Bernard's "first way" of disclosing nature's meaning? It was in fact the empirical classical process of abstractive generalization, as we shall further explore below: "The first consisted in placing myself in front of nature and in rigorously simplifying it."[20] Second, what does Bernard mean by "conception and memory"? Do those faculties achieve an "unforgetting" in the Neoplatonic sense, as Cheetham claims? Or are they thoroughly informed by empirical data and normative mental functions? Bernard's distinction between his "two ways," as we shall see, is not one between transcendent and empirical methods, but between direct synthesis (simplification in front of the motif) and indirect synthesis (relying on the natural distilling effects of a normative memory). It is my aim here to offer a sort of pendant or complement to Cheetham's work on the transcendent rhetoric of Symbolist art theory by outlining the empiricist side of Symbolist theories of idealization, especially in two practitioners, Denis and Bernard, who later openly embraced the term "classicism" to define their art and aspirations. Indeed, my own aim is similar to Cheetham's: to trace a genealogy of abstract art from within a long tradition of Western thought, but here that tradition is empirical classicism and its pursuit of the ideal through abstraction and generalization. To explore this aspect, it is necessary to turn our attention from Symbolist *goals* (the rhetoric of purity), which frequently imply transcendence, to Symbolist *means*: the epistemological and formal process of purification.

Synthetism and the Empirical Ideal

In an 1892 review of three Symbolist-influenced exhibitions, Remy de Gourmont, like Aurier, opposed the new movement to Impressionism, but unlike Aurier he did so in a way that explicitly maintained the empirical analysis characteristic of the Impressionists at the center of the Symbolists' process:

> Two schools . . . remain evident: the Impressionists and the Symbolists: those who tend to convey on canvas, vividly and crudely, the impression pure and simple, and wholly objective, which one aspect of things has produced on their sensorial imagination; [and] those who decompose that same impression in order to recompose it at their leisure and following their will to express in their work, not the ephemeral, but permanent,

eternal meanings, representations meant to be definitive.[21]

Gourmont's sympathies are obviously with the Symbolists: the Impressionist project is again characterized as one that attempts to convey an ephemeral, purely objective, and purely sensory aspect of nature, where the Symbolist attempts to produce a permanent, definitive, and eternal representation. Gourmont continues by pretending to validate both schools, but actually subsumes the Impressionist project to the Symbolist project: "These two approaches are valid in proportion to their sincerity: in practice they conjoin and complete each other, for the Symbolist needs a fund of Impressionism, and any Impressionist who should seek only to capture nuances would plunder the landscape in vain."[22] In Gourmont's formulation, the Impressionist "impression" represents the empirical and analytic aspect of artistic creation. Gourmont insists upon the necessity of this aspect, but places it as a moment within the Symbolist project, which will "decompose" and "recompose" the fund of empirical impressions in order to produce an eternal and definitive representation.

The works under review in Gourmont's essay are characterized as attempts to create "un art synthétique, idéaliste," and in a specific consideration of a Denis landscape, this synthetic and idealist art is characterized as modern in its subject matter but "classique" in its order.[23] Although advanced without any detailed epistemological apparatus, Gourmont's understanding of the Symbolist project is recognizably classical not only in its reference to compositional order, but also in its "idealist" aspirations and attempt to find "permanent, eternal meanings." It is recognizable more specifically as empirical classicism in its insistence upon close analytic observation of the motif. Gourmont's description of the Symbolist "decomposition" and "recomposition" of the motif in order to derive that ideal is relatively vague as an indication of epistemological process, but his use of the term "synthétique" suggests that Symbolist art is characterized by a distilled coalescence of the fragmentary and several Impressionist "analyses"—in other words, by generalization.

The term synthesis and its derivatives are ubiquitous in Symbolist art theory and criticism; indeed, both Aurier and Denis used "synthétisme" as a synonym for "symbolisme" in describing the new school.[24] It is the notion of synthetism, understood as an empirical process of distilling sensory data to discover the essence of nature, that allows Denis to assert the fundamental identity of Symbolism and classicism despite their apparent differences. In "Les Arts à Rome, ou la méthode classique" (1898 or 1899), Denis, like Gourmont, claims Impressionism as the necessary basis of a new classicism: "Realism and impressionism are two fertile periods that are perhaps preparing the way, with their new elements, for another classical Renaissance."[25] Thus, although in a journal entry of 1898 he asked for "a way of escaping from empiricism and impressionism," in the next breath Denis subsumes their analytic projects to an overall process that intends to "concentrate quotidian efforts and sensations in a restrained number of motifs."[26] In his 1905 article on Aristide Maillol, this "concentrating" epistemological activity is again identified with "the Classical notion of Art":

> All reflecting artists come sooner or later to prefer this [that is, classical] beauty to all others. The ideal of art is to condense, to sum up, in a small number of clear and concise forms, the infinite variety of relations [*rapports*] that we perceive in nature. It is to reduce our most particular sensations to the essential, to make the simple out of the complicated.[27]

Here, then, classicism is defined against the infinite variety and particularity of our sensations, but at the same time is explicitly based on those sensations and those relations: "L'idéal . . . c'est de faire du simple *avec du compliqué*." The word "sensation" should be taken here, as elsewhere in Denis, as both subjective and objective, as signifying both the optical impression of the object and the feeling induced by that impression—Denis's idea of synthesis is simultaneously responsible to expressive, formalist, and ontological criteria.[28] Classical art, for Denis, attains the ideal through synthesis understood in an almost Hegelian sense as a sublation of the two major poles of nineteenth century art: Realist objectivity and Romantic subjectivity. Classical art starts from a close observation of nature and a self-awareness of internal affective states, but these are only the data of art: idealization entails a synthesis of such data. The process of synthesis is correspondingly described as "to condense, to sum up," "to reduce our most particular sensations to the essential." "Thus, in the Classical notion of Art, what dominates is the idea of synthesis. There is no classicism that is not economical of means, that does not subordinate all of the graces of detail to the beauty of the ensemble, and that does not attain grandeur by concision."[29]

It is clear from these citations that the dominant formal move of synthesis and of classicism is simplification. This is a strong, but not necessarily exclusive, indication that Denis's notion of synthesis is a form of generalization: "simplicity" is commonly ascribed to classicism in many of its forms, and indeed the quality of simplicity unites a host of modernist values, including not only classicism but also primitivism, formalism, geometric rationalism, and so on. In 1913, Clive Bell described *all* art since the time of Manet and Cézanne as characterized by "simplification," as opposed to "anything we have seen since the twelfth century," and especially as opposed to the "Victorian slough" of the early- to mid-nineteenth century.[30] And Bell was, of course, primarily formalist in his aesthetic. Both formalism and primitivism are also clearly evident in Denis's writings, especially his seminal "Définition du néo-traditionnisme" (1890). However, at least by the time of his "Les Arts à Rome" article later in the decade, Denis had explicitly rejected the "agreeable little sensation obtained by the felicitous combination of three or four fine tones" that he had found earlier in the "Primitives."[31] By the later 90s, Denis had redefined his aims, or, more precisely, rearranged his emphases to argue for a distinctly classical notion of synthesis and beauty: synthesis is simplification in the sense of eliminating the contingent (abstraction), and synthesis bundles or comprehends (generalizes) the multitude of particular sensations that constitute its empirical and analytic basis.

Denis is more thorough than Gourmont in describing the epistemological process of synthesis, although it is also true that his description is evocative rather than analytic. The central metaphor for synthesis in both his journal and in the "Les Arts à Rome" article is "crystallization." Remarking that "the same [sensations] are reproduced in front of different objects," Denis concludes that we must "classify similar sensations."[32] The classification of sensations marks the difference between Impressionism, which for Denis exhibited both subjective and objective fragmentation, and classicism, which exhibits synthesized sensations as class-ideas. Based on their similarity, a certain number of sensations group together and become concentrated: "Our sensations have connections among themselves; they accumulate in our minds to determine durable states, veritable crystallizations."[33] The classification of sensations is "a task that will form centers of crystallization . . . to concentrate around each one all the sensations that can be associated with it."[34]

Another key metaphor employed by Denis for the process of synthesis is "digestion," and here the word signals not only the concentration of sensations, but also the slow and ruminative process that digestion implies. Denis contrasts such slowly digested and concentrated syntheses with the lamentable tendency of art since Impressionism toward "immediate synthesis," a regurgitation of the motif within "five minutes."[35] Great artists like Rubens and Poussin "understood the need to digest their sensations, not to employ them while they were new; sometimes a very slow digestion, and one which permits a homogeneous and rational work."[36] Denis notes that this classification of similar sensations is at first a "laborious" process for those "who have never attempted it," but it becomes nearly "instinctive" for great artists, "and Ingres, among others, must have done so without difficulty."[37] Reynolds and Diderot had also remarked on the "long laborious" or "slow, tentative, painfully groping" nature of the comparative-abstractive process of generalization.[38] For Denis as for those theorists, the difficulty of generalization is due to the fact that it is a firsthand, empirical process—not a direct, divine revelation, and not one that can be achieved by means of "scholastic rules and technical recipes."[39]

We can begin to see the confluence of this "synthetist" process with both the Symbolist and the classical style in one of the most unlikely heroes of the Symbolists, Puvis de Chavannes.[40] From one point of view, Puvis is obviously classicizing in his use of Greco-Roman motifs, in his clear and balanced compositions, and in his restrained emotional tone, but neither Denis nor Emile Bernard extol Puvis for sustaining the tradition of togas and temples in the modern era. Instead, they commend Puvis's process, which shows him to be the "true creator of symbolism and synthetism" and "the highest revelation of idealist French art."[41]

In support of Puvis's status as inventor of Symbolist synthetism, Bernard records a series of the older artist's dicta. It is remarkable the extent to which these dicta summarize the empirical classical project as we have been exploring it:

> Puvis loved the [old] masters, but taught: Let us take nothing but from ourselves; let us prefer a little charm to a lot of empty science.
>
> He said: "To simplify is to extract the thought; the simplest conception will be found to be the most beautiful."
>
> To the materialists he responded: "Painting is not an imitation of reality, but a *parallelism* to nature."
>
> He acknowledged that [one must]: "Strive to paint real spectacles, but having a general sense."
>
> Such was his symbolism: "For me," he confessed, "I have always sought to divine the body under its robe of changing reflections; I have sought things in their permanent character, in their profound appearance, that is to say in their essence. My way of working is interior, if I dare say so; before any execution, my creation is almost completely achieved in my head."
>
> He furthermore said: "It is necessary to prune from nature everything that is contingent, accidental, everything that is momentarily inexpressive, that is to say everything that would not tend to translate our thought. Art achieves what nature sketches, pronounces the word that she stammers. How does one arrive at aiding nature in her effort to talk? By abbreviation and simplification. Set yourself to express the essential, pass over the rest; this is the secret of composition, the secret of drawing, and even the secret of eloquence and of the spirit.[42]

Nature is covered by a "robe aux reflets changeants," she only sketches and stammers. To find nature's "caractère permanent," her "sens général," her "essence," we must "élaguer de la nature tout ce qui est contigence, accident." This process of "abréviation" and "simplification" will "dégager la pensée," and will also result in "la plus belle" conception; this is the secret of composition, drawing, eloquence, and even of the spirit. The "maîtres" were right, but we must pursue the ideal "de nous mêmes," and we must "s'efforcer de peindre des spectacles réels." There is little or nothing in these statements that Reynolds would not have agreed to, and together they form a relatively full, if somewhat aphoristic, statement of the discourse of generalization or "synthesis," and suggest that either Bernard or Puvis or both knew of or had independently determined the central cluster of ideas defining that discourse.

Denis also cites Puvis's words to establish the nature of his influence on the young Symbolists; and once again that influence resides in the older artist's ability to (as Denis would put it) "digest" and "crystallize" his sensations. Elaborating on his "interior way of working," Denis's Puvis says:

> ". . . ideas most often come to us tangled and vague. It is necessary thus to extract them first of all, to be able to hold them, in pure form, under the internal eye. A work is born out of a sort of confused emotion in which it is contained as the animal is contained in the egg. The thought that resides in this emotion, I roll it and roll it until it is elucidated before my eyes and until it comes into view with the greatest possible clarity. . . . That's symbolism, if you wish."[43]

Puvis is uncertain whether his aims and process are "symbolist," but for Denis they clearly are, and are simultaneously an example of "la méthode classique" (the subtitle of the article in which this citation appears). The notion of synthetism unites the two: the "tangled," "vague" and "confused" sensations of empirical reality are synthesized until they are crystallized, pure and clear.

For both Denis and Bernard, then, what is simultaneously classical and Symbolist about Puvis's work is its revelation of nature's essence through a directed simplification of form based on an epistemological process of synthesis or generalization. And indeed, in this respect Puvis's style has a good deal in common with that of Denis and Bernard around 1890. In works such his *Poor Fisherman* (figure 28), as in Bernard's and Denis's "synthetist" works of around 1890 (figures 29 and 30), the ground is formed very simply by flat tints: the nearly unvaried gray of the water punctuated by four gray-green wedges of land, three from the right and one from the left, meeting the lighter gray of the sky. The background is thus a highly simplified backdrop to the figures, which stand out against that ground rather than upon it. Puvis's way of laying on those figures is also close

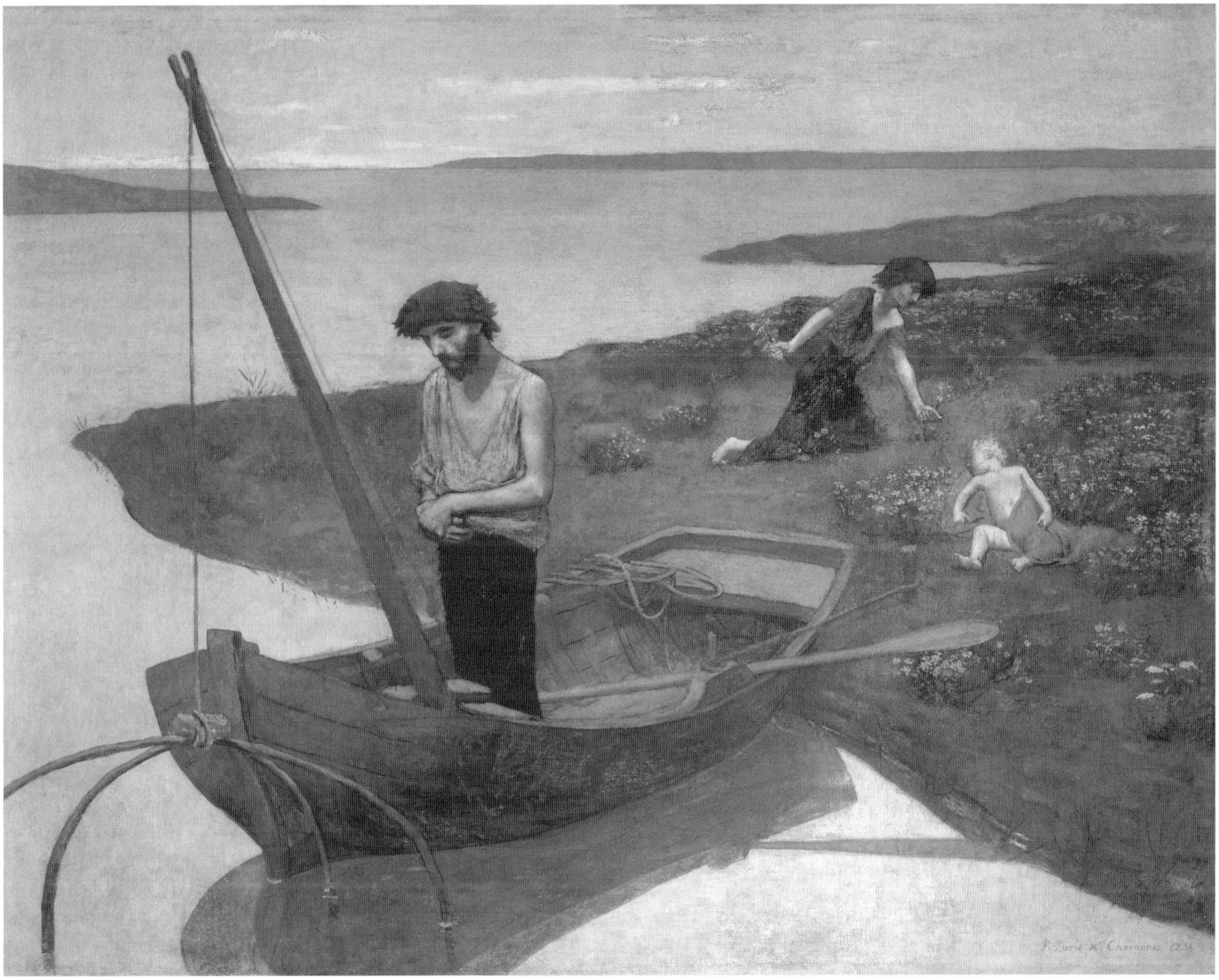

28. Pierre Puvis de Chavannes, *The Poor Fisherman*, 1881. Musée d'Orsay, Paris. Photo Credit: Erich Lessing/Art Resource, NY.

to that of later Symbolist practice. First a relatively broad, dark outline delineated the basic pose of the figure in a relatively schematic way, generalizing contours by the continuous trajectory of the strokes. A few, basic internal anatomical features were fixed by interacting with this contour. With a large brush and a thin but fairly opaque flesh tone, Puvis would begin to indicate the underlying bone and muscular structure, in places staying well within the contour, and in others completely covering it to form an edge with the ground. The brushwork describing the left arm of the fisherman, for example, overlies the contour line at the bottom of the forearm, forming an edge with the pinkish white of the shirt. On the inside of the elbow and in the wrist and thumb, however, the original contour remains nearly untouched. The effect is highly descriptive of the anatomical structure of the figure: through high value contrasts where the flesh tone abuts the darker contour, Puvis articulates the bony hardness of the joints of the fisherman; and through long strokes parallel to the described limb and overlapping the contour, Puvis simulates the stretching of the flesh over the rounded muscles between the joints. Further, increasingly light and opaque flesh tones continue to build up the internal masses of the major muscle groups, again forming sharp edges of high value contrast at key anatomical points, as for example the spur on the outside of the elbow or the large, rounded termini of the radius and ulna at the wrist. A few, directed strokes describe the general structural makeup of the

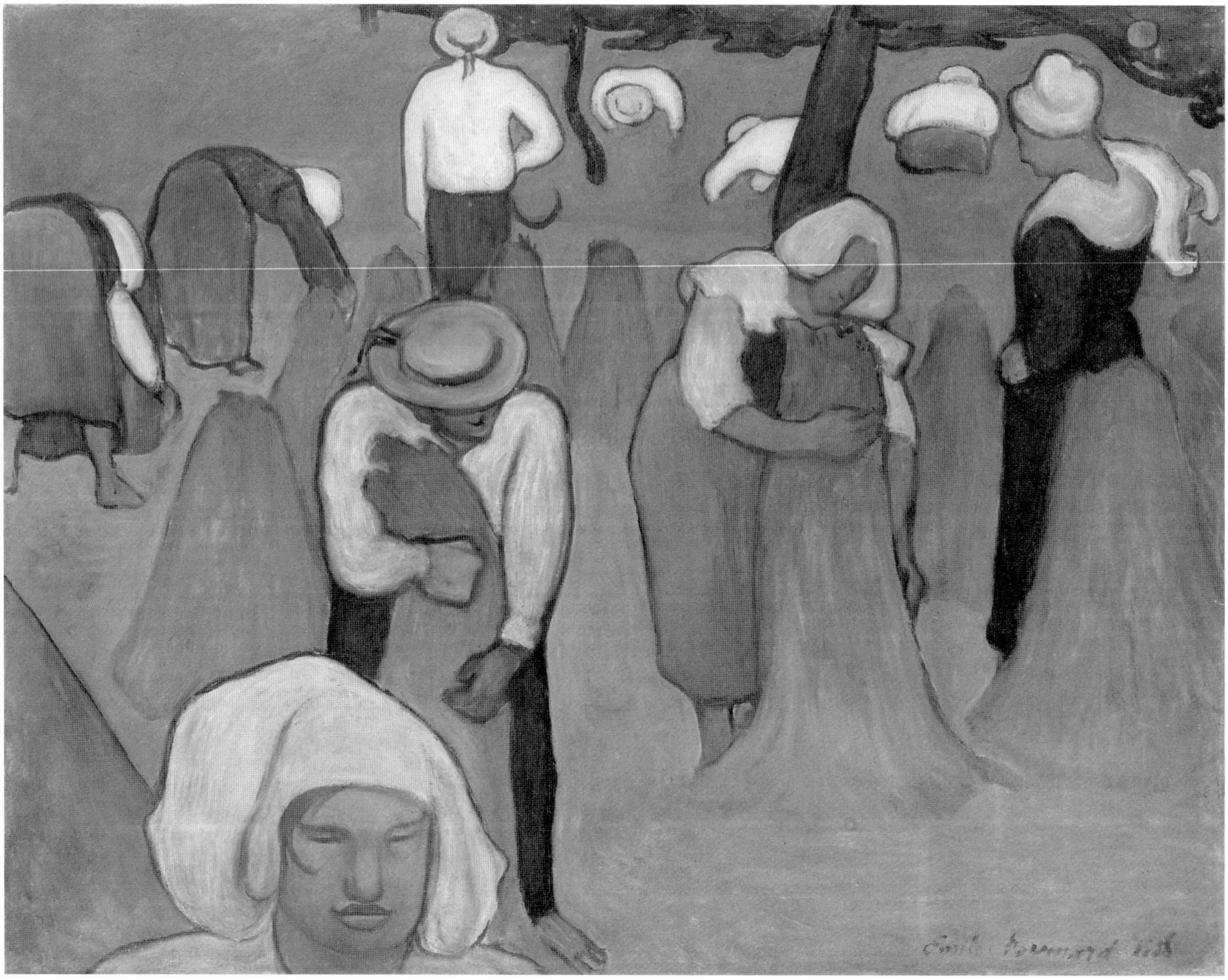

29. Emile Bernard, *Le blé noir (Buckwheat Harvest)*, 1888. Private collection on loan to the Metropolitan Museum of Art, New York, L. 2004.56. © 2006 Artists Rights Society (ARS), New York/ADAGP, Paris.

object, and once laid on, those strokes are not blended or smoothed, but remain evident on the surface of the work as indices of the artist's generalization.

Symbolism, Abstraction, and Memory

Of course, Puvis's "syntheses" were not as radical as those of Denis and Bernard around 1890. In Bernard's *Buckwheat Harvest* of 1888 (figure 29) and Denis's *Sunlight on the Terrace* of 1890 (figure 30), the rendering of the contour is generalized into a continuous line or edge that is now almost hieratic in its simplicity, and the features between those contours, such as the folds and wrinkles of the clothing and the skeletal and muscular armature under the flesh, are almost completely eliminated. Even facial features, which are normally rendered in much greater detail than those of the body, are reduced to a very few basic lines, almost like a child's drawing. Justifying this schematic style in his 1919 article "Mémoire pour l'histoire du symbolisme pictural de 1890," Bernard wrote:

> I wanted to reject everything that was an obstacle to my vision of generality and I approached symbolism through synthesis. I wrote at the time: "everything that overcharges a spectacle [of nature] covers it with reality and occupies our eyes to the detriment of our mind [*esprit*]. We must simplify the spectacle in order to disclose its meaning. We must more or less make a schema out of it,"

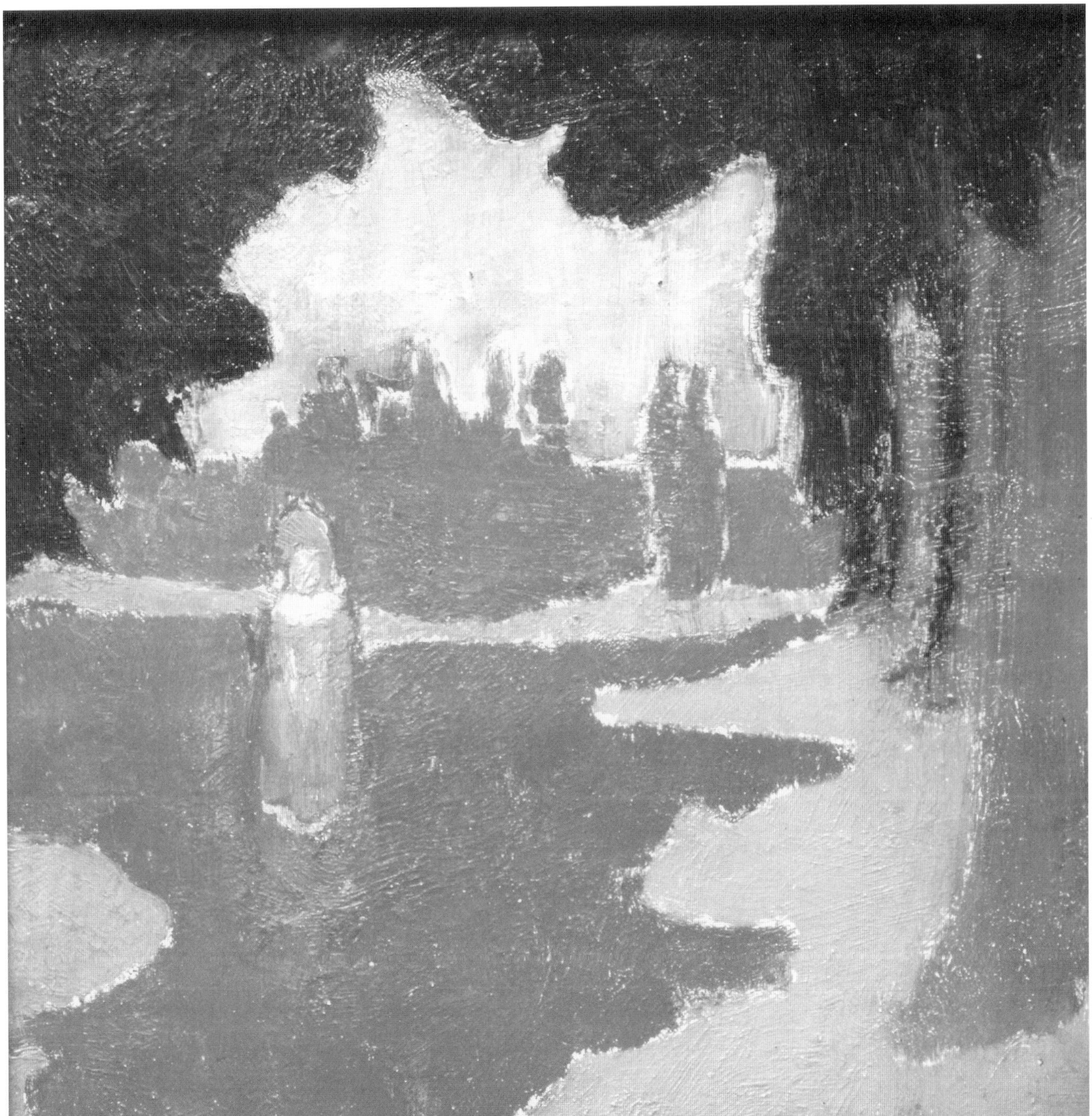

30. Maurice Denis, *Taches de soleil sur la terrace (Splashes of Sunlight on the Terrace)*, 1890. Musée d'Orsay, Paris. Photo Credit: Réunion des Musées Nationaux/Art Resource, NY. © 2006 Artists Rights Society (ARS), New York/ADAGP, Paris.

and I arrived, in effect, at more or less significant schemas.[44]

This passage is a brief but relatively full statement of generalization-theory: reality is "overcharged," and occupies the eyes rather than the mind or spirit; proper "significance" is derived from the spectacle by means of "synthesis," and the "vision of generality" offered by the work is proportionate to its simplification of mimetic form. The Symbolist takes such simplification to the point of making "schemas."

Bernard's direct connection between the Symbolist/classical process of synthesis and the highly simplified "schemas" of Symbolist art completes the linkage that this chapter is pursuing between the radical style of the modernist movement and the traditional goal and means of empirical classicism. Before we can examine the cogency of this linkage, however, we must make a further digression into theoretical matters, centering on the meaning of the term "abstraction" in Symbolist art theory. As we saw above, Bernard cited two distinct processes for arriving at his schemas, which I now cite in full:

> The first consisted in placing myself in front of nature and in rigorously simplifying it. The result was sometimes very grand. The basis of my system was to reduce nature's lines to eloquent contrasts, and her nuances to the seven fundamental colors of the prism. I wrote: "See the style and not the object. Draw out the abstract sense, and not the objective."
>
> The second way to arrive at this result consisted in relying on conception and memory and in disengaging myself from all direct contact [with nature]. With this way, I manifested myself more; and it was really myself that I was depicting, while in front of nature it was the invisible significance hidden under the mute form of exteriority.[45]

This first way is the most obviously empirical way: to "tirer le sens" out of nature, which is the "abstract" rather than the merely "objective," it is necessary to confront the motif and "la simplifier jusqu'à la rigueur." Bernard's second process, by contrast, rejects direct contact with nature in favor of working from *souvenir* and *conception*. Significantly, by 1919 Bernard had rejected this second method as achieving only a personal, rather than an ontological significance: working from memory, Bernard "manifested himself more," whereas working directly from nature, he achieved "the invisible significance hidden under the mute form of exteriority." However, working from memory was originally intended to achieve the same goal. Cheetham has described the Symbolist notions of abstraction and of memory in terms of Neoplatonic philosophy: abstraction as a thoroughgoing rejection of sensory data and memory as a collection of innate Ideas that the artist seeks to "unforget." As an aspect of Symbolist rhetoric—the subject of Cheetham's chapter—this is undoubtedly true. There is another way of conceiving of the operation of memory, though: rather than the Elysian field of Platonic Ideas, the memory can be seen as the factory and warehouse of empirical "general ideas."

The operation of the memory had been an uneasy partner to generalization-theory since at least Reynolds. In British empirical epistemology, the memory is nothing but "decaying sense," as Hobbes put it: the gradual atrophy of originally distinct and detailed sensory impressions.[46] Although in one place Reynolds advised his students not to depend on their memories because the "impressions . . . which are there deposited . . . are for ever wearing out," the same "wearing" or "decaying" effects of the memory make it a potential tool of abstraction and generalization.[47] In the eleventh Discourse, reiterating his constant point that "The detail of particulars . . . is worse than useless, it is mischievous," Reynolds noted that "the impression which is left on our mind, even of things which are familiar to us, is seldom more than their general effect. . . . [Capturing the details] presupposed *nicety* and *research*, which are only the business of the curious and attentive, and therefore does not speak to the general sense of the whole species; in which common, and, as I may so call it, mother tongue, every thing grand and comprehensive must be uttered."[48] Although he later rejected the notion of working from memory, the conclusion could coherently be drawn that the decaying effect of the memory naturally helps to generalize ideas. In the memory, aspects of an object that are not repeated dissipate, and those that are repeated become reinforced—the same process of comparison and elimination of contingent variables that helps to form the "general sense of the whole species" as opposed to the appearance of one of its individual members in a single context. Bernard's argument that the memory aids in abstracting details in favor of the general ideal may not be a transcendent or Neoplatonic process, then, but a sort of shortcut to empirical generalization.

In Van Gogh's letters of 1888–89, the debate over whether to synthesize directly from the motif or instead to rely on memory is related to the question of painting "abstractions," here describing works that have recognizable subject matter, but which were made without direct study of the motif. Both Bernard and Gauguin had suggested that Van Gogh should try to paint such abstractions, but Van Gogh was dissatisfied with the results, and apparently his brother Theo discouraged the practice. Van Gogh wrote in a letter to Theo of November 1889:

> I certainly agree with you that it is perhaps better to attack things with simplicity than to seek after abstractions. . . . Lately I have seen the women picking and gathering the olives, but as I had no chance of getting a model, I have done nothing with it. However, now is not the moment to ask me to admire our friend Gauguin's composition, and our friend Bernard has probably never seen an olive tree. Now he is avoiding getting the least idea of the possible, or of the reality of things, and *that is not the way to synthesize* [emphasis added].[49]

This letter confirms Bernard's assertion that the Symbolists of the late 1880s had "two ways" of achieving synthesis: Van Gogh contrasts the process of "attack[ing] things with simplicity" (Bernard's first way) with "seek[ing] after abstractions" in the memory (Bernard's second way). Van Gogh rejected the latter method, and indeed gently attempted to dissuade Bernard from practicing abstraction as well. In an earlier letter to Bernard, Van Gogh had written:

> to tell the honest truth, my attention is so fixed on what is possible and really exists that I hardly have the desire or the courage to strive for the ideal as it might result from my abstract studies. . . . I find it all ready in nature, only it must be disentangled.

Softening the blow to Bernard's ego, Van Gogh allows that

> others may have more lucidity than I do in the matter of abstract studies, and it is certainly possible that you are one of their number, Gauguin too . . . and perhaps I myself when I am old. But in the meantime I am getting well acquainted with nature.[50]

The implication is that painting from memory should be practiced only by older artists, because only after an extensive acquaintance with nature can memory-ideas have significance—the reverse would be true in most Platonic interpretations of the memory.[51] Ironically, Bernard was twenty at the time of this letter, and Van Gogh was still too young to rely on his memory at thirty-five.

As we saw, Bernard also eventually rejected memory-abstractions as of limited ontological significance, as revealing "himself" rather than "the invisible significance hidden under the mute form of exteriority." He clearly identified the memory with normative mental operations, at least in his later years, as is evident in his interpretation of "that phrase of Saint Denys l'Aréopagite, the Platonist: '*The idea is the form of things outside of things*.'" In the context of Platonism, of course, the word "idea" carries an ontological, and not merely a psychological significance. But while the context here is explicitly Platonic, Bernard's answer to the question of "how to represent things *en idée*" is thoroughly empirical:

> The answer seemed to me to be simple. Since the idea is the form of things taken in by the imagination, it was necessary to paint no longer in front of the thing, but in consultation with the imagination that took it in, *which conserved its idea* [Bernard's italics]. Thus the idea of the thing would take a form proper to the subject of the tableau, or rather, proper to its ideal (sum of ideas).[52]

While this exegesis of Saint Denys seems at first to be a sleight-of-hand (substituting idea for Idea), it is in fact an empirical translation of the Platonist's ideas, a substitution of the general idea for the Platonic Idea. The parenthetical phrase makes a crucial distinction, for in the memory or imagination are not only the important "general ideas," but also trivial ideas and mere fantasies. In 1894 Bernard distinguished between two notions of the imagination, the faculty that "sees" and combines the sensory impressions left in the memory. On one hand, there is the "vulgar" notion of imagination that would represent "in a considerable disorder, all sorts of bizarre and deformed things." On the other hand, there is a "less well-known" imagination, which performs "a work of logical transposition. . . . Here is not a strange conglomeration, but a nature seen, completely remade, completely transformed and fully alive with the life of order and of the will."[53] It is the latter ideas that are worthy of artistic creation: not individual ideas of particular nature or of Horatian fantasy,[54] but the "ideal" as the (synthesized) "sum of ideas." For Bernard, the memory performs a sort of automatic synthesis of empirical reality:

> Simplification or synthesis is inherent to ideas, since ideas keep only the essential of the perceived things, and, by consequence, reject from them the details. The memory does not retain everything, but only what strikes the spirit. Thus forms and colors became simple, of an equal unity. In painting from memory, I had the advantage of abolishing the useless complication of forms and of tones. Only a schema of the perceived spectacle remained . . . the color-types of the prismatic palette . . . the typical forms of all the objective forms. This was the form my symbolism took in 1888.[55]

The opposition of the Symbolist style to that of Impressionism is clear: ideas synthesized in the memory do not retain all of the subtleties of hue and tone that were discriminated by the eyes of a Monet or a Renoir, but are unified in the simplicity of elemental form and color. Although indirect, and although Bernard would later reject memory-abstraction for direct methods, the goal is still the ideal, the process is still normative and empirical (not transcendent), the dominant move is still synthesis, the elimination of the "useless complication" of the "details" to find the distilled "essence" of the "ideal," and the ideal is explicitly conceived as the "typical form" as opposed to the "objective form." For Bernard, then, both direct and indirect synthesis were empirical and classical epistemological processes, and directly resulted in the "schematic" ideal of late-eighties Symbolism.

Classicism, Primitivism, and the Schema

While both Bernard and Denis used the notion of epistemological synthesis and stylistic simplicity to define their earlier Symbolism as a form of classicism, it would be willfully myopic to assert that they did not change their styles as they changed their allegiances from Symbolism to classicism. Bernard's *Buckwheat Harvest* of 1888 (see figure 29), which the artist cited as evidence that his own practice of synthetism predated and indeed inspired Gauguin's more famous *Vision after the Sermon*, seems to have relatively little in common with his *After the Bath* of around 1908. The latter, a vaguely Arcadian scene in which idealized female nudes lounge in somewhat contrived Academic poses, is more obviously classically inspired. By contrast, the earlier work is distinctly unclassical both in style, with its bright, flat color areas and highly schematic rendering, and in subject matter, which is the annual Breton harvest. Primitivism rather than classicism seems to have inspired both the rural subject and the radically schematic style.

Frances Connelly has characterized the Western concept of the "primitive" in the period between 1725 and 1907 as "the inverse of classicism." In contrast to the austere and ordered rationality exemplified by Western classicism, the primitive was defined by its "unreason," and especially by its tendency toward the mere "physicality" of ornament and the purely imaginative "disorder" of the grotesque.[56] Although this broad framework does articulate one facet of the heterogeneous Western notion of the primitive, for many theorists the primitive was not categorically opposed to the classical. In his *Lectures on Fine Art*, Hegel characterized the primitive or "Symbolic" period of art as an early manifestation of the same aim as classicism, to grasp the Idea. More significantly for our purposes, in his *Essai sur l'idéal*, Quatremère de Quincy explicitly identified the primitive as the source not only of the ontological aspirations of the classical but also of the abstract simplicity of its form.

As we saw, throughout his essay on the ideal, Quatremère was above all concerned with combating the notion of art as primarily mimetic, as aspiring only to a faithful reproduction of nature. In contrast to the narrowly mimetic "style de portrait" or "style de modèle," Quatremère advocated an abstractive or generalizing system. In what was perhaps his most original and startling contribution to generalization-theory, Quatremère examined the evolution of the practice of generalization in Greek art where it was first manifested. Like Egyptian art, early Greek art was primarily an art of *signes* rather than *images*: that is, rather than attempt to "imitate" objects through a close mimesis, the primitive art of the Egyptians and the Greeks at first only "indicated" objects through a "représentation informe ou syncopée."[57] In Egypt, this mode of representation became their alphabet, and thus devolved into a purely arbitrary and conventional system, but in Greece, primitive signs "did not create letters, but instead recalled [*retracèrent*] ideas, and thus they became the most generalized expression of objects or subjects, the ideas or memories of which they were intended to communicate. Faithful to their original usage, they retained throughout the course of the subsequent development of art the purpose of perpetuating for the eyes and for the mind a more or less abstract system of execution."[58] The exact same terms are used by Quatremère to describe "primitive" Greek art as are used to describe classical idealization: the primitive *signes* are "ideal" in the "définition originelle" of the term,[59] because they "retracèrent des idées" (rather than imitating reality); their syncopated form is "l'expression la plus généralisée" of the objects they serve to indicate; and while Greek art undergoes considerable evolution away from this early mode, it remains faithful to its origin—that is, rather than devolving into a mimetic *style de portrait*, Greek classicism maintains its original character as "un système d'exécution plus ou moins abstrait." For Quatremère, primitive Greek art is not the inverse of the classical, nor indeed a radically different mode from the classical, either in goal or in style: the *signes* were an early form of classicism, "un système incomplet d'idées abstraites et d'images générales."

In fact, for Quatremère it was the derivation of Greek classicism from primitive *signes* that allowed it to maintain its ideality, generalization, and abstraction in the face of a growing tendency toward a pernicious naturalism. Although Quatremère valorizes the evolution of Greek art toward increasing mimetic fidelity in opposition to the "incomplete" nature of the primitive *signes*, mimesis always tends dangerously toward the *style de portrait*. The High Classical period of Greek art around the time of Phidias is described as the perfect balance between the abstract generality and ideality of primitive *signes* and the newer system of mimetic *images* that grounds those signs in empirical reality and makes them suitable for universal communication rather than conventional communication, as in the Egyptian hieroglyphic alphabet. In a few, remarkable pages, Quatremère draws a parallel between the historical development of Greek art and the creation of an individual work of art. The same is true of the ontogenesis of an individual painting as of the phylogenesis of Greek art: the artist's *croquis* or *esquisse* is equated to the "rough sketches [*ébauches*] of the first centuries of art" as "a truth in embryo, which could only embrace that which is the least particular or detailed in the form of things."[60] The artist begins with a rough "plan" of the work, which renders only "the most general form of the large parts of the figure, considered in its ensemble, before entering into its details. Thus, for example, the treatment of an arm or of a leg will appear, in this first layout, only as nearly straight and parallel lines. If the artist wished to indicate a head according to this method, it would begin in the form of an egg."[61] The artist's first *plan* or *croquis*, Quatremère says, is equivalent to the "style of Egyptian hieroglyphics" and "the style of the infant state of art in Greece." It is also "the most *ideal* imitative style, inasmuch as it gives the most abstract, the most generalized, and the least detailed idea of the object [Quatremère's italics]."[62] Explicitly, then, the primitive schema, with its parallel lines for limbs and egg for a head, is the most ideal, the most abstract, and the most general.

While the schema is subsequently modified by approaching it toward the mimetic *image*, and while this process helps to correct the intuitive *signes* in light of further study of empirical reality, mimesis contributes *nothing whatsoever* to further the ideality of the representation. In fact, it always threatens to detract from that ideality. In the next phase of production, the artist "will round the contours a bit; will fix the broad proportions and designate the articulations and attachments of the principal muscles." This moment corresponds to "the style of the second manner of Greek art," and is "the second degree of abstractive imitation," in which "the influence of the so-called *imitative truth* of nature plays but a little part."[63] Although typically Western art theory valorizes its own productions over primitive productions precisely in measure as they approach imitative fidelity, Quatremère decries even the very slight influence of *mimesis* here: it is a "prétendue vérité imitative." The third moment, both of individual artistic production and of Greek cultural evolution, sees the artist gradually fixing "the subordinate parts and forms, such as are revealed by anatomical study," and again Quatremère quickly insists that this increase of detail is permissible only insofar as it is subordinated to the "formes générales" established at the work's foundation. This period is "the medium of the two extremes," that of the "hieroglyphic manner" and that of what Quatremère again derides as "so-called true imitation, which we are calling the individual or portraitic style."[64] The fourth period is the High Classical period in Greece, and is the point at which the individual artist should stop his or her gradual approach to mimetic detail: although the artist continues to embrace "more and more minute details," these details must be "subordinated to one another" and should not extend to "fortuitous or individual accidents, such as wrinkles or other such variables of the skin, the softness and plumpness of the flesh," and so forth.[65] Art after Phidias continues this increasing bent for accidental nuance, as a result of which it marches right away from the ideal toward a detailed naturalism that Quatremère dismisses as "individual or particular," and which is also the decadence of modern art.[66] Throughout this unfolding history of Greek art, then, the entire portion of ideality, abstraction, and generality in the work, even that exhibited by the High Classical Greek art of the time of Phidias, is due to nothing other than the guiding influence of the primitive *signe*. It is the primitive, with its egg-shaped heads and its tube-like limbs that represents the truly ideal, the truly abstract, and the truly general.

Although I would not assert the direct influence of Quatremère's ideas on the Symbolists, they do provide a coherent theoretical matrix that explains the otherwise puzzling parallels that Denis and Bernard draw between classicism and the radically "schematic" and "primitive" Symbolist productions of around 1890. By now we should be prepared for the counterintuitive form that the ideal takes in this theory. Throughout this study I have emphasized the potential of generalization-theory to produce some surprising formal results; results that appear to be well outside of the tradition of classical art as it is traditionally (and rather narrowly) conceived, but which were logical conclusions to the idealizing process as it was framed in generalization-theory. Whether produced by direct synthesis in front of the motif, or indirectly by means of the distilling effects of the memory, Symbolist "schemas" can be cited as extreme generalizations.

Indeed, the schema is perhaps the most successful instance we have yet seen of a "general idea" taking visual form. The problem for classicism as I am exploring it is to find a visual equivalent of general nouns such as "man": nouns that embrace a broad class of objects or entities without specifying any of the individual members of that class. Verbal language succeeds admirably in this regard, but only because its signs are arbitrary and conventional. As such, linguistic signs are neither derived from empirical reality, nor are they intuitively or universally understood. Although the word "men" on a bathroom door nominally allows access to all males, no matter what their race, age, nationality, or physical build, it does so only by virtue of an arbitrary convention. By contrast, a schema or stick figure of a man (figure 31) *embodies* the general idea of "man" or "men" (though not necessarily of "men's restroom") in a way that is directly derived from empirical reality and is universally comprehensible.

Recall Berkeley's objection to Locke's notion of visual general ideas. In 1710, Berkeley asked how it was possible to abstract, from multiple individual men, a coherent image of man-in-general:

> wherein it is true, there is included colour, because there is no man but has some colour, but then it can be neither white, nor black, nor any particular colour; because there is no one particular colour wherein all men partake. So likewise there is included stature, but then it is neither tall stature nor low stature, nor yet middle stature, but something abstracted from all of these.[67]

How can the general idea simultaneously represent *no* particular quality—no particular color, no particular height—and yet be referentially adequate to or "bundle" *all* particular qualities? This is the reductio ad absurdum of generalization-theory. The bathroom door schema easily resolves this objection: its white color is obviously an abstraction or *lack* of any color specification (black would, and often does, serve as well in this regard); and the lack of any markers of scale within the frame of the image also serves to embrace *any* stature. The simplification of the structure of the body into an upright torso with two supportive lower limbs, two available upper limbs, and a head is perhaps the most abstract possible indication of the human form that is easily distinguishable from all other animal forms, including chimpanzees or gorillas, whose proportions and postures would be significantly different.[68] And of course the absence of clothing abstracts the schema from

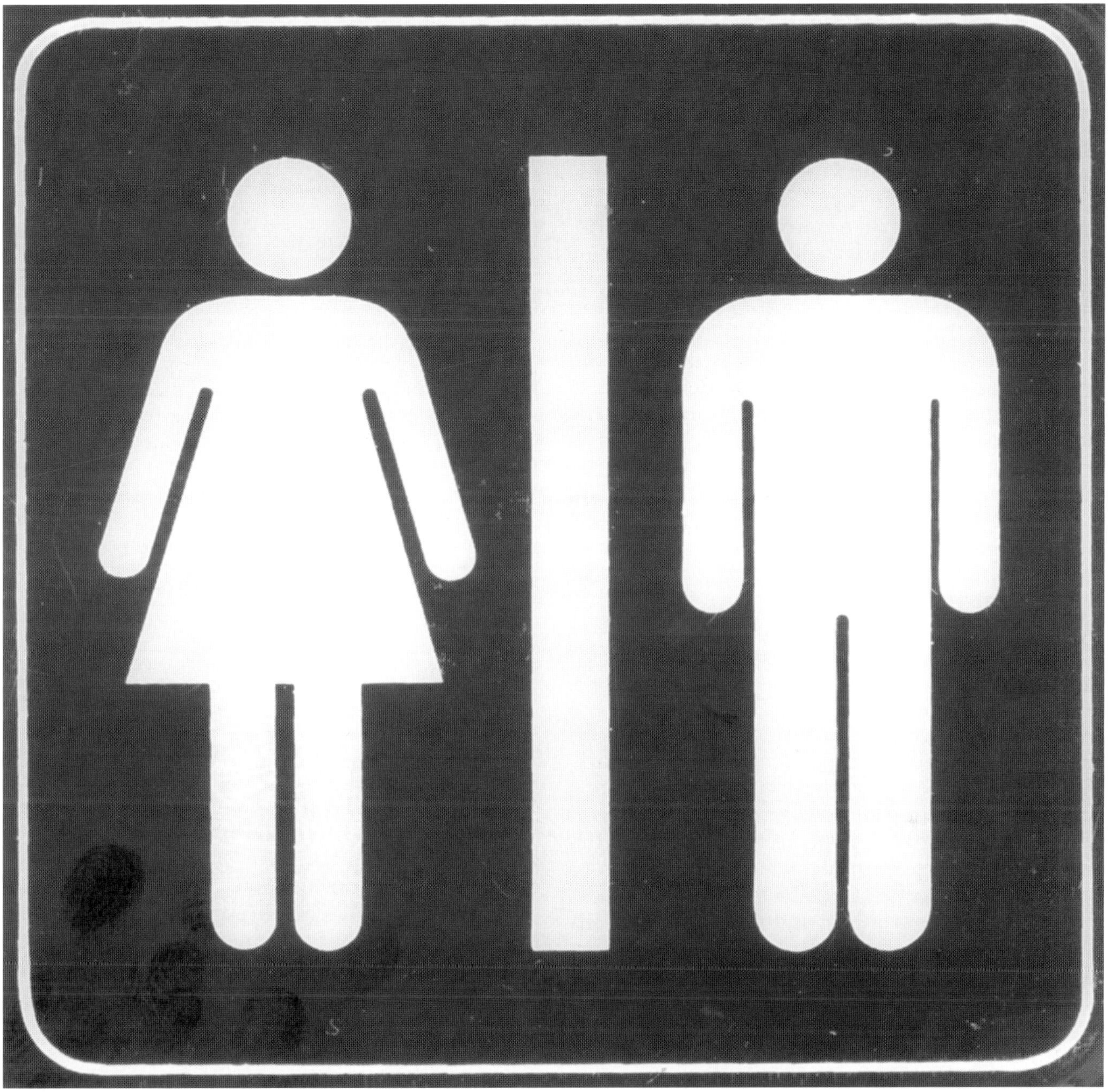

31. Restroom door sign, 2005.

any fashion or time period: it would be as adequate to an eighteenth-century English bathroom door, a late nineteenth-century French bathroom door or a fifth-century B.C.E. Greek bathroom door as it is to a twenty-first-century American bathroom door.

A number of further qualifications and questions could continue to probe this connection between the schema and the general idea. The schema for the women's restroom is somewhat less successful as a universal representation, as its inclusion of a dress is a fashion-specific, and largely outmoded, distinction between the sexes. However, in some signage the spread-legged stance of the man versus the straight-legged (or even, occasionally, tapering monopedal) stance of the woman serves to indicate a generic difference in the hip structure of the sexes (if, that is, it is not an implicitly sexist contrast between assertive authority and diffident modesty). In signage featuring children, such as school crossing or "children at play" signs, the schema for child is identical to that for the adult with the exception of the head, which is proportionately larger, as indeed children's heads are. In any case, a crucial difference is remarkable between this type of iconic signage, which is the more-or-less successful result of an abstractive, empirical generalization, and the arbitrary linguistic signage "men" or even the metonymic, but only slightly less arbitrary pictorial sign ♂ (originally a shield and spear). If we have a mental picture corresponding to the general idea "man," then, bathroom door signage and Symbolist art may be close to the form it takes. Berkeley's objection to the notion of pictorial general ideas ultimately turns on an illogical and surely philosophically unauthorized presumption that the mental image of a general idea must be empirically *plausible*; that is, that such an image could walk out of the mind (or the painting) into the real world without raising any eyebrows.

Interestingly, just as in Quatremère we can find a theoretical justification of the Symbolists' radically schematic practice within the context of the classical tradition, we may have a direct formal anticipation of that practice in the obviously classicizing work of John Flaxman. For the most part, Flaxman's illustrations to Dante's *Divine Comedy* (1793) are in a relatively traditional neoclassical style. The distinct, continuous contours of the figures are generally similar to the Greek vase painting that Flaxman clearly studied, and can thus with little difficulty be called both "classical" (that is, generalization achieved through line) and "neoclassical" (that is, they are recognizably similar to Ancient productions). However, perhaps the most startling illustration in the series (figure 32), Dante's culminating vision of God Himself, cannot by any stretch be called neoclassical. Robert Rosenblum has remarked on the "astonishing simplicity" of the image, which "leaps across the nineteenth century into the language of modern abstraction."[69] However, with a properly late-eighteenth-century understanding of abstraction, the work can be spared its decontextualizing leap. In illustrating this passage of Dante's poem, Flaxman confronted the eighteenth century's "character versus the ideal" problem head on: how can the artist represent the "universal shape"?

> In its profundity I saw—ingathered
> and bound by love into one single volume—
> what, in the universe, seems separate, scattered:
> substances, accidents, and dispositions
> as if conjoined—in such a way that what
> I tell is only rudimentary.
> I think I saw the universal shape
> Which that knot takes.[70]

In his third Discourse, as we saw, Reynolds noted that

> though the most perfect forms of each of the general divisions of the human figure are ideal, and superior to any individual form of that class; yet the highest perfection of the human figure is not to be found in any one of them. It is not in the Hercules, nor in the Gladiator, nor in the Apollo; but in that form which is taken from them all, and which partakes equally of the activity of the Gladiator, of the delicacy of the Apollo, and of the muscular strength of the Hercules. For perfect beauty in any species must combine all the characters which are beautiful in that species.[71]

As Reynolds, Barry, and Hegel all noted, Greek polytheism never had to address this problem, and thus Flaxman could find no prior solutions within Ancient production; nor could he find a solution in prior Christian production, with its almost universal illustration of God in the specific character of white-bearded male wisdom. The solution that he fixed upon here is the logical conclusion of the British Academic practice of abstraction and an anticipation of the Symbolists' practice of a hundred years later: all particular or distinguishing features of age, race, gender, action, hairstyle, build, time, and place are completely eliminated, as a result of which nothing remains but a schema.

Symbolism and Classicism

Although Denis and Bernard argued a continuity between their Symbolist and classical "phases" on the basis of shared ontological aspirations (the quest for the ideal), shared epistemological processes (synthesis or generalization), and even shared technique (simplification), and although I believe that their argument is cogent, three caveats must be kept in mind. First, that argument is largely retrospective: although contemporaneous letters

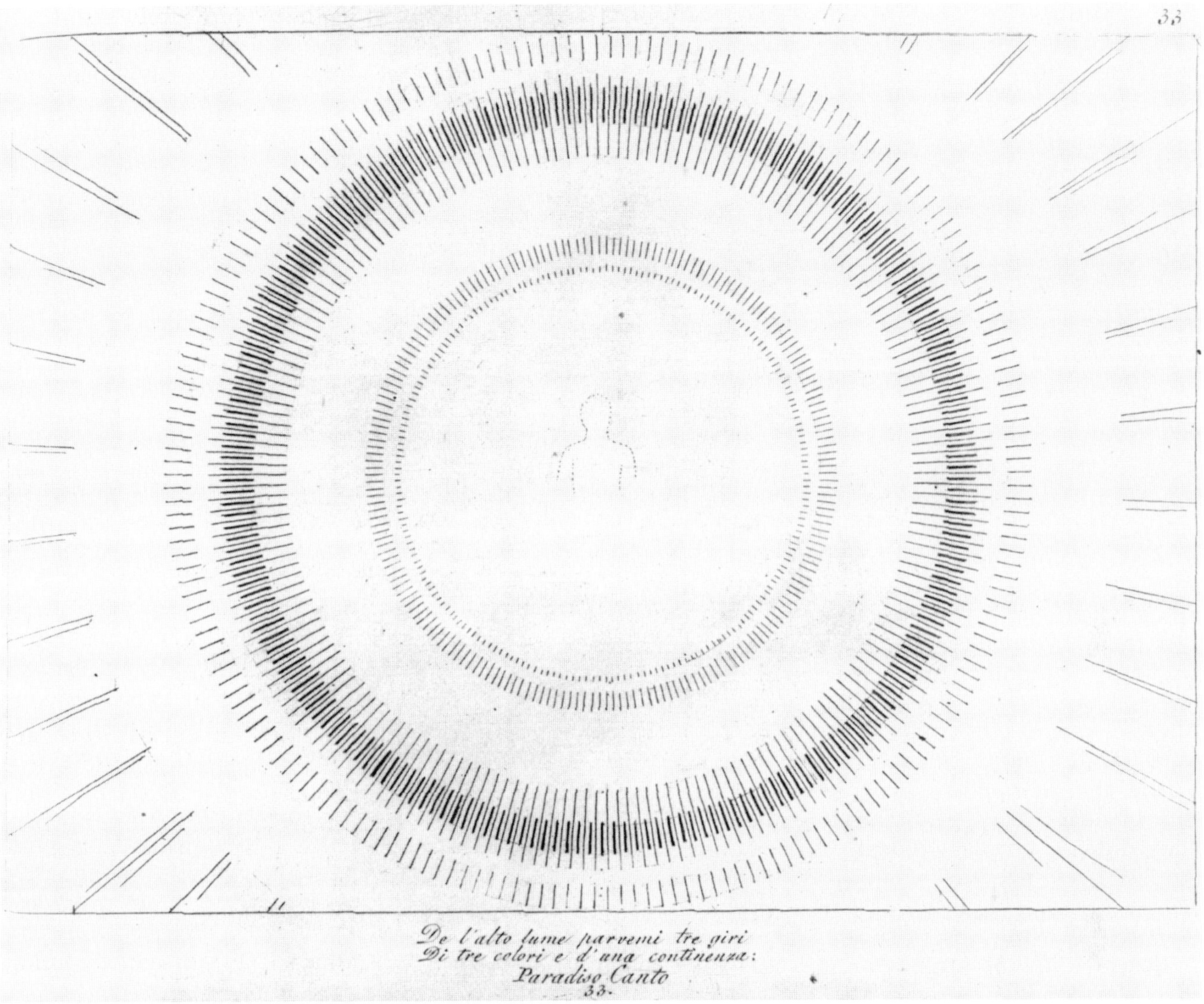

32. John Flaxman (engraved by Thomas Piroli), Illustration from *Paradiso* Canto 33, in Thomas Piroli, *La Divina Comedia di Dante Alighieri* (Amsterdam: In Possesso di Tomasso Hope, 1793). Yale Center for British Art, Paul Mellon Collection.

hint at it, the clearest explanations of synthetism as generalization are enunciated only some ten years after the schematic practice that Denis and Bernard claimed resulted from that process.[72] Second, once they clearly defined synthesis as generalization, both Denis and Bernard practiced a less extreme, and indeed occasionally quite traditional form of classicism. And third, generalization-theory is only one strand in the heterogeneous aggregate of Symbolist theory; only one way in which the radical simplicity of certain Symbolist works was justified, either contemporaneously or in retrospect. For all of these reasons it would be tendentious to assert unequivocally that generalization-theory was the *sole* cause of Symbolist schemas, although I hope to have demonstrated that Denis and Bernard were correct: generalization was part of the Symbolist discourse from very early on, and it could be seen as a *sufficient* cause.

It is also important to note that Denis and Bernard both argued that Symbolism was not quite classicism, although the way in which they formulated the relation between Symbolism and classicism confirms the main contention of this chapter: Symbolist schemas were an *extreme* classicism, a too-radical generalization of things. In his 1909 article "De Gauguin et de Van Gogh au classicisme," Maurice Denis confessed that

> under the pretext of synthesis, we frequently satisfied ourselves, let us acknowledge it, with hasty generalizations; [and] in becoming schematic our art remained fragmentary, incomplete. We made too many sketches and too few tableaux. We did not know how to finish, then; even in ancient works, we preferred the sketch to the completed work.[73]

For Denis as for Quatremère, the schema is an "incomplete" manifestation of the classical ideal. Looking back, Denis felt that although the Symbolists had correctly identified the classical process as one of abstraction and synthesis, they had embraced that process too enthusiastically and concluded that the ideal resided in the schema, the *esquisse* and the *ébauche* rather than in the finished *tableau*. In his increasing alarm at the directions taken by modern art and society, Denis's main distinction between Symbolism and classicism denounces the former as an over-radical "généralisation hâtive" versus the more moderate "digestion lente" that should characterize true classicism. While the Symbolists synthesized, then, they did so only intuitively and too radically, and they did not properly classify their sensations, preferring to produce a hundred "fragmentary" works rather than two or three "crystallized" works that would distill the sensations of all.

Because it was a more or less intuitive and ill-understood leap toward the farthest extreme of the classical, Denis identifies another problem: Symbolism quickly reduced the quest for the ideal to a mere stylistic convention. In a 1907 essay on Cézanne, Denis attempted to distinguish between a pseudo-synthetic style and a truly motivated synthesis:

> To synthesize is not necessarily to simplify in the sense of suppressing certain parts of the object: it is to simplify in the sense of *making intelligible*. It is, in brief, to hierarchize: to submit each work to a single rhythm, to a dominant [idea]; it is to sacrifice, subordinate—to generalize. It is not sufficient to *stylize* an object, as they say at the school of Grasset—to make a simple copy of the object and then to emphasize the exterior contour with a thick line. Simplification thus obtained is not synthesis.[74]

Here Denis describes a mechanical way of obtaining a recognizably "synthetist" formal appearance—copy the object, and then exaggerate the contour with a broad, continuous outline—but this mode of simplification is not true synthesis because it completely elides the laborious epistemological aspect of synthetism, the slow classification, digestion, and crystallization of multiple sensations. Bernard makes the same point in a consideration of Eugène Carrière's monochromatic, smoky paintings:

> Starting with the principle that a broad and simple technique is the index of an elevated conception, and that there is no discord between the means adopted and the thought expressed, the work in which these means are but a diluted and indirect imitation of this principle will appear as eminently routine and deformed. This is the case of Eugène Carrière. In truth, the breadth of his brushwork is only scholastic; it is a facture without significance. Indeed, the patent to his brushwork is held by the Ecole des Beaux-Arts.[75]

A "technique large et simple" is "l'indice d'une conception élevée"—this is one of the main connections that I am exploring in this study. As both proponents and opponents of generalization-theory had long remarked, there is the risk that once this connection has been made, it could become a mere conventional sign, rather than a motivated index of generalization. Opie had similarly warned his students of nearly a hundred years earlier against their mistaken notion that they "approached the heroic and poetical in proportion as they . . . became muddy, tame, and monotonous in the effect."[76]

In essays written between 1904 and 1906, Bernard used the motivation problem to distinguish between Symbolism and classicism despite their shared goals and means. The "error" of his "first forays into symbolist expression," Bernard says,

> was to represent nothing but an abstraction, by peeling away the aspects of nature with a technical, immutable, and more or less mechanical system. I would even cut them off from life; they were not magnified, amplified or aggrandized, but mummified, immobilized in a methodological and simplistic stratification.

We have elsewhere seen this system valorized by Bernard; and indeed here he is not rejecting abstraction or synthesis per se, but rather its "mechanical" application. His motive for questioning the process he was otherwise eager to claim as his own is made clear as he turns to Gauguin:

> Gauguin continued this practice without adding anything to it. In a word, Gauguin, blind follower of this process, replaced sensitivity with routine, suppressed the emotion and mutilated his works with dryness and deformation. . . . Definitively, then, Gauguin preserved only the exterior, decorative maneuver of symbolism, without pouring into it anything of the spirit. He did not proceed by conception; he was actuated only by a formulaic system.[77]

Like Denis, Bernard regrets the immediate conventionalization of the synthetic technique, its mobilization by pseudo-idealists who never had any notion of the epistemological process that should motivate its simplified form. The work of Gauguin

> offers the appearance of symbolism, but without any symbol; it fools the spectator by an abstract appearance, and even that appearance is not personal to him, because he borrowed it. . . . He would have been incapable of conceiving [this system], of discovering it . . . he applied it only mechanically, taking only its surface appearance, and as such his works are only the formal contradictions of an ignorant child.[78]

With this formulation, Bernard could assert that he not only *invented* the synthetic technique (intuitively), he was the first consciously to realize its significance and potential and hence was the only artist qualified to practice it in an engaged manner. This realization marks the difference between Bernard-the-impetuous-Symbolist and Bernard-the-mature-classicist—but also their identity, as he suggested in 1906. In contrast to Gauguin's stultification in an ill-understood, secondhand Symbolism, and in contrast to the intuitive leap that characterized the "hasty generalizations" of his early work, Bernard underscores his own artistic evolution toward a mature and conscious classicism. He cites a 1901 review of his work by Roger Marx in which the critic compliments this evolution:

> "Having logically chosen, in the beginning, *the most summary and immediate modes of expression, you* [Bernard] *have continued to ornament and complete yourself each year*. In isolation, and by means of reasoned study you have added to your native gifts the acquisitions that would permit and guarantee *an approach to consistent and certain truth* [Bernard's italics]."

Like Quatremère's primitive Greeks, Bernard began with an intuitive and radically "summary" mode of expression, a "schema," and has gradually worked to "complete" it. Bernard concludes:

> Where would this process lead me but to the definitive state of my art, the constant thought of my life, *the realization of Symbolism in its highest and most complete form; that is to say in its union with classicism* . . . I sought nothing less, by an increasingly "conscious" study, than the achievement of *classical symbolism*, the strict union of the truth of human spectacles with the divine majesty of Intelligence fertilized by the Ideal [Bernard's italics].[79]

7
Mondrian and the End of Classicism

It is a commonplace of art-historical scholarship to assert that Mondrian was in some way a classicist. Generally, however, this assertion is made only at the level of formal rhyming, connecting Mondrian and classicism on the basis of a common sense of compositional order, rationalism in color, and a hard-edged linear treatment of form. The tenth edition of *Gardner's Art Through the Ages*, for example, states that Mondrian's *Composition in Blue, Yellow, and Black* of 1936 "resonates with the calm external order that we saw in ideal Classical works such as Raphael's *School of Athens*, Poussin's *Burial of Phocion*, and Ingres's *Apotheosis of Homer*."[1] Michel Seuphor described the 1919–38 period of Mondrian's work as "The development of Neo-Plastic classicism," although he did not elaborate on that idea.[2] In the catalog to the 1994 Mondrian retrospective, Yve-Alain Bois described a set of eight paintings produced between 1929 and 1932 as "classical," in a section entitled "Poussin?"—again because of compositional order.[3] Although this connection between Mondrian's abstract work and the classical tradition is perhaps cogent according to a formalist understanding of both, it could merely be an example of what Erwin Panofsky called "pseudomorphosis: the emergence of a form A, morphologically analogous to, or even identical with, a form B, yet entirely unrelated to it from a genetic point of view."[4] A more coherent and pervasive connection can be found by examining the parallels between Mondrian and the classical tradition in terms of goals and processes. Like the classicists, Mondrian sought to discover and render the essence of nature; like the empirical classicists more specifically, Mondrian sought that essence through a close examination of nature on an individual level; and like the generalizers, Mondrian described the essence as that which is "common" to all nature and achieved that essence by means of a gradual elimination of the accidents of particular difference. In other words, Mondrian validated the connection that this study has repeatedly approached between "abstraction" in its empirical classical sense and "abstraction" in its formal sense.

Mondrian and Theosophy

Mondrian began his career as a landscape painter in the fairly traditional painterly naturalism of the Hague School style. A major change is visible in his work starting around 1907, when he began rather idiosyncratically to assimilate the major movements of the modernist tradition: Symbolism, Pointillism, and eventually Cubism. At the same time, Mondrian's theoretical writings begin to cite a higher ontological goal than the regional naturalism of the Hague School, that of finding the "finer regions," the "spiritual," or "universal." This goal would remain with him at least through his European period, and eventually consolidate in his signature style of black horizontal and vertical lines bounding flat areas of white and primary color.

The influence that is usually cited as catalyzing this shift in both goal and style is Mondrian's interest in theosophy, a popular occult science of the late-nineteenth and early-twentieth centuries. Indeed, within the writings of theosophists such as Madame Blavatsky scholars have discovered some statements about the spirituality of certain geometric forms such as ovals and crosses that seem to

*Unfortunately, we were unable to obtain permission to reproduce the relevant Mondrian images for this chapter. Reference is made instead to the illustrations in Marty Bax, *Complete Mondrian* (Burlington, VT: Lund Humphries, 2001).

transcribe directly into Mondrian's paintings. Robert Welsh's 1971 article "Mondrian and Theosophy" is the seminal treatment of this aspect of Mondrian's oeuvre and thought.[5] Welsh there gives what remain the standard interpretations of Mondrian's *Passion Flower*, *Devotion* and the *Evolution* triptych, the last of which (Bax p. 149) lends itself particularly well to direct theosophical interpretation. Read in the order left, right, then center, the three women represent an allegorical "evolution" from matter to spirit, or an allegorical representation of the "three spirits"—terrestrial, astral, and divine—that comprehensively inform both the human soul as microcosm and the universe as macrocosm. The geometric shapes forming aspects of the anatomy and background of the figures point first downward (symbolizing matter), then downward and upward (forming above the shoulders of the right-hand woman the theosophical emblem, a six-pointed star), then upward alone (symbolizing pure spirit).[6]

I find this interpretation convincing, and with it the notion that Mondrian fulfilled his spiritual aspirations through a more or less direct illustration of theosophical doctrine, at least for a time. However, Welsh extrapolates an equally concrete presence of such theosophical schemas and symbols in Mondrian's later art. I would argue that his interpretations become tendentious when he sees a direct illustration of the "world egg" of Hindu mythology in Mondrian's oval compositions, a Greek cross in the intersecting lines of the plus-minus compositions, and an implied such cross or the theosophical "double triangle" in the diamond compositions.[7] More recent scholarship has questioned, not the general influence of theosophy on Mondrian's goals and aspects of his art theory, but the concreteness of that influence on his practice. Carel Blotkamp, for example, cites three ways in which theosophy was used in Dutch Symbolist art around the turn of the century: 1) artists would "accentuate renderings of visible reality in ways that could be interpreted theosophically"; 2) artists would directly copy the "auras and astral bodies" as revealed to theosophical seers; or 3) artists would parallel theosophy's project of amalgamating world religions by utilizing symbols from ancient Eastern and Western spiritual traditions.[8] For Blotkamp, Mondrian's work is theosophical only in his somewhat vague first way, and the *Evolution* triptych was "exceptional in his entire oeuvre because of its unnatural character and overt symbolism."[9] In his book *Mondrian: The Art of Destruction*, Blotkamp concludes that Mondrian's Paris period shows theosophical influence "not [through] symbols, perhaps, but [through] theories on the relationship between the material and the spiritual world, and the evolution of all being."[10] Mark Cheetham and Yve-Alain Bois add that there seems to be no reason to stop at theosophy as the direct cause of Mondrian's spiritual interests or even his terminology: theosophy was itself an aggregation of multiple philosophical and occult theories of spirituality, and a symptom of a larger cultural phenomenon, which has occasionally been mistaken as the root of that phenomenon.[11] From a matter of "influence," the relation between Mondrian and theosophy becomes one of "recognition," and Mondrian's forays into direct illustration of theosophical doctrine, as in the *Evolution* triptych, can be seen as an exploration of the extent to which direct theosophical symbolism could be adequate to illustrate and help to catalyze a general spiritual evolution.

It is not my intent to evacuate all theosophical influence from Mondrian's work but rather to address a more fundamental epistemological question, similar to the debate between transcendent and empirical theories of classicism. Did Mondrian work deductively, starting from a received wisdom that spiritual art will take a certain form, or inductively, attempting to discover the form of a spiritual art for himself? In the first scenario, Mondrian's evolution toward abstraction must be seen as a gradual imposition of an a priori form onto nature, while in the second scenario the same works reveal a gradual discovery of that form based on his own a posteriori research into nature. Although both postulates are to a certain extent consistent with his practice, Mondrian frequently and explicitly rejected the mindset of transcendent mysticism in his theory, insisting that his approach to the problem of spiritual art was inductive and empirical. While he was a member of the Theosophical Society until the end of his life, whenever he refers to theosophy in his writings he carefully qualifies its relevance to his art. In his 1917–18 series of articles on "The New Plastic in Painting," for example, Mondrian refers to theosophy as follows: "In *On the Spiritual in Art* Kandinsky points out that theosophy (*in its true meaning* and not as it commonly appears) is another expression of the same spiritual movement we now see in painting [Mondrian's italics]."[12] Although the catalog *Abstraction: Towards a New Art* cites this passage as establishing "the importance of Theosophy" to Mondrian, Mondrian quadruply qualifies that importance: the reference is relegated to a footnote, attributed to Kandinsky, noted as *not* the common understanding of theosophy, and cited as "another expression" of the spiritual—not the same expression.[13]

In 1909, the Dutch critic Israël Querido wrote a series of articles on an exhibition that included Mondrian, Cornelius Spoor, and Jan Sluyters, in which he warned Mondrian about too great a reliance upon theosophical dogma. Mondrian wrote a response to the second installment of that critique, and Querido decided to publish Mondrian's letter in lieu of the continuance of his own review. Although Mondrian there admits that he is attempting to acquire an "occult knowledge" of the spiritual side of things, or the "finer regions" as he called them, he denies Querido's contention that his work is "like that of others, who do the same." Despite "much similarity," Mondrian insists, "there is a great difference":

> I do not know how I shall develop, but for the present I am continuing to work within ordinary, generally known terrain, different only because of a deep substratum, which leads those who are receptive to sense the finer regions. Therefore my work still remains totally outside the occult realm, although I try to attain occult knowledge for myself in order better to understand the nature of things.[14]

Ironically, this letter is also usually cited as reflecting the influence of theosophy on Mondrian,[15] although Mondrian asserts that his work "remains totally outside the occult realm," and although Querido's reading of it concludes, "Now that he acknowledges himself to be aware that, despite the undercurrent of a different spiritual life, as a painter he works like other non-occult or non-theosophically inclined persons, further warning is unnecessary."[16] The "great difference" between Mondrian's approach and that of "others" who are interested in a spiritual art is that where others begin with occult symbols, Mondrian begins "within ordinary, generally known terrain," that is, with empirical nature. From this basis, he attempts to discover (inductively—he "does not know how he shall develop") a "deep substratum, which leads those who are receptive to sense the finer regions." The last paragraph of this letter sums up his project of the early teens:

> For the present at least I shall restrict my work to the customary world of the senses, since that is the world in which we still live. But nevertheless art already can provide a transition to the finer regions, which I call the spiritual realm, perhaps erroneously, for I have read [that] whatever has form is not yet spiritual. But it is nonetheless the path of ascension; away from matter.[17]

An empirically based art can convey higher ontological truths: this is the starting postulate of empirical classical art.

Abstraction as a Transition to the Finer Regions

The traditional problems immediately raised by this project are three, and Mondrian recognized them all. First, how can an art based in nature ever transcend nature in ontological status? Second, how can the artist discover the objective truth of nature from within the terrain of a subjective mind? Third, how can art, with its sensuous means (colored pigments, for example), ever transcend that sensuality to convey a spiritual content? Mondrian's general solution to all three of these problems was identical to that of Reynolds some hundred and fifty years earlier: although the fully spiritual is nonmimetic and formless, there exists a *sliding scale* and not an insuperable gulf between the real, the subjective, the sensuous, and the spiritual. As his letter to Querido already insists, art, despite its empirical basis and its sensuous means, can nonetheless "provide a *transition*" to the finer regions, a "path of *ascension*; away from matter." In a sketchbook of 1912–14, Mondrian explicitly redefined the term "spiritual" to make it accept this scale:

> In speaking about the impulse in the spirit of the age towards spiritual art, one must carefully take into consideration that this word "spiritual" has a comprehensive meaning. The spiritual (i.e. the supersensory) has many degrees; thus the term "spiritual" is used both for the scale of degrees away from the physical towards the spirit, but also only for the spiritual proper. If we concern ourselves with the purely spiritual alone, we are led astray because this needs to be expressed.[18]

Although Mondrian agrees with Hegel that the fully spiritual must be "supersensory" and thus inexpressible in art, he preserves the possibility of a spiritual art as indicating an approach to the universal. For Mondrian, "all art is *more or less* direct aesthetic expression of the universal," and again he notes that "this more or less implies *degrees* [Mondrian's italics]."[19]

Mondrian asserted in his 1909 letter to Querido, "I do not know how I shall develop" along this path from the sensory world to the spiritual (cited above). Only by the time of his 1917 essay "The New Plastic in Painting" did Mondrian feel confident that he had achieved a "*direct* (aesthetic) *expression of the universal*." The parenthetical word qualifies that universality: it is still an aesthetic (sensuous) expression of the universal, not fully spiritual. But again, it is the existence of this scale of degrees from the materiality of nature and paint to the formlessness of "the spiritual proper" that allows Mondrian to practice the apparently oxymoronic "spiritual art." The above citation continues, "and it is precisely this difference of degree . . . that raises the new plastic to the purest manifestation of art."[20] In the same essay, Mondrian traces the phylogenic "impulse in the spirit of the age towards spiritual art" within his own ontogenic development along this scale of spirituality through Symbolism and Cubism: "Throughout modern painting we see a trend to the straight line and planar, primary color. Shortly before Cubism we see the broad contours emphasized as strongly as possible and the colors within them made flat and intense." This Symbolist approach to the universal had affinities with the "profound" art of Mantegna and with early Christian, ancient Eastern and Indian art, but unfortunately "the modern age soon abandoned the old way of intensifying nature and tended to proceed from the decorative." These assertions parallel Bernard's and Denis's contentions that Symbolism, intuitively right, devolved into mere formal maneuvers. Later, Mondrian continues:

> Cubism broke the closed line, the contour that delimits individual form; but because it also represents this *breaking*, it falls short of pure unity. While it achieves greater unity than the old art because its composition has strong plastic expression, Cubism loses unity due to the fragmented character of the natural appearance of things. For objects remain objects despite their fragmentation.

The new plastic painting, because it replaces fragmentation with "*the intensification of form to the straight line*," approaches the unity of the universal more closely; but Mondrian again notes that this is not a purely formal move: "In order to achieve this, Abstract-Real painting had to follow the same path as Cubism: by *abstracting natural appearance* [Mondrian's italics]."[21]

These observations suggest a certain teleology—an inevitable progression toward the straight lines and planar, primary color of Mondrian's mature style—but importantly, it is an unconscious teleology, legible only in retrospect. The process of discovering the spiritual by abstracting natural appearance must remain open-ended. The moment a certain form is identified and deployed as spiritual, it ironically becomes the opposite of the spiritual; it becomes mere sensual decoration. It is my argument that this notion of an open-ended approach to the spiritual along a sliding scale, starting from empirical reality and human subjectivity and always responsible to art's sensuous means, better accounts for the evolution of Mondrian's style from naturalism to abstraction than does the notion that he blindly accepted, but for some reason only gradually imposed, transcendent theosophical "revelations" onto natural form.

How, then, did Mondrian derive the universal and spiritual from the contingency of empirical nature, within the subjectivity of his own mind, and consistent with the concrete sensuous means of art? In his essay "The New Plastic in Painting," which was composed during the crucial period of his evolution in early- to mid-teens,[22] Mondrian describes the epistemological aspect of his process as "aesthetic vision." Aesthetic vision is for Mondrian a special way of looking at nature, a subject-object relation that starts from the conditions of ordinary subjectivity (the artist's senses and feelings) and ordinary objectivity (the contingency of "particular nature"), but nonetheless transcends them both and approaches the spiritual.

The "first degree" subject-object relation—that which is operative in everyday life—is called "ordinary vision" by Mondrian. He notes that this is the sort of vision that is incorrectly called objective and true: "There is a common, a more literal naturalistic vision that to some extent is determined by things themselves. A horse, for instance, is a horse for everyone. This objective vision is true, or rather has the appearance of truth, to the extent that it exists outside of our own human ideas."[23] Such is our intuition about the relationship between vision and reality: we presume that there is a real extramental horse that incurs our vision of that horse, and that will also incur a corresponding (and potentially identical) vision in others. But this presumed objective truth is in fact impossible to grasp, for it is true only "to the extent that it exists outside of our human ideas." As soon as we perceive the horse, of course, it is no longer objective reality but rather a subjective idea. Mondrian agrees with the German Idealists that there is strictly speaking no such thing as "objective vision," for vision is by definition subjective, a property of the subject or viewer, not of the object or view.

Mondrian's solution to this problem is similar to that of multiple occult traditions, as well as the teleological history of Hegel and others. Human subjectivity itself is evolving:

> A great *heightening* of subjectivity is taking place in man (evolution)—in other words a *growing, expanding consciousness*. Subjectivity remains subjective, but it diminishes in the measure that objectivity (the universal) grows in the individual. Subjectivity ceases to exist only when the mutationlike *leap* is made from subjectivity to objectivity, from individual existence to universal existence; but before this can happen there *must be a difference in the degree of subjectivity* [Mondrian's italics].[24]

Although Mondrian characterizes this evolution as a "heightening of subjectivity," it is in fact a growth in objectivity, an "expanding consciousness" that is again marked out as a scale of degrees. More specifically, aesthetic vision achieves the objective within the terrain of the subjective through a process that German Idealist philosophers called "disinterested contemplation." Disinterested contemplation was for Kant, Schopenhauer, and Hegel a way of resolving the paradox of "objective ideas" (where ideas are by definition subjective) by eliminating or abstracting all appetitive interest from the consideration of objects. In ordinary life, we tend immediately to relate to objects through appetite, that is in relation to our own concepts and purposes: this is an apple, it is to be eaten; this is a chair, it is to rest in. Clearly such ideas of apples and chairs are relative, and not absolute or objective, because they literally relate those objects to a subjective, human purpose. Similarly, the ordinary notion of beauty (especially sensual human beauty) requires the actual existence of the beautiful individual as capable of satisfying a sensual appetite. When we see an object (as beautiful) without having a vested interest in the actual existence of the object as capable of satisfying an appetite, then we see (the beauty of) the object "in itself," that is, objectively.

Mondrian adapts this notion of disinterested contemplation to his own notion of aesthetic vision:

> In *aesthetic vision*, man possesses the means to unite himself with the universal *abstractly*, that is *consciously*. Through all vision as disinterested contemplation (as Schopenhauer calls it), man transcends his naturalness. . . . [I]n the moment of aesthetic contemplation the individual as individual falls away. *The universal now comes to the fore* . . . [Mondrian's italics].[25]

Aesthetic vision is a way of relating to sensory experiences "abstractly" and "consciously," as opposed to the sensuous and reflexive appetitive mode of ordinary vision. Although he associates aesthetic vision with "artistic temperament," which in most modernist art theory is associated with the individual and even idiosyncratic subjectivity of the artist, Mondrian's notion of aesthetic vision as disinterested contemplation is in fact a "universal" (shared) subjectivity.[26] The abstraction of appetitive interest from the mind's grasp of the object does away with the conditions that differentiate individual responses to the object, such as judgments of pleasure or praxis. As the German Idealist philosophers insisted, "disinterested" judgments of beauty are not, like judgments of pleasure, individual and subjective; they are universal in the sense that they are the same for all viewers, and objective in the sense that they judge the object in itself, and not in relation to a subjective human appetite or purpose.

As we saw in chapter 2, the British empirical tradition also attempted to resolve the problem of the subjectivity of human ideas. Reynolds was similarly concerned that the artist's judgment should be disinterested, a matter of universal truth rather than one of mere individual taste or local custom, although he, like Hume, resolved the paradox of "objective ideas" differently. For the British empirical tradition, consultation with others will reveal what is idiosyncratic or subjective about our own taste and what is (or approaches) the universal or objective. More directly similar to the empirical classical tradition is an aspect of Mondrian's notion of aesthetic vision that does not form part of the German Idealist tradition of disinterested contemplation: for Mondrian, aesthetic vision will *transform the appearance of the object*. In the German Idealist tradition disinterested contemplation changes the viewer, not the view. The disinterested viewer sees the same object as everyone else; he or she simply relates to that object differently. For Mondrian, aesthetic vision changes the view as well as the viewer: the appearance of the object itself changes in a way that begins to reveal its underlying "universal" form.

In effect, Mondrian's "aesthetic vision" amalgamates the German Idealist notion of disinterested contemplation to the British empirical notion of abstraction (the elimination of the accidents of nature) and generalization (the discovery thereby of the essential commonalities of nature). Aesthetic vision will not only transcend the individual subjectivity of the artist in favor of universal intersubjectivity, it will also discover the universal order of objective nature: "The universal in the artist causes him to see through the individuality that surrounds him, to see order free from everything individual." The way in which Mondrian describes the problems of the low-order "individual" reality of nature and the proper method of deriving a high-order truth from this imperfect source is identical to that of generalization-theory. Empirical nature "veils" its order under capricious multiplicity, and the artist must therefore "reduce" nature to its essential unity:

> This order, however, is veiled. The natural appearance of things has evolved more or less capriciously: although reality shows a certain order in its articulation and multiplicity, this order does not often appear clearly but is obscured by the conglomeration of forms and colors.[27]

> We can *see* unity in the natural. In the natural, however, unity is manifested only in a veiled way. Although inexactly expressed in the natural, all appearance can nevertheless be reduced to this manifestation [Mondrian's italics].[28]

To indicate the conformity of this aspect of Mondrian's thought with generalization-theory, we should recall that in other theories, the truth may be categorically different from empirical appearances, and may not be derived from empirical appearances at all. Mondrian's theory and practice are a suitable subject for this study because he, like the other artists and theorists we have considered, believed that the universal order of nature can be derived from the individual disorder of its empirical appearances by means of a purification that eliminates the "accidents" in favor of an underlying "essence" that is common to all objects.

Already in his sketchbooks of 1912–14, before he had arrived at what he announced in 1917 to be the "direct (aesthetic) expression of the universal," Mondrian articulated his "scale of degrees" from the real (the individual and empirical) to the ideal (the universal and spiritual) as a gradual simplification or purification of natural appearances:

> The spiritual is expressed firstly in physical form, but also in other intermediate forms (*which we do not see*). If one conceives these intermediate forms as increasingly simple and pure, commencing with the physical visible forms of appearance, then one passes through a world of forms ascending from reality to abstraction. In this manner one approaches Spirit, or purity itself [Mondrian's italics].[29]

This passage amounts to a statement of intent, and it is a statement of empirical classical intent: "commencing with the physical visible forms of appearance," the artist can simplify and purify those forms to reveal the "intermediate forms" of spirit, which we do not see through ordinary vision, but which the artist can discern through aesthetic vision and render through style. In 1917, calling now upon Aristotle, Mondrian explicitly asserts that the abstractive function of aesthetic vision (here called "pure vision") will reveal the "original unity" of nature; the general, that which all things have in common:

> Pure vision shows us this original unity as the *enduring force* in all things, as the *universally shared force common to all things*. This *deepest universal element* was termed by Aristotle *substance—that which is*, the *thing-in-itself*, existing of itself, independent of those accidents of size, form, or qualities which constitute only the *outwardness* by which substance is manifested [Mondrian's italics].[30]

By abstracting the "accidents" the artist discovers the "substance," the "universally shared force common to all things"—the general, the ideal.

The Ideal as Structure

The order of nature that Mondrian discovered through this process differs considerably from that of the other artists we have examined hitherto: Mondrian took the abstractive classical process to the point of abstraction. This is due to two differences in the way in which Mondrian conceived the artistic project. First, he insisted that art consists in a *determination* of nature, which allowed him to resolve, at least rhetorically, the hitherto problematic notion that the process of generalization results in an approach to indeterminacy: "If [the universal] is to be expressed determinately, it is illogical to identify the new art with the vaguely plastic—as is often done."[31] It was partially this rhetorical move that allowed Mondrian to take the empirical classical process to its outermost limits—for him, abstraction in art is not the unfortunate byproduct of a reductio ad absurdum, but on the contrary the determinate expression of the universal in its most pure possible (aesthetic) form. Accordingly, where many critics used this approach to abstraction to discredit generalization-theory, Mondrian validated it as a "logical conclusion"—the logical conclusion that I have suggested was implicit in generalization-theory since the late-eighteenth century:

> [The artist] learned to represent *exactly* what is *vaguely perceptible* in nature, he *reduced and destroyed the concreteness* of appearance (by simplification), yet he did no more than carry the *concept of art to its logical conclusion*. And so our age arrived at *abstract-real* painting [Mondrian's italics].[32]

Again, Mondrian's linkage of the empirical classical notion of abstraction (as a purification that discovers essence) to the notion of abstraction in its formal sense is emphatically not new. What is new here, as he recognized, is only his validation and completion of that process.

So far, this validation is more or less rhetorical, however; a reversal of the normal application of the terms "vague" and "determinate." For Mondrian, it is *nature* that is vague and indeterminate in relation to the ideal, where for prior theorists, the generalized ideal was (or threatened to become) vague and indeterminate in relation to nature. A second difference in the way in which Mondrian conceived of the idealizing project is more fundamental, and more crucial to his conviction that the process of abstraction in its empirical classical sense will result in abstraction in the formal sense. For Mondrian, the underlying essence of nature consists, not in shared features and archetypal shapes, but rather in shared *forces* and *structural elements*. The "original unity" of nature is to be found in the "universally shared force common to all things." Mondrian thus examined objects in nature in order to discover, not commonalities of shape, as had Reynolds, for example, but rather commonalities in the structural elements that go into making shape and the forces at work in that making. An analogy may help to clarify this distinction. A rough equivalent of Mondrian's project is the physicist's discovery that all matter is made up of three basic units: the protons, electrons, and neutrons that combine to make different chemical elements such as hydrogen, carbon, oxygen, and so forth; and which in more and more compound and complex combinations make up water, sugar, protein, muscle tissue, ponies, and pigs—all natural objects. Protons, neutrons, and electrons can be described both as structural elements and as structuring forces—protons as positively charged forces, electrons as negatively charged forces, and neutrons as neutral. The elements of De Stijl—horizontal and vertical lines, the colors red, yellow, and blue, and the values black and white—are essential and universal in this sense, the basic structural and structuring units of all form; structural units that are obscured by their combinations in nature, but to which all natural and artificial objects can ultimately be "reduced."

Despite this shift in focus, the parallels between Reynolds's process and Mondrian's process are as visible on the level of technique as they are on the level of theory. For both artists, the ideal or spiritual must be derived from the individual and natural by means of a process that approaches the general (that which things have in common) by means of abstraction (an elimination of the accidents of difference). In his 1919 *Dialogue on the New Plastic*, Mondrian (B) explains the technical aspects of this process to an interested interlocutor (A):

> A. But I still don't understand why you favor the *straight line* and have come *entirely* to exclude the curved.
>
> B. The search for the expression of vastness led to the search for the *greatest* tension: the straight line; because all curvature resolves into the straight, no place remains for the curved.
>
> A. Did you come to this conclusion suddenly?
>
> B. No, very gradually. First I abstracted the capricious, then the freely curved, and finally the mathematically curved.
>
> A. So it was through this abstracting that you came to exclude all naturalistic representation and subject matter?
>
> B. That's right, *through the work itself*. The theories I just mentioned concerning these exclusions came afterward [Mondrian's italics].[33]

It is worth noting first of all that Mondrian here as elsewhere asserts that his process was inductive and empirical: he did not "come to this conclusion suddenly" as a matter of divine revelation or a priori theory, but "very gradually" and a posteriori, "through the work itself." Although here the goal is articulated as a matter of structural elements and not representational features, it results from the same process as Reynolds's. The "straight line" was discovered by "abstraction" in gradual stages from empirical objects; and this abstraction is an elimination by way of comprehension or generalization: "all curvature *resolves into* the straight."

A direct comparison between Reynolds's and Mondrian's notions of generalization will help to underscore the fundamental similarity of their processes and at the same time this shift of emphasis. Reynolds's specific discussion of the problem of generalizing a rather variable feature, the human nose, ultimately transfers that problem to a question of form, the "central form" that is articulated as a certain type of line:

> To instance in a particular part of a feature, the line that forms the ridge of the nose is beautiful when it is straight; this then is the central form, which is oftener found than either concave, convex, or any other irregular form that shall be proposed.[34]

This is virtually identical to a certain stage of Mondrian's process, as we shall see; the only major difference is a matter of emphasis: for Reynolds it is always a question of discovering commonalities in representational features (the straightness *of the nose*), where for Mondrian it becomes a question of the commonalities of abstract structural elements (the *straightness* of the nose).

It is of course a commonplace of Mondrian scholarship to illustrate his arrival at the style of De Stijl through a series of works that demonstrate a gradual "reductive" progression. My aim here is simply to elicit the linkages of this process with the classical tradition of generalization, and to note how Mondrian's change of emphasis from representational form to structural elements and forces allowed him to resolve some of the longstanding problematics of that tradition. Mondrian's works of the early teens quite literally exemplify his contemporaneous statement of intent to "simplify" the "physical visible forms of appearance" in order to "pass through a world of forms ascending from reality to abstraction" and thus to approach "Spirit, or purity itself" (cited above). Here I will especially concentrate on the moves in this trajectory relating to line. I follow Mondrian in describing the stages of that trajectory as a progression from the "capricious curve" to the "free curve" to the "mathematical curve" to the "straight line"—but really only as a suggestion of a progress that could appear so orderly and inexorable only in retrospect.

In the 1909 Stedelijk exhibition Mondrian submitted a painting of a tree, shot with red, against a background of deep blue sky (Bax p. 157). In the same exhibition was a work entitled *Molen [Mill]*, the bright, hot colors of which caused the critic Querido to interpret it as "not the mill as a beautiful mill . . . but the moment of sensation of the height of the glowing day" where

> everything, but everything, is in the service of a hymn to the sun, the resounding blaze of summer light, the whirlpools of color from summer daylight, ferocious and vehement, in the face of which, stunned and blinded, you slam your eyes shut.[35]

The *Red Tree* is susceptible to the same sort of analysis. It is worth remarking that the tree is identical to one represented in a sketch that Scuphor dates to 1909–10. Although perhaps drawn from a slightly different angle (the negative shapes between the branches are more spread out in the painting), there are rather singular configurations of branches that suggest that this was indeed a specific tree. The lean of the trunk and the extension of the major branches toward the right is the same in sketch and painting, for example, as is the rogue branch that starts just right of center and grows across this dominant lean to end on the left. This is a specific tree, then, painted in colors that suggest a specific moment of observation—now a "moment of sensation" of the cool blue evening, against which the tree and ground still retain some of their glowing warmth. Although Querido's use of the word "hymn" may hint at a deeper, more spiritual underpinning, his interpretation is basically sensual or impressionistic: the radical use of intense color, which other critics had the usual difficulties with,[36] is explicable as an attempt to simulate the sensation of a specific place at a specific time: "everything, but everything" can be explained in relation to optical "sensation."

In stark contrast to this quasi-impressionistic work is Mondrian's *Gray Tree* of 1911 (Bax p.186). A sketch, dated by Seuphor to around 1910 or 1911, again suggests that this is a specific tree. In both sketch and painting, the trunk leans to the right near the ground, and then curves toward the left in a reversed *C*. Just below the middle of both compositions a single branch reinforces that curve. Indeed, given the relatively abstract appearance of the work, it is surprising the extent to which Mondrian carefully conformed the painting to the sketch (or vice versa, or both to the same tree). In the ground just to the right of the trunk in the sketch, for example, there is a slight dip that is faithfully transcribed in the painting as a shallow *U*-shaped brushstroke punctuating the horizontality of the ground line. In this work, however, Mondrian has eliminated all color. Reynolds had noted that a monochromatic use of color was one way of achieving "ideal simplicity," a notion that I suggested was responsive to the idea that *all* color is merely an accidental feature of objects (Reynolds's other way was, of course, the restriction of color to red, yellow, and blue!). Whether or not this was also Mondrian's intent, the elimination of color does eliminate any obvious reference to a specific temporal moment such as evening or dawn, and, more importantly, it helps to concentrate attention on the *structure* rather than the surface appearance of the tree. Rather than mobilize relatively short, thin strokes to describe that surface appearance, Mondrian here uses broad, sweeping strokes. Rather than simulating the rough texture of the bark stroke-by-stroke and describing the divagations of the branches joint-by-joint, Mondrian reduces that capricious surface appearance to a notion of directional growth, rendered in sweeping strokes. Although this is still a specific tree—and Mondrian is very faithful to certain idiosyncratic details that mark its specificity—the *Gray Tree* now represents only the general pattern of growth of that tree, that which is the same at morning, noon, or night; in fall, winter, spring, or summer. Note that his technical means are at this stage virtually identical to that of Reynolds some hundred and fifty years earlier: Mondrian's "free curves" are freehand, gestural strokes whose continuous trajectories elide minute interior details (the barky surface and the variations of surface color) and the most clearly accidental vagaries of contour (slight deviations in trajectory) in favor of the tree's general structure. In Mondrian's own terms, then, the *Gray Tree* can be seen as reducing the "capricious curves" of the branches to the "free curves" that inform their general pattern of growth.

Despite its nearly abstract appearance, the *Flowering Apple Tree* of 1912 (Bax p. 187) seems to represent the exact same tree.[37] In this painting, the reversed *C* curve of the trunk is straightened in the brown (trunk) area bounded by two black lines in lower center, but is recalled just to the right of that area in a gentle curve. Certainly the line starting in the middle of the trunk (about a third of the way up the composition) and moving from a slight right diagonal into a sweeping leftward curve is the same branch as that just below center in the earlier drawing and in the *Gray Tree*. To the left of this curve is a set of overlapping, horizontal, pointed ovals made up of paired parenthetical lines that almost exactly embrace the suggested negative shapes between branches in the earlier painting. The "free curves" of the *Gray Tree* are here reduced again, to more "mathematical curves"—that is to say, the repertory of curves is much more restricted and regularized, and as such obviously represents variations on a single mathematical theme. This restricted repertory is particularly evident at the top of the composition, where the earlier, rather random pattern of overlapping subdivisions of branches reaching toward the sky is rendered as a set of repeated, scooped parabolas, differing only in relative steepness.

Two differences between Mondrian's process and that of Reynolds begin to become evident at this point. First, as I have emphasized, Mondrian is insistently working here with a *single* apple tree, rather than many. For Reynolds, in order to discover the ideal form of the apple tree in general, the artist must make a "long, laborious comparison" of multiple individual apple trees that will allow him or her to recognize and eliminate that which is merely accidental to any individual tree and retain only that which is common to all. However, this comparative and bundling process was also the root of the major problematics of generalization-theory, as we saw. What is the "type" of a given individual object? Is that particular apple tree a specific instance of the class of apple trees? Of deciduous trees? Of trees in general? Of plants? Which if any of these types is a true class, authorized by natural law or divine creation? Even more problematic, how can the artist represent a type or class-idea without individualizing the representation? While it is true that the branches of apple trees tend toward low, horizontal spread, as soon as the artist makes a low, horizontal mark, that mark is fixed as a particular instance of that type of growth, and not as the general rule.

What saves these objections and allows Mondrian conclusively to resolve the reductio ad absurdum of generalization-theory is the second difference between his and Reynolds's conceptions of the general: the shift of focus from the shape of features to the structural elements of shape that I outlined above. When Mondrian begins to distill "free curves" into "mathematical curves," he is tacitly beginning to consider, not the exact form of a specific curve, but rather a type of curvature as the essence of the object. The formula for the type of curve represented in the parabolas at the top of the *Flowering Apple Tree*, for example, would be $y = ax^2 + bx + c$ (the general formula for a parabola). Just as the "free curves" of the *Gray Tree* represent the general pattern of the tree's growth without undue attention to accidental deviations, the "mathematical curves" of the *Flowering Apple Tree* subsume those free curves to their underlying geometric basis: this particular free curve is an example of this type of geometric curve, a parabola. All free curves thus "resolve into" one or another family of geometric curves. In turn, the formula $y = ax^2 + bx + c$ is "general" in the sense that it can be used to produce any parabola, with any degree of steepness, depending on what values are selected for the variables a, b, and c.

In "The New Plastic in Painting," Mondrian describes the theoretical revelation of this shift from individual appearances to the mathematical basis of those appearances. "Through painting itself the artist became conscious that the appearance of the *universal-as-the-mathematical* is the essence of all feelings of beauty as pure *aesthetic* expression":

> Through the very culture of representation through form, we have come to see that the abstract—*like the mathematical*—is *actually* expressed in and through all things, although not determinately. In other words, the new painting achieved of its own accord a determinate plastic expression of the universal, which, although veiled and hidden, is revealed in and through the natural appearance of things [Mondrian's italics].[38]

The universal is revealed by a "determination" of the appearances of things into the mathematical forces that inform their underlying structural patterns. Because Mondrian is still working with a specific, individual tree in the *Gray Tree* and *Flowering Apple Tree*, he can cogently depict particular free curves and parabolas to represent that tree's growth. However, at the same time he is increasingly departing from the surface appearance of the specific tree and gradually emphasizing the structural elements and forces underlying that growth; first by rendering the general structure of that tree in the "free curves" of the *Gray Tree*, and then the underlying geometric basis of that structure in the "mathematical curves" of the *Flowering Apple Tree*.

As described retrospectively in the *Dialogue on the New Plastic*, the next step in Mondrian's process involved the "determination" of all curvature into straight, and ultimately horizontal and vertical, lines. This step is a further revelation based on the discovery of the mathematical basis of curvature. In any formula for a curve, such as the formula for a parabola $y = ax^2 + bx + c$, what is being expressed is fundamentally a relationship between two axes: x (the horizontal axis on a Cartesian grid) and y (the vertical axis). In other words, *any* type of regular or "mathematical" line on a planar surface can be described as a relationship between two directional forces, horizontality and verticality.[39] The formula $x = y$, for example, would describe a forty-five degree diagonal line that ascends one vertical unit for every horizontal unit. In sketches dating to around 1913 (Bax p. 555), Mondrian is seen superimposing a step-pattern of dark horizontal and vertical lines over the lighter diagonal lines of the branches of a tree, as though literally deriving the slope of their diagonal trajectory as a ratio of these elemental horizontal and vertical forces. In *The Tree 'A'* of 1913 (Bax p. 189), this move has been used to render almost all of the curved or diagonal spread of the branches of the tree.

The same two forces underlie everything that has shape—all matter that Mondrian examined, from Domburg church to piers and oceans to damaged façades. The shape of all bodies consists in *extension*, and all extension in two dimensions can be described in terms of two interacting forces on a Cartesian grid: horizontality and verticality. (A third dimension could be added with a third axis for depth, or depth could be considered another manifestation of horizontality; to my knowledge, Mondrian did not explore this question.) The horizontal and vertical lines of De Stijl, in other words, are representations of the two fundamental elements or forces underlying all extension, the shapes of all bodies.

Much the same can be said of the other elements of De Stijl. In addition to extension, all bodies have color and value. Red, yellow, and blue and black and white are the primary colors and primary values inasmuch as all of the other colors and values found in nature can be produced by mixing them, and no mixture of any other colors can in turn produce red, yellow, or blue, black or white; they are the basis and purified essence of all color and value in nature. The elements of De Stijl are thus precisely that which all things have in common: the fundamental structural elements of *all* form, the absolute and irreducible essence of everything.

De Stijl and Style

It is this shift in focus from the shapes of individual features to the structuring elements of all shape that is signaled by Mondrian's insistence that "artistic temperament, aesthetic vision . . . perceives style." For Mondrian as for the classical tradition, style is (or should be) an attribute of nature, not of the artist. Style consists not in a more or less idiosyncratic or historical way of rendering the features of nature but rather in looking through these features to the universal underpinnings of natural forms. Above we traced the way in which aesthetic vision allows the artist to rise from the subjective to the objective within his or her own mind, and from the capricious disorder of empirical nature to the essential order of its structural basis. Aesthetic vision achieves both of these objectives by seeing the style and not the object: the universal structural elements and forces rather than the individual shapes of features. For Mondrian, the problem with ordinary vision (and the traditional naturalism that results from it) is precisely its failure to shift its view from features to style. Traditional naturalistic art is based in "ordinary vision," which "does not *want* style in art, it demands a detailed reproduction. The artist, on the contrary *wants* and *searches* for style: this is his struggle."[40]

The naturalistic art that results from ordinary vision is not a thoroughgoing error, however, for style (the absolute) is manifested in nature and must be derived from nature, as Mondrian always insists. However, it is the special virtue of the artist to make that absolute more determinate than it is in nature through the transformative capability of aesthetic vision:

> Although the universal expresses itself *through* nature as the *absolute*, the absolute in nature is plastically expressed only through natural color and concealed or veiled by form. Although the universal is plastically expressed as the absolute . . . it is revealed in nature only as a *tendency* toward the absolute.[41]

The transformative capacity of aesthetic vision, then, rests specifically in its ability to see through the individuality of features to discern the underlying style, the structural elements and structuring forces of the object. The sliding scale from the individual and natural to the universal and spiritual will thus take the form of a gradual reduction of the representational shapes of objects to abstract style; a style that reveals (makes determinate) the elements and forces informing the structure of that object, and ultimately the elements and forces that are common to *all* objects.

Note that at no point do Mondrian's paintings claim to represent the *class-idea* of any given object in the sense understood by Reynolds. The *Gray Tree* and *Flowering Apple Tree* are not attempting to represent apple trees in general, but only the underlying structure of one particular apple tree. The advance of a progressive classicism occurs for Mondrian not as a gradual embrace of more and more individuals in broader and broader taxonomic classes but rather as a gradual discovery or determination of the fundamental structural elements and forces underlying every individual object. In this way Mondrian resolves the reductio ad absurdum of generalization-theory: there is no "general idea of an oak" that is sensuously determinate but at the same time nonspecific as to exact form; no moment at which the artist must compromise between the different shapes of ponies and pigs. Only two classes exist for Mondrian: the individual, where accidents of difference prevail, and the absolute, where all individuality disappears in the universal commonalities of structural elements. The sliding scale in between is merely the struggle of the artist to achieve the latter.

Furthermore, it is in this way that Mondrian resolves the paradox of "spiritual art," where the spiritual proper is by definition supersensory and art is by definition sensuous. The paradox of spiritual art becomes evident only when the sensuous means of art are contrary to its spiritual goal, but before this happens, art and nature share a common *aesthetic* (sensuous) absolute in the elements of De Stijl. The fundamental structural elements of all natural form—horizontal and vertical lines, the primary colors, and the primary values—are also the fundamental units of all artistic form: all *art* as well as all of nature meets its aesthetic absolute in the elements of De Stijl.

Mondrian and the End of Classicism

Mondrian thus took the classical project to its outermost limits, to the one, absolute unity that embraces the entire multiplicity of nature and of art. In the "Dialogue on the New Plastic," Mondrian's interlocutor remarks that, as he follows Mondrian's arguments, his project will "make everything look *alike*." Mondrian confirms, "That is a necessity rather than a hindrance, if we wish to express plastically what all things have in common rather than what sets them apart. Thus the *particular*, which diverts us from what is essential, disappears; only the universal remains."[42] The absolutely universal will by definition be one, and therefore necessarily the same. In this sense Mondrian's mature work marks the "end of classicism," the culmination of its abstracting project in its final goal: the discovery of the irreducible essence of all nature, the universal basis of all individual forms.

However, all Mondrians do not look alike, of course. What we have examined here is only one aspect of Mondrian's project: the discovery, through the empirical classical process of abstraction, of the universal structural elements of form. A second, and equally important aspect of Mondrian's project is what he did with these elements once he discovered them: he began to use them to compose his own works, works based not in the structure of natural objects, but in a quest for harmonious and balanced "equilibration" of form. Although it may appear seamless in a survey of his oeuvre, there is a major shift in his process at this point: a shift from abstraction in its empirical classical sense to abstraction in something more like its modernist sense.

As Mondrian himself noted, none of the works examined above are, strictly speaking, absolute. Although "in painting a tree I progressively abstracted the curves" and thus "you can understand that very little 'tree' remained," a tree abstracted in this sense is still fundamentally naturalistic: "Merely to express the natural with straight lines still remains *naturalistic* reproduction even though the effect is already much stronger." Therefore, Mondrian asserts, "*abstraction alone* is not enough to eliminate the naturalistic from painting. Line and color must *be composed otherwise* than in nature . . . an entirely different composition, more mathematical but not symmetrical, is needed in order to achieve pure plastic expression of equilibrated relationship [Mondrian's italics]."[43] Mondrian articulates this shift in his process from "abstraction" to "composition" at several points in his writings. In the introduction to "The New Plastic in Painting," for example, he divides his own artistic evolution into two stages, the discovery of the "universal plastic means," and the subsequent mobilization of those means in "an exact plastic of pure relationship":

> The universal plastic means were discovered in modern painting by carrying through the process of consistent abstraction of form and color: once

> these were discovered there emerged, almost of its own accord, *an exact plastic of pure relationship*—thus the essence of all emotion of plastic beauty.[44]

In the second stage, the universal plastic means—the elements of De Stijl—are released from any immediate reference to natural form and are used to create entirely new compositions, equilibrated in relationship to one another rather than demonstrating the underlying structural essence of any given object. Later in the same essay, Mondrian extrapolates this shift in his own development to the wider evolution of art in general:

> Abstract-real plastic evolved through and from naturalistic plastic: it emerged directly from an art that was still of the previous generation. The modern artist has performed the arduous task of creating a mode of expression for the future generation, after destroying that of the previous one. The artist of the future will not have to follow the path of gradual liberation from natural form and color: the way has been cleared for him; the mode of expression is ready; he has only to perfect it. *Line and color as plastic means in themselves* (i.e. free from particular meaning) are at his command so that he can express the universal determinately.
>
> Increasingly, then, the artist of the future will be able to begin from the universal, whereas the artist of today had to start from the natural (the individual). Our time is to be seen as the great turning point: from now on humanity will *no longer move from individual to universal, but from the universal to the individual through which the universal can be realized* [Mondrian's italics].[45]

The first, "abstracting" stage moves from the individuality of nature to the universality of nature's plastic means; the second, "composing" stage mobilizes these universal means to create individual instances of the equilibrated absolute. Sketches dating to around 1920 clearly show Mondrian moving lines and areas of color around on the surface of the work—without beginning in empirical observation—in order to achieve various individual manifestations of "equilibrated relationship" using the universal plastic means. Importantly, the equilibration of those elements in composition is not a matter of imposing a human concept of balance on nature, but rather of eliciting nature's own "tendency towards . . . the equilibrated" (as well as toward "the straight, the plane, the pure").[46] As was the case with the elements of De Stijl, "equilibration" is a state toward which nature always tends but never perfectly achieves. The artist only makes that tendency determinate, he or she does not impose it a priori.

Ironically, it is the works of this later stage that are said to embody both "classicism" and "abstraction" in Mondrian's body of work. If this is true, it is in very different senses of the terms from those which I have been using. The "classicism" of these later works is apparent only as yet another manifestation of the commonplace formalist understanding of classicism as inevitably linear, planar, balanced, and so forth. The "abstraction" of these later works consists in conceiving them—mistakenly—as *pure form*, as unmotivated by any of the careful basis in nature that Mondrian always emphatically reconfirmed. Mondrian's works of the teens better exemplify both classicism and abstraction in the senses used by the artists and theorists in this study: classicism as the quest for the ideal or essence of nature (no matter what form that quest takes); and abstraction as one of the means to that end, a gradual "pulling away" of the accidents of natural appearance in order to discover the underlying essence of nature.

Conclusion

THE CLASSICAL PROJECT IS NOW LARGELY DEFUNCT. The goal of classicism—to discover and render ideas of absolute truth and perfect beauty and to judge both art and nature by those truths—is anathema to those exhorted by Michel Foucault to "prefer . . . difference over uniformity, flows over unities, mobile arrangements over systems" and to "develop action, thought, and desires by proliferation, juxtaposition, and disjunction, and not by subdivision and hierarchization."[1] Barbara Maria Stafford has mobilized this Foucauldian preference across her studies of Enlightenment art and science, contrasting the "'lean' images of deprivation and want" that issued from "the external and atemporal standpoint of a Platonic-Cartesian geometrical model" of Enlightenment thought (such as classicism) to the "'fat' images of multiplicity and deviant excess" that issued from the "lively, changeable, and organic milieu" of the Epicurean and sophistic model.[2] Foucault's exhortation appears in preface to a book that he called an "introduction to the non-fascist life." The charge of fascism is also easily leveled against the classical project, especially since the adoption of its most obvious stylistic manifestation by Adolf Hitler as the model for his conception of Aryan man. In *Bodyscape*, Nicholas Mirzoeff collapses the entire "nineteenth century discourse of the ideal body in representation" into this fascist project: "The notion of the Classical body . . . was from the very outset designed to demonstrate the superiority of the Northern, white 'races' and to justify their imperial policies."[3] I should emphasize that this study of the classical tradition is intended neither as a defense of nor as a basis for furthering such a project. However, it is an attempt to better understand the history of that project.

My approach has been to examine idealization as a mental and technical *process* rather than the ideal as a formal or iconographic product. Most scholarship has more or less completely elided the notion of process from the idealizing project by assuming that the ideal was always already defined by the fixed proportions and rigidly bound linear contours of its Apollonian and Neoclassical paradigm. There is of course some support for this assumption in the primary literature. Ingres, for example, unequivocally stated that, as far as ideal beauty is concerned, "there is nothing essential to discover after Phidias and after Raphael."[4] I do not question the existence of the Apollonian-Augustan-Raphaelesque-Poussiniste-Ingriste paradigm of ideality, nor the fact that for a number of artists and theorists the ideal existed as an object to be recovered, not discovered. However, the dominance of that paradigm and the doctrine of imitation that helped to perpetuate it may well be overemphasized in the scholarship. Certainly its presence in the nineteenth century was far from secure and hegemonic: it was tenuous and under continuous assault; hence Ingres's reactionary retrenchment. In an essay on Manet, and in company with innumerable other modernist critics in the nineteenth century, Emile Zola mobilized Ingres's "defense" of idealization as a brief for the prosecution:

> Here is the popular opinion concerning art. There is an "absolute" of beauty which is regarded as something outside the artist or, to express it better, there is a perfect ideal for which every artist reaches out, and which he attains more or less successfully. From this it is assumed that there is a common denominator of beauty. This common denominator is applied to every picture produced, and according to how far the work approaches or recedes from this common denominator, the work is declared good or less good. Circumstances have elected that the Classical Greek should be regarded as the standard of beauty, so that all works of art created by mankind have ever since been judged on their greater or lesser resemblance to Greek works of art.[5]

It is surely ironic that this passage, written by a passionate critic of the tradition of ideal beauty, coincides with so much of the scholarship on that tradition that it sounds like a neutral description. It is not. There is a significant and unjustified elision between Zola's description of the classical aesthetic goal (a common denominator of ideal beauty) and his assertion that the Classical Greek standard entirely fulfills that goal. Zola intentionally conflates idealization with a dogmatic and unexamined neoclassicism in order better to extol, by contrast, Manet's originality, truth, forcefulness, and above all his assiduous attention to *métier* and to the life and nature around him. In this way, modernist critics prewrote much modern art history on the nineteenth-century idealizing project. Following Zola's logic of conflating idealization with imitation, Ernst Gombrich is forced to conclude that "the world of the 'ideal,' in which patterns 'borrowed' by the master could be conceived and could grow, has also become threadbare in this clash with reality."[6] For Rensselaer Lee as well, the idealizing tradition, practically defined by its doctrine of imitation, almost unavoidably tended toward an "uninspired traditionalism" and "an artificial and forever invariable canon of beauty."[7]

I have demonstrated that this impoverished and academicized formulation of classical imitation was a construct, not of modernist critics or modern historians, but of the classicists themselves, who used it to draw qualitative distinctions within their own practice. Bellori castigated those artists who "follow common practice in everything," producing works "that are not natural children but bastards of nature"; Diderot scorned those who copy the Antique as "servile, almost stupid imitators of their predecessors"; and Reynolds carefully distinguished between "bad copies of good painters" and "excellent imitators of the great universal truth of things."[8] Indeed, I have traced this qualitative distinction within the idealizing discourse throughout this study: it recurs in the British Royal Academy's treatments of the "motivation problem"; in Aurier's distinction between the "idéalistes" and the "idéistes"; in Denis's and Bernard's critiques of the "pseudosynthetic" practice of Gauguin, Carrière, and the school of Grasset; and in Mondrian's insistence that his was an engaged and inductive discovery of ideal form, and not a dogmatic recourse to a priori doctrine. The pitfall of academicism is a metacategory of aesthetic discourse throughout the modern period, and not one especially reserved for classicists or even Academic artists.

A broader methodological question underlies this issue and has informed the approach used in this study. Under what circumstances and according to what logic can we speak of an idealizing or classical tradition in Western art? The general consensus from Wölfflin to Stafford is that such a tradition existed primarily in the form of a recurrent style. That style is in turn both defined and recognized by a set of formal characteristics: a certain approach to composition, proportion, line, and color embodied in works such as the *Apollo Belvedere*, the *Ara Pacis Augustae*, Raphael's *School of Athens*, Poussin's *Burial of Phocion*, Ingres's *Apotheosis of Homer*, and so on. It is ironic that even the scholarship that questions the veracity of classicism's proposed atemporal and homogenous truths has thus tended to reinforce that atemporality and homogeneity. The problem with defining classicism as a recurrent style is not only that it reduces the classical tradition to a thin veneer of surface appearances but also that it has no context and no history. The description, comparison, and taxonomic grouping of works according to internal formal characteristics remains confined within the edges of the picture frame and the facets of the sculpture's block, creating a world of aesthetic affinities among objects divorced from their historical contexts. Although disciplines that deal with physical artifacts should be able to deal with the visible, tangible aspects of those artifacts, how can they do so without becoming mired in those aspects with no way out? The methodology of formal analysis and formal taxonomy takes place on an axis between the artifact and its current viewer, and not between the artifact and its context. How can we explore the extrinsic relations between the object and its historical context when our methodology is centered on the intrinsic characteristics of the object? Too often, indeed, the study of form attempts to elide the viewer as well, pretending to the status of neutral, disembodied description. These are of course the objections that recent art history has directed against formalist art history, but the widespread turn to extrinsic, contextual issues and emphasis on the arbitrary nature of the physical signifier (and by implication of interpretation) has to a large extent only reversed the problem, turning to context and interpretive aporia at the expense of ignoring the physical art object and its peculiar properties and motivations.

We can resolve this problem by examining style, not in terms of the final formal appearance of the art object or artifact, but in terms of the *process of making* that artifact. I prefer the term "artifact" in this context not only because the examination of style as process can be applied to any made object, but also because the word artifact retains the root "facere," to make, that the word art now elides, despite its own etymology. As Ernst Gombrich and Kendall Walton have noted,[9] a second meaning of style relates to the way in which something is done, "a method or custom of performing actions or functions."[10] By studying style as process, we can link the form of the artifact to the actions or functions that produced that form: most immediately, to the corporeal or mechanical actions of its maker, but from there to the mental processes and goals that motivated those actions, and then to the wider social and intellectual context that motivated those goals and that specific way of achieving them. The study of process is a study of *events*, not of static, self-contained form. Events are inherently relational, linking visible, tangible effects to their manual, mental, and social causes—and thus we can consider the relations between context and form. The mental and manual events of a human process happen at and according to the logic of a particular time and a particular place, and thus the study of process is necessarily historical, social and cultural. The form of the artifact becomes legible as the cumulative effect of a matrix of historical events that expand outward to comprehend the full context of that work.

Rather than a disembodied internal description, then, the study of style as process requires a methodology suitable for dealing with cause-and-effect, and one that can serve to divide a complex matrix of informing causes into manageable units. As a preliminary approach to this problem, we can turn to Aristotle's fourfold concept of causality. As we saw above, in Book Two of his *Physics* (194b17–195a27) Aristotle distinguished four different causes that intersect to make any given object come into being: the material cause, the efficient cause, the formal cause, and the final cause. A thorough examination of these four causal factors will constitute a contextual statement of the style of any artificial object.[11]

First, anything that is made is made out of some material or materials, and those materials have certain properties that inform the nature of the objects that can be made out of them: this is the *material* cause. Bronze has a higher tensile strength than marble, and thus Cellini's bronze statue of *Perseus* can dramatically cantilever the arm holding the Gorgon's head where Michelangelo requires a tree trunk to buttress the right leg of his marble *David*. The potentialities of different materials are an ahistorical matter of physics, but the use and invention of materials is not, and thus already important aspects of the form of the object are rooted in the natural environment and trade system of its culture, and reveal the degree to which that culture sought, recognized, and exploited the material potentials of the media available to it.

In addition to the material cause, any made object has a maker or makers who work that material. This aspect is what Aristotle called the *efficient* cause of the object, the maker and the sequential physical acts that molded the raw material into its eventual form. Even within the limitations of a given material there is a wide variety of possible manipulations. A clay bowl can be pressed into shape by hand, or it can be made by the coil method, or it can be thrown on a wheel. Any given instance of these acts is partially individual, an aspect of the personal style of the maker, and partially cultural, issuing from the technologies and customs of the maker's context. With the study of efficient cause we ground the style of the object not only in the physical acts of its maker but also, by further analysis and comparison, in the technologies of his or her culture, its system of technical training, its invention or use of methods and of tools, machines, and other prosthetic devices, its division of labor, and so forth.

In most cases, before the maker begins work on the object, he or she has an idea of what the final state of the object should be, and the choice of material and efficient causes will be motivated by that idea.[12] Aristotle called this mental plan or blueprint the *formal* cause of the object. Under the aegis of the formal cause we can study the object in terms of the extent and limitations of the imagination of its maker and of his or her culture and, with the help of additional documents, the epistemological aspects of the making process that obtained in a given context for a given type of object. The artifact enters the world of the mind and thus the history of ideas: the causes of style are not only material and technical but also mental.

As much recent art history has stressed, the artifact is also created within a nexus of economic and social relations. These facets enter the analysis of style as process through what Aristotle called the *final* cause of the object, the function or purpose (indeed, generally many purposes) for which any given object is made, and which may be semiotic, social, and economic as well as physical: to hold wine, to be transported in a ship's hold, to be used in certain rituals, to be sold on the open market, to promote the divine authority of the king, and so forth.

I should emphasize that each of these causal factors exist, not in isolation, but in complex imbrication and interpenetration with the others. The final cause or intended function will naturally help to determine the formal cause. The efficient cause is directed on one hand to realizing the formal cause, but is confined or inflected on the other hand by the material cause. A material may be chosen, not only for its physical properties, which are aspects of the material cause, but also for its signifying value, which involves an arbitrary (or rather conventional) linkage between the material and the final cause, and so forth.

In short, if we consider the form of the artifact not in isolation, but as the result of a process, then we can trace the causes of that result, the causes of style, deep within the material, technological, mental, and social life of its culture. Static, ahistorical form renders up its rich and dynamic context. In my understanding, then, the constants of the idealizing project are not the Apollonian proportions and Wölfflinian form of classical commonplace, but rather the overall goal (the final cause) of discovering and rendering the underlying truth of nature, a truth that in turn was usually postulated to exist in the form of a set of Ideas, universals, or archetypes that embodied absolute essence and perfect beauty.[13] Another constant of the idealizing project was the characterization of empirical nature by classicists from Plato to Piet Mondrian as bewilderingly diverse, misshapen, and contingent, an unlikely source from which to derive such a transcendent product. The problem for the classical artist is to visualize the ideal as a formal cause susceptible to being rendered through a judicious choice of material and of efficient actions. The classical discourse on art is thus comprised, not exclusively by a reiteration of the absolute perfection of prior models and the endless mantra of imitation, but rather by debates about how to achieve that end; in a word, by debates about classical process.

With this examination of classical process we began to see considerable divergence in what is usually taken as a homogenous and monolithic project, and significant effects of context and history entering into what is usually taken as an ahistorical project. The quest for the ideal is, at the level of formal cause, an epistemological enterprise that depends upon the model of knowledge assumed in various intellectual contexts. Imitation itself is revealed, in the looser sense privileged by the Academies, as an aspect of the artist's epistemological process: a way of acquiring, not the ideal itself, but the "principles" and "mode of study" that characterized the Ancient approach to the ideal.[14] Other processes emerge alongside imitation, most crucially a longstanding distinction between two very different models of epistemological process that I distinguished as "transcendent classicism" and "empirical classicism." Reynolds's and Blake's contentious distinctions between these two different approaches constitute only one moment in a debate that stretched across more than two millennia of Western history, from Plato to Piet Mondrian. Within each of these basic epistemological models we find further subdivision and further debate: within the transcendent model, a distinction between "inspiration" and "unforgetting," and within the empirical model, a distinction between "selection" and "generalization." Examined as a process, there is not one classicism; there are at least five (including imitation or neoclassicism). Much further work remains to be done to understand the differences between, and potentially finer distinctions within, each of these epistemological approaches. Imitation, one of the most extensively studied, is still too often conflated with mere "borrowing." I have here examined the selective process only through the lens of the abstractionists who rejected it, and thus I have provided a view of it that is both incomplete and biased. The transcendent classical processes of inspiration and unforgetting have also received short shrift in this study for the same reasons.

If both the transcendent and the empirical formulations of classical process are transhistorical, they are not therefore ahistorical. A closer consideration of classical art theory in the eighteenth century revealed the very close engagement of theorists such as Reynolds, Diderot, and Quatremère de Quincy with the specific epistemological models of their day. Much of the vocabulary of these theorists and, as I have also argued, much of the structure of their thoughts as well were pervaded by the new empirical epistemology of John Locke and his followers. That epistemology reemphasized not only the ineluctable particularity and contingency of sensory data—a commonplace of classical art theory—but also the mind's tendency to further perplex that data with its own associative deflections in a hey-go-mad cluttering of the stock of ideas, the crucial *fons et origo* of all empirical knowledge. The classical aesthetic project, which since Plato and Aristotle had been defined by its classification of ideas of nature into archetypal universals, took its specific historical cogency and urgency in the eighteenth century from its ability to subdue and control this empirical and noetic cacophony, countering associative madness with its structured, taxonomic rationality. Eighteenth-century classicism instructs not only morally, through its presentation of didactic narratives, but also epistemologically, through its presentation of class-ideas. The Lockean process of abstractive generalization that responded to those problems and achieved that end provided a new procedural model for classical idealization, one coherently grounded in the new empirical epistemology of the Enlightenment, and one explicitly replacing the long-hallowed but now denigrated processes of imitation, inspiration, and selection.

However, further examination of the peculiar logic of that epistemological process immediately revealed a fundamental paradox. Embedded within generalization-theory was the reductio ad absurdum articulated by Berkeley, Hazlitt, and Ruskin that always threatened to generalize things generically different and to annihilate the formal coherence of mimetic representation. The debates around the reductio inflected crucial aspects of the eighteenth- and early nineteenth-century discourse on philosophy, religion, and natural science as well as art: How do we visualize class-ideas? What was the nature of God's creative ideas? Does the monotheistic concept of God challenge the Moderns to surpass the polytheistic Ancients? Or does the sensuous nature of art preclude any general ideas beyond the level of "specific character"? These debates demonstrate the complex involvement of the nineteenth-century classical aesthetic discourse, not just with a dead past, but with its own intellectual milieu. They also offer a different perspective on certain aspects of late eighteenth- and early nineteenth-century aesthetic thought that I have by no means exhausted: one bifurcated not between an outmoded idealism and an emergent naturalism, but between two contemporaneous, equally matched and (at the time) equally plausible ways of thinking about morphology and the natural order of things: the one, exemplified by Reynolds, Geoffroy, and Richard Owen, giving priority to the formal causes of Creation, and the other, exemplified by Ruskin, Cuvier, and Buckland, to function or final causes. In effect, these two ontologies solicit two different modes of seeing, two different reasons for representing, neglecting, or correcting aspects of empirical nature. All of these debates become legible when we examine classicism as an historical problem on the level of the formal cause, not a foregone conclusion; and recognizing the fecundity and contentiousness of these debates helps to restore to the classical tradition some of the vitality and challenge that was undoubtedly one condition of its uncanny longevity.

An examination of style as process also has the potential to link theory and practice, the final and formal causes of style to the efficient and material causes of its execution. These two aspects of artistic creation are too often separated in the scholarship. It is unfortunate that Panofsky, who called attention to the differences between the transcendent and empirical epistemological bases of classical art theory, and David Morgan, who called attention to the Lockean abstractive process in late eighteenth-century aesthetic discourse, did not examine the practice of these ideas, and indeed did not illustrate their arguments at all. The separation of theory and practice in considerations of the ideal has tended to reconfirm that, while idealization has a rich philosophical background, its practice tended to stultify in dogmatic poverty. With the study of classicism as process, theory and practice are inextricably linked. The formal cause of classicism includes the understanding that its ideals should be able to take visible form susceptible to material realization. The abstruse theoretical problem of the reductio ad absurdum is actually a very concrete technical problem, arising even in philosophy out of the (questionable) assumption that general ideas take static and coherent visual form in the mind.

Nowhere is the potential to link the theory and practice of classicism more clearly exemplified than in the art theory of Joshua Reynolds, whose emphasis on classicism as a process led him to a close, if not seamless, interrelation of its mental, manual, and material aspects.

The epistemology of abstraction and generalization was insistently embodied, for Reynolds, in a broad, elisive brushwork that simultaneously obviates the minute, distracting particularity of adventitious detail and articulates the "central form" of the depicted object as a species rather than a particular individual. The sophistication of Reynolds's frequent considerations of the utility of brushwork in art not only belies the reflexive association of classicism with a linear treatment of form, but also lends a much needed texture to premodern considerations of the manual performance of the artist. The scholarly distinction between the "painterly" and the "linear," which describes only a certain final formal appearance in artworks, is far too blunt to cover the various modes of and rationales for painterly application. The analysis of brushwork as an aspect of the efficient cause of style will call attention to the various goals that motivate a painterly performance, which include classical generalization as well as inspired enthusiasm, Romantic expression, picturesque atmospherics, Rococo elegance, and so forth.

Reynolds's theory and practice of painterly classicism also provide the first hints that the proponents of abstraction-theory radically altered not only the epistemological means of the classical tradition; they also demonstrated a remarkable willingness to allow radical new visions of its end. Reynolds, his fellow Academicians and his critics explicitly distinguished the new, painterly route to ideal form from its commonplace (Raphaelesque-Poussiniste-Mengsian) linear paradigm. The potential of the new mental and manual process to result in "muddy," "tame," "monotonous," "slovenly," "unfinished," "insipid," "vague," and "indeterminate" form was warned against by Reynolds and John Opie, cautiously acknowledged by James Barry, embraced by Alexander Cozens, and severely castigated by William Hazlitt and William Blake, but was in all cases reconfirmed, suggesting that we need to alter our identikit of British eighteenth-century ideality accordingly.

Subsequent history corroborates the revolutionary effects of the new epistemological process on the practice of idealization, and places at least the generalizing faction of the classical tradition squarely within, and not futilely arrayed against, the theoretical engagement and innovative fecundity of the modernist tradition. We have seen the general idea take the form of an inkblot, a primitive fish, a "primitivist" schema, and finally a set of abstract structural elements. Ingres's above-cited assertion that "there is nothing essential to discover after Phidias and after Raphael" does not apply to the artists and theorists under consideration in this study. Although these very different visions of ideality are perhaps not classical in a Wölfflinian formal sense, they are emphatically classical in terms of the artists' goals and process. Hazlitt, Ruskin, and the later Denis and Bernard exemplify the uneasiness with which we face the notion that ideality may take the form of an indeterminate blob or a decorticated and eviscerated fish, or that the schema on a bathroom door may be more ideal than a Raphael. But all of these are coherent ends to a procedural logic that was widely accepted, at least for a certain time, as cogent. Indeed, the central and mediating term of that process, abstraction, embodies both the epistemological and technical means of this discourse and its end product.

I do not intend by this reconceptualization of the classical project to replace previous scholarship on the idealizing tradition, but only to extend the scholarly view of that tradition. Imitation, linearity, the Apollonian paradigm, the pitfall of academicism, the pernicious social aspects of the idealizing project: all of these are important facets of the classical tradition, but they are all well covered in the scholarly literature already. Where I redescribe or even directly contradict some of those aspects, it is not in order to replace them with "better" views, but to supplement them with more views. I am not surprised to find heterogeneity and even internal contradictions in the classical tradition; indeed, I am more surprised that that tradition should for so long have been seen as homogenous.

The spirit of this study is best articulated as an instance of what Hayden White called "discourse." In the introduction to *Tropics of History*, Hayden White notes that the root of the word discourse originates in *discurrere*, suggesting a movement "back and forth" or a "running to and fro."

> This movement, discursive practice shows us, may be as much prelogical or antilogical as it is dialectical. As antilogical, its aim would be to deconstruct a conceptualization of a given area of experience which has become hardened into a hypostasis that blocks fresh perception or denies, in the

> interests of formalization, what our will or emotions tell us ought not to be the case in a given department of life. As prelogical, its aim is to mark out an area of experience for subsequent analysis by a thought guided by logic.
>
> A discourse moves "to and fro" between received encodations of experience and the clutter of phenomena which refuses incorporation into conventionalized notions of "reality," "truth," or "possibility." It also moves "back and forth" (like a shuttle?) between alternative ways of encoding this reality, some of which may be provided by the traditions of discourse prevailing in a given domain of inquiry and others of which may be idiolects of the author, the authority of which he is seeking to establish.[15]

This notion of discursive "shuttling" describes the intent of this study and its place in the wider terrain of the scholarship. It is a sort of antilogical deconstruction (though not in Derrida's special sense) of an understanding of the classical tradition that has become "hardened into a hypostasis that blocks fresh perceptions." It is also a more or less prelogical attempt to mark out an area of study: the study of classicism, and of style in general, as process. It attempts to incorporate phenomena into the classical pantheon that do not seem possible: brushwork, blots, fish, schemas, and abstraction. And of course it is an attempt to establish the authority of a particular idiolect within the classical tradition: the idiolect of abstraction and the classical ideal. However, its authority is emphatically conceived not as transcendent, but rather as another throw of the shuttle, another weft in the loom.

Notes

Introduction

1. Joshua Reynolds, *Discourses on Art*, ed. Robert R. Wark (New Haven, CT: Yale University Press, 1997), 44.

2. Morgan cites Otto Stelzer, *Die Vorgeschichte der abstrakten Kunst: Denkmodelle und Vorbilder* (Munich: Piper, 1964); Andrew Kagan, "Representation, Abstraction, and the Absolute in Art," *Arts Magazine* 52, no. 3 (1977): 136–40; and Barbara Maria Stafford, *Body Criticism* (Cambridge, MA: MIT Press, 1991): chapter 2. Mark Cheetham's book *The Rhetoric of Purity* (Cambridge: Cambridge University Press, 1991) also examines the concept of abstraction as a certain process of idealization in modern art theory, but as we shall see, his notion of abstraction is fundamentally different from the one under consideration here.

3. See David Morgan: "The Idea of Abstraction in German Art Theories of Ornament from Kant to Kandinsky," *Journal of Aesthetics and Art Criticism* 50 (1992): 231–42; "The Concept of Abstraction in French Art Theory from the Enlightenment to Modernism," *Journal of the History of Ideas* 53 (1992): 669–85; and "The Rise and Fall of Abstraction in Eighteenth-Century Art Theory," *Eighteenth-Century Studies* 27 (1994): 449–78.

4. For example, in his essay "The Concept of Abstraction in French Art Theory from the Enlightenment to Modernism," Morgan begins with a consideration of the entirely empirical and idealist notion of abstraction held by Denis Diderot, François-Jean de Chastellux and Quatremère de Quincy, and concludes with an examination of the Neoplatonic and symbolist/expressive notion of abstraction in the art theory of Victor Cousin, Théodore Jouffroy, Paul Gauguin, and Wassily Kandinsky. Although Morgan links all of these theorists by noting that "in each phase, . . . abstraction entailed the removal of what was considered (by whatever means and for whatever reason) *inessential*," as his parenthetical statement indicates, this is a very vague link (685).

5. My approach in this sense is initially similar to that of Arthur O. Lovejoy in *The Great Chain of Being: A Study of the History of an Idea* (Cambridge, MA: Harvard University Press, 1964). There, Lovejoy identifies what amounts to a leitmotif of intellectual history from the Neoplatonists to the nineteenth century: a model of the universe as a hierarchical sequence from the lowest existents through the highest, composed of the linked ideas of "continuity," "plenitude," and "gradation." For a further examination of the methodology of this study, and in particular an examination of how I attempt here to connect the theoretical issues of intellectual history to artistic production, see the Conclusion.

6. Benjamin Jowett, trans., in *Plato: The Collected Dialogues*, ed. Edith Hamilton and Huntington Cairns (Princeton, NJ: Princeton University Press, 1994), 1161. Plato makes this point in reference to divine creation, but subsequent Neoplatonic art theorists drew the analogy to artistic creation.

7. R. Kassel, trans., in *The Complete Works of Aristotle*, ed. Jonathan Barnes, 2 vols. (Princeton: Princeton University Press, 1991), 2:2323.

8. See Heinrich Wölfflin, *Principles of Art History: The Problem of the Development of Style in Later Art*, trans. M. D. Hottinger (New York: Dover, 1950), 14–16 passim, and J. J. Winckelmann, *Reflections on the Imitation of Greek Works in Painting and Sculpture*, trans. Elfriede Heyer and Roger C. Norton (La Salle, IL: Open Court, 1987), 33ff.

9. I am not, of course, suggesting that the "naturalistic" project of representing phenomenal nature is easy or unproblematic. There is a wide literature on the problems and paradoxes of naturalism from Ernst Gombrich's *Art and Illusion*, 2nd ed. (Princeton, NJ: Princeton University Press, 1961); to Nelson Goodman's *Languages of Art* (Indianapolis: The Bobbs-Merrill Company, 1968); to Dominic Lopes's "Pictorial Realism," *Journal of Aesthetics and Art Criticism* 53 (1995): 277–85; and beyond. There is very little comparable literature on the idealizing project.

10. The scholarship on the process of idealization is considerably less vast than that on the neoclassical concept of the ideal. Besides David Morgan's and Mark Cheetham's work, cited above, the most notable examples include Erwin Panofsky, *Idea: A Concept in Art Theory*, trans. Joseph J. S. Peak (New York: Harper & Row, 1968); Anthony Blunt, *Artistic Theory in Italy, 1450–1660* (Oxford: Oxford University Press, 1982); and Rensselaer Lee, *Ut Pictura Poesis* (New York: W. W. Norton & Co., 1967). None of these latter studies examine the period from the late eighteenth century to the early twentieth, and, more significantly, none of these studies except for Cheetham's attempts to trace its theoretical findings into artistic practice.

11. G. P. Bellori, "The Idea of the Painter, Sculptor and Architect, Superior to Nature by Selection from Natural Beauties," in *Le Vite de' Pittori, Scultori e Architetti Moderni* (Rome, 1672), as translated in Panofsky, 171.

12. "Le peintre ne sauroit donc mieux faire que de tâcher à pénétrer l'excellence de ces Ouvrages, pour connoître la pureté de la Nature," in Roger de Piles, *Abrégé de la vie des peintres*, rev. ed. (Paris: J. Estienne, 1715), 26–27.

13. Winckelmann, 5.

14. See Panofsky, *Idea*, 25–32 (on Plotinus), 56–57 (on Ficino), and 95–99 (on Lomazzo). Throughout this book Panofsky makes a general division of the process of idealization into an *aprioritic* or "transcendent" mode and an *apostereoritic* or "empirical" mode.

15. See, for example, Plato, *Ion* 533c–535a.

16. See, for example, Plato, *Phaedrus* 246b–250b.

17. Cited in Panofsky, *Idea*, 12.

18. *The Poetry of Michelangelo*, trans. James M. Saslow (New Haven, CT: Yale University Press, 1991), 322. For recent studies on the notion of Michelangelo as divinely inspired and the rhetoric of transcendence in Renaissance and Mannerist art theory, see Stephen J. Campbell, "'*Fare una Cosa Morta Parer Viva*': Michelangelo, Rosso, and the (un)divinity of art," *The Art Bulletin* 84, no. 4 (2002): 596–620, and Maria Ruvoldt, "Michelangelo's Dream," *The Art Bulletin* 85, no. 1 (2003): 86–113.

19. The most thorough Ancient account of this story is Cicero, *de Inventione* 2.1.1.

20. As translated in J. J. Pollitt, ed., *The Art of Ancient Greece: Sources and Documents* (Cambridge: Cambridge University Press, 1990), 155.

21. Aristotle, *De anima* 403b1 and *Posterior Analytics* 81b 1. See Julius Weinberg, "Abstraction in the Formation of Concepts" in Philip P. Wiener, ed., *Dictionary of the History of Ideas*, 5 vols. (New York: Charles Scribner's Sons, 1973), 1:1–9.

22. Interestingly, recent studies in psychology have examined and tended to confirm a connection between averageness and attractiveness (if not ideality) of facial features. See Judith H. Langlois and Lori A. Roggman, "Attractive Faces are Only Average," *Psychological Science* 1, no. 2 (March 1990): 115–21, a report on a study that created digitized "average" faces out of 2, 4, 8, 16, and 32 randomly-selected individual faces and found that "the composite faces became more attractive as more faces were entered" (115). Gillian Rhodes and Tanya Tremewan, "Averageness, Exaggeration, and Facial Attractiveness," *Psychological Science* 7, no. 2 (March 1996): 105–110 confirmed these findings. I should emphasize, however, that this study is an essay in the history of ideas, and is in no way concerned with the accuracy of those ideas.

23. As translated in Pollitt, ed., 76–77.

24. In *Phaedrus* 250b–d, Plato suggests that the Idea of beauty is particularly available to recollection through the contemplation of earthly beauties, and in the *Symposium* 211b–212a, Plato's spokeswoman Diotima describes a gradual ascent to the "final revelation" of "universal beauty . . . starting from individual beauties" (trans. Michael Joyce, in *Plato: The Collected Dialogues*, 562–63).

25. Mathematics makes technical distinctions between terms like "mean" (the average of multiple numbers), "median" (the middle value of a range of numbers placed in ascending order), and "mode" (the most common value in multiple measurements) that will not concern us here, partly because the process of abstraction or generalization was rarely mobilized in the overtly mathematical way that Galen and Alberti suggest, and partly because in many cases it is unclear which meaning the theorists intend.

26. Alberti, *De statua*, in Alberti, *On Painting and On Sculpture*, trans. Cecil Grayson (New York: Phaidon, 1972), 123.

27. Ibid., 133–35.

Chapter 1. The Epistemology of Classicism

1. Galen, *De temperamentis* 1.9, as translated in J. J. Pollitt, ed., *The Art of Ancient Greece: Sources and Documents* (Cambridge: Cambridge University Press, 1990), 77.

2. Alberti, *On Sculpture*, in Alberti, *On Painting and On Sculpture*, trans. Cecil Grayson (London: Phaidon Press, 1972), 135.

3. Denis Diderot, *Diderot on Art II: Salon of 1767*, trans. John Goodman (New Haven: Yale University Press, 1995), 15.

4. Ibid., 13.

5. Ibid., 15.

6. Bellori, "The Idea of the Painter, Sculptor and Architect," as translated in Erwin Panofsky, *Idea: A Concept in Art Theory*, trans. Joseph J. S. Peak (New York: Harper & Row, 1968), 171; Roger de Piles, *Abrégé de la vie des peintres* (Paris: J. Estienne, 1715), 26–27.

7. Bellori, in Panofsky, 169.

8. "Il faut qu'il regarde l'Antique comme un Livre qu'on a traduit dans une autre langue, dans laquelle il suffit de bien rapporter le sens et l'esprit, sans s'attacher servilement aux paroles de l'Original" (de Piles, 26–27). De Piles was a strong advocate of imitation, and he makes this point with reference to the fact that only Ancient sculptures have survived, and the modern painter will literally have to translate them into the language of the different medium. However, de Piles's language does explicitly recognize a certain "servility" in the imitative process.

9. Joshua Reynolds, *Discourses on Art*, ed. Robert R. Wark (New Haven: Yale University Press, 1997), 203–04.

10. Ibid., 261.

11. James Barry, *Works of James Barry*, ed. Edward Fryer, 2 vols. (London: Cadell and Davies, 1809), 1:382.

12. John Opie, *Lectures on Painting*, ed. P. Hoare (London: Longman, Hurst, Rees and Orme, 1809), 29–30. Opie, like many in the eighteenth century, uses "it's" as a possessive. I have silently modernized this usage throughout this study.

13. Henry Fuseli, *Life and Writings of Henry Fuseli*, ed. John Knowles, 3 vols. (London: H. Colburn and R. Bentley, 1831), 2:59.

14. Albert Boime, *The Academy and French Painting in the Nineteenth Century* (London: Phaidon, 1971), 6–7.

15. Quatremère de Quincy, *Histoire de la vie et des ouvrages de Raphaël*, 2nd ed. (Paris: Ad. Le Clère et Cie., 1833; facsimile reprint by Elibron Classics, 2003), 77. Richard Shiff calls attention to this passage and to this looser sense of imitation in "Phototropism (Figuring the Proper)," *Studies in the History of Art* 20 (1989): 166.

16. Good examples of this approach in the study of Reynolds's works include: Edgar Wind, "'Borrowed Attitudes' in Reynolds and Hogarth," *Journal of the Warburg Institute* 2 (1938): 183–5, reprinted in Wind, *Hume and the Heroic Portrait*, ed. Jaynie Anderson (Oxford: Clarendon Press, 1986), 69–73; Ernst Gombrich, "Reynolds's Theory and Practice of Imitation: *Three Ladies Adorning a Term of Hymen*," *Burlington Magazine* 80 (February 1942), reprinted in Gombrich, *Norm and Form* (London: Phaidon, 1978), 129–134; Malcolm Warner, "The Sources and Meanings of Reynolds's *Lady Sarah Bunbury Sacrificing to the Graces*," *Art Institute of Chicago Museum Studies* 15 (1989): 7–19; and Martin Postle, *Sir Joshua Reynolds: The Subject Pictures* (Cambridge: Cambridge University Press, 1995). While all of these studies are informative, Wendy Roworth has noted the way in which the "persistent search for pictorial sources and borrowings from Old Master Paintings" in artists such as Reynolds has tended to

"obscure rather than illuminate our understanding of the pictures within a wider cultural context" ("Book Review: The Subject Pictures, The Painter in Society," *Eighteenth-Century Studies* 31 [1997], 142). Indeed, this tracing of pictorial models into distant (and occasionally very obscure) sources serves not only to displace the works from their contemporary social matrix, it is often implicitly used to denigrate the entire concept of idealized representation. Gombrich, for example, fully conflates idealization in art with the process of borrowing from prior models, remarking that "the world of the 'ideal,' in which the patterns 'borrowed' by the master could be conceived and could grow, has also become threadbare in [a] clash with reality" (Gombrich, 133).

17. Lee, 12.

18. Gustave Courbet, "Statement on Realism," in Charles Harrison, Paul Wood, and Jason Gaiger, eds., *Art in Theory 1815–1900* (Oxford: Blackwell, 1998), 372.

19. It is worth recalling, with Edgar Wind, that Reynolds's "borrowings" frequently take the form of irreverent wit rather than solemn homage (Wind, 69–73).

20. Diderot, *Salon of 1767*, 12.

21. For an examination of the general philosophical affinities of Reynolds's art theory, see Louis Bredvold, "The Tendency toward Platonism in Neo-Classical Esthetics," *English Literary History* 1 (1934): 91–119; Hoyt Trowbridge, "Platonism and Sir Joshua Reynolds," *English Studies* 21 (1939): 1–7; Walter Hipple, "General and Particular in the Discourses of Sir Joshua Reynolds: A Study in Method," *The Journal of Aesthetics and Art Criticism* 11 (1953): 231–47; David Morgan, "The Rise and Fall of Abstraction in Eighteenth-Century Art Theory," *Eighteenth-Century Studies* 27 (1994): 449–78; and Amal Asfour and Paul Williamson, "On Reynolds's Use of de Piles, Locke, and Hume in his Essays on Rubens and Gainsborough," *Journal of the Warburg and Courtauld Institutes* 60 (1997): 215–229. I follow Trowbridge, Morgan, Asfour and Williamson in emphasizing the empirical and especially Lockean epistemological basis of Reynolds's theories. Unfortunately, this issue has to date never been brought to bear on the matter of Reynolds's artistic practice, although there are clear practical consequences to Reynolds's empiricism and his concept of generalization, as we shall see.

22. Reynolds, *Discourses*, 44.

23. David Hume, "Of the Rise and Progress of the Arts and Sciences," in Hume, *Essays Moral, Political and Literary*, ed. Eugene F. Miller (Indianapolis: Liberty Classics, 1985), 114.

24. Of course, Reynolds was by no means the first. Joseph Addison's *Spectator* papers on "The Pleasures of the Imagination" (1712) are an early example, and in *Jonathan Richardson: Art Theorist of the English Enlightenment* (New Haven, CT: Yale University Press, 2000) Carol Gibson-Wood traces the Lockean underpinnings of many of Richardson's ideas.

25. Reynolds, *Discourses*, 94–95.

26. Ibid., 94.

27. Ibid., 272.

28. Ibid., 281.

29. For an exploration of Reynolds's solution to this problem, see chapter 2, "Generalization from the Customary to the Universal."

30. Reynolds, *Discourses*, 45.

31. Ibid., 43.

32. Diderot, *Salon of 1767*, 11.

33. "Pour bien saisir cette théorie très abstraite, il faut remarquer que ce que notre Platon moderne appelle ici l'idée générale, le Platon ancien l'appelait la vérité ou le premier type. Ce type, cette vérité existait, suivant lui, dans l'entendement de Dieu, et les φαντασματα, les formes, ce que notre Philosophe appelle la chose individuelle, étaient autant d'émanations de ces premiers types, de ces vérités existantes dans l'entendement de Dieu. Ainsi la vérité, le type, l'idée générale n'existe pas dans la nature; le Platon ancien vous dira qu'elle existe dans l'entendement divin, le Platon moderne, que c'est un être idéal." Denis Diderot, *Salons*, 3 vols., ed. Jean Seznec and Jean Adhémar (Oxford: Clarendon Press, 1979), 3:57. This passage is omitted from Goodman's translation.

34. "ce que ce n'est point, mais ne nous dit rien de ce que c'est." Diderot, "Recherches philosophiques sur l'origine et la nature du beau," in Diderot, *Oeuvres esthétiques* (Paris: Garnier Frères, 1965), 414; see also 392. Diderot goes on to ground ideal beauty in a purely empirical epistemology, asserting that any notions of order, proportion, relation, or harmony that may be cited as "règles essentielles du beau" must have "passé par nos sens pour arriver dans notre entendement" (416).

35. Plotinus, *The Enneads* 1.6.8, trans. Stephen MacKenna (n.p.: Larson Publications, 1992), 71. Interestingly, Plotinus suggests that if by "withdraw[ing] into yourself and look[ing]," you do not yet find beauty, you should "act as does the creator of a statue that is to be made beautiful: he cuts away here, he smoothes there, he makes this line lighter, this other purer, until a lovely face has grown upon his work" (71–72). This sounds at first like abstraction, but importantly, Plotinus still does not tell us how to know *what* to cut away or *where* to smooth. The abstraction-theory of the late eighteenth century answers this question: cut away that which is uncommon, and smooth out that which departs from the "central form" or average. For Plotinus, there is an a priori model that guides the artist's abstraction, the innate Idea; for the empirical classicist, this ideal model does not exist beforehand, but is to be *discovered* through abstraction.

36. Cicero, *de Inventione* 2.1.1, as translated in J. J. Pollitt, *The Art of Ancient Greece: Sources and Documents* (Cambridge: Cambridge University Press, 1990), 151.

37. Diderot, *Salon of 1767*, 9.

38. Ibid., 11.

39. Ibid.

40. Ibid., 10.

41. Ibid., 9.

42. Ibid., 11.

43. "Le style idéal . . . ne doit pas encore être entendu, comme étant l'imitation formelle d'une collection de parties du corps humain, répétés ou copiées servilement." A. C. Quatremère de Quincy, *Essai sur l'idéal* (Paris: Adrien Le Clère, 1837), 55–56.

44. "Certainement [Lysippe] ne . . . conseilloit pas de faire venir chez lui cette multitude, pour copier en détail, à l'un un bras, à l'autre une jambe ou un pied, à un autre un torse, etc. . . . On ne saurait donc concevoir, ni comme physiquement practicable, ni par conséquent comme théoretiquement admissible, une réunion formelle de toutes sortes de parties d'individus, pour imaginer ou pour exécuter une statue." Quatremère de Quincy, *Sur l'idéal*, 79–80.

45. "*réunion des beautés éparses* chez les individus." Quatremère de Quincy, *Sur l'idéal*, 61.
46. "un chef-d'oeuvre des discordances." Quatremère de Quincy, *Sur l'idéal*, 77.
47. "une métaphore employée par la théorie de l'art." Quatremère de Quincy, *Sur l'idéal*, 85.
48. "Ce n'est là, qu'une manière adroite, pour produire dans l'imagination du lecteur, par le souvenir des beautés principales de chacun de ces ouvrages, l'image d'un ensemble complet de beautés et de perfections. . . . Lucien, comme écrivain, devoit avoir recours à cette réunion . . . afin de faire comprendre à l'esprit, ce qu'il ne pouvoit pas montrer aux yeux." Quatremère de Quincy, *Sur l'idéal*, 76.
49. Diderot, *Salon of 1767*, 12.
50. "Sur quoi reposera le jugement de la préférence dont on parle? sur quoi se fondera le choix?" Quatremère de Quincy, *Sur l'idéal*, 65.
51. Diderot, *Salon of 1767*, 14. Quatremère de Quincy similarly reminds his readers that there is a difference between the *beau* and the *beau idéal*: "On peut s'en convaincre par la comparaison des belles têtes *idéals* de femmes, et des belles têtes de femmes, *portrait*, dans l'antique. Quelle différence entre elles!" Quatremère de Quincy, *Sur l'idéal*, 57.
52. Although as Hutcheson notes his theory of "internal senses" does not presuppose any innate ideas of beauty such as Plato posited, it does presume "natural Powers of Perception," the "final cause" of which is presumed to rest in Divine providence (Francis Hutcheson, *An Inquiry into the Original of Our Ideas of Beauty and Virtue* 1.6.10 [Indianapolis: Liberty Fund, 2004], 67, 78–81).
53. Diderot, *Salon of 1767*, 12.
54. Ibid., 14.
55. Ibid., 12–13.
56. Reynolds, *Discourses*, 44.
57. "la puissance d'idéer, ou de généraliser en abstraction." Quatremère de Quincy, *Sur l'idéal*, 31.
58. "Or, on sait que ces figures modernes dont j'ai parlé, et auxquelles on donnoit le nom d'*académiques*, procèdent du principe d'imitation, que j'appelle *particulière* ou *individuelle*, et forment visiblement le style contraire à celui de l'*idéal*. Il est par conséquent très-naturel de conclure que les figures antiques, où domine le style *idéal*, ont dû être le produit d'un principe opposé, c'est-à-dire de celui que l'on doit appeler *abstrait* ou *généralisant*." Quatremère de Quincy, *Sur l'idéal*, 42.
59. "Généraliser un sujet, c'est, dans le sens de cette théorie, ramener autant qu'il est possible l'objet imitable, ou le modèle, à la simplicité de son principe, à l'unité morale de sa nature; ce qui signifie, par contrecoup, porter l'objet imitant au plus haut point de sa valeur significative, en la dégageant de ces accessoires." Quatremère de Quincy, *Sur l'idéal*, 194.
60. See above and Quatremère de Quincy, *Sur l'idéal*, 7, 8, 12, 16, 17, 31, 42, 47, 48, passim.
61. "manière de voire particularisée et minutieuse"; "manière de voire généralisée." Quatremère de Quincy, *Sur l'idéal*, 97–98.
62. "privation;" "négligence véritablement systématique." Quatremère de Quincy, *Sur l'idéal*, 96–97.
63. "En Grèce, le corps de l'homme parut, dans son image, comme épuré, et comme purgé de toutes ces minuties accidentelles, qui appartiennent au caractère de l'individualité. C'est l'homme, en quelque sort, tel qu'on pourroit croire, que le Créateur l'avoit formé, tel que la nature de son type élémentaire veut qu'il soit." Quatremère de Quincy, *Sur l'idéal*, 53.
64. "peu de détails, de larges divisions, et surtout de la simplicité." Quatremère de Quincy, *Sur l'idéal*, 128.
65. Diderot, *Salon of 1767*, 12.
66. Reynolds, *Discourses*, 120.
67. Diderot, *Salon of 1767*, 13.
68. "Lorsqu'il s'agit des beaux-arts, cette expression [idéal] . . . désigne souvent le plus haut point de perfection. . . . La peinture ne connoît que deux genres bien distincts, le genre imitatif, & le genre *idéal*; ce qui renferme trois objets différens: imitation exacte de la nature, genre vulgaire & borné qui ne consiste proprement qu'à copier ce qu'on a sous les yeux; choix de la belle nature, ce qui demande déja du goût & de l'élévation; recherche de la beauté abstraite & *idéale*, ce qui exige plus que du talent, & qui est vraiment l'ouvrage du génie. De ces trois opérations de l'art, deux appartiennent au genre imitatif, une seulement au genre *idéal*. Nulle personne un peu initiée dans les beaux-arts qui croie avec le peuple que le choix de la belle nature suffise aux peintres ou aux statuaires pour donner naissance à un modele de beauté, tel que l'*Apollon* du Belvedere, la *Vénus* de Médicis, la *Madonna della Seggiola*, ou la *Magdelaine de Parme*. Lorsque Zeuxis rassembla les plus belles filles de Crotone pour copier les beautés particulieres & locales que chacune d'elles possédoit éminemment, il ne voulut faire que de simples études, & ce fut sans doute par le secours de l'abstraction qu'il parvint à peindre une figure parfaite." François-Jean de Chastellux, "Idéal," in Denis Diderot, ed. *Supplément à l'Encyclopédie*, 4 vols. (Amsterdam: M. M. Rey, 1777), 3:514. The *Encyclopédie* attempted to reform the use of accents in written French, eliminating the use of the *accent grave* over words such as "particuliere," for example.
69. "Consulter n'est pas toujours imiter, encore moins copier des parties séparées." Quatremère de Quincy, *Sur l'idéal*, 85.
70. "En effet, s'il donne à quelque partie du corps d'un modèle, la préférence sur la même partie d'un autre, il ne se décide à cette préférence, que par la confrontation qu'il fait de telle ou telle partie, au *type intérieur* qu'il possède." Quatremère de Quincy, *Sur l'idéal*, 67.
71. "un ensemble de connoissances acquises;" "que ses études et ses observations lui ont fait aquérir." Quatremère de Quincy, *Sur l'idéal*, 65, 67.
72. Quatremère de Quincy, *Sur l'idéal*, 15–16.
73. "C'est là le vrai type général, le véritable exemplaire, auquel peut se confronter chaque partie du modèle particulier." Quatremère de Quincy, *Sur l'idéal*, 66.
74. Lorenz Eitner, ed., *Neoclassicism and Romanticism, 1750–1850* (New York: Harper & Row, 1989), 93.
75. Instances of this type of explanation include ("animal spirits") René Descartes's *Les Passions de l'âme* (Paris: Henry Le Gras, 1649) and ("pressing") Thomas Hobbes's *Leviathan* (London: Andrew Crooke, 1651). The most thorough subsumption of aesthetic considerations to this materialist model of the mind ("nervous fibers") is that of Edmund Burke, *A Philosophical Enquiry*, 3rd ed. (London: R. and J. Dodsley, 1761), although Joseph Addison had considered the operation of Cartesian "animal spirits" in aesthetic phenomena in his essays "The Pleasures of the Imagination," *Spectator* 411–21 (21 June–3 July 1712).

76. John Locke, *An Essay Concerning Human Understanding* 2.2.1–3 (Oxford: Clarendon Press, 1990), 119–21.
77. Locke 2.11.2, 156.
78. Walter Jackson Bate, *From Classic to Romantic* (New York: Harper & Row, 1961), 96.
79. See Martin Kallich, *The Association of Ideas and Critical Theory in Eighteenth-Century England* (The Hague: Mouton, 1970). See also Kallich, "The Association of Ideas and Critical Theory: Hobbes, Locke, and Addison," *English Literary History* 12 (1945): 290–315; "The Associationist Crisis of Frances Hutcheson and David Hume," *Studies in Philology* 43 (1946): 644–67; and "The Argument against the Association of Ideas in Eighteenth-Century Aesthetics," *Modern Language Quarterly* 15 (1954): 125–36.
80. David Hume, *A Treatise of Human Nature* 1.1.4, (Oxford: Clarendon Press, 1990), 11. Hume also notes a third principle of association, cause-and-effect, which unlike resemblance and contiguity would seem to be necessary and objective, rather than contingent and subjective. However, Hume's most famous contribution to epistemology was his dismantling of the cause-and-effect association into a repeated contiguity of certain sense-impressions, effectively divorcing mental associations from any valid basis in the natural order of things.
81. "une suite d'idées fondamentales. . . . Au-dessus de chacune s'éléveroient d'autres suites d'idées qui formeroient des espèces de chaînes. . . . On peut même remarquer qu'à mesure que la chaîne s'étend, elle se soudivise en différens chaînons; ensorte que, plus on s'éloigne du premier anneau, plus les chaînons s'y multiplient. Une première idée fondamentale est liée à deux ou trois autres; chacune de celles-ci à un égal nombre, ou même à un plus grand, et ainsi de suite." Etienne Bonnot, abbé de Condillac, *Essai sur l'origine des conoissances humaines* 1.2.3.29, in Condillac, *Oeuvres philosophiques de Condillac*, ed. Georges Le Roy, 3 vols. (Paris: Presses Universitaires de France, 1947), 1:17.
82. Hobbes, *Leviathan* 1.8 (Indianapolis: Hackett, 1994), 39.
83. Locke 2.11.13, 161.
84. Locke 2.33.18, 401.
85. "Le principal avantage qui résulte de la manière dont j'ai envisagé les opérations de l'âme, c'est qu'on voit évidemment comment le bon sens, l'esprit, la raison et leurs contraires naissent également d'un même principe, qui est la liaison des idées les unes avec les autres." Condillac, *Essai* 1.2.11.107, in *Oeuvres*, 1:36).
86. "Je suppose deux hommes; l'un, chez qui les idées n'ont jamais pu se lier; l'autre, chez qui elles se lient avec tant de facilité et tant de force, qu'il n'est plus le maître de les séparer. Le premier seroit sans imagination et sans mémoire, et n'auroit, par conséquent, l'exercice d'aucune des opérations que celles-ci doivent produire. Il seroit absolument incapable de réflexion; ce seroit un imbécille. Le second auroit trop de mémoire et trop d'imagination, et cet excès produiroit presque le même effet qu'une entière privation de l'une et de l'autre. Il auroit à peine l'exercice de sa réflexion, ce seroit un fou." Condillac, *Essai* 1.2.3.34, in *Oeuvres*, 1:18.
87. Laurence Sterne, *The Life and Opinions of Tristram Shandy* 1.1 (London: Penguin Books, 1985), 35.
88. Locke 2.33.6, 396.
89. Locke 2.33.5, 395.
90. Sterne 1.4, 39.
91. Sterne 1.1, 35.
92. Sterne 1.2, 36–37.
93. Locke 2.33.8, 397.
94. Locke 2.32.6, 385–86.
95. Locke 2.11.9, 159.
96. "Si je me représente un être reel, & que je pense en meme tems à toutes les qualités qui lui sont particulieres, alors l'*idée* que je me fais de cet individu, est une *idée* singuliere; mais, si écartant toutes ces *idées* particulieres, je m'arrête seulement à quelques qualités de cet être, qui soient communes à tous ceux de la même espece, je forme par-là une *idée* universelle, générale.

"Nos premiéres [sic] *idées* sont visiblement singulieres. Je me fais d'abord une *idée* particuliere de mon pere, de ma nourrice; j'observe ensuite d'autres êtres qui ressemblent à ce pere, à cette femme, par la forme, par le langage, par d'autres qualités. Je remarque cette ressemblance, j'y donne mon attention, je la détourne des qualités par lesquelles mon pere, ma nourrice, sont distingués de ces êtres; ainsi je me forme une *idée* à laquelle tous ces êtres participent également. . . . Je me fais donc une *idée* générale, c'est-à-dire, j'écarte de plusieurs *idées* singulieres, ce qu'il y a de particulier à chacune, & je ne retiens que ce qu'il y a de commun à toutes: c'est donc à l'*abstraction* que ces sortes d'*idées* doivent leur naissance. . . .

"[I]l suit qu'en observant cette ressemblance des *idées* singulieres, on se forme des *idées* générales; qu'en retenant la ressemblance des *idées* générales, on vient à s'en former de plus générales encore; ainsi l'on construit une sorte d'échelle ou de pyramide qui monte par dégrés, depuis les individus jusqu'à l'*idée* de toutes, la plus générale, qui est celle de l'être." Denis Diderot, ed. *Encyclopédie, ou Dictionnaire Raisonné*, s. v. "Idée," 17 vols. (Neufchastel: Samuel Faulche, 1765), 8:491–92.
97. "Qui pourroit en effet imaginer & retenir des noms propres pour tous les êtres que nous connoissons? A quoi aboutiroit cette multitude de noms singuliers? Nos connoissances, il est vrai, sont fondées sur les existences particulieres, mais elles ne deviennent utiles que par des conceptions générales des choses, rangées pour cela sous certaines especes, & appellées d'un même nom." *Encyclopédie* 8:492.
98. Locke 2.11.9, 159.

Chapter 2. Classicism and Generalization

1. Joshua Reynolds, *The Works of Sir Joshua Reynolds*, ed. Edmond Malone, 2 vols. (London: T. Cadell, Jr. and W. Davis, 1797), 1:362.
2. Samuel Johnson, *Rasselas* 10, in Donald Greene, ed., *The Oxford Authors: Samuel Johnson* (Oxford: Oxford University Press, 1984), 352–53.
3. Aristotle, *Poetics* 1451a1–1451b1, trans. R. Kassel, in *The Complete Works of Aristotle*, ed. Jonathan Barnes, 2 vols. (Princeton, NJ: Princeton University Press, 1991), 2:2322–23.
4. It is worth remarking that Reynolds seems to have come to the concepts of contemporaneous empirical epistemology through a medium other than Johnson. Edmund

Burke wrote in a letter to Edmond Malone that "[Reynolds] has always told me that he owed his first disposition to generalise and to view things in the abstract to old Mr. [Zachariah] Mudge, Prebendary of Exeter" (cited in Louis I. Bredvold, "The Tendency toward Platonism in Neo-Classical Esthetics," *English Literary History* 1 [1934]: 114). The Mudges were acquaintances of Reynolds in Devonshire. He painted Zachariah c. 1761–62, his son the physician John Mudge c. 1752, and Dr. John's son c. 1758.

5. Reynolds, *Works*, 2:212–13.

6. Joshua Reynolds, *Discourses on Art*, ed. Robert R. Wark (New Haven, CT: Yale University Press, 1997), 269.

7. Reynolds, *Discourses*, 44–45.

8. Ibid., 45 passim.

9. Reynolds, Letter to *The Idler* 82 (10 November 1759), in *Works*, 1:358–59. By "oftener found," Reynolds specifies, he does not mean that the ideal occurs commonly in nature, but that whereas there are many different kinds and degrees of deformity, the influence of the "central form" is pervasive, and thus the general idea is more prevalent (though implicit) in nature than "any one kind of deformity."

10. Reynolds, *Discourses*, 50.

11. Ibid., 58.

12. Ibid., 77.

13. Ibid., 126.

14. Ibid., 157.

15. Ibid., 192.

16. Ibid., 99–100.

17. Ibid., 277.

18. Cited in James Northcote, *The Life of Sir Joshua Reynolds*, 2 vols. (London: Henry Colburn, 1819), 2:78.

19. If this note postdates 1776, Tucker's use of the example of a pin maker may have been intended to pronounce allegiance to Adam Smith's new economic theory. In the first chapter of the first book of his *Wealth of Nations* (1776) Smith uses the example of pin making to demonstrate the productive power of the division of labor.

20. Reynolds, *Discourses*, 44–45.

21. Ibid., 47.

22. Reynolds, Letter to *The Idler*, in *Works*, 1:360–61. Reynolds's suggestion that Europeans and Ethiopians constitute different "species" may strike some readers as odd, or even as resonant with "polygenecist" theories of human diversity. I should therefore clarify that although in 1749 Buffon had defined the taxonomic category of the species as a group of individuals who can interbreed and produce offspring, Reynolds is using the term in its more general philosophical sense as a class of similar objects. Ernst Mayr has noted that there is still some confusion between what he calls the "classical concept" of the species, which simply signified the idea of a class of similar objects, and the "biological species concept," heralded by Buffon but not common even in biological literature until the second half of the nineteenth century, which defined species as an interbreeding population. See Ernst Mayr, "What is a Species, and What is Not?" *Philosophy of Science* 63 (1996): 262–77. Throughout this study, theorists such as Reynolds and Opie continue to use the terms "species" and "genus" in what Mayr conveniently calls the "classical" sense.

23. Actually, Reynolds's argument here is not that *all* judgments of beauty are a matter of custom, but that judgments from "custom" or the "association of ideas" hold sway only in comparisons between *different species* or types of object; comparisons between Ethiopian and European types of beauty or between two different types of bird. The idea of beauty *within* a given type or species is not merely a matter of custom or association, but is based in the universal judgment of the "central form," as Reynolds asserts immediately after the above: "in creatures of the same species, beauty is the medium or centre of all its various forms" (Reynolds, *Works*, 1:361). The obviously crucial question of what constitutes the boundaries of a species or type will be examined in chapter 5.

24. John Barrell, *The Political Theory of Painting from Reynolds to Hazlitt* (New Haven, CT: Yale University Press, 1986), 70–72.

25. Ibid., 72.

26. David Hume, "Of the Rise and Progress of the Arts and Sciences," in *Essays Moral, Political and Literary*, ed. Eugene F. Miller (Indianapolis: Liberty Classics, 1985), 112.

27. Hume, "Of the Standard of Taste," in *Essays*, 231.

28. Reynolds, *Discourses*, 122–23.

29. "The Mind makes the particular *Ideas*, received from particular Objects, to become general; which is done by considering them . . . separate from . . . Time, Place, or any other concomitant Ideas. This is called *ABSTRACTION*," John Locke, *An Essay Concerning Human Understanding* 2.11.9 (Oxford: Clarendon Press, 1990), 159.

30. Johnson, 352–53.

31. Reynolds, *Discourses*, 132.

32. Ibid., 47–48.

33. On the relation of issues of what we would call "race" to Reynolds's theory and to late eighteenth-century aesthetics in general, see Paul Youngquist, "In the Face of Beauty: Camper, Bell, Reynolds, Blake," *Word & Image* 16 (2000): 319–34, and David Bindman, *Ape to Apollo: Aesthetics and the Idea of Race in the Eighteenth Century* (Ithaca: Cornell University Press, 2002).

34. Reynolds, *Discourses*, 137.

35. Ibid., 135.

36. Ibid., 137.

37. Ibid., 128. Accordingly, Reynolds employed professional drapery painters for much of the clothing in his own portraits. Susan Rather has analyzed the attempt to distinguish between the fine art of painting and the artisanal practice of the tailor or drapery painter in her article "Carpenter, tailor, shoemaker, artist: Copley and portrait painting around 1770," *The Art Bulletin* 79 (1997): 269–90.

38. Reynolds, *Discourses*, 138–39.

39. Ibid., 136.

40. Ibid., 139.

41. Ibid.

42. Ibid., 122.

43. Ibid., 141.

44. Ibid., 122–23.

45. Ibid., 45.

46. Ibid., 96.

47. Ibid., 222; see also *Discourses*, 279, in which the student is recommended to make a *pasticcio* of the works of Michelangelo.

48. See, for example, Edgar Wind, "'Borrowed Attitudes' in Reynolds and Hogarth," *Journal of the Warburg Institute* 2 (1938): 183–5, reprinted in Wind, *Hume and the Heroic Portrait*, ed. Jaynie Anderson (Oxford: Clarendon

Press, 1986), 69–73; Ernst Gombrich, "Reynolds's Theory and Practice of Imitation: *Three Ladies Adorning a Term of Hymen*," *Burlington Magazine* 80 (1942), reprinted in Gombrich, *Norm and Form* (London: Phaidon, 1978), 129–134; Malcolm Warner, "The Sources and Meanings of Reynolds's *Lady Sarah Bunbury Sacrificing to the Graces*," *Art Institute of Chicago Museum Studies* 15 (1989): 7–19; and Martin Postle, *Sir Joshua Reynolds: The Subject Pictures* (Cambridge: Cambridge University Press, 1995).

49. Reynolds, *Discourses*, 25–26.

50. Ibid., 204; see also above and *Discourses*, 222.

51. Ibid., 247; see also 103–04, where it is argued that Raphael became a "model for all succeeding painters" as the result of "having taken so many models" himself.

52. Ibid., 170.

53. Ibid., 171; see also 225–26, where the attainment of perfection before death indicates too low an aim.

54. Ernst Cassirer, *The Philosophy of the Enlightenment* (Princeton, NJ: Princeton University Press, 1979), 13.

55. *Oxford English Dictionary*, 1979 edition, s. v. "generalize."

56. See Iain Pears, *The Discovery of Painting* (New Haven, CT: Yale University Press, 1988), especially chapter one.

57. Ann Bermingham, *Landscape and Ideology: The English Rustic Tradition, 1740–1860* (Berkeley: University of California Press, 1986), 14–28.

58. Cited in David Solkin, "Great Pictures or Great Men? Reynolds, Male Portraiture, and the Power of Art," *Oxford Art Journal* 9, no. 2 (1986): 43.

Chapter 3. Techniques of Generalization

1. See Joshua Reynolds, *Discourses on Art*, ed. Robert R. Wark (New Haven, CT: Yale University Press, 1997), 27, 93, 158, and 266.

2. Ibid., 60 and 146.

3. Ibid., 65. Reynolds's use here of the term "sublime" is vexed. He generally uses it as a synonym or epithet for the highest form of classical art, the Grand Manner, although certainly by then the word had been clearly defined by some as meaning something radically different from the classical or beautiful—see Burke's explicit opposition of the two terms in his *Philosophical Enquiry*, 3rd ed. (London: R. and J. Dodsley, 1761), for example. However, as Robert Wark notes, Reynolds very seldom used the term sublime in the sense understood by Burke (see Reynolds, *Discourses*, 119n.), and in a note appended to the published version of the eighth Discourse, Reynolds confessed that he "did not recollect" at the time he was composing it "the admirable treaties *On the Sublime and Beautiful*" (162), suggesting that he never internalized Burke's usage.

4. Reynolds, *Discourses*, 50 and 157.

5. James Northcote, *The Life of Sir Joshua Reynolds*, 2 vols. (London: Henry Colburn, 1819), 2:58. Alberti had similarly suggested that the artist should "squint" or "close the sight with the eyelashes so that the lights are dimmed and seem painted in intersections," but only as a way to help "in evaluating the lights," and not, as Reynolds suggests, in order to abstract the "little unimportant parts" (Alberti, *On Painting*, trans. John R. Spencer [New Haven, CT: Yale University Press, 1979], 94).

6. Reynolds, *Discourses*, 194, 192.

7. Ibid., 251.

8. Nicholas Penny, ed., *Reynolds* (exh. cat., London: Royal Academy of Arts, 1986), 176.

9. Reynolds, *Discourses*, 59. The persistent belief, despite textual, pictorial, and as we shall see contemporary critical evidence to the contrary, that Reynolds advocated a polished and "linear" finish is still evident in studies such as Richard C. Sha's *The Visual and Verbal Sketch in British Romanticism* (Philadelphia: University of Pennsylvania Press, 1998), 40–51.

10. Reynolds, *Discourses*, 202.

11. Ibid., 193–94.

12. Ibid., 194.

13. Ibid., 201.

14. Ibid., 202.

15. Ibid., 199.

16. Ibid., 44.

17. Ibid., 236–37. Balthasar Denner (1685–1749) was a portraitist and miniature painter, but more than that: he served Reynolds, Ruskin, and everyone in between as an example of a "high finisher" in art and consequently a "narrow, vulgar, untaught or rather ill-taught" mind (see also chapter 5).

18. Ibid., 81 and 103. Similarly, John Opie accuses David's work of "barren coldness," Poussin's of "brick-dust" coloring, and Raphael's of "dryness" (Opie, *Lectures on Painting*, ed. P. Hoare [London: Longman, Hurst, Rees and Orme, 1809], 18).

19. West to Copley, 4 August 1766, as cited Paul Staiti, "Accounting for Copley," in Carrie Rebora and Paul Staiti, eds., *John Singleton Copley in America* (exh. cat., New York: Metropolitan Museum of Art, 1995), 39.

20. Captain R. G. Bruce to Copley, 4 August 1766, as cited in Rebora and Staiti, 215.

21. Reynolds's opinion is reported by West, letter to Copley, 20 June 1767, as cited in Rebora and Staiti, 238.

22. Capt. R. G. Bruce to Copley, 20 June 1767, as cited in Staiti, 39.

23. Reynolds, *Discourses*, 248–49.

24. Cited in John Engamells and John Edgcumbe, eds., *The Letters of Sir Joshua Reynolds* (New Haven, CT: Yale University Press, 2000), 46n2. What Reynolds meant by the "French school" is difficult to determine, since Northcote does not date Reynolds's remark and David came to prominence relatively late in Reynolds's career. Reynolds was certainly familiar with David's work, however, even writing a laudatory review of David's *Death of Socrates* for the *Courier Anglais*. See Edgar Wind, "A Lost Article on David by Reynolds," *Journal of the Warburg and Courtauld Institutes* 6 (1943): 223–24.

25. William Hazlitt, "William Hazlitt's Essays on Reynolds's *Discourses*," in Reynolds, *Discourses*, 324.

26. Ibid., 329.

27. See Mary Sheriff, *Fragonard: Art and Eroticism* (Chicago: University of Chicago Press, 1990), especially chapters 4 ("Easel Painting and the Aesthetics of Brushwork") and 5 ("Representing Genius: Fragonard's *Portraits de Fantaisie*").

28. This observation does not hold for the rendering of certain fabrics like velvets and satins, which even Copley rendered in broad, sweeping strokes, and which were in

any case largely dismissed by Reynolds, along with other ornaments, as merely fashionable or "secondary truths," not worthy of great art or a great artist; and were indeed in many cases painted by a professional drapery-painter rather than by Reynolds himself. My observations about Reynolds's brushwork of generalization in this chapter are derived mostly from his rendering of the flesh of his figures, which, as an aspect of natural anatomy and not of customary accouterments, should be susceptible to generalization.

29. Reynolds, *Discourses*, 63, 64, and 66.

30. Ibid., 195.

31. Ibid., 196.

32. Cited in Martin Kemp, *The Science of Art* (New Haven, CT: Yale University Press, 1990), 276.

33. Reynolds, *Discourses*, 61.

34. Kemp, 281.

35. Reynolds, *Discourses*, 102.

36. Ibid., 84–85.

37. Ibid., 102.

38. Ibid., 85.

39. John Hayes, ed., *Gainsborough* (exh. cat., London: Tate Gallery, 1980), 140.

40. See, for example, Ann Bermingham's reading of Gainsborough's *Mr. and Mrs. Robert Andrews* in *Landscape and Ideology* (Berkeley: University of California Press, 1986), 28–33.

41. Reynolds's analysis of Salvator Rosa marks a special case where the artist's "peculiar" marks are well attuned to his subject matter: "What is most to be admired in him, is, the perfect correspondence which he observed between the subjects which he chose and his manner of treating them. Everything is of a piece: his Rocks, Trees, Sky, even to his handling, have that same rude and wild character which animates his figures" (*Discourses*, 85). The legend of Rosa as a bandit naturalizes a certain handling to him and his correspondingly "savage and uncultivated" subject matter makes that handling naturally appropriate to his works.

42. Reynolds, *Discourses*, 202.

43. *British Royal Academy General Assembly Minutes* (1782) 1:161–64, Royal Academy Library, London.

44. Reynolds, *Discourses*, 194.

45. Opie, 17.

46. Robert R. Wark, introduction to *Discourses*, by Joshua Reynolds, xvii.

47. Ibid., xx–xxi.

48. William Blake, "William Blake's Annotations to Reynolds's *Discourses*," in Reynolds, *Discourses*, 295, 315.

49. Ibid., 310.

50. Ibid., 313.

51. Ibid., 316.

52. Ibid., 298.

53. Ibid.

54. Ibid., 296.

55. Ibid., 319.

56. Hazlitt, 321.

57. Ibid., 327.

58. Ibid., 328.

59. Ibid., 327.

Chapter 4. The Practice of Generalization

1. Joshua Reynolds, *Discourses on Art*, ed. Robert R. Wark (New Haven, CT: Yale University Press, 1997), 72.

2. The *Keppel* was "the picture that made Reynolds's name" (Nicholas Penny, ed., *Reynolds* [exh. cat., London: Royal Academy of Arts, 1986], 181); it was "the first key salvo in [Reynolds's] ultimately successful campaign" (David Solkin, "Great Pictures or Great Men? Reynolds, Male Portraiture and the Power of Art," *Oxford Art Journal* 9, no. 2 [1986]: 45); it "made his reputation" (Ellis Waterhouse, *Painting in Britain 1530 to 1790* [London: Penguin Books, 1988], 204).

3. Solkin, 46. David Mannings has more recently considered and rejected the direct or indirect derivation of the *Keppel* from Ramsay's *Macleod*, proposing instead a French bronze *Apollo* after Legros as "without question Reynolds's model," apparently on the basis of "the very distinctive motif of the downwards pointing arm," although he also notes that the French *Apollo* "is itself loosely based on the Apollo Belvedere." Mannings also reinforces the derivation of Reynolds's style in the work from "the Tintorettos he had been studying just a few months earlier" on his Grand Tour through Italy. These observations are typical of a scholarship dedicated to tracing "borrowings" in Reynolds's (and ultimately all classical) work. However, more significantly for my purposes, Mannings's analysis of the "pictorial unity" and "colour scheme" of the portrait resonates with Reynolds's own advice on the utility of brushwork and monotony of color in generalizing objects (see chapter 2): the color scheme is "more subtle than is usual in eighteenth-century naval portraits"; it is "a study in sea-green, slate grey and silver" (David Mannings, ed., *Sir Joshua Reynolds*, 2 vols. [New Haven, CT: Yale University Press, 2000], text:288).

4. Solkin, 47–48.

5. Reynolds, *Discourses*, 72.

6. Ibid., 140–41.

7. Like most eighteenth-century portraitists, Reynolds made use of professional assistants to paint the drapery, accessories, landscape backgrounds, and so forth, at least in the final, most visible layer of paint—in short, almost everything except the flesh of the figure. See David Mannings, "At the Portrait Painter's: How the Painters of the Eighteenth Century Conducted their Studios and Sittings," *History Today* 25 (1977): 279–87.

8. Reynolds, *Discourses*, 181–82.

9. Joseph Baretti, *A Guide through the Royal Academy* (London: T. Cadell, 1781), 17.

10. Reynolds, *Discourses*, 131.

11. Ibid., 123–24.

12. Cited in Mannings, ed., *Sir Joshua Reynolds*, text:545.

13. See the table of Reynolds's prices in Mannings, ed., *Sir Joshua Reynolds*, text:21.

14. William Mason described Reynolds as starting the initial "dead-color" of a portrait "without making any previous sketch or outline" (cited in Mannings, "At the Portrait Painter's," 285).

15. Warton, *Verses on Sir Joshua Reynolds's Painted Window at New-College Oxford*, (Oxford: Oxford University Press, 1930), 1, 5–6.

16. Reynolds, *Discourses*, 100.
17. Warton, 24.
18. Ibid., 7–8.
19. Reynolds to Warton, 13 May 1782, as cited in Warton, iii.
20. Peter and Linda Murray, *The Penguin Dictionary of Art and Artists* (New York: Penguin Books, 1989), s.v. "caricature."
21. Kieran Lee, Graham Byatt, and Gillian Rhodes, "Caricature Effects, Distinctiveness, and Identification: Testing the Face-Space Framework," *Psychological Science* 11 (2000): 379–385.
22. Reynolds, *Discourses*, 72.
23. William Hazlitt, "William Hazlitt's Essays on Reynolds's *Discourses*, written for *The Champion* 1814–15," in Reynolds, *Discourses*, 330.
24. John Constable, *John Constable's Discourses*, ed. R. B. Beckett (Ipswich, England: Suffolk Records Society, 1970), 83.
25. Ibid., 65–66.
26. Ann Bermingham has analyzed Constable's Bergholt works in relation to his personal "Mapping the Self" in the landscape (*Landscape and Ideology* [Berkeley: University of California Press, 1986], 86–155).
27. Cited in C. R. Leslie, *Memoirs of the Life of John Constable* (Chichely: Paul P. B. Minet, 1971), 16.
28. Reynolds, *Discourses*, 261.
29. Constable, 9–10.
30. Reynolds, *Discourses*, 199.
31. William Gilpin, "The Art of Sketching Landscapes," in Gilpin, *Three Essays* (London: R. Blamire, 1792), 63.
32. Malcolm Andrews, *The Search for the Picturesque* (Stanford: Stanford University Press, 1989), 239.
33. "On Picturesque Travel," in Gilpin, 42, 48–49.
34. "On Picturesque Beauty," in Gilpin, 7–12.
35. Gilpin, *Forest Scenery* 2:225, as cited in Andrews, 69.
36. "On Picturesque Beauty," in Gilpin, 19.
37. "The Art of Sketching Landscapes," in Gilpin, 64.
38. Ibid., 65, 74.
39. "On Picturesque Beauty," in Gilpin, 16–17.
40. "On Picturesque Travel," in Gilpin, 50–51.
41. Ibid., 42.
42. Portions of what follows have been published in my article "Alexander Cozens's *New Method*: The Blot and General Nature," *The Art Bulletin* 79 (1997): 112–129.
43. Reynolds, *Discourses*, 199.
44. Alexander Cozens, *A New Method of Assisting the Invention in Drawing Original Compositions of Landscape* (London: J. Dixwell, 1785), 23.
45. See Jean-Claude Lebensztejn, *L'art de la tache* (Paris: Editions du Limon, 1990), 25–29, and Cramer, 113.
46. Cozens, 2–3.
47. Reynolds, *Discourses*, 25–27.
48. Cozens, 12–13.
49. Ibid., 13.
50. Samuel Johnson, *A Dictionary of the English Language* (London: W. Strahan, 1755), s. v. "blot."
51. Jonathan Swift, *A Tale of a Tub and Other Satires*, ed. Kathleen Williams, rev. ed. (London: J. M. Dent & Sons, 1975), 1–2.
52. Oliver Goldsmith, "Preface to the *History of England*," in Goldsmith, *The Works of Oliver Goldsmith*, ed. James Prior, 4 vols. (New York: Siegel-Cooper, 1837), 1:576.
53. Cozens, 14–15.
54. Ibid., 16.
55. Ibid., 6–7.
56. Ibid., 13–14.

Chapter 5. Reductio ad Absurdum

1. John Ruskin, *Modern Painters*, in *The Works of John Ruskin*, ed. E. T. Cook and Alexander Wedderburn, 39 vols. (London: G. Allen, 1903), 3:149–51.
2. [John Eagles,] "Modern Painters," *Blackwood's Edinburgh Magazine* 54, no. 336 (1843), 495; George Darley as cited in Ruskin, 3:34.
3. Ruskin, 3:34–35.
4. Joshua Reynolds, *Discourses on Art*, ed. Robert R. Wark (New Haven, CT: Yale University Press, 1997), 50.
5. Reynolds, *Discourses*, 70.
6. Ibid., 44.
7. William Hazlitt, "William Hazlitt's Essays on Reynolds' *Discourses*," in Reynolds, *Discourses*, 332–33.
8. Reviewing certain similarities of argument in Hazlitt's and Ruskin's criticism of Reynolds's Discourses, William C. Wright has suggested that Ruskin directly knew Hazlitt's writings ("Hazlitt, Ruskin, and Nineteenth-Century Art Criticism," *Journal of Aesthetics and Art Criticism* 32 [1974]: 509–23).
9. George Berkeley, *Principles of Human Knowledge* 9–10, in *The Works of George Berkeley*, ed. A. A. Luce and T. E. Jessop, 9 vols. (London: T. Nelson, 1948–1957), 2:28–29.
10. We shall see that Berkeley's tacit assumption that the mental or visual representation of the general idea is isometric with its referent is, indeed, only an assumption: a pictographic representation of a man on a bathroom door does not reserve the facilities inside only to individuals who exactly resemble its schematic form. However, this argument leaps more than a century of debate about the theory of generalization, and it is with this debate that this chapter is concerned.
11. David Hume, *A Treatise of Human Nature* 1.1.7 (Oxford: Clarendon Press, 1990), 17–21.
12. See Anthony Kenny, "The Homunculus Fallacy," in M. Green, ed., *Interpretations of Life and Mind* (New York: Humanities Press, 1971), 65–74.
13. Hazlitt, 332.
14. Ibid., 330. Nadia Tscherney has noted that the set of portraits to which this work belongs is unusual in Reynolds's oeuvre for the works' "honesty in representing individual quirks and physical imperfections," and has traced their relation to a corresponding transformation in the art of biography ("Reynolds's Streatham Portraits and the Art of Intimate Biography," *Burlington Magazine* 128 [1986]: 7).
15. Immanuel Kant, *Critique of Judgment* 17, trans. Werner S. Pluhar (Indianapolis, IN: Hackett, 1987), 81.
16. Ibid., 80–82. Actually, of course, the image would be most heavily colored in the area of the smallest and slenderest individuals, but Kant's general point is clear.
17. Ibid., 82–83.
18. Ibid., 81.
19. Ibid., 83.

20. Ibid., 81n57.
21. Reynolds, *Discourses*, 47.
22. G. P. Bellori, "The Idea of the Painter, Sculptor and Architect, Superior to Nature by Selection from Natural Beauties," in Erwin Panofsky, *Idea: A Concept in Art Theory*, trans. Joseph J. S. Peake (New York: Harper & Row, 1968), 165.
23. Reynolds, *Discourses*, 79.
24. Joshua Reynolds, *The Works of Sir Joshua Reynolds*, ed. Edmond Malone, 2 vols. (London: T. Cadell, Jr. and W. Davies, 1797), 1:360.
25. Reynolds, *Discourses*, 47.
26. James Barry, *The Works of James Barry*, ed. Edward Fryer, 2 vols. (London: Cadell and Davies, 1809), 1:398.
27. John Opie, *Lectures on Painting*, ed. P. Hoare (London: Longman, Hurst, Rees and Orme, 1809), 15–16.
28. Barry, 1:365–66.
29. Opie, 29.
30. Reynolds, *Discourses*, 79.
31. Ibid., 170–71.
32. G. W. F. Hegel, *Hegel's Aesthetics*, trans. T. M. Knox, 2 vols. (Oxford: Clarendon Press, 1998), 1:7–8.
33. Hegel, 1:175.
34. Ibid., 1:486–87.
35. Ibid., 1:236.
36. Ibid., 1:9–10.
37. Ruskin, 3:27–30.
38. Reynolds, *Discourses*, 50.
39. Ibid., 62.
40. Ruskin, 3:32–33.
41. Ibid., 3:27.
42. Ibid., 3:38.
43. Ibid., 3:34.
44. Ibid., 4:64; see also 4:146.
45. Ibid., 4:164.
46. Ibid., 4:173.
47. Ibid., 4:64.
48. Ibid., 4:146–47.
49. Ibid., 4:170–172.
50. Ibid., 4:170.
51. Ibid., 4:172.
52. See George P. Landow, *Victorian Types, Victorian Shadows* (London: Routledge & Kegan Paul, 1980), and *William Holman Hunt and Typological Symbolism* (New Haven, CT: Yale University Press, 1979).
53. Beverly Seaton, "Considering the Lilies: Ruskin's 'Proserpina' and other Victorian Flower Books," *Victorian Studies* 28 (1985): 261.
54. Cited in Nicolaas A. Rupke, *Richard Owen: Victorian Naturalist* (New Haven, CT: Yale University Press, 1994), 129–30.
55. Ibid., 118.
56. William Buckland, *Geology and Mineralogy Considered with Reference to Natural Theology*, new ed. (Philadelphia: Lea & Blanchard, 1841), 145–46.
57. The classic study of the two schools is Edward S. Russell, *Form and Function: A Contribution to the History of Animal Morphology* (Chicago: University of Chicago Press, 1982).
58. Aristotle, *Physics* 194b17–195a27. Aristotle defines what is traditionally called the formal cause as "the form or the archetype, i.e. the definition of the essence, and its genera," linking the formal cause most closely to the essence and the class or genus of the object (194b27–29, trans. R. P. Hardie and R. K. Gaye, in *The Complete Works of Aristotle*, ed. Jonathan Barnes, 2 vols. [Princeton, NJ: Princeton University Press, 1984], 1:332). This passage may be a direct influence on Richard Owen's choice of the term "Archetype" for his visual model of the vertebrate class (see below).
59. Cited in Toby A. Appel, *The Cuvier-Geoffroy Debate* (New York: Oxford University Press, 1987), 24.
60. See Brian K. Hall, ed., *Homology* (San Diego: Academic Press, 1994).
61. Richard Owen, *On the Archetype and Homologies of the Vertebrate Skeleton* (London: R. and J. E. Taylor, 1848), 7; see also Owen, *Lectures on the Comparative Anatomy and Physiology of the Invertebrate Animals* (London: Longman, Brown, Green and Longmans, 1843), 374, 379.
62. Richard Owen, *On the Nature of Limbs* (London: J. Van Voorst, 1849), 6. Geoffroy went further than Owen, seeking homologies not merely within the class of vertebrates but across the entirety of the animal kingdom. In a series of memoirs presented in January and February of 1820, Geoffroy "reduced" the class of articulates (e.g. insects and crustaceans like lobsters) and the class of vertebrates (like llamas) by noting the similarities between the segmented exoskeletons of the former and the segmentation of the backbone in the latter, resulting in his famous maxim that "every animal lives within or without its vertebral column" (see Appel, 109–112).
63. In his *Philosophie anatomique* (1818), Geoffroy noted that nature "tends to cause the same organs to reappear in the same number and in the same relations, and it varies to an infinite degree only their form. According to this principle [the "principle of connections"], in the determination of the bones of the head of fishes, I will never have to decide according to consideration of their form, but only according to that of their connections" (cited in Appel, 89).
64. See Appel, 97–99.
65. See Rupke, *Richard Owen*, 107. For an account of the Cuvier-Geoffroy debates and their social and scientific implications, see Appel.
66. Barry, 1:384–86.
67. Owen, *On the Archetype*, 72.
68. Owen, *On the Nature of Limbs*, 40.
69. [W. J. Broderip and Richard Owen,] "Generalizations of Comparative Anatomy," *Quarterly Review* 93, no. 185 (1853): 78–79.
70. Owen, *On the Archetype*, 175.
71. Ibid., 132.
72. Ibid., 172.
73. Owen, *On the Nature of Limbs*, 2–3.
74. See Nicolaas A. Rupke, "Richard Owen's Vertebrate Archetype," *Isis* 84 (1993): 242–50.

Chapter 6. Symbolism and Classicism

1. "Cependant, pour l'observateur attentif, il était facile de démêler dès 1890 dans l'outrance des oeuvres et les paradoxes des théories les prodromes d'une réaction classique." Maurice Denis, "De Gauguin et de Van Gogh au classicisme" (1909), in Maurice Denis, *Le Ciel et l'Arcadie*, ed. Jean-Paul Bouillon (Paris: Hermann, 1993), 160.
2. "Aujourd'hui qu'en littérature nous assistons—cela commence à devenir évident—à l'agonie du naturalisme,

alors que nous voyons se préparer une réaction idéaliste, mystique même, il faudrait s'étonner si les arts plastiques ne manifestaient aucune tendance vers une pareille évolution. *La Lutte de Jacob avec l'Ange*, que j'ai tenté décrire en exorde de cette étude, témoigne assez, je crois, que cette tendance existe, et l'on doit comprendre que les peintres engagés dans cette voie nouvelle ont tout intérêt à ce qu'on les débarrasse de cette absurde étiquette d' 'impressionnistes', qui implique, il faut le répéter, un programme directement contradictoire du leur." Albert Aurier, "Le Symbolisme en peinture: Paul Gauguin" (1891), in Albert Aurier, *Textes critiques, 1889–1892* (Paris: Ecole nationale supérieur des Beaux-Arts, 1995), 29–30.

3. "L'impressionnisme, c'est et ce ne peut être qu'une variété du réalisme . . . la fidèle traduction *sans nul au-delà* d'une *impression exclusivement sensorielle*, d'une sensation." Aurier, "Le Symbolisme en peinture," 28–29.

4. "Le XIXe siècle, après avoir, quatre-vingts ans, proclamé, dans son enthousiasme enfantin, l'omnipotence de l'observation et de la déduction scientifique, après avoir affirmé qu'aucun mystère ne subistait devant ses lentilles et ses scalpels, semble enfin s'apercevoir de la vanité de ses efforts, de la puérilité de ses vantardises." Albert Aurier, "Les peintres symbolistes" (1892), in *Textes critiques*, 95.

5. ". . . une époque matérialiste, industrielle, utilitaire . . . où le mot *idéal* faisait sourire comme un vocable ridicule et vide de sens, qu'on classerait bientôt dans les dictionnaires parmi les archaïsmes inusités." Aurier, "Les peintures symbolistes," 98.

6. "Ç'aura été le propre du XIXe siècle de vouloir introduire la science partout, même dans les choses où elle a le moins affaire." Albert Aurier, "Essai sur une nouvelle méthode de critique" (1892), in *Textes critiques*, 1.

7. "La doctrine de M. Taine, on le sait, est basée sur cette idée qu'une oeuvre d'art est un phénomène essentiellement relatif et contingent, qui n'existe pas en soi, et dont la seule valeur est d'être le témoignage de l'état physiologique d'un peuple à une époque donnée." Aurier, "Essai sur une nouvelle méthode de critique," 2.

8. Hippolyte Taine, *Philosophie de l'art* (Paris: Fayard, 1985), 18–19.

9. "De ce seul mot naissent une infinité de particularités qui composent toute la manière d'être de la contrée, non seulement ses dehors physiques et ce qu'elle est par elle-même, mais encore l'esprit et les qualités morales et physiques des habitants et de leurs oeuvres." Taine, 33.

10. "On pourrait dire qu'en ce pays l'eau fait l'herbe, qui fait le bétail, qui fait le fromage, le beurre et la viande, qui, tous ensemble avec la bière, font l'habitant. En effet, de cette grasse vie et de l'organisation physique imbibée d'air humide, vous voyez naître le tempérament flamand." Taine, 34.

11. Taine does attempt to amalgamate this relativist notion of artistic production to the classical notion of an ideal in the fifth part of his *Philosophie de l'art*, and once again it is in part the duration and extent of the moral character or visible characteristic that determines its degree of ideality (see especially part 5, chapter 2). However, the bulk of his theory remains relativistic.

12. Castagnary, "The Three Contemporary Schools," introduction to the "Salon de 1863," as translated in Charles Harrison, Paul Wood, and Jason Gaiger, eds., *Art in Theory, 1815–1900* (Oxford: Blackwell, 1998), 411.

13. "Malheureusement, oui, [les artistes] subissent l'influence des milieux, plus ou moins, malgré leur désir, qui est un devoir de s'en éloigner et de s'en abstraire. Ils sont en quelque sorte des cygnes qui, par hasard tombés dans un bourbier, tâchent de se renvoler vers le Ciel, mais dont les ailes ont été souillées par la boue du marécage." Aurier, "Essai sur une nouvelle méthode de critique," 5.

14. "*L'oeuvre d'art est, en valeur, inversement proportionnelle à l'influence des milieux qu'elle a subie*." Aurier, "Essai sur une nouvelle méthode de critique," 12.

15. See Patricia Matthews, *Aurier's Symbolist Art Criticism and Theory* (Ann Arbor: UMI, 1984).

16. See Aurier, "Essai sur une nouvelle méthode de critique," 11. Aurier uses the word "idéiste" rather than "idéaliste" in order to distinguish the modern assays toward the Platonic Idea from the conventional and moribund tradition of the Academy. The *idéalistes* "se sont contentés d'*arranger* l'objectivité, suivant certaines notions de qualité conventionnelles et préjugées; ils se sont piqués de nous présenter des objets *beaux*, mais *beaux en tant qu'objets* . . . ce qu'ils ont appelé idéal ne fut jamais que le roublard maquillage des laides choses intangibles." By contrast, the *idéistes* are in pursuit of the true Platonic Idea, "la matérialisation représentive de ce qu'il y a de plus élevé et de plus vraiment divin dans le monde, de ce qu'il y a, en dernière analyse, de seul existant, l'Idée" (Aurier, "Le Symbolisme en peinture," 32). In effect, Aurier is simply repeating the commonplace distinction, established by the Academy itself, between the formulaic repetition of a conventional ideal and the engaged pursuit of the true ideal.

17. "Pour produire un chef-d'oeuvre, il faut avoir entrevu le divin" (Sâr Péladan, *L'art idéaliste*, 270); "une oeuvre, comme un être, n'a point d'autre excellence que la vision du divin suscitée" (Sâr Péladan, *Comment on devient artiste*, 300), as cited in Philippe Junod, *Transparence et opacité* (Lausanne: Editions l'age d'homme, 1975), 82, 47.

18. Ferdinand Hodler, "La mission de l'artiste" (1897), as translated in Henri Dorra, ed., *Symbolist Art Theories* (Berkeley: University of California Press, 1994), 247.

19. Mark Cheetham, *The Rhetoric of Purity* (Cambridge: Cambridge University Press, 1991), 23.

20. "Le premier consistait à me mettre devant la nature et à la simplifier jusqu'à la rigueur." Bernard, "Mémoire pour l'histoire du symbolisme pictural de 1890" (1919), in Emile Bernard, *Propos sur l'art*, ed. Anne Rivière, 2 vols. (Paris: Séguier, 1994), 1:201.

21. "Deux écoles, néanmoins, restent en présence: les Impressionnistes et les Symbolistes; ceux qui tendent à transporter sur la toile, vive et crue, l'impression pure et simple, toute objective, qu'un aspect des choses a produit sur leur imagination sensorielle;—ceux qui décomposent cette même impression pour la recomposer à loisir selon la volonté d'exprimer en leur oeuvre, non pas des fuyances, mais des permanences, des significations éternelles, des représentations voulues définitives." Remy de Gourmont, "Les Premiers Salons: Indépendants, Rose+Croix, Exposition de Mme Jeanne Jacquemin," *Mercure de France* 5 (May 1892), 60.

22. "Ces deux arts valent par leur sincérité: pratiquement ils se joignent et se complètent,—car il faut au symboliste un fond d'impressionnisme, et l'impressionniste qui ne chercherait qu'à emmener des nuances en captivité serait le plus vain des détrousseurs de paysages." Remy de Gourmont, 60.

23. "un admirable effort vers le nouveau, vers un art synthétique, idéaliste, symétrique, vers un art de signifi-

cation et de volonté"; "une ordonnance comme classique, et pourtant un viaduct de chemin de fer s'érige dans le fond: dévulgariser la nature civilisée, c'est intéressant et c'était difficile." Remy de Gourmont, 60–61.

24. Aurier, "Le Symbolisme en peinture," 30; Denis, "De Gauguin et de Van Gogh au classicisme," 160. H. R. Rookmaaker has most thoroughly explored the Symbolist concept of synthetism in *Synthetist Art Theories* (Amsterdam: Swets and Zeitlinger, 1959).

25. "Réalisme et impressionnisme sont deux périodes fécondes qui préparent peut-être avec des éléments nouveaux une autre Renaissance classique." Denis, "Les Arts à Rome, ou la méthode classique" (1898 or 1899), in *Le Ciel et l'Arcadie*, 64.

26. "D'une méthode pour échapper à l'empirisme et à l'impressionnisme et concentrer sur un nombre de motifs restreint les efforts et les sensations quotidiennes." Denis, Journal, 6 February 1898, in *Le Ciel et l'Acradie*, 51.

27. "Tout artiste qui réfléchit en vient tôt ou tard à préférer cette beauté-là [that is, classical beauty] à toute autre. L'idéal de l'Art c'est de condenser, de résumer en un petit nombre de formes claires et concises les rapports infiniment variés que nous percevons dans la nature. C'est de réduire à de l'essentiel nos sensations les plus particulières, c'est de faire du simple avec du compliqué." Denis, "Aristide Maillol" (1905), in Le *Ciel et l'Arcadie*, 101.

28. See Richard Shiff, *Cézanne and the End of Impressionism* (Chicago: University of Chicago Press, 1984), 187–89.

29. "Dans la notion d'Art classique, ce qui domine donc, c'est l'idée de synthèse. Pas de classique qui ne soit économe de ses moyens, qui ne subordonne toutes les grâces de détail à la beauté de l'ensemble, qui n'atteigne la grandeur par la concision." Denis, "Aristide Maillol," 102.

30. Clive Bell, *Art* (New York: Capricorn Books, 1958), 148–49.

31. "Le petit chatouillement agréable que procure l'heureuse réunion de trois ou quatre tons fins, ou quelques rapports de valeurs, nous l'avions cherché et trouvé chez les Primitifs: il nous faut renoncer ici à cette saveur. . . . Il y a ici des oeuvres qui s'adressent plus à notre jugement qu'à nos sens." Denis, "Les Arts à Rome," 57.

32. "Le nombre des impressions originales dont chaque esprit est susceptible est extrêmement limité: ce sont les mêmes qui se reproduisent devant les objets différents. . . . Donc: classer les sensations similaires." Denis, "Les Arts à Rome," 67; see also Denis, Journal, 6 February 1898, 54.

33. "Nos sensations ont un lien entre elles; dans notre esprit, elles s'accumulent pour déterminer des états durables, de véritables cristallisations." Denis, "Les Arts à Rome," 66.

34. ". . . tâcher que se forment des centres de cristallisation . . . pour concentrer autour de chacune toutes les sensations qui peuvent s'y rattacher." Denis, Journal, 6 February 1898, 54.

35. "Depuis l'impressionnisme . . . l'habitude de synthèse immédiate"; "Il faudrait le courage de résister . . . à notre public qui veut des impressions d'art en cinq minutes." Denis, Journal, 6 February 1898, 51, 54.

36. "Ils comprenaient la nécessité de digérer leurs sensations, de ne pas les employer trop neuves; digestion souvent très lente, et qui permet un travail homogène et rationnel." Denis, "Les Arts à Rome," 63.

37. "Classer les sensations similaires; groupement d'abord laborieux pour qui n'y a jamais pensé, mais qui doit devenir facilement instinctif et qu'Ingres, entre autres, devait faire sans difficulté." Denis, "Les Arts à Rome," 67; see also Denis, Journal, 6 February 1898, 54.

38. Joshua Reynolds, *Discourses on Art*, ed. Robert R. Wark (New Haven, CT: Yale University Press, 1997), 44; Denis Diderot, *The Salon of 1767*, trans. John Goodman (New Haven, CT: Yale University Press, 1995), 12.

39. "Les règles de l'école et les recettes de métier." Denis, "Les Arts à Rome," 61.

40. Denis cites Puvis among the predecessors of Symbolism, despite the fact that his "official glory" should normally have "displeased" the young modernists (Denis, "De Gauguin et de Van Gogh au classicisme," 158).

41. "Véritable créateur du symbolisme et du synthétisme"; "la plus haute révélation idéaliste de l'art français." Bernard, "Le symbolisme pictural, 1886–1936" (1936), in *Propos sur l'art*, 1:288.

42. "Les maîtres, [Puvis] les aimait, mais professait: Ne tirons rien que de nous-mêmes, préférons un peu de charme à beaucoup de science blafarde.

"Il disait: 'Simplifier, c'est dégager la pensée; la conception la plus simple se trouvera être la plus belle.'

"Aux matérialistes il répondait: 'La peinture n'est pas une imitation de la réalité, mais *un parallélisme* de la nature [Bernard's italics].'

"Il s'accusait de: 'S'efforcer de peindre des spectacles réels, mais ayant un sens général.'

"Tel fut son symbolisme: 'Pour moi, confessait-il, j'ai toujours cherché à deviner le corps sous la robe aux reflets changeants; j'ai cherché les choses sous leur caractère permanent, dans leur apparence profonde, c'est-à-dire dans leur essence. Ma façon de travailler est intérieure, si j'ose dire; avant de rien exécuter ma création est presque entièrement achevée dans ma tête.'

"Il disait encore: 'Il faut élaguer de la nature tout ce qui est contingence, accident, tout ce qui est momentanément inexpressif, c'est-à-dire ce que ne tendrait pas à traduire notre pensée. L'art achève ce que la nature ébauche, prononce la parole qu'elle balbutie. Comment arrive-t-on à aider la nature dans son effort pour parler? Par l'abréviation et la simplification. Attachez-vous à exprimer l'important, passez le reste, c'est là le secret de la composition, c'est là le secret du dessin, c'est même le secret de l'éloquence et de l'esprit.'" Bernard, "Puvis de Chavannes" (1903), in *Propos sur l'art*, 1:59.

43. "'Les idées nous arrivent le plus souvent emmêlées et troubles. Il importe donc de les dégager d'abord, pour pouvoir les tenir, pures, sous le regard intérieur. Un oeuvre naît d'une sorte de confuse émotion dans laquelle elle est contenue comme l'animal dans l'oeuf. La pensée qui gît dans cette émotion, je la roule, je la roule jusqu'à ce qu'elle soit élucidée à mes yeux et qu'elle apparaisse avec toute la netteté possible. . . . C'est là du symbolisme, si vous voulez.'" Denis, "Les Arts à Rome," 64.

44. "Je pensais à rejeter tout ce qui était obstacle à ma vision de la généralité et je marchais au symbolisme par la synthèse. J'écrivais alors [to Anquetin]: 'Tout ce qui surcharge un spectacle le couvre de réalité et occupe nos yeux au détriment de notre esprit. Il faut simplifier le spectacle pour en tirer le sens. Il faut en quelque sorte en faire le schéma', et je parvins, en effet, à des schémas plus ou moins significatifs." Bernard, "Mémoire pour l'histoire du symbolisme pictural," 1:201.

45. "J'avais deux moyens pour y parvenir. Le premier consistait à me mettre devant la nature et à la simplifier jusqu'à la rigueur. Il en résulta parfois des aspects fort grands. Réduire ses lignes à d'éloquents contrastes, ses nuances aux 7 couleurs fondamentales du prisme fut la base du système. J'écrivais [to Anquetin]: 'Voir le style et non pas l'objet. Dégager le sens abstrait et non l'objectif.'

"Le second de mes moyens consistait, pour arriver à ce résultat, à faire appel à la conception ou au souvenir en me dégageant de toute ambiance directe [de la nature]. Ici, je me manifestais davantage, et c'est proprement moi que j'écrivais alors que devant la nature c'était le sens invisible caché sous la muette forme de l'extériorité." Bernard, "Mémoire pour l'histoire du symbolisme pictural," 1:201.

46. Thomas Hobbes, *Leviathan* 1.2 (Indianapolis: Hackett, 1994), 8.

47. Reynolds, *Discourses*, 223–24.

48. Ibid., 192–93.

49. Vincent Van Gogh, *The Complete Letters of Vincent Van Gogh*, 3 vols. (Boston: Little, Brown and Company, 1988), 3:228–29.

50. Ibid., 3:518.

51. In some places Plato does note that empirical experience helps to key the recollection of the Ideas. In *Phaedrus* (250b–d), Plato suggests that the Idea of Beauty is particularly available to recollection through the vision of earthly beauties, and in the *Symposium* (210a–212a), Plato's spokeswoman Diotima describes a gradual ascent to the "final revelation" of "universal beauty . . . starting from individual beauties" (211b–c, as translated by Michael Joyce in Edith Hamilton and Huntington Cairns, eds., *Plato: The Collected Dialogues* [Princeton, NJ: Princeton University Press, 1994], 562–63).

52. ". . . cette phrase de saint Denys l'Aréopagite, le platonicien: *'L'idée est la forme des choses en dehors de ces choses.'* . . . Comment représenter les choses *en idée*? La réponse me parut simple. Puisque l'idée est la forme des choses recueillies par l'imagination, il fallait peindre, non plus devant la chose, mais en la reprenant dans l'imagination qui l'avait recueillie, *qui en conservait l'idée* [Bernard's italics]. Ainsi l'idée de la chose apporterait la forme convenable au sujet du tableau, ou plutôt à son idéal (somme des idées)." Bernard, "Quelques souvenirs de Pont-Aven (1888)" (1939), in *Propos sur l'art*, 1:300–1.

53. "En dehors de ce que l'on nomme vulgairement 'Imagination,' faculté qui consisterait à se représenter dans un désordre considérable toutes sortes de choses bizarres et déformées, il y a une 'Imagination' plus méconnue qui est celle qui préside à l'ordonnance et établit la solidité de l'oeuvre: travail logique de transposition qui ne demande pas moins d'effort que le précédent et d'où l'artiste surgit créateur et digne de ce nom. Ici n'est point une cohue étrange, mais une nature vue, toute refaite, toute transformée et toute vivante de vie de l'ordre et de la volonté." Emile Bernard, "Paul Cézanne" (1894), in *Propos sur l'art*, 1:51.

54. Bernard's dismissal of the "bizarre and deformed things" that the vulgar imagination is capable of producing echoes Horace's denigration of painters who "join a horse's neck to a human head and spread on multicolored feathers, with different parts of the body brought in from anywhere and everywhere, so that what starts out above as a beautiful woman ends up horribly as a black fish." Horace, *Ars poetica* lines 1–9, trans. Leon Golden, in O. B. Hardison, Jr. and Leon Golden, *Horace for Students of Literature* (Gainesville: University Press of Florida, 1995).

55. "La simplification ou synthèse, s'imposait d'abord comme inhérent à l'idée; car l'idée ne garde que l'essentiel des choses perçues, et, par conséquent, en rejette le détail. La mémoire ne retient pas tout, mais ce qui frappe l'esprit. Donc, formes et couleurs devenaient simples, dans une égale unité. En peignant de mémoire, j'avais l'avantage d'abolir l'inutile complication des formes et des tons. Il restait un *schéma* du spectacle regardé . . . [les] couleurs-types de la palette prismatique . . . les formes typiques de toutes les formes objectives. Tel fut mon synthétisme en 1888." Bernard, "Quelques souvenirs de Pont-Aven," 1:301.

56. Frances S. Connelly, *The Sleep of Reason* (University Park: Pennsylvania State University Press, 1995), 11–14.

57. Quatremère de Quincy, *Essai sur l'idéal* (Paris: Adrien Le Clère, 1837), 99–100, 105. The word "syncopated" is here being used in its rhetorical sense, as an abbreviation by means of elision (most commonly, of letters inside a word, as in "e'er" for "ever"). As such, it is perhaps intended by Quatremère to specify the abstraction of objects by eliminating features within the contour.

58. ". . . ne créèrent pas des lettres, mais ils retracèrent des idées, ils devinrent, dès lors, l'expression la plus généralisée des objets ou des sujets, dont ils devoient communiquer l'idée ou perpétuer le souvenir. Fidèles à leur emploi originaire, ils ne laissèrent pas, à mesure du développement successif des arts, de perpétuer pour les yeux et pour l'esprit, l'habitude d'un système d'exécution plus ou moins abstrait." Quatremère, 105–06.

59. Quatremère, 117.

60. "[Dans les] ébauches des premiers siècles de l'art, il y avoit, comme dans les esquisses de l'artiste dont nous avons parlé, une *vérité*, c'est celle que la nature nous montre partout aussi, dans tous les genres de créatures." This truth is "une vérité en germe, laquelle ne pouvoit embrasser, que ce qu'il y a de moins particularisé ou détaillé dans la formation des créatures." Quatremère, 120–21.

61. ". . . la direction la plus générale des grandes parties de [la] figure, considérée par lui dans son ensemble, avant de l'être dans ses détails. Ainsi, par exemple, le trait d'un bras ou d'une jambe ne présentera, dans ce premier tracé, que des lignes presque droites et parallèles. S'il veut, selon cette méthode, indiquer la tête, il commencera par tracer un oeuf." Quatremère, 124.

62. ". . . le style d'imitation le plus *idéal*, en tant qu'il donne de l'objet, l'idée la plus abstraite, la plus généralisée, la plus éloignée des détails [Quatremère's italics]." Quatremère, 124–25.

63. "[Il] arrondira un peu les contours, il désignera les articulations, les attachemens des principaux muscles, il arrêtera les grands rapports." This moment corresponds to "le style de la seconde manière de l'art en Grèce," that of the period between Homer and Pisistratus, and is "le second degré de l'imitation abstraite," in which "n'entra que pour fort peu, l'influence de la prétendue *vérité imitative* de la nature." Quatremère, 125–26.

64. ". . . les parties et les formes subordonnées, que révèle l'étude anatomique," "le milieu entre les deux extrêmes" of the "manière hiéroglyphique" and the "pré-

tendu vrai imitatif, qu'on appelle d'individu ou style de portrait." Quatremère, 126–27.

65. ". . . de plus minutieux détails, subordonnés les uns aux autres, c'est-à-dire, jusqu'aux formes qui ne sont que des accidens fortuits ou individuels, comme les plis ou les passages si variables de la peau, les mollesses et l'embonpoint de la chair." Quatremère, 127.

66. "Depuis Phidias, le style d'imitation, et ce qu'on appelle la manière des artistes, loin de se porter vers l'idéal, où le système de généralisation, dans l'imitation du corps humain, marcha progressivement vers le style imitatif des détails, et de cette vérité que nous avons appelée *individuelle* ou *particularisée*." Quatremère, 141.

67. George Berkeley, *Principles of Human Knowledge* 9–10, in *The Works of George Berkeley*, ed. A. A. Luce and T. E. Jessop, 9 vols. (London: T. Nelson, 1948–1957), 2:28–29.

68. Signage such as that typically found on restroom doors is not exclusively the result of an aposterioritic abstraction away from empirical observation but also relies on an aprioritic abstraction toward rational geometric shapes. In this respect it departs from generalization-theory. It is significant to note, then, that Bernard's *Buckwheat Harvest* does not take its synthesis toward the geometric, but rather retains a supple, organic quality.

69. Robert Rosenblum, *Transformations in Late-Eighteenth Century Art* (Princeton, NJ: Princeton University Press, 1989), 171.

70. Dante, *Paradiso* Canto 33.85-91, trans. Allen Mandelbaum (New York: Bantam, 1986).

71. Reynolds, *Discourses*, 47.

72. Bernard's 1888 letter to Anquetin, in which he outlined his "two ways" of arriving at his schemas, and Van Gogh's 1888–89 letters to Bernard and Theo regarding the question of painting "abstractions" are contemporaneous with that practice, but they are glancing references in a sea of other possibilities.

73. "Sous prétexte de synthèse, nous nous sommes souvent contentés, avouons-le, de généralisations hâtives: en devenant schématique notre art est resté fragmentaire, incomplet. Nous avons fait beaucoup d'esquisses et trop peu de tableaux. Nous ne savons pas finir, soit; mais même chez les anciens, nous préférons l'ébauche à l'oeuvre faite." Denis, "De Gauguin et de Van Gogh au classicisme," 168.

74. "Synthétiser ce n'est pas nécessairement simplifier dans le sens de supprimer certaines parties de l'objet: c'est simplifier dans le sens de *rendre intelligible*. C'est, en somme, hiérarchiser: soumettre chaque tableau à un seul rythme, à une dominante, sacrifier, subordonner—généraliser. Il ne suffit pas pour *styliser* un objet, comme on dit à l'école de Grasset, d'en faire une copie quelconque, puis d'en souligner d'un trait épais le contour extérieur. La simplification ainsi obtenue n'est pas la synthèse." Maurice Denis, "Cézanne" (1907), in *Le Ciel et l'Arcadie*, 147.

75. "Partant de ce principe qu'un technique large et simple est l'indice d'une conception élevée, et qu'il n'y a nulle discordance entre les moyens adoptés et la pensée émise, l'oeuvre en laquelle les moyens ne sont qu'une imitation vicieuse et détournée des méthodes apparaît comme éminemment routinière et déformatrice; et c'est le cas d'Eugène Carrière. En vérité, la largeur de son faire n'est qu'une facture sans portée et souvent écolière, dont l'original est détenu à l'Ecole des Beaux-Arts même." Emile Bernard, "Eugène Carrière ou l'impuissance picturale" (1905), in *Propos sur l'art*, 1:101.

76. John Opie, *Lectures on Painting*, ed. P. Hoare (London: Longman, Hurst, Rees and Orme, 1809), 17.

77. "L'erreur de ma première expression symboliste—telle que la conserva sans y rien ajouter Gauguin—fut de ne représenter qu'une abstraction, en dépouillant, par un système technique immuable et en quelque sorte mécanique, les aspects de la vie, en les retranchant de vie même, non pas magnifiés, amplifiés ou agrandis, mais momifiés, immobilisés dans une stratification méthodique, simpliste. En un mot, Gauguin, continuateur aveugle du procédé, remplaça la sensibilité par la routine, supprima l'émotion en mutilant son oeuvre de sécheresse et de déformation. . . . En définitive donc, Gauguin ne conserva du symbolisme que la manoeuvre extérieure, décorative, sans y avoir versé l'esprit. Il ne procéda point par conception; son mobile ne fut jamais que la mise en oeuvre d'un système." Emile Bernard, "Note relative au symbolisme pictural de 1888–1890" (1906), in *Propos sur l'art*, 1:122–23.

78. "Ainsi l'oeuvre de Gauguin offre l'image d'un symbolisme sans symbole, qui trompe le spectateur par un aspect abstrait, qui ne lui est en somme pas personnel, puisqu'il l'a emprunté . . . il eût été incapable de le concevoir, de le découvrir . . . il l'appliqua uniquement par système, n'en prenant que l'écorce et n'en faisant jamais qu'une contradiction formelle avec ses enfantillages d'ignorant." Bernard, "Mémoire pour l'histoire du symbolisme pictural," 1:203–4.

79. "'Après avoir élu au début, et en toute logique, *les modes d'expression les plus sommaires, les plus immédiats, vous* [Bernard] *avez été vous ornant et vous complétant chaque jour*. Dans l'isolement, et par l'étude raisonnée vous avez ajouté aux dons natifs les acquisitions qui devaient favoriser et garantir *une approche de la vérité constante et sûre*.' . . .

"Où devait me conduire cet état définitif de mon art, sinon à la pensée constante de ma vie: *la réalisation du symbolisme dans sa forme la plus haute et la plus complète; c'est-à-dire dans son union avec le classicisme*. . . .

"Je n'en poursuis pas moins, par une étude de plus en plus *'consciente*,' l'accomplissement du *symbolisme classique*, étroite union de la vérité des spectacles humains avec la majesté divine de l'Intelligence fécondée par l'Idéal [Bernard's italics]." Bernard, "Note relative au symbolisme pictural," 1:123–24.

Chapter 7. Mondrian and the End of Classicism

1. Richard G. Tansey and Fred S. Kleiner, *Gardner's Art through the Ages*, 10th ed. (Fort Worth: Harcourt Brace, 1996), 1062.

2. Michel Seuphor, *Piet Mondrian: Life and Work* (New York: Abrams, [1956]), 5.

3. Yve-Alain Bois, "The Iconoclast," in Angelica Zander Rudenstine, ed., *Piet Mondrian* (exh. cat., The Hague: Haags Gemeentemuseum, 1994), 353.

4. Erwin Panofsky, *Tomb Sculpture*, ed. H. W. Janson (New York: Harry N. Abrams, [1964]), 25–26.

5. Robert Welsh, "Mondrian and Theosophy," originally published in the exhibition catalogue *Piet Mondrian Centennial Exhibition* (New York: Guggenheim Museum, 1971), reprinted in Patricia Kaplan and Susan Manso, eds., *Major European Art Movements, 1900–1945* (New York: E. P. Dutton, 1977), 250–74.

6. See Welsh, 262–68.

7. Ibid., 268–71.

8. Carel Blotkamp, "Annunciation of the New Mysticism: Dutch Symbolism and Early Abstraction," in Maurice Tuchman et al., eds., *The Spiritual in Art* (exh. cat., Los Angeles: L. A. County Museum, 1988), 96.

9. Blotkamp, "Annunciation of the New Mysticism," 100.

10. Carel Blotkamp, *Mondrian: The Art of Destruction* (London: Reaktion Books, 1994).

11. See Mark Cheetham, *The Rhetoric of Purity* (Cambridge: Cambridge University Press, 1991), 49–50; and Yve-Alain Bois, "The Iconoclast," in Rudenstine, ed., 329 and 367n70.

12. Piet Mondrian, "The New Plastic in Painting" (1917–1918), as translated in Piet Mondrian, *The New Art, The New Life: The Collected Writings of Piet Mondrian*, ed. and trans. Harry Holtzman and Martin S. James (New York: Da Capo Press, 1993), 44, note 'u.'

13. Peter Vergo, ed., *Abstraction: Towards a New Art* (exh. cat., London: Tate Gallery, 1980), 47.

14. Piet Mondrian to Querido, in *Two Mondrian Sketchbooks*, ed. and trans. R. P. Welsh and J. M. Joosten (Amsterdam: Meulenhoff International, 1969), 10.

15. Welsh, 251.

16. Mondrian, *Two Mondrian Sketchbooks*, 10–11. Interestingly, Mondrian's letter to Querido was written before the rather overt deployment of theosophical symbolism in the *Evolution* triptych.

17. Cited in Mondrian, *Two Mondrian Sketchbooks*, 10, with the exception of the phrase "for I have read [that] whatever has form is not yet spiritual," which is taken from Martin S. James's translation in "Piet Mondrian: Art and Theory to 1917," in Mondrian, *The New Art, The New Life*, 14. The Welsh and Joosten translation of this passage makes little sense: "for not everything having form is therefore spiritual, I have read." I regret that I do not have access to the original Dutch.

18. Mondrian, *Two Mondrian Sketchbooks*, 38.

19. Mondrian, "The New Plastic in Painting," 41.

20. Ibid.

21. Ibid., 63–64.

22. In September 1915, Mondrian wrote to his friend Dr. H. van Assendelft, "The book is almost complete; it has become far more comprehensive than I expected" (see Mondrian, *The New Art, The New Life*, 27).

23. Piet Mondrian, "Natural Reality and Abstract Reality" (1919–20) in *The New Art, The New Life*, 92.

24. Mondrian, "The New Plastic in Painting," 41. In "Natural Reality and Abstract Reality," Mondrian similarly writes: ". . . there is also a more *subjective* vision that comes from ourselves and that is mainly determined by our limited human ideas. And this vision is very dangerous so long as it remains immature; when mature, it once again becomes *objective* vision, for we have then transcended the subjective" (92).

25. Mondrian, "Natural Reality and Abstract Reality," 89–90. On Schopenhauer's formulation of disinterested contemplation, see *The World as Will and Representation* 33ff.

26. Mondrian, "The New Plastic in Painting," 32.

27. Ibid.

28. Ibid., 30.

29. Mondrian, *Two Mondrian Sketchbooks*, 38, 36.

30. Mondrian, "The New Plastic in Painting," 48.

31. Ibid., 35.

32. Ibid.

33. Piet Mondrian, "Dialogue on the New Plastic" (1919), in *The New Art, The New Life*, 77.

34. Joshua Reynolds, *The Works of Sir Joshua Reynolds*, ed. Edmond Malone, 2 vols. (London: T. Cadell, Jr. and W. Davis, 1797), 1:358–59.

35. Cited in Rudenstine, ed., *Piet Mondrian*, 102.

36. Ibid.

37. Mondrian's "reversion" in the *Flowering Apple Tree* to a specific moment in time marked by the light pastel colors of spring should not be taken as confounding my argument. As will be made clear below, for Mondrian *every* object at *every* moment exhibits the "original unity" of nature to a greater or lesser extent.

38. Mondrian, "The New Plastic in Painting," 35.

39. This phenomenon is embodied in the Etch-a-Sketch toy, which enables the user to make any sort of line using just two dials, one controlling the horizontal "force" and one controlling the vertical.

40. Mondrian, "The New Plastic in Painting," 32.

41. Ibid., 31–32.

42. Mondrian, "Dialogue on the New Plastic," 77.

43. Ibid.

44. Mondrian, "The New Plastic in Painting," 28–29.

45. Ibid., 61–62.

46. Ibid., 32.

Conclusion

1. Michel Foucault, "Preface," in Gilles Deleuze and Félix Guattari, *Anti-Oedipus*, trans. Robert Hurley, Mark Seem, and Helen R. Lane (Minneapolis: University of Minnesota Press, 1983), xiii.

2. Barbara Maria Stafford, *Body Criticism* (Cambridge, MA: MIT Press, 1991), 43, 38.

3. Nicholas Mirzoeff, *Bodyscape* (London: Routledge, 1995), 28.

4. Jean Auguste Dominique Ingres, from Notebooks, as translated in Charles Harrison, Paul Wood, and Jason Gaiger, eds., *Art in Theory 1815–1900* (Oxford: Blackwell, 1998), 185.

5. Emile Zola, "Edouard Manet," (1867), in Harrison, Wood, and Gaiger, eds., 557.

6. Ernst Gombrich, "Reynolds's Theory and Practice of Imitation," in *Norm and Form* (London: Phaidon, 1978), 133.

7. Rensselaer Lee, *Ut Pictura Poesis* (New York: W. W. Norton & Co., 1967), 12.

8. Giovanni Pietro Bellori, "The Idea of the Painter, Sculptor and Architect" (1672), as translated in Erwin Panofsky, *Idea*, trans. Joseph J. S. Peak (New York: Harper & Row, 1968), 169; Denis Diderot, *Diderot on Art II: Salon of 1767*, trans. John Goodman (New Haven, CT: Yale University Press, 1995), 13; Joshua Reynolds, *Discourses on Art* (New Haven, CT: Yale University Press, 1997), 261.

9. See Kendall L. Walton, "Style and the Products and Processes of Art," in Berel Lang, ed., *The Concept of Style*, rev. ed. (Ithaca, NY: Cornell University Press, 1987), 72–73.

10. *Oxford English Dictionary*, 1979 edition, s. v. "style."

11. I should note that the study of style as process as I conceive it is a study of *intentions* and not of actual usage or derived meanings, and that I do not intend to reify the "intentional fallacy" that the only or even the privileged meaning of the artifact resides in the intentions of its creator. Once the artifact is made, it enters into complex relations with its viewers and users that may or may not have been anticipated by its maker. The study of these relations is a study of reception and not of production, and requires a different mode of analysis. However, under the aegis of the final cause the study of style as process does include all uses that the maker can conceive the user will make of his or her work, and thus will constitute one contextual understanding of the use or meaning of the artifact.

12. A brief caveat: in the mythology of "action painting," the artist begins work on the canvas without having any preconceptions about what will come out:

> The painter no longer approached his easel with an image in his mind; he went up to it with a material in his hand to do something to that other piece of material in front of him. . . .
>
> It is pointless to argue that Rembrandt or Michelangelo worked in the same way. You don't get Lucrece with a dagger out of staining a piece of cloth or spontaneously putting forms into motion upon it. She had to exist someplace else before she got on the canvas, and the paint was Rembrandt's means for bringing her there. Now, everything must have been in the tubes, in the painter's muscles, and in the cream-colored sea into which he dives. If Lucrece should come out she will be among us for the first time—a surprise. To the painter she *must* be a surprise. In this mood there is no point in an act if you already know what it contains. (Harold Rosenberg, "The American Action Painters," in *Artists, Critics, Context*, ed. Paul F. Fabozzi, 24–25 (Upper Saddle River, N.J.: Prentice Hall, 2002).

Action painting thus construed is specifically an art of material and efficient cause, to the greatest possible exclusion of formal and final causes. Conversely, Conceptual art can be construed as an art of formal and final cause, to the maximum possible exclusion of material and efficient cause. In both cases, the artists specifically dealt with those issues by negating them.

13. Of course, other final causes can also be cited and prioritized: the artist's concept of the ideal can be intended (and even where not intended can be mobilized) for pernicious social projects of qualitative evaluation, exclusion, and domination.

14. Joshua Reynolds, 203–4; James Barry, *The Works of James Barry*, ed. Edward Fryer, 2 vols. (London: Cadell and Davies, 1809), 1:382; John Opie, *Lectures on Painting*, ed. P. Hoare (London: Longman, Hurst, Rees and Orme, 1809), 29–30; Henry Fuseli, *The Life and Writings of Henry Fuseli*, ed. John Knowles, 3 vols. (London: H. Colburn and R. Bentley, 1831), 2:59; Antoine Chysostome Quatremère de Quincy, *Histoire d la vie et des ouvrages de Raphaël*, 2nd ed. (Paris: Ad. Le Clère et Cie., 1833; repr., Elibron Classics, 2003), 77.

15. Hayden White, introduction to *Tropics of Discourse* (Baltimore, MD: The Johns Hopkins University Press, 1978), 3–4.

Works Cited

Primary Sources

Alberti, Leon Battista. *On Painting*. Translated by John R. Spencer. New Haven, CT: Yale University Press, 1979.

———. *On Painting and On Sculpture*. Translated by Cecil Grayson. New York: Phaidon, 1972.

Aristotle. *The Complete Works of Aristotle*. Edited by Jonathan Barnes. 2 vols. Princeton, NJ: Princeton University Press, 1991.

Aurier, Albert. *Textes critiques, 1889–1892: De l'impressionnisme au symbolisme*. Paris: Ecole nationale supérieur des Beaux-Arts, 1995.

Baretti, Joseph. *A Guide through the Royal Academy*. London: T. Cadell, 1781.

Barry, James. *The Works of James Barry*. Edited by Edward Fryer. 2 vols. London: Cadell and Davies, 1809.

Bellori, Giovanni Pietro. "L'Idea del Pittore, dello Schultore e dell'Architetto, Scelta della Bellezza Naturali Superiore Alla Natura," from *Le vite de' Pittori, Scultori e Architetti moderni* (Rome, 1672). Translated in Erwin Panofsky, *Idea: A Concept in Art Theory*, 154–177. New York: Harper & Row, 1968.

Berkeley, George. *The Works of George Berkeley*. Edited by A. A. Luce and T. E. Jessop. 9 vols. London: T. Nelson, 1948–1957.

Bernard, Emile. *Propos sur l'art*. Edited by Anne Rivière. 2 vols. Paris: Séguier, 1994.

British Royal Academy General Assembly Minutes. Royal Academy Library, London.

[Broderip, W. J., and Richard Owen.] "Generalizations of Comparative Anatomy." *Quarterly Review* 93, no. 185 (1853): 46–83.

Buckland, William. *Geology and Mineralogy Considered with Reference to Natural Theology*. New ed. Philadelphia: Lea & Blanchard, 1841.

Burke, Edmund. *A Philosophical Enquiry into the Origin of Our Ideas of the Sublime and Beautiful*. 3rd ed. London: R. and J. Dodsley, 1761.

Condillac, Etienne Bonnot de. *Oeuvres philosophiques de Condillac*. Edited by Georges Le Roy. 3 vols. Paris: Presses Universitaires de France, 1947.

Constable, John. *John Constable's Discourses*. Edited by R. B. Beckett. Ipswich, England: Suffolk Records Society, 1970.

Cozens, Alexander. *A New Method of Assisting the Invention in Drawing Original Compositions of Landscape*. London: J. Dixwell, 1785.

Dante. *Paradiso: A Verse Translation*. Trans. Allen Mandelbaum. New York: Bantam, 1986.

Denis, Maurice. *Le Ciel et l'Arcadie*. Edited by Jean-Paul Bouillon. Paris: Hermann, 1993.

De Piles, Roger. *Abrégé de la vie des peintres*. 2nd ed. Paris: J. Estienne, 1715.

Descartes, René. *Les passions de l'âme*. Paris: Henry Le Gras, 1649.

Diderot, Denis. *Diderot on Art II: Salon of 1767*. Translated by John Goodman. New Haven, CT: Yale University Press, 1995.

[———., ed.] *Encyclopédie, ou Dictionnaire raisonné des sciences, des arts et des métiers*. 17 vols. Paris: Briasson; Neufchastel: Samuel Faulche, 1751–65.

———. *Oeuvres esthétiques*. Paris: Garnier Frères, 1965.

———. *Salons*. Edited by Jean Seznec and Jean Adhémar. 2nd ed. 3 vols. Oxford: Clarendon Press, 1975–83.

[———., ed.] *Supplément à l'Encyclopédie*. 4 vols. Amsterdam: M. M. Rey, 1776–77.

[Eagles, John.] "Modern Painters." *Blackwood's Edinburgh Magazine* 54, no. 336 (1843): 485–503.

Engamells, John, and John Edgcumbe, eds. *The Letters of Sir Joshua Reynolds*. New Haven, CT: Yale University Press, 2000.

Fuseli, Henry. *The Life and Writings of Henry Fuseli*. Edited by John Knowles. 3 vols. London: H. Colburn and R. Bentley, 1831.

Gilpin, William. *Three Essays: On Picturesque Beauty; On Picturesque Travel; and On Sketching Landscape*. London: R. Blamire, 1792.

Goldsmith, Oliver. *The Works of Oliver Goldsmith*. Edited by James Prior. 4 vols. New York: Siegel-Cooper, 1837.

Gourmont, Remy de. "Les Premiers Salons: Indépendants, Rose+Croix, Exposition de Mme Jeanne Jacquemin." *Mercure de France* 5 (May 1892): 60–66.

Harrison, Charles, Paul Wood, and Jason Gaiger, eds. *Art in Theory, 1815–1900: An Anthology of Changing Ideas*. Oxford: Blackwell, 1998.

Hegel, G. W. F. *Hegel's Aesthetics*. Translated by T. M. Knox. 2 vols. Oxford: Clarendon Press, 1998.

Hobbes, Thomas. *Leviathan*. London: Andrew Crooke, 1651.

———. *Leviathan*. Indianapolis: Hackett, 1994.

Hume, David. *Essays Moral, Political and Literary*. Edited by Eugene F. Miller. Indianapolis: Liberty Classics, 1985.

———. *A Treatise of Human Nature*. Oxford: Clarendon Press, 1990.

Hutcheson, Francis. *An Inquiry into the Original of Our Ideas of Beauty and Virtue*. Indianapolis: Liberty Fund, 2004.

Johnson, Samuel. *A Dictionary of the English Language*. London: W. Strahan, 1755.

———. *The Oxford Authors: Samuel Johnson*. Edited by Donald Greene. Oxford: Oxford University Press, 1984.

Kant, Immanuel. *Critique of Judgment*. Translated by Werner S. Pluhar. Indianapolis, IN: Hackett, 1987.

Leslie, C. R. *Memoirs of the Life of John Constable*. Chichely: Paul P. B. Minet, 1971.

Locke, John. *An Essay Concerning Human Understanding*. Oxford: Clarendon Press, 1990.

Michelangelo. *The Poetry of Michelangelo*. Translated by James M. Saslow. New Haven, CT: Yale University Press, 1991.

Mondrian, Piet. *The New Art, The New Life: The Collected Writings of Piet Mondrian*. Edited and translated by Harry Holtzman and Martin S. James. New York: Da Capo Press, 1993.

———. *Two Mondrian Sketchbooks*. Edited and translated by R. P. Welsh and J. M. Joosten. Amsterdam: Meulenhoff International, 1969.

Northcote, James. *The Life of Sir Joshua Reynolds*. 2nd ed. 2 vols. London: Henry Colburn, 1819.

Opie, James. *Lectures on Painting*. Edited by P. Hoare. London: Longman, Hurst, Rees and Orme, 1809.

Owen, Richard. *Lectures on the Comparative Anatomy and Physiology of the Invertebrate Animals*. London: Longman, Brown, Green and Longmans, 1843.

———. *On the Archetype and Homologies of the Vertebrate Skeleton*. London: R. and J. E. Taylor, 1848.

———. *On the Nature of Limbs*. London: J. Van Voorst, 1849.

Plato. *The Collected Dialogues*. Edited by Edith Hamilton and Huntington Cairns. Princeton, NJ: Princeton University Press, 1994.

Plotinus. *The Enneads: A New, Definitive Edition*. Translated by Stephen MacKenna. Burdett, New York: Larson Publications, 1992.

Pollitt, J. J., ed. *The Art of Ancient Greece: Sources and Documents*. Cambridge: Cambridge University Press, 1990.

Quatremère de Quincy, Antoine Chrysostome. *Essai sur l'idéal dans ses applications pratiques aux oeuvres de l'imitation propre des arts du dessein*. Paris: Adrien Le Clère et Cie., 1837.

———. *Histoire de la vie et des ouvrages de Raphaël*. 2nd ed. Paris: Ad. Le Clère et Cie., 1833. Reprint. Elibron Classics, 2003.

Reynolds, Joshua. *Discourses on Art*. Edited by Robert R. Wark. New Haven, CT: Yale University Press, 1997.

———. *The Works of Sir Joshua Reynolds*. Edited by Edmond Malone. 2 vols. London: T. Cadell, Jr. and W. Davis, 1797.

Ruskin, John. *The Works of John Ruskin*. Edited by E. T. Cook and Alexander Wedderburn. 39 vols. London: G. Allen, 1903.

Sterne, Laurence. *The Life and Opinions of Tristram Shandy*. London: Penguin Books, 1985.

Swift, Jonathan. *A Tale of a Tub and Other Satires*. Edited by Kathleen Williams. Rev. ed. London: J. M. Dent & Sons, 1975.

Taine, Hippolyte. *Philosophie de l'art*. Paris: Fayard, 1985.

Van Gogh, Vincent. *The Complete Letters of Vincent Van Gogh*. 3 vols. Boston: Little, Brown and Company, 1988.

Warton, Thomas. *Verses on Sir Joshua Reynolds's Painted Window at New-College Oxford, 1782*. Oxford: Oxford University Press, 1930.

Winckelmann, J. J. *Reflections on the Imitation of Greek Works in Painting and Sculpture*. Translated by Elfriede Heyer and Roger C. Norton. La Salle, IL: Open Court, 1987.

Secondary Sources

Andrews, Malcolm. *The Search for the Picturesque: Landscape Aesthetics and Tourism in Britain, 1760–1800*. Stanford: Stanford University Press, 1989.

Appel, Toby A. *The Cuvier-Geoffroy Debate: French Biology in the Decades before Darwin*. New York: Oxford University Press, 1987.

Asfour, Amal, and Paul Williamson. "On Reynolds's use of de Piles, Locke, and Hume in his Essays on Rubens and Gainsborough." *Journal of the Warburg and Courtauld Institutes* 60 (1997): 215–29.

Barrell, John. *The Political Theory of Painting from Reynolds to Hazlitt: The Body of the Public*. New Haven, CT: Yale University Press, 1986.

Bate, Walter Jackson. *From Classic to Romantic: Premises of Taste in Eighteenth Century England*. New York: Harper & Row, 1961.

Bell, Clive. *Art*. New York: Capricorn Books, 1958.

Bermingham, Ann. *Landscape and Ideology: The English Rustic Tradition, 1740–1860*. Berkeley: University of California Press, 1986.

Bindman, David. *Ape to Apollo: Aesthetics and the Idea of Race in the Eighteenth Century*. Ithaca, NY: Cornell University Press, 2002.

Blotkamp, Carel. "Annunciation of the New Mysticism: Dutch Symbolism and Early Abstraction." In *The Spiritual in Art: Abstract Painting 1890–1985*. Edited by Maurice Tuchman. Los Angeles: L. A. County Museum, 1988.

———. *Mondrian: The Art of Destruction*. London: Reaktion Books, 1994.

Blunt, Anthony. *Artistic Theory in Italy, 1450–1660*. Oxford: Oxford University Press, 1982.

Boime, Albert. *The Academy and French Painting in the Nineteenth Century*. London: Phaidon, 1971.

Bois, Yve-Alain. "The Iconoclast." In *Piet Mondrian*. Edited by Angelica Zander Rudenstein. Exhibition catalog. The Hague: Haags Gemeentemuseum, 1994.

Bredvold, Louis. "The Tendency towards Platonism in Neo-Classical Esthetics." *English Literary History* 1 (1934): 91–119.

Campbell, Stephen J. "'*Fare una Cosa Morta Parer Viva*': Michelangelo, Rosso, and the (un)divinity of art." *Art Bulletin* 84, no. 4 (2002): 596–620.

Cassirer, Ernst. *The Philosophy of the Enlightenment*. Princeton, NJ: Princeton University Press, 1979.

Cheetham, Mark. *The Rhetoric of Purity: Essentialist Theory and the Advent of Abstract Painting*. Cambridge: Cambridge University Press, 1991.

The Compact Edition of the Oxford English Dictionary: Complete Text Reproduced Micrographically. 2 vols. London: Book Club Associates, 1979.

Connelly, Frances S. *The Sleep of Reason: Primitivism in Modern European Art and Aesthetics, 1725–1907*. University Park: Pennsylvania State University Press, 1995.

Cramer, Charles A. "Alexander Cozens's *New Method*: The Blot and General Nature." *The Art Bulletin* 79, no. 1 (1997): 112–29.

Dorra, Henri, ed. *Symbolist Art Theories: A Critical Anthology*. Berkeley: University of California Press, 1994.

Eitner, Lorenz, ed. *Neoclassicism and Romanticism, 1750–1850: An Anthology of Sources and Documents*. New York: Harper & Row, 1989.

Foucault, Michel. Preface to *Anti-Oedipus: Capitalism and Schizophrenia*, by Gilles Deleuze and Félix Guattari. Translated by Robert Hurley, Mark Seem and Helen R. Lang. Minneanapolis: University of Minnesota Press, 1983.

Gibson-Wood, Carol. *Jonathan Richardson: Art Theorist of the English Enlightenment*. New Haven, CT: Yale University Press, 2000.

Gombrich, Ernst. *Art and Illusion: A Study in the Psychology of Pictorial Representation*. 2nd ed. Princeton, NJ: Princeton University Press, 1961.

———. *Norm and Form: Studies in the Art of the Renaissance I*. London: Phaidon, 1978.

Goodman, Nelson. *Languages of Art*. Indianapolis, IN: The Bobbs-Merrill Company, 1968.

Hall, Brian K., ed. *Homology: The Hierarchical Basis of Comparative Biology*. San Diego: Academic Press, 1994.

Hardison, O. B., and Leon Golden, eds. *Horace for Students of Literature*. Gainesville: University Press of Florida, 1995.

Hayes, John, ed. *Gainsborough*. Exhibition catalog. London: Tate Gallery, 1980.

Hipple, Walter. "General and Particular in the Discourses of Sir Joshua Reynolds: A Study in Method." *The Journal of Aesthetics and Art Criticism* 11 (1953): 231–47.

Junod, Philippe. *Transparence et opacité: Essai sur les fondements théoriques de l'art moderne*. Lausanne: Editions l'age d'homme, 1975.

Kagan, Andrew. "Representation, Abstraction and the Absolute in Art—Part One: Toward a Clarification of the Three Fundamental Concepts of Form." *Arts Magazine* 52, no. 3 (1977): 136–40.

Kallich, Martin. "The Argument against the Association of Ideas in Eighteenth-Century Aesthetics." *Modern Language Quarterly* 15 (1954): 125–36.

———. "The Association of Ideas and Critical Theory: Hobbes, Locke, and Addison." *English Literary History* 12 (1945): 290–315.

———. *The Association of Ideas and Critical Theory in Eighteenth-Century England: A History of a Psychological Method in English Criticism*. The Hague: Mouton, 1970.

Kemp, Martin. *The Science of Art: Optical Themes in Western Art from Brunelleschi to Seurat*. New Haven, CT: Yale University Press, 1990.

Kenny, Anthony. "The Homunculus Fallacy." In *Interpretations of Life and Mind*, edited by M. Green, 65–74. New York: Humanities Press, 1971.

Landow, George P. *William Holman Hunt and Typological Symbolism*. New Haven, CT: Yale University Press, 1979.

———. *Victorian Types, Victorian Shadows: Biblical Typology in Victorian Literature, Art and Thought*. London: Routledge & Kegan Paul, 1980.

Langlois, Judith H., and Lori A. Roggman. "Attractive Faces are only Average." *Psychological Science* 1 (1990): 115–21.

Lebensztejn, Jean-Claude. *L'art de la tache: Introduction à la* Nouvelle méthode *d'Alexander Cozens*. Paris: Editions du Limon, 1990.

Lee, Kieran, Graham Byatt, and Gillian Rhodes. "Caricature Effects, Distinctiveness and Identification: Testing the Face-Space Framework." *Psychological Science* 11 (2000): 379–385.

Lee, Rensselaer. *Ut pictura poesis: The Humanistic Theory of Painting*. New York: W. W. Norton & Co., 1967.

Lopes, Dominic. "Pictorial Realism." *Journal of Aesthetics and Art Criticism* 53 (1995): 277–85.

Lovejoy, Arthur O. *The Great Chain of Being: A Study of the History of an Idea*. Cambridge, MA: Harvard University Press, 1964.

Mannings, David. "At the Portrait Painter's: How the Painters of the Eighteenth Century Conducted their Studios and Sittings." *History Today* 25 (1977): 279–87.

———., ed. *Sir Joshua Reynolds*. 2 vols. New Haven, CT: Yale University Press, 2000.

Matthews, Patricia. *Aurier's Symbolist Art Criticism and Theory*. Ann Arbor, UMI, 1984.

Mayr, Ernst. "What is a Species, and What is Not?" *Philosophy of Science* 63 (1996): 262–77.

Mirzoeff, Nicholas. *Bodyscape: Art, Modernity and the Ideal Figure*. London: Routledge, 1995.

Morgan, David. "The Concept of Abstraction in French Art Theory from the Enlightenment to Modernism." *Journal of the History of Ideas* 53 (1992): 669–85.

———. "The Idea of Abstraction in German Art Theories of Ornament from Kant to Kandinsky." *Journal of Aesthetics and Art Criticism* 50 (1992): 231–42.

———. "The Rise and Fall of Abstraction in Eighteenth-Century Art Theory." *Eighteenth-Century Studies* 27 (1994): 449–78.

Murray, Peter, and Linda Murray. *The Penguin Dictionary of Art and Artists*. New York: Penguin Books, 1989.

Panofsky, Erwin. *Idea: A Concept in Art Theory*. Translated by Joseph J. S. Peak. New York: Harper & Row, 1968.

———. *Tomb Sculpture: Four Lectures on its Changing Aspects from Ancient Egypt to Bernini*. Edited by H. W. Janson. New York: Harry N. Abrams, [1964].

Pears, Iain. *The Discovery of Painting: The Growth of Interest in the Arts in England, 1680–1768*. New Haven, CT: Yale University Press, 1988.

Penny, Nicholas, ed. *Reynolds*. Exhibition catalog. London: Royal Academy of Arts, 1986.

Postle, Martin. *Sir Joshua Reynolds: The Subject Pictures*. Cambridge: Cambridge University Press, 1995.

Rather, Susan. "Carpenter, Tailor, Shoemaker, Artist: Copley and Portrait Painting around 1770." *The Art Bulletin* 79 (1997): 269–90.

Rebora, Carrie, and Paul Staiti, eds. *John Singleton Copley in America*. Exhibition catalog. New York: The Metropolitan Museum of Art, 1995.

Rhodes, Gillian, and Tanya Tremewan. "Averageness, Exaggeration, and Facial Attractiveness." *Psychological Science* 7 (1996): 105–10.

Rookmaaker, H. R. *Synthetist Art Theories: Genesis and Nature of the Ideas on Art of Gauguin and His Circle*. Amsterdam: Swets and Zeitlinger, 1959.

Rosenberg, Harold. "The American Action Painters." In *Artists, Critics, Context*, edited by Paul F. Fabozzi, 23–32. Upper Saddle River, N. J.: Prentice Hall, 2002.

Rosenblum, Robert. *Transformations in Late-Eighteenth Century Art*. Princeton, NJ: Princeton University Press, 1989.

Roworth, Wendy. "Book Review: The Subject Pictures, The Painter in Society." *Eighteenth-Century Studies* 31 (1997): 142–43.

Rudenstein, Angelica Zander, ed. *Piet Mondrian*. Exhibiton catalog. The Hague: Haags Gemeentemuseum, 1994.

Rupke, Nicolaas A. *Richard Owen: Victorian Naturalist*. New Haven, CT: Yale University Press, 1994.

———. "Richard Owen's Vertebrate Archetype." *Isis* 84 (1993): 231–51.

Russell, Edward S. *Form and Function: A Contribution to the History of Animal Morphology*. Chicago: University of Chicago Press, 1982.

Ruvolt, Maria. "Michelangelo's Dream." *Art Bulletin* 85, no. 1 (2003): 86–113.

Seaton, Beverly. "Considering the Lilies: Ruskin's 'Proserpina' and other Victorian Flower Books." *Victorian Studies* 28 (1985): 255–82.

Seuphor, Michel. *Piet Mondrian: Life and Work*. New York: H. N. Abrams, [1956].

Sha, Richard. *The Visual and Verbal Sketch in British Romanticism*. Philadelphia: University of Pennsylvania Press, 1998.

Sheriff, Mary. *Fragonard: Art and Eroticism*. Chicago: University of Chicago Press, 1990.

Shiff, Richard. *Cézanne and the End of Impressionism: A Study of the Theory, Technique and Critical Evaluation of Modern Art*. Chicago: University of Chicago Press, 1984.

———. "Phototropism (Figuring the Proper)." *Studies in the History of Art* 20 (1989): 161–79.

Solkin, David. "Great Pictures or Great Men? Reynolds, Male Portraiture and the Power of Art." *Oxford Art Journal* 9, no. 2 (1986): 42–49.

Stafford, Barbara Maria. *Body Criticism: Imaging the Unseen in Enlightenment Art and Medicine*. Cambridge, MA: MIT Press, 1991.

Tansey, Richard G. and Fred S. Kleiner. *Gardner's Art through the Ages*. 10th edition. Fort Worth, TX: Harcourt Brace, 1996.

Trowbridge, Hoyt. "Platonism and Sir Joshua Reynolds." *English Studies* 21 (1939): 1–7.

Tscherney, Nadia. "Reynolds's Streatham Portraits and the Art of Intimate Biography." *Burlington Magazine* 128 (1986): 4–10.

Vergo, Peter, ed. *Abstraction: Towards a New Art*. Exhibition catalog. London: Tate Gallery, 1980.

Walton, Kendall L. "Style and the Products and Processes of Art." In *The Concept of Style*, edited by Berel Lang, 72–103. Rev. ed. Ithaca, NY: Cornell University Press, 1987.

Warner, Malcolm. "The Sources and Meanings of Reynolds's *Lady Sarah Bunbury Sacrificing to the Graces*." *Art Institute of Chicago Museum Studies* 15 (1989): 7–19.

Waterhouse, Ellis. *Painting in Britain 1530 to 1790*. London: Penguin Books, 1988.

Wiener, Philip P., ed. *Dictionary of the History of Ideas*. 5 vols. New York: Charles Scribner's Sons, 1973.

Welsh, Robert. "Mondrian and Theosophy." In *Major European Art Movements, 1900–1945*. Edited by Patricia Kaplan and Susan Manso, 250–74. New York: E. P. Dutton, 1977.

White, Hayden. *Tropics of Discourse*. Baltimore, MD: The Johns Hopkins University Press, 1978.

Wind, Edgar. *Hume and the Heroic Portrait*. Edited by Jaynie Anderson. Oxford: Clarendon Press, 1986.

———. "A Lost Article on David by Reynolds." *Journal of the Warburg and Courtauld Institutes* 6 (1943): 223–24.

Wölfflin, Heinrich. *Principles of Art History: The Problem of the Development of Style in Later Art*. Translated by M. D. Hottinger. New York: Dover, 1950.

Wright, William C. "Hazlitt, Ruskin and Nineteenth-Century Art Criticism." *Journal of Aesthetics and Art Criticism* 32 (1974): 509–23.

Youngquist, Paul. "In the Face of Beauty: Camper, Bell, Reynolds, Blake." *Word & Image* 16 (2000): 319–34.

Index

Page numbers for figures are in boldface type.

```
proc gmap data=both;
   id _map_geometry_;
   choro region/discrete;
run;
quit;
```

Close the HTML destination and open the listing destination. The HTML destination must be closed before you can view the output with a browser. ODS LISTING opens the Listing destination again so that the destination is again available for displaying output during this SAS session.

```
ods html close;
ods listing;
```

Printed in the United States
28746LVS00003B/34